Issues and Options in Language Teaching

Issues and Options in Language Teaching

H. H. Stern

Edited by Patrick Allen and Birgit Harley

Oxford University Press

Oxford University Press
Walton Street, Oxford OX2 6DP

Oxford New York Toronto Madrid
Delhi Bombay Calcutta Madras Karachi
Kuala Lumpur Singapore Hong Kong Tokyo
Nairobi Dar es Salaam Cape Town
Melbourne Auckland

and associated companies in
Berlin Ibadan

Oxford and *Oxford English* are trade marks of Oxford
University Press

ISBN 0 19 437066 6

© H. H. Stern 1992
First published 1992
Second impression 1993

All rights reserved. No part of this publication may be reproduced, stored in a retrieval system, or transmitted, in any form or by any means, electronic, mechanical, photocopying, recording, or otherwise, without the prior permission of Oxford University Press.

This book is sold subject to the condition that it shall not, by way of trade or otherwise, be lent, re-sold, hired out or otherwise circulated without the publisher's prior consent in any form of binding or cover other than that in which it is published and without a similar condition including this condition being imposed on the subsequent purchaser.

Set in 10½/12 pt Sabon.
Typeset by Wyvern Typesetting Ltd, Bristol.
Printed in Hong Kong

An Appreciation

I would like to extend my deepest gratitude to Patrick Allen and Birgit Harley for having so ably tackled the difficult and time consuming job of piecing together David's manuscript. It was no mean feat. Birgit, Patrick, and David were long-standing friends and colleagues. They worked together on a daily basis for many years and were very much in tune with each other's thoughts and ideas.

It was with this in mind that I approached them both after David's death and asked for their help in preparing David's manuscript for publication. In spite of their own heavy commitments their response was unhesitatingly enthusiastic. I am deeply indebted to them for giving their time, energy, and expertise so generously and for their unfailing enthusiasm throughout the project. They have made David's cherished vision a reality.

David derived much of his inspiration from a lively interaction with colleagues, teachers, and students. I hope that, in turn, this book will be an inspiration to some of them.

Rhoda Stern

Contents

Acknowledgements

The editors and publishers would like to thank the following for permission to reproduce material that falls within their copyright:

Harcourt Brace Jovanovich and the authors for a figure from *Modern Language Performance Objectives and Individualization: A Handbook* (1972) by R. M. Valette and R. S. Disick.

TESOL and the author for adaptations of figures from 'Making informed decisions about the role of grammar in language teaching' (1985) by M. Celce-Murcia, in *TESOL Newsletter* Vol. 19/1.

Harcourt Brace Jovanovich and the authors for extracts from *Classroom Techniques: Foreign Languages and English as a Second Language* (2nd edn., 1977) by E. D. Allen and R. M. Valette.

National Textbook Co. for extracts from *Teaching Culture* (1984) by H. N. Seelye.

Multilingual Matters and the authors for a figure from *Learner Language and Language Learning* (1984) by C. Faerch *et al.*

Northeast Conference on the Teaching of Foreign Languages for an adapted figure from 'Toward a multidimensional foreign language curriculum' by H. H. Stern, in *Foreign Languages: Key Links in the Chain of Learning*, edited by R. G. Mead (1983).

Every effort has been made to trace the owners of copyright material in this book, but we should be pleased to hear from any copyright holder whom we have been unable to contact.

Editors' preface

Dr H. H. (David) Stern, founder and former head of the Modern Language Centre at the Ontario Institute for Studies in Education, was a well-known authority on second language teaching and one of Canada's most distinguished educators. When Dr Stern retired from the Institute he set himself the task of writing two books which together would provide a comprehensive survey of the field of second language education. The first volume, *Fundamental Concepts of Language Teaching*, gave an account of the theoretical foundations and rapidly established itself as a key reference. The second volume, left unfinished at Dr Stern's death, dealt with practical implications for the second language curriculum. Thus, although this book is designed to stand alone, it will be apparent that the two volumes complement one another, the first in an important sense being incomplete without the second.

Shortly after Dr Stern's death, we were asked by Mrs Rhoda Stern to prepare the second volume for publication, and we gladly agreed to undertake the important task of making this work available to the field. The manuscript we received was at various stages of completion. Some sections were in almost final form, some were in first draft form, and some were missing entirely. At an early stage in the work we decided that our aim as editors was to revise and reorganize the existing material, but that we would not add to the main text, apart, for example, from updating references and inserting footnotes. The reader can be confident, therefore, that the Introduction and Chapters 1–12 closely follow the author's rough draft, and that they convey his intentions with reasonable accuracy.

The present text provides a carefully argued and richly exemplified analysis of a number of central issues in second language curriculum design. The reader should nevertheless bear in mind that it has not been possible to carry out the author's original intention in every respect. We know that Dr Stern intended to include chapters on vocabulary, social strategies, curriculum resources, and evaluation, but these chapters were either non-existent or only in rough note form. Also missing was the Conclusion, in which Dr Stern planned to discuss how the various components of the multidimensional curriculum might be combined into an integrated whole. In order to fill the gap left by the missing chapters, we have provided a new Conclusion, in which we briefly round out the framework and discuss the issue of curriculum integration, based wherever possible on source material from Dr Stern's files.

The original manuscript consisted of 23 chapters of varying lengths. These have been reorganized into 12 chapters, divided into four parts, with an Introduction and Conclusion. In Part One the author discusses a general approach to language teaching analysis, which forms the basis for his multidimensional curriculum framework. Part Two is concerned with the four language teaching objectives of proficiency, knowledge, affect, and transfer. These objectives relate in turn to the four content syllabuses—language, communicative activities, culture, and general language education—which are dealt with in Part Three. Finally, in Part Four, the author discusses a number of teaching strategies which are represented as options on three dimensions: intralingual–crosslingual, analytic–experiential, and explicit–implicit. A Conclusion has been provided by the editors, as already indicated.

We wish to acknowledge the help of the many individuals who have assisted us in the preparation of this volume. Our greatest debt is to Mrs Rhoda Stern, who generously made available to us all of Dr Stern's books and papers, and who helped us to trace a number of important documents. We are grateful to the Ontario Institute for Studies in Education for administrative and financial assistance, to Oxford University Press for their encouragement and support, and to three anonymous reviewers who provided detailed comments on the manuscript. We would like to thank Roger Stern who helped us to transfer the text from Dr Stern's home computer to the Institute VAX. We are grateful to Ellen Jeske, text-processing specialist, without whose expertise and dedicated work it would have been impossible to complete the project. Our thanks are extended to Alice Weinrib, MLC librarian, who provided valuable assistance in tracing bibliographic references. We would also like to express our appreciation for the role played by our graduate assistants Iva Baltova, Michael Clouston, Sonia Fiorucci, Xiaowei Liang, Li Paper, Stephanie Paulauskas, Kathryn Shred-Foley, Yilin Sun, and Wenxia Wang, who performed a variety of editorial tasks with great efficiency.

Stern's hope was that this book would provide an impartial yet critical overview of language teaching methodology as a basis for educational decision-making and future research. In presenting this edited version of Stern's work, we hope that we have succeeded in capturing the essence of his thinking on the need for a more comprehensive perspective on language teaching theory and practice. It should be clearly recognized, however, that the present formulation is only a beginning. As the author himself put it in a book published over twenty years ago (Stern 1970: 42): 'Nowhere in the world can language teaching claim to have found an easy and final answer to its instructional problems . . . The continuous questioning of our own efforts and the persistent dissatisfaction among learners do suggest that we are by no means at the end of the road.'

Patrick Allen
Birgit Harley

Toronto
December 1990

Introduction

Aim of the book

This book is addressed to second or foreign language teachers in general. It is not specific to any one language and therefore concerns, for example, the teacher of English as a second language (ESL) or English as a foreign language (EFL) as much as the teacher of French, Spanish, Russian, or Japanese. The book is also general in another sense. It is not only meant for teachers who work in a particular type of institution, such as a comprehensive school, high school, or grammar school; it has in mind equally the teacher of young children as well as of adult learners; it ranges from kindergarten to university; it is for teachers of students who are taught informally through private tuition or formally in conventional classes of ten, twenty, or thirty pupils; it is also meant for teachers who reach mass audiences through radio or television. It should be of interest to teacher trainers, supervisors, administrators, and others whose business is second or foreign language teaching or some aspect of it.

The settings in which language teaching occurs are very diverse, but they all have two things in common: (a) the teachers must be able to analyse and interpret the situation within which they teach, and (b) they must be able to plan, develop a policy, and come to decisions in the interests of their students and their programme, so that the new language is learnt as effectively as possible. Consider, for example, a teacher who has been asked to take on a new ESL class. He[1] would immediately want to know something about the students: How old are they? How much English do they know already? How long have they been learning English? How did they acquire their knowledge of the target language? Moreover, the teacher would want to know whether there is a syllabus, programme, or plan which determines how this class should be taught. This kind of questioning is the beginning of planning, which is part of the curriculum process. As the lessons proceed, the teacher has to decide what to do in particular weeks or on particular days. He must choose activities which he believes will help his class to learn English. He will no doubt ask himself from time to time how his teaching is received, whether the pace is right for the class, and whether the students are making progress. Even more so, after the course is over, a conscientious teacher will review the success of the entire programme. Would he teach like that again the next time round? What changes would he wish to introduce? And so on.

Whatever the objective, the setting, or the scale of the operation, second language education requires us to think about the teaching/learning process. Such reflection may be piecemeal, arbitrary and casual, following the whim of the moment—in short, non-professional in character. For example, some language teachers claim that they 'just do what works'; they switch from 'method' to 'method'; they staunchly assert that in language teaching 'you can't apply a theory'; and they ask questions as if language teaching was purely a matter of fashion: Is translation old-fashioned? Is grammar 'in' or 'out'? Is dictation still approved? Have you got a recipe for advanced students? Which is the right method these days? It is not our intention to offer pat answers to such flippant and naive questions, nor to present the reader with a definitive method or prescription. Rather, our purpose is to provide the necessary background knowledge to analyse particular language teaching situations, and to help readers develop the skills needed to ensure that their conceptualization of language teaching is systematic, coherent, and relevant.

With these goals in mind, we will examine language pedagogy as objectively, comprehensively, and systematically as possible. This book, therefore, is *not* a prescriptive guide for language teachers. Rather it is an attempt to analyse the main issues in language teaching practice, to define the parameters within which practitioners have to make choices, and to identify controversial questions and areas which require empirical research. The task we have set ourselves is one of fact-finding, describing, and documenting trends of thought and experience, analysing, synthesizing, and interpreting. We will draw on the past and current pedagogical literature and other relevant documentation, such as policy statements, reports, teaching materials, etc., and wherever possible we will bring together findings from North America and Europe and other parts of the world. Our hope is that this treatment of language pedagogy will not only provide an overview and a set of analytical concepts, but that it will be of direct assistance to practitioners in analysing language teaching situations and in making well-reasoned choices, that it will give direction to future experimentation and empirical research, and that, in a more general way, it will contribute to overcoming the unpredictable changes and 'bandwagon' tendencies that have been so prevalent in our field.

Relationship to *Fundamental Concepts of Language Teaching*

This book, then, like its predecessor, *Fundamental Concepts of Language Teaching* (Stern 1983a) (henceforth FCLT), is intended to help teachers to think and plan constructively. The relationship between the two books and the perspective of the present volume can best be understood if we look at a diagram which in FCLT provided the basic framework:

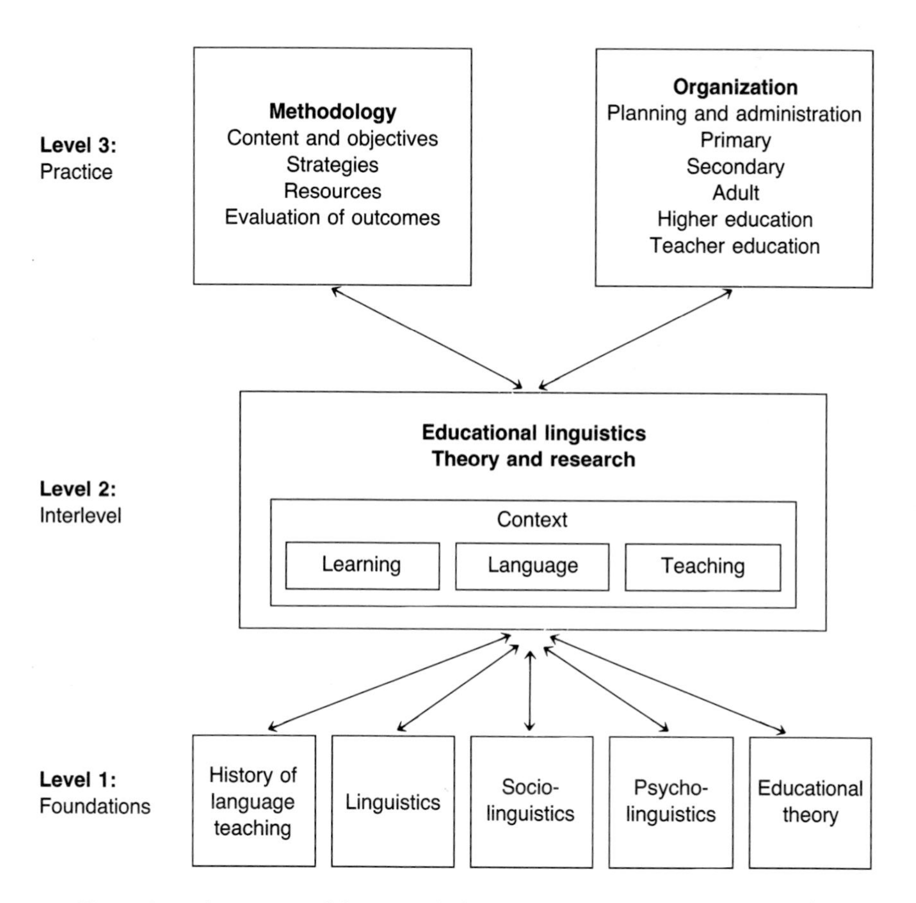

Figure I.1 A conceptual framework for second language teaching theories

This diagram makes certain assumptions about the relationship between 'theory' and 'practice'. It is well known that language teachers do not fancy themselves as great theoreticians. They tend to believe in intuitive and practical approaches to the day-to-day tasks they are facing. In fact, they are often quite negative about anything that is described as theoretical and they often look askance at 'ivory-tower' research. Nevertheless, being practical and down-to-earth does not mean being thoughtless. The earlier book gave particular attention to the theory-practice relationship which is reflected in Figure I.1. This diagram represents a theoretical framework of language teaching on three levels. The most abstract, general, and theoretical level is at the bottom and the most practical and concrete level is at the top.

The diagram can be read from the top down or from the bottom up. Starting at the first or lowest level, at least five major fields of study can be identified which have a bearing on language teaching, i.e. historical, linguistic, sociological, psychological, and educational studies. They are seen as contributing to language teaching by coming together at the second level, which is the level of applied or educational linguistics. This discipline deals with the fundamental concepts of language teaching: language, learning, teaching, and social context. Like any other scholarly discipline, educational linguistics develops theories and undertakes research, but its particular function is to provide the scholarly basis for practical language tasks, in this case second language teaching and learning. Because of its position at the second level, educational linguistics is well placed to act as an intermediary between the more general language-related disciplines at level 1 and the more specific practice of language teaching at level 3. The third level, practice, is divided into two cells, methodology (or pedagogy) and organization. *Methodology* deals with the practical concepts we need in teaching and learning languages, while *organization* refers to the institutions which provide opportunities for such teaching and learning. In this model, we visualize the practitioner operating at the third level. Practitioners are not only language teachers but also others directly or indirectly concerned with language teaching, such as politicians, advisers, administrators, curriculum makers, and so on.

In FCLT our main task was to delineate the four main concepts of language, society, learning, and teaching and to study the relationship between these and the underlying disciplines. In other words, FCLT was concerned with the first and second levels in Figure I.1. The chief purpose of FCLT was to help teachers and others concerned with language education to clarify these fundamental concepts in their own minds and thus to define the philosophy underlying their own practice. In the present work the focus has shifted from the relationship between levels 1 and 2 to the relationship between levels 2 and 3 in Figure I.1. At level 3 our interest is directed to the cell on the left, methodology, rather than the one on the right, organization. Methodological issues present themselves in all types of institution in which languages are taught. The institutional aspect of language teaching is a distinct topic which will not be dealt with in the present volume.

In order to locate the treatment of pedagogy in this book as clearly as possible we will refer to a second diagram (Figure I.2) which is, so to speak, carved out of the basic framework in Figure I.1. It is once more a three-level model:

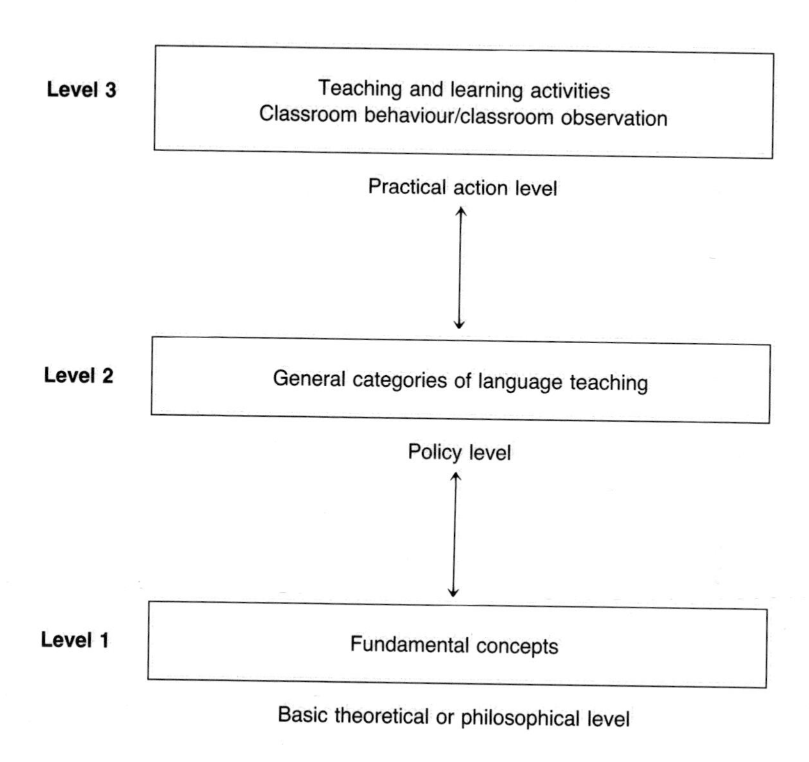

Figure I.2 From deep to surface levels in language pedagogy

At the base, which corresponds to level 2 in Figure I.1, we find the fundamental concepts which were thoroughly explored in FCLT in relation to the theoretical disciplines. In the present model they constitute the basis of fundamental beliefs and represent the philosophical level of the model. The methodology/pedagogy cell of Figure I.1, which is the principal focus of the present book, is for the purpose of our discussion divided into two levels. The second level is the policy level which gives language teaching its characteristic shape and direction. At the third level we reach the surface of the model and consider the classroom manifestations of teaching which consist of the concrete behaviour of teachers and learners, materials in use, examination records, classroom tests, video or audio recordings of classroom episodes; in short, the actual situations in which teachers and learners find themselves in a particular classroom in a given school or college. We will refer to this as the practical action level.

Historical perspective

The theoretical position we are adopting can best be understood against the background of historical developments in language pedagogy. It is sufficient for our purposes to provide a brief overview of the one-hundred-year period which began in the 1880s. At that time, there was a remarkable upsurge of interest in foreign language teaching in several European countries which made itself felt in all the educational systems of the Western world. The entire time span is characterized by three major trends of development which created the ideological climate within which present-day thought on language teaching has evolved. These trends represent the three major ways in which language pedagogy throughout this period has attempted to renew and improve itself:

1 Innovation through changes in teaching method;
2 Innovation through the language-related sciences and research;
3 Technological innovation.

Innovation through changes in teaching method

One of the main features of the development of language pedagogy has been the continuous attempt to renew language teaching through changes in teaching method. These efforts have gone on unabated from the late nineteenth century up to the present time. During the final decades of the last century a vigorous reform movement arose in Western Europe and spread to most countries in which modern languages were part of the school curriculum. This movement focused on classroom teaching and initiated a century of debate on teaching method. The traditional grammar–translation method, then current in schools, came under heavy fire. The reformers advocated a new direct method, which emphasized oral practice and dispensed with translation as a technique of language teaching. The controversy about the new method was prolonged and often bitter. It had repercussions on language teaching not only in Europe but also in North America.

The debate on language teaching methods continued into the period between the two world wars, a period which from the point of view of language pedagogy is characterized by the search for realistic solutions to the method controversy. Some language teaching theorists recommended a compromise between the traditional method and the direct method. Others advocated the search for practical limited objectives, emphasizing in particular the usefulness of reading as an appropriate goal for language training.

With World War II a sudden demand emerged for language capability in the pursuit of military objectives, and the next two decades were a time of extraordinary efflorescence of new ideas and bold experiments in language pedagogy, culminating around 1960 in the audiolingual method, the spread of language laboratories, research on language teaching methods, and the extension of second language teaching into primary education. The initiative for many of these efforts came from the United States but they were echoed in many countries around the world.

By the late 1960s, radical changes in linguistic and psychological thought were precipitating the erosion and decline of audiolingualism and a search for a more satisfactory teaching approach. Some looked to cognitive theory as the answer to the shortcomings of audiolingualism. Others, however, disturbed by the constant shifts in methodological prescriptions, argued that the importance of teaching methods had been exaggerated; they thought that the focus should be on other more important aspects of language training. Several new directions were pursued in the 1970s. One was to look for improvements through more attention to curriculum and curriculum design. A lead in this respect was given by the Modern Languages Project of the Council of Europe. This remarkable international enterprise tried to determine the content and objectives of language teaching in a more systematic way by focusing on the needs of learners.

A second new direction was an emphasis on the human aspect of language teaching and learning. What matters more than teaching method, it was argued, is the interaction between teacher and learner, and the personal characteristics of the learner. This conviction led to various experiments, all designed to modify the traditional teacher-centred language class. Some writers advocated individualization of language instruction, some emphasized cultivation of the learner's initiative and sense of responsibility, while others tried to influence human relations in the language class by sensitizing teachers to the social and emotional aspects of language teaching.

Another development during the 1970s, a surprising phenomenon of the time which in some ways contradicted the 'break with method' concept, was a definite method renaissance. Several distinct methods of teaching, some of which had been developed earlier, for example Community Language Learning and the Silent Way, were suddenly rediscovered and widely discussed. They were soon joined by a whole spate of new methods, including Suggestopedia, the Dartmouth Method, and the Natural Approach, which aroused much interest and attracted a definite following. Other teachers, however, did not adopt any one method in its entirety; they saw in all of them certain valuable and distinct features which could be adopted eclectically.

Innovation through new teaching methods has continued to flourish to this day. The methods which aroused interest in the 1970s continue to be examined, and new ones have been added. These evoke a good deal of attention among language teaching theorists, even among those who have reacted against the narrowness and dogmatism of a rigid method formula.

Innovation through the language-related sciences and research

The one-hundred-year period of language-teaching method development coincides with the growth of the human sciences: linguistics, psychology, sociology, psycholinguistics, sociolinguistics, and related disciplines. It is important to recognize their influence on the development of language teaching. Between 1880 and World War I, the first major linguistic discipline that influenced language teaching was phonetics. It gave the language teaching reform around 1900 its characteristic shape. Phonetics was in many ways the applied linguistics of the last decades of the nineteenth century.

During the inter-war years, language teaching reforms, especially in the United States, were influenced by the growth of educational psychology and research in education. For example, the important Modern Foreign Language Study, carried out from 1924 to 1928, was a major attempt to renew language teaching with the help of various scholarly projects, and based its approach to vocabulary on word frequency studies that educational psychologists had undertaken for reading instruction. Likewise, language tests were modelled on the new objective tests that had been introduced into school systems after the experience with psychological testing in World War I.

The period 1940–1965 was characterized by the increasing influence of linguistics on language teaching. The audiolingual method was the first language teaching method claiming to be based on linguistics and psychology. It was also during this period that psycholinguistics developed as a new discipline on the border between linguistics and psychology. However, the changes in linguistic theory around 1960 and the criticism of the linguistic and psychological bases of audiolingualism led not only to a shift towards a more cognitive or rational approach to language teaching, but also to serious questions about the role of the different disciplines. Just as there was a constant shift from one teaching method to another, the language-related sciences seemed to necessitate periodic changes from one underlying discipline to another or from one theory to a newer and better theory. It was in response to this concern that educational or applied linguistics evolved in the early 1960s as a buffer between linguistics and language teaching.

An important development in the wake of the scientific movement was the increasing use of empirical research methods in the attempt to solve problems of language pedagogy. The 1960s witnessed vigorous attempts to come to grips with the method controversy through empirical research. Several research projects were initiated with this purpose in mind. They were only partially successful in that the evidence they produced for one or the other methodological option was not very conclusive. These studies gave rise to further controversies, and the researchers were drawn into the debate. In the 1970s, researchers abandoned the central emphasis on teaching method and, as already mentioned, initiated a new and productive series of studies on language learning. Those exploring this avenue argued forcefully that no improvement in language teaching could be expected unless the characteristics of second language learners and the learning process were better understood. Many studies in the 1970s and the 1980s were carried out with this objective in mind. Gradually also research on language teaching was tried again, but this time more cautiously and with greater sophistication, and with more safeguards to ensure validity.

Research and the language-related sciences have gained a place in the development of new approaches to language pedagogy and have decisively influenced current thought on language teaching and learning. While a research approach is by no means universally accepted, many practitioners and administrators now recognize it as an appropriate way of discovery and of arriving at decisions on language teaching questions. The contact with various disciplines has been fruitful, but it has also presented problems. The constant shift in theoretical viewpoints and the shift of emphasis from one discipline to another has been unsettling and confusing from the practitioner's point of view. On the other hand, it has led first to the acceptance of a multidisciplinary basis for language pedagogy; and second to the conviction that the relationship between the disciplines and pedagogy cannot be simple and direct. There is new recognition that an intermediary between the foundation disciplines is needed in order to arrive at a satisfactory relationship between language pedagogy and the underlying sciences, a role which is usually assigned to applied linguistics.

Technological innovation

A third development in language teaching during the past one hundred years has been the influence of technology. Technological innovation has occurred in three waves, the first of which began to make itself felt around 1900. At this time the invention of the phonograph soon led to the recognition of its usefulness as a language teaching aid, and by the early 1920s, language courses were already available on gramophone records.

Between World War II and 1965, a second wave of technology occurred. The invention of the magnetic tape recorder and its mass production led to the concept of the language laboratory. Moreover, the filmstrip projector in combination with the tape recorder gave rise to the idea of audio-visual language teaching which was developed and perfected in France. Technology became a central feature of the new audio-lingual method and the language laboratory raised hopes of a new era in language instruction. But, as has so often happened in language teaching, the innovation did not fulfil its promise. Language laboratories have remained part of the modern equipment of language teaching, but by the early 1970s they were being looked upon more soberly as useful adjuncts for certain specific purposes rather than as a 'breakthrough' in language pedagogy.

Towards the end of the 1970s a third wave of technology gathered momentum as a result of the development of microcomputers. It has opened up a new era of computer-assisted language learning (CALL). The use of computers in the classroom offers a number of important advantages. Computers offer interactive learning, personalized instruction, and considerable versatility in handling different types of material. On the other hand, computers cannot effectively conduct an 'open-ended' dialogue with the student, which means that they can be used only for certain types of activities. It is necessary, therefore, for teachers to come to terms with the computer, to weigh up its advantages and disadvantages, and to work out the most effective way it can be used to serve their own purposes. According to Ahmad *et al.* (1985: 10), for example, the computer 'is not a self-sufficient means of language teaching, but rather a valuable aid which should take its place alongside other already established devices for helping the language learner'.

Of the three main trends of development in the continuing efforts to improve language teaching, technology has been the least problematical and probably also the least influential. Language teaching has not changed radically as a result of technology. None the less, the resources that technology has put at the disposal of language teaching have been of immense value. Nowadays, we take for granted the use of tape or cassette recorders, and overhead and filmstrip projectors, as well as the use of radio, television, and video in the service of language teaching. Certainly the development of microcomputers offers opportunities for new programs and for useful individualized approaches. However, there are as yet no indications of any very significant changes merely because a new technology has come into use. Those who work in the area of computer-assisted language learning tend to be cautiously optimistic without making the excessive claims that accompanied the introduction of language laboratories in the 1960s.

Some recent trends

Various theoretical positions found among theorists and practitioners today can be characterized either as: (a) eclecticism, or (b) variations on the theme of communicative language teaching. In Chapter 1, another position, the theoretical model we are adopting for the purposes of this book, will be explained.

Eclecticism

At the end of the 1970s, several writers—prominently among them Grittner (1977) and Rivers (1981)—reacted to the profusion of theories, methods, research studies, and pedagogical innovations of the previous decade with the view that none of them is comprehensive or powerful enough to command single-minded support. On the other hand, they all contain germs of truth and none of them can be dismissed out of hand. In the light of this conviction, these and other authors have recommended a judicious eclecticism as the best approach for our time. They try, in this way, to overcome unnecessary confrontation and approach the whole range of modern thought in a positive frame of mind. The weakness of the eclectic position is that it offers no criteria according to which we can determine which is the best theory, nor does it provide any principles by which to include or exclude features which form part of existing theories or practices. The choice is left to the individual's intuitive judgement and is, therefore, too broad and too vague to be satisfactory as a theory in its own right.

The communicative approach

Of all the concepts in language teaching which have been widely used in recent years, the terms 'communication' or 'communicative' no doubt top the list. In the titles of books and articles, in the names of language courses and in curriculum guides, communication is a word which occurs with remorseless regularity. While some years ago everything in language pedagogy was 'audiolingual' and 'structural', 'communication' and 'communicative' have taken over the dubious privilege of being the fashionable terms today.

We can distinguish two scientific and three pedagogical sources originating in the 1970s which have contributed to the modern concept of communicative language teaching. The first of the scientific sources is the tendency to widen the scope of language studies and to adopt an increasingly social and semantic view of language learning, a trend which became marked in the late 1960s and early 1970s. Since then, many linguists have turned their backs on the highly abstract structural view of language which had dominated linguistics since the 1930s. The continued growth of psycholinguistics, the rapid development of socio-linguistics, the renewed interest in semantics, and the study of pragmatics, or language in relation to the real world, strongly emphasized the language user and real-world language use. These developments had implications for language teaching which were quickly recognized and taken up by educational linguists. The second scientific source was the explosion of research on second language learning, which led to the conviction that the learner constructs his own second language competence relatively independently and not necessarily following the graded steps of a planned syllabus. All this has given rise to questions about the learner's own role, his perceptions, motivations, and initiative, and to the demand for a more flexible, open, individualized, and more 'negotiable' approach to teaching.

Besides these changes in the language sciences, several pedagogical developments of the 1970s contributed to the concept of communicative language teaching. Two of these were novel approaches to the language curriculum, while a third concerned classroom treatment. The first curriculum approach is represented by the Modern Languages Project of the Council of Europe. This project was the first systematic attempt to base teaching on the communicative needs of specified groups of learners and to develop a curriculum in terms of situations, social roles, notions, and language functions, thus giving concrete expression to one interpretation of the concept of communicative teaching. A parallel development has been English for Special Purposes, which has resulted in courses designed to prepare adult second language learners for the kinds of discourse they need in order to study and practise their chosen profession in English.

The other approach to a communicative curriculum is content-based. It can be illustrated by the Canadian experiments in French immersion which had been initiated as early as 1965 but spread across Canada in the 1970s and the 1980s. In an immersion class the emphasis is not on language *per se*. Rather, the emphasis is on substantive, non-language content, and on experiencing the language in actual use. There is no sequencing according to grammatical or speech act categories. In this approach, language is almost 'deschooled', as if to say 'Take care of the content and let language take care of itself.' In reality, immersion programmes in Canada have not adopted the position of deschooling language in its most radical form, but the underlying rationale is to place the language learner in a situation in which the target language is used for 'real' communication, rather than for rehearsal, play, pretence, or simulation. Immersion, therefore, interprets communicative language teaching as an experiential or activity approach to learning. As we will see later, such an experiential approach is not confined to this Canadian experiment. Teaching a language with an emphasis on message rather than on form has had advocates elsewhere, too.

A third significant pedagogical development with a bearing on communicative language teaching is one that occurred in the United States during the 1970s and which can be described as the human relations or humanistic emphasis. In the previous decade, audiolingualism and the language laboratory had encouraged an efficient but relatively impersonal approach. The teacher's role was directive and authoritarian, and in a way ran counter to the prevailing educational philosophy. Individualization of instruction, group work, and humanistic techniques changed the social climate of the language class and expressed a new awareness of human relations as an important factor in language teaching. The widespread interest in new methods such as Suggestopedia, the Silent Way, and Community Language Learning reflected interest in the key role of interpersonal relations in the language class. Here, then, was another aspect of classroom treatment that contributed to the interpretation of what is involved in a communicative approach.

The different emphases of the 1970s described above suggest two main directions in the interpretation of communicative language teaching. The first can be called analytic or 'formal' and is based largely on linguistic and sociolinguistic considerations. It reflects the European work on needs analysis, speech act theory, and discourse analysis, and more generally the growth of sociolinguistics and related disciplines. The other is non-analytic, experiential, or participant in character and reflects the mainly North American experience of immersion, emphasis on content, awareness of human relations, and language acquisition research. It is important to recognize that there is no necessary conflict between a more analytic and a more experiential or non-analytic approach.

The communicative approach, understood in this comprehensive way, has had a bearing on second language curriculum, on teaching methodology and materials, and also on evaluation. Today, many language teaching methodologists subscribe more or less consciously to one or other aspect of communicative teaching. Although it has incorporated many of the characteristics of earlier language teaching innovations, communicative language teaching has avoided the narrowness and dogmatism of the method concept and covers a wider range of components. Many of its advocates are seeking a synthesis with aspects of earlier methodologies. These qualities give communicative language teaching the potential for greater strength and durability and for making a more lasting contribution than was the case with earlier innovations.

Concluding comments

The recent history of language pedagogy is a history of constant movement, of ups and downs and remarkable efforts to deal constructively with the unsolved issue of how to effect a radical improvement in language teaching. If we ask ourselves why language teaching, in spite of all these efforts in so many directions, is still struggling, a general answer might be that the efforts have been piecemeal and fragmentary. This is most obvious in the 'method' approach. Each new approach has presented a plausible case for its particular emphasis, but ultimately no single method has been sufficient in itself to deal with the great variety of circumstances, types of learners, and levels of instruction that constitute second language pedagogy.

In some ways, the search for a more systematic approach through the language-related sciences and research fell into a similar trap. Like methods, disciplines are limited, although in a different way. A discipline necessarily focuses on one aspect of reality as its central concern; linguistics, for example, has often had a particular thematic interest, such as phonetics in the 1890s, grammatical structure in the 1950s, and discourse in the 1970s and 1980s. But the language that the teacher has to cope with is always more than any one of these, not just sounds or syntax or vocabulary or discourse, but all of them combined. Research studies are limited, too. They must focus on specific aspects, excluding other equally important issues. This is in the nature of research and is one of its assets. But one research study cannot adequately represent the complex totality that the language teacher has to deal with.

Eclecticists have intuitively grasped that practitioners cannot limit themselves to one teaching method, the results of a single research direction, or the approach offered by one or other of the disciplines. They are, therefore, ready to shift ground, and their openness to everything—technology, teaching innovations, new theories, emphasis on this or that discipline, various research studies—has been an advantage. Yet, unselective openness can also be self-defeating, since it leaves us without direction. We cannot choose everything, or our choices eventually become indiscriminate and unfocused.

As for the communicative approach, the reliance on a single overriding concept, 'communication', is a disadvantage which prevents communicative language teaching from being entirely satisfactory as a theoretical framework. In order to account for all varieties and aspects of language teaching we either stretch the concept of communication so much that it loses any distinctive meaning, or we accept its limitations and then find ourselves in the predicament of the 'method' solution: an excessive emphasis on a single concept.

With these considerations in mind, we have reached the point where we will develop a theoretical framework which aims to be wide and differentiated enough to cover language teaching in all its various manifestations, and yet coherent and well-integrated enough to avoid the imprecision and vagueness of unqualified eclecticism. The description of this framework is the subject of Chapter 1.

Note

1 In a footnote to the Introduction of *Fundamental Concepts of Language Teaching*, Stern made the following observation: 'He/she? Him/her? While I accept the principle of non-sexist language in scholarly writing commonly recommended in recent years, I have tried not to make too much of an issue of it in this book and have used masculine forms he/his/him, etc. whenever they seemed natural and stylistically convenient on the argument that they can be understood as unmarked for sex unless otherwise indicated by the context.' Stern continued to use generic, masculine forms in early drafts of the present volume, and in editing the text we have allowed this convention to remain.

PART ONE

Policy and practice

Policy and practice

It is easy enough to see that a language cannot be learned in one big stride, but deciding how best to organize the language learning activities is much more difficult. We face here the problem that every instructor is up against when he or she undertakes to teach a language class. What do I teach them? In what order? How should I plan my programme? Some school systems prescribe what is to be taught, and when, and how. The system provides a 'course of study', a 'curriculum guide', or a 'syllabus'. Sometimes, a textbook serves as the curriculum planning instrument. In other cases, the language programme is determined by an examination syllabus. There are, however, situations where teachers are left to their own devices. There is no curriculum guide, not even a textbook to fall back on, and the teachers themselves have to decide how to proceed. Some teachers welcome such freedom; others find it a considerable burden. On a larger scale, the problems of curriculum design have to be faced by those who write textbooks or develop courses of study. How important is a curriculum or syllabus? What should it consist of? Who should be responsible for it? As a start we need to clarify the use of these terms.

A specialized terminology is employed in language teaching, and certain distinctions are made, which derive from educational theory and more specifically from curriculum theory. The term 'curriculum' itself can be used in two ways. In one sense, it refers to the programme of studies of an educational institution. When we talk, for example, of the school curriculum or the university curriculum, we think of the overall functions of schools or universities and how these functions are manifested in the distribution of subjects and activities. In this sense, foreign languages have their place in the curriculum of most educational institutions. In a more restricted sense we use the term curriculum to describe the substance of what is taught in a given subject, say mathematics, history, or French. We refer, accordingly, to the mathematics curriculum, the history curriculum, or the French curriculum. The use of the term curriculum in the second sense usually involves at least three aspects: (a) defining objectives, (b) determining content, and (c) indicating some sort of sequence or progression. Together, these aspects constitute the essential minimum of what is meant by curriculum.

In Britain, the term 'syllabus' is roughly equivalent to curriculum in the more restricted sense above. It is widely used in all kinds of educational contexts, particularly in connection with external examinations. Examining bodies issue 'syllabuses' for a subject, which are consulted by teachers and examination candidates. In more recent years, British applied linguists have used the term 'syllabus' to characterize the content, or the underlying principle of selecting and sequencing, of second language courses. In this book we use the term *syllabus* to refer to content components of the curriculum, and the term *curriculum* itself more globally to refer to the plan for teaching a language. The term *course* refers to the administrative unit of instruction, and a series of courses or a variety of courses offering different options constitutes a *programme.*

In some formulations, curriculum is restricted to the three aspects we have identified—objectives, content, and progression—and the concept of curriculum is contrasted with instruction. In this way, ends and means, or product and process are clearly differentiated. In other formulations, however, curriculum is more widely interpreted and includes instruction. At its most comprehensive, curriculum is a full and detailed statement covering every aspect and phase of teaching a language. Understood in this broad sense, the curriculum of a language course becomes virtually synonymous with language pedagogy and can be defined as a comprehensive, explicit or implicit plan of language teaching which organizes into a more or less coherent whole the goals, content, strategies, techniques, and materials, as well as the timing, sequential arrangement, social organization, and evaluative procedures of a course or programme or of a set of courses or programmes.

This comprehensive interpretation of curriculum, to which we subscribe, is not accepted universally. Some authorities prefer to restrict the scope of the curriculum concept to the definition of content and objectives and to omit from it all instructional aspects on the grounds that this gives greater freedom to the teacher to determine the appropriate teaching methodology. In its most radical interpretation (for example, Candlin 1983), a curriculum is not determined in advance; it is 'negotiated' by each teacher in contact with a class. According to Candlin (1984), as well as Breen (1984), what happens in a given class is always the result of the encounter between what the teacher offers and the unpredictable response of a given group of learners.

The apparent conflict between a view of curriculum as a detailed teaching plan carefully designed in advance and curriculum as a spontaneous event which can only be described after the fact can perhaps be resolved if we adopt a distinction between the *curriculum itself* and the *curriculum processes* which specify how, by whom, and when the curriculum is developed, delivered, and modified. Our aim in the following two chapters is to set the scene by taking up some of the broader issues of policy and practice. In Chapter 1 we will deal with language teaching analysis which forms the basis for the curriculum itself. Then, in Chapter 2, we will discuss a number of topics relating to the processes of curriculum development, implementation, evaluation, and research.

1 Language teaching analysis

At this point we refer back to the three-level model which we briefly outlined in the Introduction (Figure I.2). The aim of the present chapter is to present the model in more detail, beginning with the basic theoretical or philosophical level and going on to a consideration of the policy and practical action levels.

The basic level

At the basic theoretical or philosophical level we consider four central concepts to be the essential building blocks of any theory of language teaching. They are concepts of:

1 language
2 society
3 learning
4 teaching.

These concepts are not necessarily formulated in any deliberate kind of way; they may be implicit in acts of teaching, in policy decisions, and in the learner's conduct. They could also be implicit in the categories of a classroom observation scheme. It was a weakness of past debates on teaching methods that these underlying assumptions were often not spelt out and therefore caused misunderstanding simply because it was not recognized that there were deep-seated differences in certain fundamental beliefs underlying a particular method.[1]

It should be noted that there are four concepts which are treated as fundamental, and not simply one. Time and again language teaching has fallen into the trap of making a single belief, concept, or principle paramount, with a resulting loss of perspective. It is easy to see how this can happen. An inspiring teacher or a persuasive new theory suddenly draws our attention to a neglected concept, such as 'language acquisition', 'comprehensible input', or 'communication', which consequently becomes a major preoccupation. It is not easy to keep several basic concepts in mind simultaneously and to give each its due place. Yet, the painful collective experience of the history of language teaching theory makes it imperative that we should do so. Why four basic concepts and not three or five or six? Readers might try to think which in their own view are the most important and most pervasive concepts, the universals of language teaching, and they may well come up with a different list. The assumption we make is that these four concepts are the basic minimum, the essential ones without which any type of language teaching is unthinkable.

In the first place, a language course always implies a view of the nature of *language* in general and of the target language itself. How is language treated in the curriculum, and in the teacher's day-to-day work in the classroom? Is importance attributed to the analysis of language, or is the language treated non-analytically? Is language treated mainly as sounds, or words, or grammatical patterns, or is reference made to discourse structures and sociolinguistic appropriateness? Changes in linguistic theory have a bearing on the treatment of language in the curriculum. Since the 1970s the interest in notional syllabuses and in communicative language teaching, for example, reflects a more semantic and a more social view of language than the one previously held. Fundamental questions about standard language, the role of dialects, and the acceptability of regional and social varieties present themselves regularly in teaching.

Our view of society and of *language in society* permeates our approach to language teaching. If we take the view that language and society are closely intertwined we would probably want our curriculum to reflect this view, since it is difficult to see how one could teach a language without constant references to society and culture. A social view of language would make us conscious of the sociolinguistic context of the learners we are concerned with. It is obvious to most teachers that the presence or absence of the second language in the wider milieu will have a profound effect on student motivation; the opportunity to use the language and the resources available outside the classroom affect the success of language learning. Social sensitivity should also make us responsive to sociopolitical issues in language teaching and to attitudes in society with regard to foreign languages, bilingualism, and ethnic diversity.

It is hardly possible to teach a language without having an underlying conception of the *language learner and learning*, however dimly it may be perceived. Recent research on language acquisition has called into question a number of assumptions. A controversial issue, for example, is whether second language learning follows rules which are similar to the regularities of first language acquisition and whether L2 teaching should be based on such 'natural' first language experience. If we adopt the latter point of view, there is a great deal that a teacher could learn from the way a mother intuitively handles the language acquisition of her young children. The insistence on the predominance of subconscious acquisition processes in the development of proficiency, which has been advocated by Krashen (1981a, 1982), could have a profound effect on syllabus design and teaching practices, because it attributes far less importance to conscious learning than do traditional ways of teaching. On the other hand, a pedagogy that demands learner autonomy takes a much more cognitive view of the learner and the learning process.

From what has been said above, it is clear that the concept of *language teaching* and the role of the teacher are bound to be modified by changes in the other basic concepts. But our views of teaching are not only shaped by current concepts of learning, language, and society, important though these concepts may be. They are also influenced by educational traditions and educational thought. Sometimes students come to the language class with very fixed ideas of what to expect from a teacher and what they think teaching should be like. Their view may be quite different from the self-image that teachers themselves wish to project. Moreover, views of language teaching are affected to some extent by historical developments in the discipline. Some methods imply a specific teaching approach. For example, in an audiolingual programme the teacher is firmly in command, directing the class step by step in a benevolent but authoritarian manner. This view of teaching is in contrast to an approach in which the teacher and students are viewed as participants in a joint enterprise, democratically negotiating with each other about what to learn and how to learn it, a point of vew which is vigorously upheld by some writers (for example, Breen and Candlin 1980; Nunan 1988a). In the method revival of the 1970s (see, for example, Oller and Richards-Amato 1983), one striking feature was the difference in conception of what role the teacher should play. For example, in Counseling-Learning the teacher is seen as a helper, in Suggestopedia he is encouraged to adopt a friendly but somewhat detached role, while in the Dartmouth Method he is expected to dramatize and create excitement.

These are a few examples to show how the four fundamental concepts that were examined in detail in FCLT permeate the other two levels of our model. Therefore, the more clearly these underlying assumptions on the nature of language, social context, language learning, and language teaching are understood, the better we will be able to analyse the other two levels.

The policy level

The second level of the model is that of policy or principal instructional options. It is the level of planning and decision-making, the locus of control and consequently also of the main controversies in language pedagogy. Decisions at this level go to the heart of what this book is mainly concerned with. We can identify four broad categories at the policy level which are implicit in our teaching, but which have been made explicit to some extent partly through earlier debates on teaching methods, and partly through more recent discussions of curriculum:

1 categories of content
2 categories of objectives
3 categories of treatment or procedures
4 categories of evaluation.

A sound analytical scheme must concern itself with all four categories. A weakness of the method controversies of the past was that they focused too exclusively on treatment factors, and did not pay enough systematic attention to the other three categories. This led to a certain lopsidedness in the method debate and to periodic shifts of perspective in the evolution of language pedagogy. In the early 1970s, the Council of Europe's Modern Languages Project set out quite deliberately to counteract this preoccupation with teaching procedures by ignoring method and emphasizing only content and objectives. However, ten years later, when this point had been adequately made, the new Council of Europe Project, which got under way in 1982, could adopt a broader perspective ranging widely over all the factors suggested by our four categories (Council of Europe 1981).

Content and objectives

Let us look briefly at the first two categories at the policy level: content and objectives. These are represented in Figure 1.1 by a cross-tabulation, in which four content categories and four sets of objectives have been identified. It is not claimed that language teaching must pursue all these objectives and content areas simultaneously and always to the same extent. However, it could be argued that a language teaching policy is better to the extent that it identifies as clearly as possible both the objectives and the content of teaching, and justifies on rational grounds why it emphasizes one or the other content area or this or that objective. Four content categories or syllabuses are distinguished in the diagram:

1 language;
2 culture;
3 communicative activities;
4 general language education.

The *language syllabus* represents the objective and analytic study of the second language (L2) concerned. It is based on the assumption that a systematic approach to the second language contributes significantly to the proficiency of the learner. What is included is dependent on the

Content	Objectives			
	Proficiency	Knowledge	Affect	Transfer
Language syllabus (L2)				
Culture syllabus (C2)				
Communicative activities syllabus (L2/C2)				
General language education syllabus (language and culture)				

Figure 1.1 A curriculum model for language teaching adapted from Stern (1980a) and Ullmann (1982)

current state of knowledge in linguistics in general and in descriptive studies of the L2. Potentially, a language curriculum can draw on the whole range of studies of the target language: phonology, grammar, lexicology, and discourse, and it can approach the language from formal, semantic, or sociolinguistic perspectives. The main point is that language cannot be taught in isolation from the other content categories. Our scheme implies that language must be complemented by other substantive areas which we have called 'culture', 'communicative activities', and 'general language education'.

The *culture syllabus* refers to the life of the target language community. Underlying this second content area is the belief that language and culture interact. This syllabus, which so far has not figured prominently in the curriculum debate, constitutes a deliberate and intellectual approach to the target culture (C2). The study of C2 is directed to specified contact groups since languages are used by geographically diverse communities. Thus, for immigrants to North America the primary C2 would be the United States or Canada. In a foreign language teaching situation, for example the teaching of English in France or Germany, the primary target community is more likely to be Britain or the United States. In India, on the other hand, where English is used internally as a language of communication, the appropriate C2 would be India itself. Both language and culture are cognitively guided areas of study. Language and culture form the object of study and enquiry. Practice activities involved in both syllabuses are directed to deliberately chosen features of the language and the society or culture. Both syllabuses represent a particular viewpoint about language learning, i.e. that the analytic study of L2 and C2 has a significant role to play.

The *communicative activities syllabus* contains topics, interests, and activities which learners pursue in order to establish personal contact with the target language community in real-life situations involving the use of the second language. This is a non-analytic or experiential approach to the target language and culture. Communicative activities represent aspects of the programme that bring the learner into personal contact with the speech community whose language is being learnt, and they comprise topics or activities other than the target language or target culture which can be regarded as worthwhile in their own right either for their educational value or for their interest to the language learner. One such topic area may be the target literature. In many instances of adult language learning, communicative activities are likely to include topics arising from the professional interests of the learner. In the case of school children, hobbies, sports, and other personal interests fall into this category. The main point of this approach is that the focus is on the message, on content, or on the activity itself rather than on language aspects. Where language is emphasized, it is subordinated to the purpose of the message. On the basis of this content area, the learner is enabled to establish a personal bond between himself and the target language, the target community, or some of its members.

All three of the syllabuses we have so far considered are concerned with different approaches to the particular L2. The fourth area adds yet another dimension. The *general language education syllabus*, reaching beyond the particular L2, is composed of topics on language, culture, society, and language learning in general. It encourages the learner to stand back from his immediate work with the new language and to make observations about language or culture in general and to reflect about his own language learning experience. In this way, the learning of the target language will become more efficient, and the student will be encouraged to view it as an exemplar enabling him to apply his experience to other languages at a later stage. This syllabus would be introduced wherever the transfer objective is of special significance.

Each of these content areas can, in principle, claim equal attention for serious curriculum development. Together the four areas represent a multidimensional approach to the target language curriculum. Whether the emphasis is spread equally over all four areas or restricted to mainly one or two should be a decision deliberately made and justified by the curriculum developer. It should not be a decision based merely on convention. By and large, it can be said that language curriculums have been too narrowly focused on linguistic content in isolation. In this book, our working hypothesis is that a language programme will be more successful if the language component is not isolated from the other three syllabuses. In other words, we believe that curriculum content should normally be multidimensional, particularly in language courses taught at school or university, unless there are specific circumstances which make this arrangement inappropriate.

The objectives in Figure 1.1 have also been broadly conceived. They originate in the well-known Bloom taxonomies of educational objectives and their application to language teaching worked out by Valette (1977, 1981) over a number of years. The objectives—like the content categories—are once again multidimensional; *proficiency* is not the only objective of language learning, but is accompanied by three other objectives: *knowledge*, *affect*, and *transfer*.

In planning a language programme, the centrality of proficiency is beyond question. In our scheme it is especially relevant to the language and communicative activities syllabuses. What is much more debatable is the degree of proficiency that is appropriate for a given language course. What can a teacher reasonably expect after one term, one year, or five years of language training? The definition of proficiency levels is an issue which is crucial for policy development. The other three categories of objectives are less obvious. In fact they are often not recognized at all or regarded as marginal, because language courses generally aim at a practical command, not at knowledge, information, or other cognitive outcomes. We will try to show that cognitive or knowledge objectives should not be dismissed a priori.

Under affective objectives we pay attention to the creation of a positive outlook on the target language and culture, and the development of a favourable emotional set towards the self as learner of a particular language. The term transfer is used to represent the idea of learning a language not only for its own sake but also as a means of generalizing beyond the particular language and culture. This category includes learning about languages in general, generalizing techniques of language learning, and developing a positive attitude towards all languages and cultures. This objective, which is particularly relevant to the curriculum area of general language education, is obviously not equally applicable in all situations. It may, however, be regarded as particularly relevant for school and university programmes where languages form part of a general educational curriculum. With this scheme of content areas and objectives we have a sufficiently broad, yet precise, set of categories to interpret curriculum policy in a variety of language teaching situations.

We can represent the options with regard to content and objectives as being somewhere on a continuum ranging from narrow and unidimensional at one end to an extreme of multidimensionality at the other end:

Figure 1.2 The scope of the second language curriculum

While plausible arguments can be advanced for a shift in either direction, the curriculum scheme we have just outlined suggests that a greater diversity of objectives and content is desirable. But there are of course circumstances where concentration on a specific curriculum component, such as language proficiency, or even some aspect of it, for example reading, is entirely justified. Languages for special purposes offer such a unidimensional concentration on the interests of particular groups of learners.[2]

Another question concerns the degree of planning and control of content and objectives, expressed on the following dimensions:

Planned	**Partly planned**	**Flexible**	**Partly unplanned**	**Unplanned**
Organized Structured				Open Unstructured

Figure 1.3 Flexibility options in the second language curriculum

Here, too, a good case can be made for either option. If a curriculum is to be carefully controlled linguistically, we will sacrifice adaptability. If we want students to have a say in the development of their curriculum, this aspect cannot be planned in advance. The trade-off between these two options has been extensively debated and we will have to consider their respective merits and drawbacks.

The treatment options

Turning now to the most controversial part of language pedagogy, the treatment, we need categories which, as Bosco and Di Pietro (1970) and Krashen and Seliger (1975) recognized, are more fundamental and less rigid than the concept of method which has dominated language pedagogy for so long. We suggest three broad categories which we will call treatment 'strategies' because they are pervasive features at the policy level. At the surface level they manifest themselves in all kinds of different techniques and activities. The three categories are:

1 teaching strategies
2 timing strategies
3 social or interpersonal strategies.

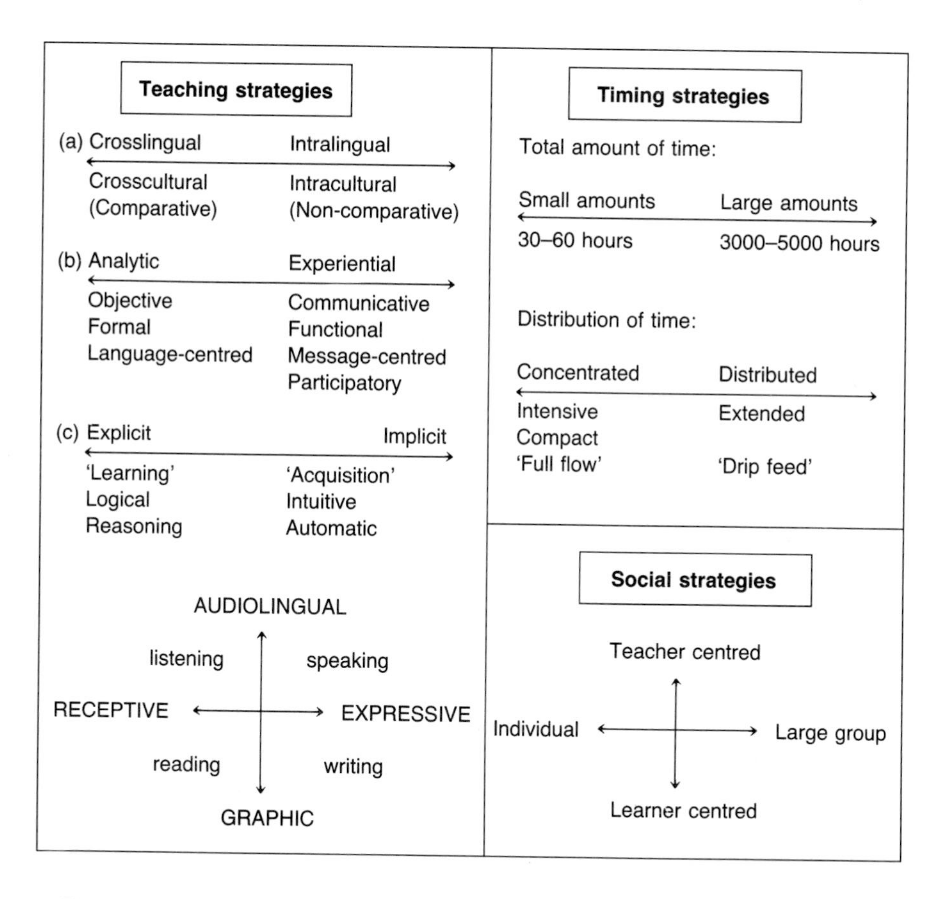

Figure 1.4 Treatment options in language teaching (adapted from Stern 1983a)

Teaching strategies. The teaching strategies displayed in Figure 1.4 are largely derived from the method controversies that have been debated at different times during the last hundred years. The intralingual–crosslingual dimension concerns the use or non-use of L1 in L2 learning. For example, the central characteristic of the direct method is an intralingual strategy, i.e. the exclusion of the native language, while the main distinguishing feature of the traditional or grammar translation method is a crosslingual strategy, namely learning the new language through the medium of the language of origin. The conflict of the late 1960s between cognitivism and audiolingualism reflects the explicit-implicit option, on the one hand problem-solving and reasoning, and on the other a less intellectually demanding, more intuitive way of learning. Degrees of communicativeness in the language class are represented in the third dimension of Figure 1.4 where we find on one side a more analytic-objective strategy matched on the other by a more experiential-communicative one. The audiolingual-graphic dimension and the receptive-expressive option also included in Figure 1.4 are based on the experience of half a century of isolating and recombining in various ways the 'four skills' of listening, speaking, reading, and writing.

All these strategy options—like the method conflicts which preceded them—can be said to originate in deep-seated issues concerning the second language learning process. However, the conflicts they have aroused in the past cannot be resolved by representing them as adversaries. They are best viewed, in this teaching analysis, as continua. There is no implicit positive or negative quality judgement on one or the other side of a pair of strategies. Rather they are complementary options which find concrete expression in the 'more or less' of classroom techniques and activities. Considering the four content syllabuses outlined in the previous section above, we can see, however, that there are interdependencies between certain strategy and content options, with the analytic strategy being characteristic of the language and cultural syllabuses, the experiential strategy closely identified with the communicative activities syllabus, and the crosslingual strategy most obviously associated with general language education.

Timing strategies. While teaching strategies are largely policy options on which practitioners can make decisions for themselves, timing strategies are only partially under the control of the individual teacher. They are generally more the responsibility of the administrator or curriculum designer. Many experiments since World War II have related to the possibility of varying the amount of time given to language instruction, the degree of concentration, and the starting age for language learning. Some writers, for example Carroll (1975) and Burstall *et al.* (1974), and some systems of education have attributed a great deal of importance to the time aspect of language learning. Beside the system-wide policy issues with regard to time, there are some timing options available to the individual teacher. Within a course or a single class a teacher can segment lessons in many small episodes or in larger 'chunks', with consequences for other strategies and ultimately for effective learning.

Social or interpersonal strategies. These refer, first, to the size and composition of language learning groups; this aspect again is partly an issue for administrators rather than for the individual practitioner. The second social dimension, however, is one over which the individual teacher can exercise much more choice; it is the strategy which reflects the increasing interest in human relations and the emotional aspect of language learning:

Large group	**Small group**	**Individual**
←		→

Teacher directed learner dependence	**Learner initiated** learner autonomy
←	→

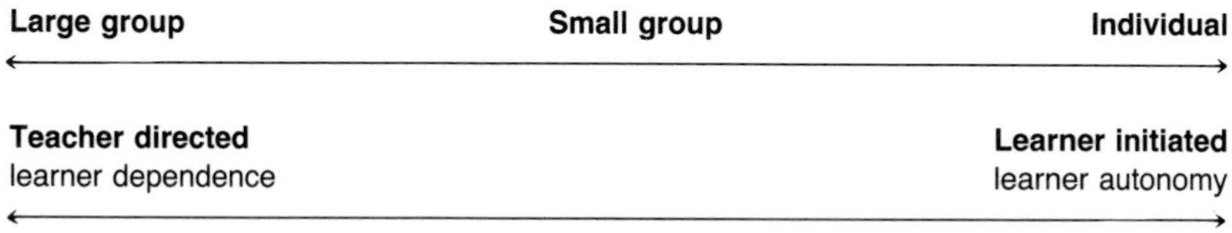

Figure 1.5 Social strategies options in language teaching

While none of the strategies can by themselves be regarded as either 'right' or 'wrong', their application in a given teaching situation is not a matter of personal whim. They may be modified in relation to different objectives, the stage of language learning (beginners, intermediate, or advanced), the age, maturity, and previous experience of the students, and the sociolinguistic context, i.e. whether a language is learnt with or without environmental support. These are all factors which the practitioner has to bear in mind in deciding on the balance of the strategies to employ. These adjustments of teaching policy to given circumstances are likely to be made intuitively by the teacher or curriculum developer. On the other hand, the choice of a given strategy can also be the subject of experimental hypotheses and then become a variable in a research study. The main point is that in a language teaching analysis we do not look for a fixed combination of strategies; rather we try to find out whether there is an awareness of the range of instructional options and on what grounds different choices are being made.

Evaluation of student progress

The next area for policy decisions concerns student evaluation, an important component of the teaching plan. Some of the issues can be expressed as follows:

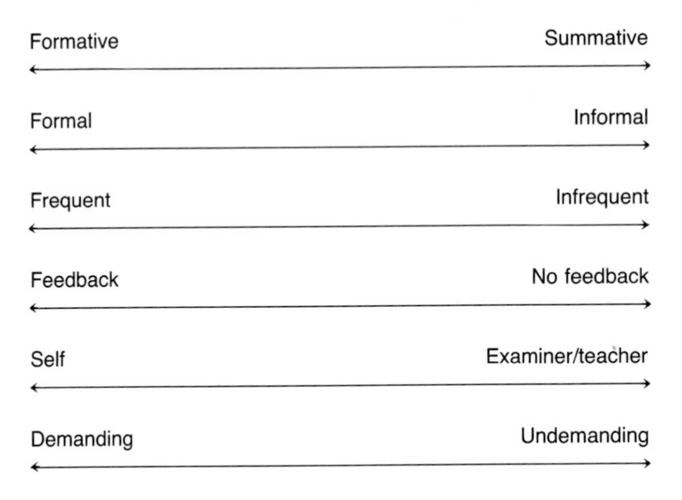

Figure 1.6 Evaluation options in language teaching

In this area, as in the others, much serious thought has been given to the merits of different options. For a language teaching analysis one would look for a rational choice of evaluation procedures which give students a realistic appraisal of progress, represent a fair judgement, and lead increasingly to self-monitoring and self-assessment.

Resources

A final and most important policy issue concerns the number and kinds of resources that come into use. We consider resources last because ideally they should be compatible with the entire curriculum policy—content, objectives, strategies, and evaluation procedures—and should reflect that policy. In fact the relationship is often the other way round, in that curriculum materials determine and sometimes distort policy. Curriculum resources, which include human resources as well as teaching materials and technological equipment, can be analysed on a scale from limited/simple at one end to extensive/varied on the other. The advantage does not necessarily lie with extensive and varied materials. Too many and too varied materials may be confusing, whereas restricted and simple resources may be more effective because they are easier to handle. There are other options to consider: print versus non-print, authentic versus contrived material, the role of technology, particularly computer-assisted learning, and so on. Clearly, it is no longer merely a question of 'What's your textbook?'

The policy context

So far we have treated instructional policy as if it could be based entirely on general principles without considering the particular circumstances and the context in which it is to operate. This is perhaps valid up to a point. We can no doubt formulate policy directions which are widely applicable in many different settings and which express our basic beliefs and convictions. However, most of our plans relate to particular groups of learners with a particular background working in a specified milieu. In formulating our policy we must take note of these context and presage variables (Dunkin and Biddle 1974), which ultimately also affect practice. Since they apply equally to the policy level and the practical action level, it is appropriate to discuss them between the two. A policy should be developed in relation to the needs, demands, and conditions of the learners who constitute the target group. The interpretation of the context is likely to be made intuitively by a teacher working with a group of students. But it can also be done systematically, and it can be carefully documented, as would be necessary in a research study or a formal programme evaluation. The following factors should be taken into account:

1 Social factors;
2 Learner factors;
3 Educational framework and teacher factors;
4 The curriculum context.

Social factors. In all language teaching we must take note of the social factors which are likely to influence language teaching. We must, therefore, ask what the characteristics of the environment are in which the teaching occurs. This means paying attention to sociocultural, historico-political, linguistic, geographic, and economic-technological factors. We might have to find out the opinions of politicians, examine language legislation, and assess public attitudes to languages in general, to the particular language in question, and to various ethnolinguistic communities. Even if we are unable to make systematic enquiries, we should at least be sensitive to these social factors (cf. Ashworth 1985).

Learner factors. It is of the utmost importance for policy and practice as well as for evaluation and research to have as deep an understanding as possible of the learner group, its social and educational background, its previous language learning experience, and its ethnolinguistic attitudes, motivations, and expectations.

Educational framework and teacher factors. It is obvious that we should be thoroughly familiar with the educational framework of the language programme. We must familiarize ourselves with the organization and structure of the system and its institutions and learn how the programme fits into the overall educational plan. Under this heading we should also include information about the teachers themselves. What is their educational and professional background? What access do they have to advice, supervision, and in-service training? How much freedom do they have to design their own courses? Do they mainly carry out a policy which is prescribed by others, or are they in a position to shape the policy for themselves?

The curriculum context. In order to understand what goes on in a particular class we must be able to place it in the context of the language course of which it forms a part. We should also be able to relate the particular class to the entire language programme of the institution in question and ultimately to its overall curriculum. We should in addition have a clear picture of the length of the total language programme, its division into stages, streams or sets, and the ways in which learner groups in the institution have been arranged.

With this brief outline of the policy context we have completed the language teaching analysis at the second or policy level of our model, and we can now turn to the third level of the scheme.

The practical action level

At the third level of the model in Figure I.2 we come to the specific manifestations of language teaching, the concrete reality of language classes in school A, college B, adult evening class C, and university language department D. Here teachers and learners come together, and it is as a result of action at this level that we expect students to learn language X, Y, or Z. We are concerned here with the activities of teachers and learners and with learning outcomes. We call this the practical action level, because it is at this point that the plans and policies of level 2 are translated into reality and manifest themselves in concrete behaviour. This is the point where the assumptions at level 1 and the policy decisions at level 2 come to the surface, and this is where the crux lies. It is here, after all, that the whole enterprise must justify itself: learning either does or does not occur.

We can look at level 3 from the point of view of the teacher responsible for teaching a particular group of students, or from the perspective of an observer of the language class. As teachers we act as we see fit according to the circumstances we find ourselves in. We constantly make split-second decisions in relation to the intentions we have brought to the teaching situation, and we make intuitive moment-to-moment assessments of student reactions, for example, Does what I planned lead to learning? Are my students improving in their proficiency? Do they understand what I am saying? Does my teaching help them to make progress? Do they learn what I am teaching them? How do they respond to my intentions? In other words, what the teacher in action is looking for is congruence or fit between planning at level 2 and concrete actions and outcomes at level 3.

Teachers use certain indicators which tell them whether what they teach is effective. In the language class we intuitively assess from our students' reactions the extent to which the strategies we employ are successful and the objectives we have set ourselves are being met. If our students are old enough to have insights into their own learning, we can ask them for their opinion. We can also use more objective and systematic measures such as tests, we can examine other aspects of students' work, for example their written work, or we can conduct student interviews. On the basis of our observations and interpretations of student progress we can revise our teaching plan. In this way there is a constant movement between the policy level and the action level in an attempt to achieve the best possible fit for successful learning. In the long term, we may gradually revise our view of fundamental concepts at level 1 as well. The advantage of a three-level scheme for the practitioner lies in the direction that it gives to the natural self-observation of classroom action at level 3 by relating classroom events systematically to decisions at the policy level and beliefs at the basic philosophical level.

If we consider level 3 from the point of view of an observer, we should note that there are several kinds of observers who have reason to examine the events of the classroom: teacher trainers; advisers, supervisors, and others in some kind of authority relationship to the class teacher; programme evaluators; and researchers. The first two groups, teacher trainers and advisers or supervisors, must observe systematically for similar reasons: they are called upon to assist teachers by making them more aware of factors which could lead to improvements in teaching; and they must make judgements about the quality of teaching for certification or promotion. Both tasks involve some sort of teaching analysis including classroom observation. The third group, programme evaluators, are not concerned with the actions of particular teachers and learning outcomes of specific groups of students or individual learners; they are mainly interested in the characteristics and quality of the programme as a whole, as it is being implemented in a school or school system. For this group, therefore, observations provide documentation on how the programme is being implemented.

In order to interpret teaching in action at level 3 we will use the same concepts that we have outlined for the planning and policy level. However, we must introduce two new features which distinguish this level from level 2. The first distinguishing feature is that we must focus on specific documentation and concrete teaching and learning activities which have to be analysed and interpreted in terms of the categories we have already established. In short, what we need at this level can be described as case studies of teaching. The second major feature that distinguishes this level from level 2 is that we are not only concerned with teaching acts but also with the corresponding behaviour of learners, with learner reactions, and with learning outcomes.

Thus, we visualize a teacher first developing a plan of action at the policy level, carrying out the plan and assessing the effect on the learner at the practical action level, and, finally, either continuing the action or revising it in the light of the assessment. This means that teaching can be viewed as a sequence of planning—acting—assessing—revising the plan—acting again, and so on. This sequence is in many cases one of numerous split-second decisions within a single class period. It can also be regarded as a longer stretch of time extending from lesson to lesson and, beyond that, as a long-term process involving development of a major policy plan for a course or programme, followed by implementation, formative evaluation, and a review process which could stretch over several years.

In other words, the sequence we have described can represent the day-to-day decision-making and actions of the class teacher as well as the planning and implementation of a curriculum by a course designer or administrator. It is equally relevant to the different categories of observers of classroom teaching. In classroom observation we have to be sensitive not only to the overt teaching acts and their effect on learners at level 3. We must equally understand the context of the teaching situation and the underlying intentions of the teacher or curriculum designer at level 2. Classroom observation will be considered in more detail in the next chapter, within the context of the curriculum planning process.

Concluding comments

The expectation is that our multidimensional framework for the analysis of second language teaching will not only provide more choice for the curriculum designer, but will ultimately lead to the enhancement of second language teaching and learning. It is also expected that the four-syllabus approach to curriculum content will be educationally more productive than curriculum content which is exclusively linguistic. The four syllabuses provide four interlocking content areas. Each offers a different perspective and a particular angle on the language learning task. The language syllabus deals with the language in a systematic way, the cultural syllabus deals with relevant aspects of society and culture, the communicative activities syllabus involves students in interesting activities in the second language, and the general language education syllabus gives them the opportunity to reflect and to gather their thoughts with regard to the language learning process. At the same time this fourfold approach increases the language teacher's repertoire and should ultimately lead to greater professional expertise and satisfaction.

Whether the broadened conception of language teaching fulfils these expectations cannot be stated a priori. It must be regarded as a hypothesis. Its implementation should, therefore, be the subject of experimentation and systematic evaluation. The priorities indicated in Figure 1.1 both in terms of objectives and the scope of content areas are likely to vary in response not only to the different aims of language courses, but also to differences in language learning contexts, the age of the students concerned, their maturity, and their previous language learning experience. The grid, as pointed out previously, is intended to be a flexible framework which is widely applicable to a great variety of language learning situations.

What are the main problems in putting a wide-ranging scheme of this kind into effect? They are principally those of curriculum development, and later those of implementation and evaluation (see Chapter 2). None of our syllabuses have been fully implemented. We have to remember that, in the past, language syllabuses have been mainly grammatical. The curriculum movement of the 1970s and 1980s widened the scope of syllabus design, and offered interesting modifications of the traditional curriculum. It has been difficult enough to broaden the grammatical syllabus by adding even one new linguistic perspective—that of notions and functions. It is an even more demanding task if we add further syllabuses of a totally different character, as suggested by our multidimensional framework. All four syllabuses are meant to be powerful and distinct approaches to second language learning in their own right. Yet, they are not to be thought of as separate entities. Rather, we should aim to integrate them with one another as much as possible, thus providing a variety of perspectives on the language our students are attempting to learn.

In Chapter 2, we will briefly consider a number of factors that, although they do not form part of our framework for the analysis of the curriculum itself, will necessarily come into play whenever we embark on the processes of curriculum development, implementation, and evaluation. While our prime concern in Parts Two to Four of this volume is to develop the analytic framework that has been outlined in this chapter, we cannot afford to ignore the real-time curriculum management processes through which we must pass in planning a curriculum.

Notes

1 For analysis of the different assumptions underlying some labelled 'methods' (e.g. grammar–translation, the direct method, the audio-lingual method), see FCLT, Chapter 20. See also Richards and Rodgers (1986).

2 Issues concerning curriculum objectives in English for Specific Purposes are discussed by Hutchinson and Waters (1987); Mackay and Mountford (1978); Robinson (1980); Trimble (1985); and Widdowson (1978, 1983).

2 Managing the second language curriculum

Curriculum processes

What the curriculum should consist of; how detailed and complex it should be; how much of it should be determined in advance; what the areas of freedom and momentary decision should be—these are all questions about the scope of the curriculum itself. A totally different set of questions is how the curriculum should be arrived at; who should be responsible for curriculum development; and what procedures should be established for curriculum making. Beyond the curriculum development process a further set of questions is how and by whom the curriculum should be 'applied', 'delivered', or 'implemented'. What steps must be taken to ensure implementation? In other words, we distinguish between the process of developing or creating a curriculum and learning materials, and that of implementing, applying, or delivering the curriculum through the use of materials in the classroom.

A further important aspect of curriculum processes is curriculum evaluation, that is, the task of monitoring the strengths and weaknesses of a course or programme. Evaluation must include mechanisms for bringing about change, in order to ensure that all language programmes are as effective and adaptable to changing circumstances as possible. In short, curriculum processes are cyclic: (a) curriculum research and development, (b) curriculum implementation, (c) curriculum evaluation, (d) renewed research and development, and so on. The processes of curriculum management—development, implementation, and evaluation—are receiving increasing attention in the literature on second language education (for example, White 1988; Johnson 1989).

The responsibility for curriculum development

A persistent question in curriculum decision-making is where the responsibility for curriculum development should lie. There is uncertainty on this issue because it has not always been made sufficiently clear which language teaching situation is being thought of. Thus, some curriculum theorists think of courses to be developed by the teachers themselves for particular groups of students, while others have in mind curriculum development which is system-wide. There are other variations one can think of between these extremes; for example, curriculum development at the institutional, local, or regional level. It is clear that the responsibilities are differently distributed in these situations. In the school systems of some countries curriculum is determined centrally by the Ministry of Education or its equivalent, and this principle applies to foreign languages just as much as to other curriculum subjects. In other countries the role of curriculum developer is divided between the central, regional, local, and institutional levels. It is often falsely assumed that a centrally determined curriculum is inevitably inflexible. But flexibility can be built into a centrally defined curriculum. On the other hand, a locally produced curriculum is not necessarily flexible. It can be just as rigid as a centrally prepared curriculum.

Much curriculum development appropriately occurs at the classroom level and is, therefore, in the hands of individual teachers. On the other hand, where languages such as English, French, or Spanish are taught in entire school systems, it is customary for a central agency to play a leading role in curriculum development. In these situations, which arise in most countries with fully developed educational systems, class teachers by and large rely on someone else, an education authority, a ministry of education, an examination board or some other body, to present them with a curriculum or syllabus. Their main function as teachers is the application or 'delivery' of the curriculum to the class with the help of prepared curriculum materials. Under these conditions, the classroom practitioner has relatively little input into the curriculum development process. In other situations, for example in the teaching of English as a second language to adults, English for Specific Purposes (ESP), or in the teaching of rarely taught languages, the teacher may find that no ready-made curriculum exists, and there may even be no readily available teaching materials. In these circumstances the teacher is completely on his own. He must design his own curriculum, make or find his own materials, and teach his curriculum to the class. In this situation the development of the curriculum and its implementation in the classroom are carried out by one and the same person, the teacher himself.

Whatever the situation, we must distinguish between the processes of curriculum development and those of curriculum implementation. These are two distinct functions, one a planning and the other a delivery function, but both are part of language teaching, whether they are carried out by one person, the teacher, or whether they are divided up so that some curriculum decisions are made by people who are relatively removed from the classroom setting, such as an inspector, an adviser, an examiner, or an official in a ministry of education. In the 1960s, the expertise of the applied linguist was often added, and curriculum development became very much the task of 'experts'. Gradually, it has become recognized that it is important to involve classroom practitioners at the school and class level much more directly and systematically in curriculum decisions and in materials development.

There has recently been much concern about the importance of obtaining input from various sources including the learners themselves, so that curriculum making can be brought closer to the classroom (Breen 1983, 1987; Nunan 1988a). This is in line with general trends in educational administration where there has been a marked tendency to devolve responsibility from a central authority closer to the local and individual setting in which the curriculum comes into operation. We believe it is right to take a number of points of view into account, including those of teachers, parents, citizens in general, and above all the reactions of students. Eventually, however, the responsibility for curriculum must lie where it has been placed by society, often upon the teachers themselves, sometimes upon a local authority, examination board, or ministry of education. The responsibility cannot be abandoned merely by declaring that we are 'negotiating' the curriculum with our students. The refusal to plan in advance is as much a curriculum decision as imposing a rigid preordained curriculum.

The planning process

Language needs analysis was an important development of the 1970s (Richterich and Chancerel 1977; Munby 1978) designed to make it possible to adjust language courses to the needs of groups of students working in various countries at different levels of proficiency and with a variety of objectives in mind. As Yalden (1983) has indicated, needs analysis remains an important first stage of curriculum development in many types of language teaching, serving as a key source of input for decisions to be made with respect to content, objectives, and treatment strategies (see also Brindley 1989).

In some circumstances needs analysis can try to do too much, because the detailed information it assembles about the learner cannot be operationalized, that is, it cannot be matched by the curriculum or the teaching approach because the resources that can be mustered are not sufficiently diversified and refined. In other instances, however, a needs analysis in the manner of Richterich or Munby is not enough, as is clearly acknowledged by Richterich (1980). It is important to find out what the individual learner wants but it is also important to determine what society requires. Therefore, as Trim (1980) has pointed out, curriculum development often demands as a first step an analysis of the entire learning context, including social and individual motivations and needs, as well as a realistic study of the conditions under which language learning is likely to occur. Within such a broadly based study, there are particular situations such as language courses for specific purposes in which a needs analysis of the type developed by Richterich or Munby, although probably in a much simplified format, has a role to play (see, for example, Hutchinson and Waters 1987). It still happens all too often that language courses are prepared and conducted with very little thought being given to the specific needs of the particular audiences which are to be served by the language programme.

The desired end product of the teaching process must be defined as clearly as possible, in answer to such questions as: What should the learner know or be able to do at certain stages and after completion of the course? The more realistically the expected intermediate or end results can be defined, the better it is for the process of curriculum development. Language objectives, for example, can be expressed in the form of a general descriptive statement and illustrated concretely by samples of spoken and written texts at the expected mastery level. Objectives may also be formulated as inventories of functions the learner is expected to be able to perform at the end of the training period. They can further be represented by a grid of various categories of content and objectives, as suggested by Valette (1971, 1981). In our own conceptual framework, in Chapter 1, by developing a scheme of content and objectives as a grid of broad categories, we are following this last pattern.

The proposed end product can be related to the total language course, the point of entry, the total time available for teaching, and the expected distribution of time from the beginning to the end of the course. In most instances of planning, suitable stretches of time can be found by relating them to the framework of the educational institution for which the curriculum is being developed. For example, in a school system divided into primary and secondary stages, it is reasonable to define the end of primary school as an intermediate level of second language instruction, and to consider how far on the way to the expected end point the learners will be at that time. For a university language course, on the other hand, a university term, semester, or academic year can be used to determine the intermediate stages.

A preliminary outline of the whole course and a tentative indication of how it is divided into stages serves to delimit the task of curriculum development. At this point, the curriculum developer reviews the resources at his disposal. There may be existing curriculums, teaching materials, and other resources to examine and compare. Curriculum development also requires access to research which may be linguistic, sociolinguistic, cultural, historical, sociological, or literary. If the relevant research has not been carried out, curriculum development has to proceed on the best information available. On this basis a detailed description of the curriculum is undertaken. Much of it must be experimental and intuitive, and the more creative and inventive the curriculum maker is, the better it will be. Different tasks in the development of the total curriculum such as the design of a language syllabus or a cultural syllabus can be allocated to different individuals or groups.

It is in the nature of curriculum that it imposes a certain structure and regularity on language teaching and learning. A constant concern has been the narrow and restricted nature of a curriculum which is imposed on the language class, which does not serve the purposes of the students, and which is frustrating for the teacher. In Figure 1.3, we represented the flexibility options for the language curriculum on a continuum, envisaging at one end a curriculum which is completely planned and structured down to the most minute detail, and at the other end one which has been left open and which is defined only in contact with the learners. Between these extremes we visualized various degrees of flexibility and partial planning. There may be instances in which a curriculum is a straitjacket which allows no freedom to the teacher to adapt the curriculum to particular circumstances. However, in many instances of language instruction the problem is not so much one of forcing the teacher into a preplanned mould. Rather there is a much greater danger of lack of planning and an absence of any systematic preparation of content.

The process of planning does not necessarily mean rigidity. Areas of choice and freedom can always be built into the most carefully designed curriculum. Moreover, any plan must allow for adaptation to particular circumstances in the process of implementation. There is no contradiction between planning and negotiating the curriculum with the students we teach. On the contrary, if the programme is not planned, the teacher has nothing to negotiate about. As we shall see in Part Three, several linguists have expressed scepticism with regard to the ordering of language data. There are indeed many aspects of syllabus design which cannot be determined by linguistic logic. Not even grammatical sequencing can be wholly based on hierarchical or logical ordering. However, this is no reason for abandoning the principle of sequencing altogether. It is possible, in a purely practical way, to develop an order on psychological and pedagogic grounds which can always be modified and refined on the basis of experience. Here, again, we see the need for making decisions but allowing for flexibility and adaptability in practice.

A final misconception has arisen out of the desire to encourage the learner to take responsibility for his own learning. This is a very promising trend which can be built into any language curriculum. But an emphasis on learner autonomy does not absolve the curriculum designer of his responsibility to plan the options within which the learner will be encouraged to exercise his judgement. In short, careful and comprehensive curriculum planning is compatible with adaptability at the class level for both teachers and students. Therefore, the laudable intention to give freedom to the teacher and responsibility to the student must not serve as an excuse for not planning the curriculum. Too much planning and over-detailed direction are not the most common defects of language curriculums; a much more likely deficiency is an absence of planning, a lack of preparation, or too restricted a scope for the curriculum.

Issues in implementation

Since, by definition, designing a curriculum takes place at the planning and preparatory stage, it is usually undertaken away from the classrooms in which the curriculum is eventually to come into operation. The translation of a curriculum into classroom reality—its implementation by teachers who have not necessarily participated at the preparation and design stage—is, therefore, likely to present problems. Teachers do not always share the preoccupations and concerns that prompted the curriculum change in the first place. They may not be aware of what the innovation is supposed to achieve. They may not understand in what way it is different from existing practice. They may recognize the nature of the change but resist it. They may regard it as unnecessary or feel threatened by it, or they may feel inadequate to carry it into effect. The more radical the new curriculum, the greater the possibility of difficulties in its application.

For these reasons, it is advisable to consider the implementation of a new curriculum as a phase of development which needs to be as carefully planned as the curriculum itself. The importance of attending to implementation is recognized in general curriculum theory (Park and Fullan 1986) but far less so in language pedagogy (see Johnson 1989, however). In order to make the transition from curriculum design to implementation as smooth as possible, it is best to envisage it as a three-stage process. To begin with, there should be small-scale try-outs which will lead to revisions of the curriculum at the second stage. After that a larger field trial will give further evidence of the practicality of the new curriculum and the steps that need to be taken to make a large-scale implementation successful. This large-scale implementation constitutes the third and final stage of curriculum development.

Implementation involves the selection or preparation of appropriate learning materials. It also involves dissemination of information about the new curriculum. It may also require plans for in-service or pre-service teacher education. The absence of implementation plans can mean that the intentions of the new curriculum design are misunderstood, misinterpreted, or misapplied. It may even mean that the new curriculum is simply ignored or does not come into operation in the way that was intended, whatever its inherent merits.

Curriculum evaluation

Although the education literature contains well-developed theories and established techniques of curriculum evaluation (for example, Lewy 1977), relatively little attention has been given to this aspect of second language pedagogy (see, however, Beretta 1986; Brown 1989; Lynch 1990). In view of the questions and concerns about the quality of programmes in many settings, the relative neglect is surprising. It is true that a few language programmes have been evaluated. A well-known evaluation study was that of French in British primary schools between 1964 and 1974 (Burstall *et al.* 1974). In Canada, French immersion programmes have been extensively monitored for about two decades (for example, Lambert and Tucker 1972; Stern *et al.* 1976; Swain and Lapkin 1982; Genesee 1987). But these tend to be the exceptions. Generally speaking, curriculum evaluation has not been accorded a prominent place in second language pedagogy.

The distinction between formative and summative evaluation that was introduced by Scriven (1967) into general curriculum theory can also be applied to second language curriculum development. Thus, the evaluation of French in British primary schools was summative: it concluded that on balance the teaching of French in the early years of schooling should not be endorsed. By contrast the Canadian immersion evaluations, which were also largely summative in character, supported the innovation. Summative studies are designed to help in arriving at policy decisions: should a given course be continued, discontinued, or modified?

Formative evaluation, on the other hand, is directed more at the curriculum developer. It checks every phase of the development process and thus helps in its improvement. Since the developer necessarily becomes personally committed to his creation, it is important to allow someone else who adopts a more objective research outlook to ask questions along the way: Are the needs and aims identified really the right ones? Does the curriculum content stand up to scrutiny? How do teachers during the initial try-outs and the field trials cope with the new curriculum? Does the curriculum meet the expectations of those who initiated it? How is the implementation proceeding? Has enough been done to assist teachers in presenting the curriculum to their classes? How is the course received by the students for whom it is intended? Is the programme successful? If it does not meet expectations what changes can be recommended?

The evaluator seeks answers to these kinds of questions by sympathetically observing classes and interviewing teachers, students, or parents. The evaluation may also involve the judicious use of tests or questionnaires. The evaluator must, of course, interpret these findings and communicate his interpretations to the developer. In this way, the curriculum developer as well as the education authority, which most likely has initiated the curriculum innovation, obtains an ongoing assessment and analysis which provides feedback for further development and change. The formative evaluation also gives the responsible authority a guarantee that the new programme has been scrutinized by knowledgeable persons and will stand up to criticism. An evaluation of a second language programme may combine a number of different approaches which together constitute a kind of qualitative audit (Mackay and Palmer 1981; Jarvis and Adams 1979; Long 1984; Brown 1989).

Curriculum research

The role of research in curriculum development

So far we have identified various stages of curriculum development. In many ways, however, it would be better to describe the process as one of research and development. A research component is, or should be, woven into the process at every stage. Some of the curriculum processes which have just been described, particularly the study of the language teaching context, needs analysis, and evaluation should in effect be regarded as research procedures. Research, however, is needed at other phases of curriculum development, particularly in the selection of curriculum content. The required research sources will include linguistic, sociolinguistic, cultural, historical, sociological, or literary documentation, depending on the nature of the topic. Unfortunately, it would be unrealistic to expect that basic research should always precede curriculum development, and in the absence of research data short-term measures must be taken. The planning of notional syllabuses has illustrated what can be done even when the research evidence lags behind developmental demands (see, for example, Wilkins 1976).

On a long-term basis, however, curriculum needs can stimulate research studies of a more systematic kind. In many instances a research approach could be a fruitful follow-up to intuitive curriculum decisions and could strengthen and refine the curriculum process. Thus, the concept of a threshold level in the Modern Languages Project of the Council of Europe served as an intuitively developed guide, and as such formed a hypothesis for what might be a minimal or threshold level of second language mastery. Ideally, it should have been followed up by an empirical research study to verify that the selected inventory truly reflects the minimal language resources needed by learners when they are exposed to the situations which were the target for the threshold level inventories, but such a study has never been undertaken. In other words, the importance of research support for curriculum development has not yet received the attention it requires.

Classroom observation

One area of research which has recently gained in importance is classroom observation. In the past, researchers relied mainly on the study of learning outcomes; studies were largely product-oriented, designed to compare the relative effectiveness of different teaching methods. But much of this research turned out to be rather inconclusive. This is why, during the 1970s, scholars were increasingly led to the conclusion that a better understanding of 'what goes on in the classroom' was needed to account for the research results. This conviction has brought about a growing interest in classroom research and in observation as a research technique (for example, Allwright 1988; Chaudron 1988; van Lier 1988). The various observation schemes created for use in the L2 classroom complement our three-level language teaching analysis, particularly at the practical action level. We will now briefly consider some recent classroom observation schemes and see what they can contribute to the process of curriculum design.

Although the importance of observing 'what goes on in the classroom' has long been recognized, research on the language class has been slow to develop and is only now beginning to come into its own. In other areas of educational research, classroom observation has been pursued for much longer and has yielded an enormous number of schemes. To begin with, in the 1960s, it was thought that the needs of language teaching could be met by simply adapting schemes designed for other curriculum areas. An early scheme for foreign language classroom observation was one such adaptation of the widely known Interaction Analysis by Flanders, devised by Moskowitz (1978). This scheme, known as FLINT (Foreign Language Interaction Analysis), assesses mainly the socio-affective climate of the language class and the degree to which it is teacher-centred or learner-centred. In other words, it is geared primarily to assessing the language teacher's social strategies. FLINT has prompted the question of whether it is appropriate for an observation scheme for language classes to be based on categories developed for another curriculum area. It was subsequently severely criticized on several grounds (Bailey 1976), and these criticisms are no doubt justified. Nevertheless, FLINT was a pioneer effort on which further developments in language classroom observation could be built.

In the meantime, other schemes were created which were intended to reflect more specifically a given language teaching policy. For example, a scheme by Jarvis (1968), based on the audiolingual method, was designed to observe whether the target language or the native language was used in the language class, and whether the L2 was used in natural spoken communication, in audiolingual drills, or through the written medium. According to its author, the model of language learning underlying this scheme

> assumes that in language skill acquisition the student must proceed through the stages of "encountering" (hearing or seeing) elements of the language, imitating them, manipulating them, and finally using them in innovative real communication language.
> (Jarvis 1968: 336)

In other words, the scheme was clearly based on language teaching considerations, and did not simply apply categories which had been developed with other curriculum subjects in mind.

Other investigators have focused on particular aspects of the language class. For example, a study on error correction (Allwright 1975a) attempted to develop a typology of errors and of error correction. This study showed that error correction can create misunderstandings rather than help students learn from their errors. A study on turn-taking (Allwright 1980) revealed subtle kinds of interaction between students and teachers at the practical action level, demonstrating that the teacher's lesson plan needs to be constantly adjusted in response to unforeseen reactions of the class.

Another scheme (Fanselow 1977) represents an attempt to analyse the language class objectively and comprehensively without making assumptions about underlying language teaching philosophy. This scheme, called FOCUS (Foci for Observing Communications Used in Settings), is deliberately kept general to capture a great variety of language learning contexts; but it can also be used differentially to focus on specific aspects of the language class. It could even be applied to verbal exchanges in a non-teaching setting. The author of the scheme wanted to provide a simple technical terminology for the observation of the language classroom which avoids the 'ill-defined and inconsistently used' vocabulary that is common in talking about classroom activities (Fanselow 1977: 18).

Of special interest for our purposes are two British and two Canadian projects involving classroom observation. The first of these was undertaken by a research team at the University of York, England. The object of this investigation was to study the classroom behaviour of a small number of outstanding professionals with a view to discussing what constitutes good language teaching. On the recommendation of national and local inspectors the project had identified a number of foreign language teachers who were held in high regard. The team recognized that research of this kind lacked 'a good conceptual system for classifying and discussing the activities which go on in the classroom' (McNair 1980, quoted in Sanderson 1982: 9). This project established the following categories which incorporated a number of hypotheses about good language teaching derived from earlier studies:

Uses the foreign language predominantly. Did the foreign language dominate the lesson or was it subservient to the mother tongue?

Is vigilant about pronunciation, intonation and stress. Was there much evidence of overt or oblique correction in this area?

Uses the foreign language for classroom instruction. Were the normal classroom directives given in the foreign language or in English?

Uses the foreign language for the teaching/learning message. Was the foreign language used for talking about the material used, discussing and amplifying it, or not?

Praises correct responses. Was the correct response acknowledged frequently, sometimes, or not at all?

Is sympathetic/positive about wrong responses. What was the teacher's reaction to a wrong response?

Conveys warmth in delivery of the message. How did the teachers speak to their pupils? What 'came through' in the way that they addressed them?

Conveys warmth through facial expression. What attitude was discernable in the way teachers looked at their pupils?

Engages in intensive oral exploitation of material. Did the materials appear to be used a great deal for oral work, or not?

Promotes understanding by non-verbal cues. Was there any evidence of understanding being helped by means other than speech? If so, how significant did these other means appear to be in the teaching observed?

Relates the foreign language to target culture. Was the foreign language used to convey either information about, or a feel for the country whose language was being studied?

Explains tasks clearly. Were clear explanations an important element in the teaching observed or not? When explanations occurred, how were they communicated?

Is varied with regard to materials. Was it important to the teachers to use a variety of materials within one lesson, or not?

Is flexible with regard to objectives. Was there much evidence of diversion from the apparent aims of the lesson?

Builds up on pupil error. Did there appear to be evidence, or not, of teachers using an error to make the correct answer more clear?

Provides a variety of language activity. Did there appear to be much variety of activity within the lesson, or not?

Involves the whole group. Was participation encouraged for the whole class, or just for certain individuals?

Is skilled in handling equipment. Did skill in handling equipment appear to be an important factor in the lessons observed, or not?

Promotes use of foreign language by pupils. Was there much evidence that the teaching observed prompted the pupils to use the foreign language productively?

(Sanderson 1982: 9)

The aim of the project was to find out whether the hypotheses could be confirmed by observation of practice. The expectation was that omissions would become apparent, but that the research would end with a revised list of well-established principles of good language teaching. This study was, therefore, not concerned with establishing a precise observation scheme. Instead, it collected detailed observations on a small number of teachers with a few definite criteria in mind. These nine teachers were observed for sixteen lessons, eight at the observers' first visit and eight at their second visit. When the observations had been completed the teachers were also interviewed with the following questions in mind:

Which of the project's hypotheses appeared most important to you? Did you feel that there were any important omissions? Were you surprised by anything in your own teaching pattern?
(Sanderson 1982: 14)

The study is based on the interpretation of these observations and the conversations with the nine teachers, so that it provides level 3 empirical data and policy statements by the teachers themselves. In later chapters we will refer to the findings of this and similar studies.

A second British study was undertaken in Scottish secondary schools by a research team at the University of Stirling. The purpose of this project was once more the empirical investigation of classroom teaching, this time 'to investigate the skills of foreign language teaching (FLT) at an elementary level, and to produce materials for the training of teachers in some of these skills' (Mitchell *et al.* 1981: 1). As a first stage, this long-term enquiry set itself the task of describing 'the FLT teaching process in a number of first year French classrooms' (ibid.: 2). With that objective in mind, the team constructed a lesson analysis scheme which it attempted to base on current theoretical conceptions of language teaching. The Stirling scheme had four dimensions:

1 topic of discourse;
2 type of language activity;
3 student and teacher involvement;
4 class organization.

Under each of these broad headings, carefully thought-out and detailed categories were listed enabling the observer to collect data on language classes. The empirical application of this scheme in seven comprehensive schools in Scotland yielded information on several classes of seventeen teachers of first year French. This research therefore illustrates another source of data for analysis at the practical action level.

Finally, we should take note of two Canadian language classroom observation schemes which were both developed by research teams in the Modern Language Centre at the Ontario Institute for Studies in Education. These two schemes have much in common, but they also differ in certain respects because they were devised for different purposes and reflect different emphases on what to observe. What makes these two schemes particularly interesting from the point of view of our three-level analysis is the fact that they were designed to reflect theoretical positions and instructional policy in a more deliberate way than the other schemes we have considered, except perhaps the Jarvis scheme (Jarvis 1968).

COLT (Communicative Orientation of Language Teaching), is an observation instrument with a specific focus (Allen, Fröhlich, and Spada 1984). It was developed as part of a large-scale long-term project on the development of bilingual proficiency. As its name indicates, its main purpose is to assess the degree of communicativeness in different types of language class. Ultimately, COLT is intended to help find out whether classes which are more or less communicative will result in characteristic and measurable differences in proficiency. COLT as a classroom observation scheme does not attempt to capture everything in the language class. Its main preoccupation is the communicative–non-communicative dimension, and every item in the scheme is clearly and explicitly related to language acquisition research and beliefs on communicative language teaching.

The scheme consists of two parts. Part A, which is observed and coded directly by the observer in the language class, records the pedagogic events as they occur. The main categories are, broadly speaking, similar to the Stirling scheme: activity type, participant organization, content, student modality, and type of material. But under these headings the scheme directs particular attention to aspects of teaching which characterize either communicative or non-communicative approaches. Part B of COLT, which is based on an audio recording of the same material observed in Part A, is a detailed analysis of the verbal exchanges that have taken place, and it uses a set of distinct criteria to distinguish the communicative from the non-communicative use of language: (1) use of target language, (2) information gap between interlocutors, (3) sustained speech, (4) reaction to message rather than code, (5) incorporation of preceding utterances in an exchange, (6) discourse initiation by students, (7) relative lack of restriction on linguistic form. With the help of this instrument the investigators were able to distinguish the communicativeness of different types of French and ESL classes. This scheme and some of its findings are likely to be particularly useful to the analysis of the content of language classes and to observations on formal or communicative classroom strategies.

The other observation scheme, TALOS (Target Language Observation Scheme), was developed wth a broader objective in mind (Ullmann and Geva 1984). It forms part of a battery of instruments assembled for the purpose of evaluating French programmes in Canadian school systems. Besides TALOS, the battery includes French proficiency tests, questionnaires for parents, teachers, and school personnel, materials analysis, and other measures for a detailed curriculum evaluation. In this battery, classroom observation is intended to contribute information on the implementation of the curriculum in language classes. TALOS is, therefore, less specific in intention than COLT. It has a 'low inference' section in which classroom events are recorded, providing a quantitative analysis of the events of a lesson. This part of the scheme records types of activity, substantive and linguistic content, the skill focus, and the teaching medium. It records information about students separately from the input provided by the teacher. TALOS has also a 'high inference' section in which characteristics of the class, teachers, and students are rated by the observers in a more global fashion. The whole scheme is based on categories which are at least partly derived from the kind of policy considerations we have already discussed at the second level. TALOS has been used in connection with the evaluation of the French programme of a school board in the Toronto area (Ullmann *et al.* 1983). Thus, TALOS and its findings are a further data base for examples of language teaching in action.

The case study approach

The case study approach incorporates some of the features of the observation schemes we have briefly reviewed, but case studies are different from observation schemes in several respects. They are broader, they are less precise, and they are more interpretive. They are broader in that they include objectives and intentions which a purely behavioural study does not cover. None of the observation schemes we have discussed includes a description of objectives. A case study is broader also in that it may emphasize the contextual factors which we have discussed above. Observation of an isolated language class out of context makes little sense. The originators of classroom observation schemes usually take these contextual factors into account implicitly or through interviews. But these factors are not an integral part of the observation schemes themselves and they may, therefore, be overlooked. On the other hand, the case study is less precise in that it provides ratings and interpretations rather than quantitative data. Where precise data are needed, such as exact proportions of communicative versus non-communicative activities, we must use the less impressionistic methods of the observation schemes.

In addition to the treatment factors which have already been discussed, a case study of classroom teaching requires reference to objectives, content, evaluation, and resources. Not only does a case study systematize areas of interest to a classroom observer, but it can also serve as a baseline for self-observation by classroom practitioners. The following summary indicates the range of questions which need to be answered.

Objectives. Are the objectives of the class explicitly stated or must they be inferred from the activities in progress? Examples of what students are expected to know or do would indicate what the objectives are.

Content. What is the content of teaching? This can be documented by providing examples of topics at different stages of the course.[1]

Procedures (classroom treatment variables). These include:

(a) Descriptions of teaching-learning activities, in answer to such questions as: What does the teacher do? What do the students do? Examples of lessons or teaching learning units illustrate the descriptions. If the teacher is asked to outline his plan beforehand and then to comment on what happened after the lesson is finished, the degree of congruence between an observer's view and that of the participant can be noted.[2]

(b) The time distribution of language learning activities: hours per week/term/year; total time available; length of teaching episodes and time distribution within one class.[3]

(c) Interpersonal relations: the teacher's role, teacher-pupil interaction, grouping of students, degree of individualization.[4]

Evaluation of progress. Note should be taken of informal and momentary judgements and error correction, as well as of tests, examinations, and other recorded or written products of formal evaluation procedures.[5]

Resources. Materials in use including textbooks and media facilities.[6]

Although the importance of research tends to be overlooked, it is advisable to include a research component at various stages in curriculum development. Curriculum designers can gain important insights into the nature of their task, not only by familiarizing themselves with the research literature, but also by incorporating their own empirical studies into the development process.

Concluding comments

To sum up, certain aspects of the curriculum process are by now widely recognized and have been thoroughly discussed, but other aspects have been left in a quite rudimentary state or have been ignored altogether. This particularly applies to research, the importance of which has not always been clearly recognized. Much remains to be done before curriculum decisions in language pedagogy are routinely handled in a truly professional manner. Keeping in mind the importance of such curriculum decision-making processes for effective planning, we now turn to a closer investigation of the categories of our multidimensional curriculum framework, focusing on issues and options involved at level 2 in the design of the curriculum itself, and some manifestations of these options in classroom practice at level 3.

Notes

1 Several observation schemes include content categories. For example, the Stirling scheme lists the following eleven categories: civilization, general linguistic notions, course book language points, other language points; situations in course material, other situations, real life, fragmented or non-contextualized formal aspects of language, routine procedures, talk about pupils' previous performance, and other topics (Mitchell *et al.* 1981). Under the same heading, COLT has the following less explicit and somewhat simpler categories: management (classroom procedures or disciplinary routines);

explicit focus on language (form, function, discourse or sociolinguistics); other topics (narrow, limited or broad range of reference); and topic control (by teacher, by student, or shared between teacher and student) (Allen *et al.* 1984: 236–7).

2 Observation schemes focus particularly on this categorization and have developed a number of different ways to describe procedures which will be discussed in a later chapter. TALOS, for example, distinguishes activity type (e.g. drill, spelling, free communication); skill focus (listening, speaking, reading, writing); and teaching act (e.g. explaining, questioning, correcting, disciplining) (Ullmann and Geva 1984). The Stirling scheme distinguishes language activities (e.g. translation, presentation, drill/exercise); teacher mode of involvement (e.g. instructing, interacting, watching/helping, participating); and pupil mode of involvement (listening, speaking, doing, reading, writing, and looking).

3 The time dimension of learning activities is curiously left unspecified in most observation schemes. Some, for example the Stirling scheme, allow for it by noting the length of each teaching segment.

4 Interpersonal relations are addressed in most schemes. This aspect is central to FLINT (Moskowitz 1978). In COLT, it is coded under the heading of participant organization and in Stirling as class organization. It is similarly classified in TALOS.

5 Some observation schemes include isolated aspects of evaluation but, on the whole, this area has not been handled systematically. However, studies on error correction such as Allwright's (1975a), make a contribution to this particular aspect of evaluation.

6 Resources constitute another important facet of the language class which observation schemes have not handled consistently. Nevertheless, this facet is categorized in some, for example, Stirling, TALOS, and COLT.

PART TWO

Defining objectives

Defining objectives

One aspect of most curriculum statements is an indication of objectives, if not a clearly formulated definition. Purposes, reasons, and values have in some way always been thought about in language pedagogy. But in the past these were not usually formally stated. They were determined more by tradition than by deliberate policy. According to Kelly (1969), language pedagogy over the centuries has pursued three major objectives: social (language as communication); artistic-literary (language as a means for artistic creation and appreciation); and philosophical (language analysis). At different periods, these broad aims have been emphasized to varying degrees. The teaching of Latin in medieval Europe, or French in England at the time of the Tudors and Stuarts, as well as present-day second language teaching, appears to have laid the main emphasis on the social purpose of communication. In nineteenth century schools, however, Latin was taught more for artistic or literary reasons, i.e. as a preparation for reading the great classical writers, and also as a training in language analysis, or more generally as a training of the mind.

The teaching of modern languages in the nineteenth century followed the example of the classical language instruction and largely pursued the same objectives. But the language teaching reforms of that period stressed once again the social function of languages in the modern world of industrialization, railways, and international trade. The great method debate which was initiated by the late nineteenth century reformers was implicitly a debate about a change in ends as much as a change in the means of language teaching. Equally, the enthusiasm for phonetics in the last decades of the nineteenth century reflected not only a new scientific approach to teaching method, but also a criticism of those who placed the dominant stress on written expression and literary language; it was a demand for a greater emphasis on the spoken language. The direct method, too, implied a shift of purpose: it restricted the use of translation and advocated 'thinking in the foreign language', leading to a closer and more immediate contact with native speakers. In intention, the direct method was, therefore, close to the modern emphasis on communication.

In the 1920s, the reading method was strongly promoted by some

American language educators (for example, Coleman 1929) and by Michael West in Bengal (West 1926). This method represented a deliberate restriction of language learning objectives to the one skill that was believed to be of the most direct utility to most language learners, namely reading. Some ten years later, the reading method was severely criticized, not because it had failed to achieve its objective, but because it was thought that the wrong objective had been pursued. At that stage, with a war in the offing, facility in the previously neglected skills of speaking and listening comprehension was regarded as the most important purpose of language training. Most of the approaches to language training after World War II—whether they were called 'audiolingual', 'audio-visual' or something else—were based on the primacy of oral communication not only as a method of teaching, but also as its principal aim.

In short, in the history of language pedagogy language teaching objectives have periodically changed, but until recently these changes remained hidden in the succession of methods which did not make a clear distinction between ends and means. In the following chapter we will begin with a survey of the background of teaching objectives in educational testing, and then go on to discuss the four objectives of the multidimensional framework.

3 Language teaching objectives

Explicit approaches to language teaching objectives

In recent decades, the definition of language teaching objectives has played an increasingly major role in the development of second language curriculums. This development can be traced to the practical needs of government language training in wartime, but even more to the increasing influence of educational psychology and educational theory on language pedagogy.

Practical language training requirements

During World War II, preparation for overseas military operations had made 'crash programmes' in foreign languages a necessity. Until then, language teaching had mainly taken place in academic contexts in which the objectives were broadly humanistic or educational and were not always too closely specified. Under the pressure of a large-scale war, language teaching had to be geared to quite specific purposes, such as the duties of military occupation, contact with civilian populations, gathering information from local inhabitants, interrogating prisoners of war, and analysing captured documents. Consequently, language training in the armed forces was intensive and concentrated on the war needs.

In the post-war era the lessons derived from this kind of purpose-specific language training were not forgotten. The principle of directing language training to definite ends was widely applied to language training in government and industry. Even for peacetime language training programmes it was not good enough merely to state that an officer needed to know French, Arabic, or Hindi. Standards of language proficiency and specified skills in relation to the demands of professional tasks and positions had to be more accurately described. Such definitions were needed for at least three reasons: one was to be able to state precisely the language requirements for particular positions; a second was to have criteria to test applicants' language command for these positions; and a third was to give direction to language training programmes. In short, as governments in the post-war era became more and more aware of the need for language proficiency, they also recognized the advantage of specifying levels and other characteristics of the language proficiency required.

Obviously, not all learners in government service needed the same standard of proficiency, nor did they necessarily require a comprehensive and equal command of all language skills. Accordingly, various agencies in the United States, such as the language schools of the Foreign Service Institute and the Defense Language Institute, developed ratings which described a range of language proficiency standards. In outline, such ratings were already available in the 1950s; but in subsequent years they were further refined, and a standard version was agreed upon in 1968 by several United States government agencies (Jones and Spolsky 1975). These ratings comprise five levels ranging from elementary proficiency to native or bilingual proficiency, as follows:

1 Elementary proficiency;
2 Limited working proficiency;
3 Minimum professional proficiency;
4 Full professional proficiency;
5 Native or bilingual proficiency.

At all five levels language proficiency was defined for each of the four skills: speaking, listening comprehension, reading, and writing; and for each of these, detailed descriptions were prepared in largely linguistic terms. Thus, the speaking skill was divided into accent, grammar, vocabulary, fluency, and comprehension (Wilds 1975).

Similar analytical descriptions of types and levels of proficiency have been attempted elsewhere. In Canada, for example, bilingual positions in the federal public service were described in detail during the 1970s. In Sweden, where jobs in industry often require a specified command of English, similar scales were developed. The scales differed in descriptive categories and number of levels. Some of them described proficiency in linguistic terms. Others indicated what communicative functions could be expected to be carried out at a given level, for example, 'can read newspaper articles of personal interest', 'can deal with visitors', 'can take part in a training programme offered in the second language'. The description of proficiency standards and characteristics and the definition of learning objectives have continued to be a preoccupation of those concerned with the planning of language instruction and the development of language curriculums at almost every level.

The influence of educational psychology and educational theory

In the 1940s and the 1950s, the dominant behaviouristic orientation in psychology gave preference to statements of objectives which described overt behaviour rather than those which postulated mental categories. In vocational selection and guidance and in industrial training, for example, objectives were often expressed by observable descriptions of performance rather than in terms of abstract categories.

The development of educational tests led to the establishment of similar criteria: What is the learner supposed to be able to do at the end of the educational process that he was not able to do at the beginning? In other words, what is the difference between 'entry' and 'exit' behaviour? Such questions would lead the test constructor to establish an inventory of items of behaviour. His task was to devise tests that would represent a fair sample of this inventory. Accordingly, the objectives of educational processes were expressed in terms of expected overt behaviour or performance.

A similar interest in specifying in advance a desired learning outcome, expressed concretely as behaviour or performance, was shown by those who, from the early 1960s, developed learning units for programmed instruction and computer-assisted instruction. The listing of items to be known or performed in specified ways was regarded as an essential step in the making of a 'programme'. Again, there was insistence on defining learning objectives precisely and concretely. Finally, also in the 1960s, work in educational economics led to the concept of educational accountability. The rising costs of education demanded greater economy and, with this end in view, educational objectives were to be related to the time and resources needed to achieve these objectives.

Taxonomies of educational objectives

Developments of this kind led to an increasing attention to the operational definition of objectives in education. The task of describing objectives unambiguously in terms of learner behaviour came to be regarded as an important step in curriculum development. The first concrete effort to come to grips with the increasing demand for a closer definition of educational objectives was an ambitious project initiated in 1948 by a group of American psychologists and educationists who were concerned with the construction of educational tests. They divided the objectives of learning into three broad areas or 'domains': psychomotor, cognitive, and affective learning. Any one curriculum subject might well involve all three; but for the purpose of analysis this division was regarded as the most useful. Two handbooks were produced, one on the cognitive domain (Bloom 1956) and the other on the affective (Krathwohl *et al.* 1964). The psychomotor domain was not developed until later (Harrow 1972).

In these schemes the presentation of objectives was not merely conceived as a list or inventory but as a comprehensive scheme of interrelated objectives, in other words, a taxonomy. The major classes of objectives were placed in ascending order from simple to complex so that a higher class of objectives would build upon the classes that preceded it. Six major classes were identified in the cognitive domain:

1 Knowledge;
2 Comprehension;
3 Application;
4 Analysis;
5 Synthesis;
6 Evaluation.

Knowledge forms one hierarchy from the concrete and specific to the general and abstract. Classes 2 to 6 form another, a hierarchy of intellectual abilities and skills which involves progressively greater capacities of generalization, abstraction, and critical judgement. The entire cognitive domain indicates a series of steps in increasing intellectual awareness.

The taxonomy of the affective domain represented a progression in terms of increasing internalization. It advanced from the positive awareness of an object ('receiving') via 'responding' to 'valuing' the organization of a system, and then to the state where the value has become completely internalized as part of the individual's personality. The taxonomy of the affective domain does not operate with the common terms of the psychology of affect, such as adjustment, interest, or value, although it is possible to relate these concepts to the five major classes of the taxonomy:

1 Receiving (attending);
2 Responding;
3 Valuing;
4 Organization;
5 Characterization by a value or value complex.

Besides this remarkable effort to classify educational objectives, another major development initiated in the 1960s was to express learning objectives as concrete behavioural changes in the learner. This technique was varyingly referred to as the writing of 'behavioural', 'performance', or 'instructional' objectives. As long as objectives were stated in broad and abstract terms, such as 'knowledge', 'comprehension', 'critical thinking', or 'interest', such terms, it was believed, were open to many interpretations. Therefore, so the argument ran, it is not enough to provide an ordered classification. Objectives must be translated into action verbs that describe the outcome of teaching as observable student behaviour or performance. Accordingly, the techniques of specifying general objectives more and more concretely was further developed. At first, this was done largely with programmed instruction in mind. But gradually it was realized that classroom teaching, teacher education and supervision, as well as the evaluation of student performance and any serious discussion on educational objectives and curriculum, could greatly benefit from such closer specification of objectives.

Handbooks on the writing of performance objectives, such as Mager (1962), demanded that performance objectives should be expressed concretely by a verb of action (something the student must do) to which are added the conditions under which the action is to be performed, and the criterion that serves as an indicator that the performance objective has been reached. Valette and Disick (1972) who, as will be shown later, have applied these concepts to language teaching, offered this example of an expression of formal performance objectives:

> To demonstrate knowledge of twenty out of fifty vocabulary words . . . write out and spell correctly the word that corresponds to each of the twenty definitions given on a twenty-minute classroom test. At least thirteen of the twenty items must be entirely correct in order to pass. (Valette and Disick 1972: 17)

Analysing this statement, Valette and Disick (1972) point to four aspects of a performance objective: (a) it is an expression of purpose ('to demonstrate knowledge of twenty vocabulary words'); (b) it defines student behaviour ('write out and spell correctly the word that corresponds to each of the twenty definitions'); (c) it specifies the conditions under which such behaviour should occur ('on a twenty-minute classroom test'); (d) it indicates a clear criterion of success ('at least thirteen of the twenty items must be entirely correct in order to pass').

Those who advocated the writing of performance objectives pointed to the clarity, precision, and concreteness of objectives expressed in this way. They were convinced it would put into the teachers' hands a practical instrument which could not be matched by abstractly expressed general objectives. At the same time, they recognized that this technique of precisely defining purpose, behaviour, conditions, and criteria, as in the above example, was not always appropriate. Differences in the degree of specificity of statements of objectives had to be admitted, depending on the topic as well as on the purpose for which the objectives were stated. It was easy to see the danger of these detailed expressions of objectives. They might easily lead to a very unproductive fragmentation and to purely formal compliance. We shall see below that the principle of performance objectives has been vehemently opposed by some general educationists as well as by some language teachers.

Bloom taxonomies and language teaching objectives

At first the study of educational objectives had been carried out in curriculum areas other than languages, mainly in the social, biological, and physical sciences. Consequently, language teaching theorists faced the problem of adapting schemes and concepts originally developed with other fields of learning in mind. The American linguist Rebecca Valette was foremost in seeing the relevance of Bloom's taxonomies for language teaching and testing. In the late 1960s, she developed a series of taxonomies to fit language learning into the categories which had been devised by Bloom and his colleagues (Valette 1969, 1971, 1981; Valette and Disick 1972).

In the earliest version of the Valette taxonomies, the cognitive domain was interpreted as the receptive or comprehension aspect of language learning while the psychomotor domain represented mainly the development of speaking and writing. In a further development of the taxonomy, Valette combined the cognitive and psychomotor domain into a single progression, omitting or modifying some of the classes of the Bloom taxonomy and replacing others by categories deemed to be more appropriate for second language learning. This revised version of the taxonomy advances from relatively elementary acts of perception, knowledge, and manipulation to more complex forms of understanding and production. The affective domain was kept separate and interpreted as increasing participation in foreign language activities.

A third revision (Valette and Disick 1972; Valette 1981) greatly simplified the descriptive categories and rearranged them in five stages, thus revealing more clearly the essential characteristics of the taxonomy. In this version the cognitive and psychomotor domain were fused into a single 'subject-matter domain' while the affective domain was again offered as a separate hierarchy. The subject-matter domain was divided into internal behaviour—the receptive aspect of second language learning—and external behaviour, i.e. its productive counterpart. The five stages of the behavioural ('subject-matter') objectives, each divided into a subcategory of internal and external behaviour, are summarized in Figure 3.1.

Valette's studies represent a first major attempt to do for language teaching what the Bloom taxonomies had attempted to do for educational objectives in general, namely, to produce a coherent expression of objectives and not merely a list or catalogue which does not indicate any interrelationships among the proposed objectives. The fact that Valette, over a period of a few years, produced three or more variants of a Bloom-type taxonomy suggests that she herself was not entirely satisfied with the categories she had established in adapting the Bloom taxonomies. Her efforts in developing a rational scheme of objectives have

Stage	Subject-matter domain	
	Internal behaviour	External behaviour
1. Mechanical skills: The student performs via rote memory, rather than by understanding.	**Perception:** The student perceives differences between two or more sounds or letters or gestures and makes distinctions between them.	**Reproduction:** The student imitates foreign language speech, writing, gestures, songs, and proverbs.
2. Knowledge: The student demonstrates knowledge of facts, rules, and data related to foreign language learning.	**Recognition:** The student shows he recognizes facts he has learned by answering true-false and multiple-choice questions.	**Recall:** The student demonstrates he remembers the information taught by answering fill-in or short-answer questions.
3. Transfer: The student uses his knowledge in new situations.	**Reception:** The student understands recombined oral or written passages or quotations not encountered previously.	**Application:** The student speaks or writes in a guided drill situation or participates in cultural simulations.
4. Communication: The student uses the foreign language and culture as natural vehicles for communication.	**Comprehension:** The student understands a foreign language message or a cultural signal containing unfamiliar material in an unfamiliar situation.	**Self-expression:** The student uses the foreign language to express his personal thoughts orally or in writing. He uses gestures as part of his expression.
5. Criticism: The student analyzes or evaluates the foreign language or carries out original research.	**Analysis:** The student breaks down language or a literary passage to its essential elements of style, tone, theme, and so forth. **Evaluation:** The student evaluates and judges the appropriateness and effectiveness of a language sample or literary passage.	**Synthesis:** The student carries out original research or individual study or creates a plan for such a project.

Figure 3.1 Valette and Disick (1972) taxonomy of behavioural objectives in second language teaching

not found an adequate echo in the pedagogical literature. Instead of testing them in practice or discussing the merits of her schemes, the literature has almost entirely ignored her comprehensive and valuable efforts. In this book we will attempt to build on her work, although the scheme we propose is less detailed and less analytic.

Around 1970, taxonomies and specifications of objectives began to be criticized by some language teaching theorists and educational philosophers. There was opposition to the very idea of a model which presents a curriculum in terms of means and ends, process and product. According to this view, the effort to develop such taxonomies and the writing of instructional objectives were misguided, because the outcome of education, particularly in the humanities, could not and should not be so clearly specified as to constitute a 'system'. For example, in a spirited attack upon 'behavioural objectives, Skinnerian rats and Trojan horses', Grittner (1977) rejects the notion of a goal-directed language curriculum with a quotation from Peters, the English educational philosopher, who writes:

> Education . . . can have no ends beyond itself. Its value derives from principles and standards implicit in it. To be educated is not to have arrived at a destination; it is to travel with a different view.
> (Peters 1965: 110)

The critics saw a danger, above all, in the demand for a narrow specificity of performance objectives. In Grittner's view, this would lead to the trivialization of the curriculum and an over-emphasis upon what is measurable, quantifiable, and examinable, and would be nothing more than a modern version of the 'coercive use of performance standards' in traditional examination systems. He concludes:

> In short, behavioural objectives seem to be part of a system for doing more efficiently that which we should not be doing at all. That is, perhaps we should not be imposing pre-made decision upon students; perhaps instead we should be helping them to make their own decisions; to learn how to learn for themselves.
> (Grittner 1977: 60)

Although the passion for behavioural objectives had spent itself somewhat by the mid-1970s, the emphasis on objectives—and even behavioural objectives—has left an indelible mark on curriculum development in language teaching.

The four objectives of the multidimensional framework

In what follows we will deal briefly with the four language teaching objectives specified in our multidimensional framework. Later, in Part

Three of this book, we will deal in more detail with the content categories, which have to be related to the objectives. In talking about objectives, we will employ personal (i.e. behavioural or psychological) concepts. In other words, we will think of the changes that the language course is intended to bring about in each individual learner. At the same time, in many cases they could also be learning objectives, that is, goals the learners have set for themselves. We will discuss the objectives in the following order: language proficiency, cognitive goals, affect, transfer.

The proficiency objective

The importance of the proficiency objective is not in question. The whole 'language learning business', as Palmer and Redman (1969) called it, centres on the multifaceted proficiency concept.[1] It is the key to the success or failure of language teaching. If we ask any group of students why they are studying this or that language we are bound to hear some reference to the acquisition or improvement of proficiency in the second language:

1 I want to improve my French.
2 English is very important for me.
3 I'm going to work in Japan. I need to have some Japanese.

These and similar statements reflect learners' expectations of reaching a certain degree of proficiency by taking a language course, but they do not distinguish different aspects or levels of proficiency. At times, however, students express their intentions in a more differentiated manner:

4 All I need is a smattering of Russian.
5 I want to be completely fluent in Arabic.
6 For me a reading knowledge of French is quite sufficient; I don't think I'll ever have the opportunity to speak it.
7 I want to have conversational German; I don't need any grammar.

In these remarks there is a certain awareness among prospective language learners that courses can be geared towards a certain level of proficiency, or that they can cater to particular aspects of proficiency, for example, reading or conversation. We will leave out of consideration for the moment the question of whether it is possible to meet these demands in exactly the way they have been voiced above.

The concept of proficiency has a determining influence on curriculum development and language testing. A global 'learning to speak English' or acquiring 'a command of French' are not sufficiently precise for curriculum development or testing. Since about 1960, many attempts have been made to gain a more differentiated understanding, based on a

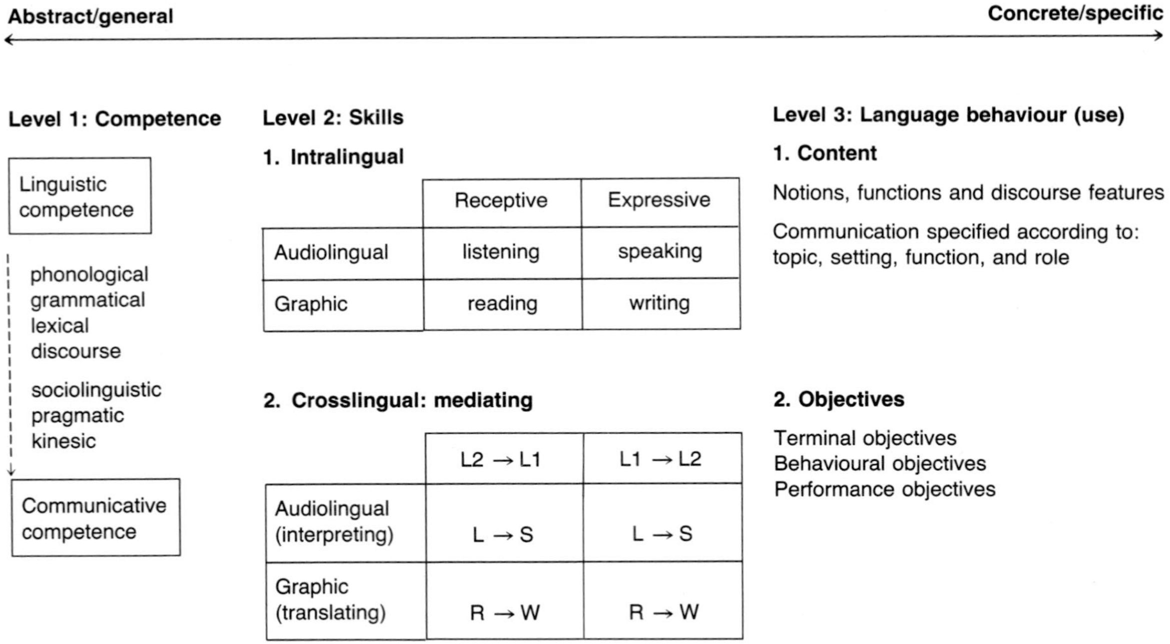

Abstract/general ←→ **Concrete/specific**

Level 1: Competence

Linguistic competence

phonological
grammatical
lexical
discourse

sociolinguistic
pragmatic
kinesic

Communicative competence

Level 2: Skills

1. Intralingual

	Receptive	Expressive
Audiolingual	listening	speaking
Graphic	reading	writing

2. Crosslingual: mediating

	L2 → L1	L1 → L2
Audiolingual (interpreting)	L → S	L → S
Graphic (translating)	R → W	R → W

Level 3: Language behaviour (use)

1. Content

Notions, functions and discourse features

Communication specified according to: topic, setting, function, and role

2. Objectives

Terminal objectives
Behavioural objectives
Performance objectives

Figure 3.2 Aspects of second language proficiency: levels of abstraction (adapted from Stern 1983a)

firmer theoretical foundation, of the structure of foreign language proficiency (Bachman and Palmer 1982; Vollmer 1983; Harley *et al.* 1990). Here it is not necessary for us to take up the long and inconclusive arguments that have been advanced in the analysis of language proficiency. From the perspective of policy and practice, which is our main concern, it is sufficient to point to two conceptualizations of proficiency. The first is the expression of degrees, stages or levels of proficiency from minimum to maximum. The view of language proficiency as a progression of stages on a continuum, which is implicit in the distribution of language classes into beginners, intermediate, or advanced, is extremely important for curriculum policy.

The other conceptualization presents another continuum: from abstract and general to concrete and specific. From the point of view of curriculum design, plausible reasons can be advanced for moving in either direction on the abstract–concrete continuum. In Figure 3.2, proficiency is represented by three categories which range from a relatively abstract and generalized knowing of the language (competence) via the more concrete communication skills to detailed specifications of language behaviour. This threefold division implies that it is legitimate to express the proficiency objective in general terms, to specify and emphasize particular skills, or to be even more specific by particularizing uses of language. An abstract general objective can claim to have very wide application while more concrete and specific behavioural categories may be relevant to clearly identified groups of learners in particular circumstances.

Proficiency as competence

Competence represents proficiency at its most abstract and psychologically deepest level. 'Competence' as a concept originated with Chomsky in the 1960s. He used it to indicate that underlying the concrete behaviour, or 'performance', of the language user, there is an abstract rule system or knowledge. We say a fluent speaker 'knows' French or English, implying that he uses the rules that govern his language without having any detailed awareness of the underlying system. He employs the right tenses, makes the necessary morphological changes, chooses the correct masculine or feminine gender, applies the usual word order, and uses the subjunctive when it is appropriate.[2] The underlying knowledge of the grammar of the language by the native speaker is his 'linguistic competence'. Hymes (1972) argued that in addition to linguistic competence the native speaker has another rule system. That is, he knows intuitively what is socially appropriate or inappropriate and can adjust his language use to such factors as the topic, situation, and human relations involved: in short, he possesses 'communicative competence'.

By applying these concepts to second language proficiency we imply that we would like the learner of L2 to approximate the intuitive command of the native speaker. Proficiency interpreted as communicative competence (including linguistic competence), therefore, means an ability to use the language without giving linguistic forms, rules, and meanings any specific thought. With competence as the proficiency objective it is immaterial whether the learner of German, for example, is aware that some prepositions govern the accusative, some the dative, and others both accusative and dative, provided that he shows by use that this complex of rules is part of his knowledge of the language. The declaration of communicative competence as an objective does not imply anything about how this intuitive command is best achieved. That is a matter of teaching methodology. Furthermore, it is understood that language learners rarely reach the native speaker's maximum competence level.

Scholars have divided up the concept of communicative competence in various ways. The characterization of competence is not merely an academic exercise, however. Differences in interpretation of what it means to know a language ultimately produce differences in teaching, learning, and testing. In other words, our concept of competence has a bearing on syllabus design and evaluation at the policy level. Defining reasonable and serviceable competence levels is a major task for language curriculum development. Linguistically speaking, native-like competence implies a mastery of phonology, morphology, and syntax, and an extensive knowledge of vocabulary. As native speakers we can also make social distinctions within the language, recognize regional and social register variations, and differentiate between the appropriate and the inappropriate, the coherent and the incoherent. In addition, we are able to interpret and actively use posture, facial expressions, and gestures which are demanded by the language. In other words, communicative competence includes a non-verbal, a kinesic, and a paralinguistic element.

Psychologically, communicative competence has perceptual, sensorimotor, cognitive, affective, and psycho-social characteristics. Language use involves the whole person. Perceptually, it demands recognition and discrimination of phonological and syntactic clues. Speaking and writing bring into action sensorimotor systems which are constantly monitored by auditory, visual, or kinesthetic perception. Cognitively, the acquisition and use of language requires planning, anticipating, and recognizing regularities of language use involving memory and habit formation. At the same time language use is 'creative', demanding the constant adaptation of the user's linguistic resources to new and changing circumstances. From an affective point of view, language evokes emotional associations in the user, many of which are shared by other members of the speech community. Consequently, the use of language predictably arouses in speakers laughter, anger, compassion, disgust, and other emotions. Most characteristic of the affective aspect of competence is the intuitive sense of right (or wrong) language use, which is often highly charged emotionally. This becomes evident in the sometimes negative reactions by native speakers to deviations from normally accepted 'correct' language use by foreigners and language learners. From the perspective of social psychology, language is closely bound up with social behaviour and social situations which spontaneously evoke in the native speaker feelings of social appropriateness or inappropriateness.

Most of the more recent formulations of proficiency as communicative competence have singled out a few major linguistic features and one or two psychological ones. In assessing a particular competence theory, it is less important to consider whether the theory in question covers the entire ground of linguistic and communicative competence. It is much more a matter of asking which aspects are emphasized and why. Thus, one of the most widely used interpretations, first developed by Canale and Swain (1980) and in its final version slightly modified by Canale (1983), distinguishes three competencies which are linguistic in nature (grammatical, discourse, and sociolinguistic competence) and one which is more psychological (strategic competence). This analysis of communicative competence is intended to emphasize discourse and sociolinguistic features without neglecting the formal (grammatical) aspects. Canale and Swain's discussion of strategic competence stresses the cognitive versatility needed by the second language learner in using an imperfectly known language for effective communication. Other possible psychological aspects of communicative competence could be, but are not, singled out in this interpretation.

Proficiency, expressed as communicative competence, has the advantage of being very general and applicable to a wide range of situations. It is, therefore, useful when a comprehensive but unspecified command of the second language is the goal. However, it has the disadvantage of being removed from particular situations and uses of the L2. It is abstract and intangible and therefore difficult to apply. Competence as a construct is not directly accessible and can only be reached through manifestations in some form of behaviour or output. Only through inferences from such output or behaviour can the characteristics of competence become known.

Proficiency as the mastery of skills

Proficiency as the mastery of skills such as listening, speaking, reading, and writing is closer to the concrete reality of performance, but leaves unspecified the uses and situations in which the skill comes into action. As a simple and straightforward expression of proficiency, this perspective was particularly popular in the 1960s when audiolingualism focused on the sequence of introducing the 'four skills'. Since that time, it has been somewhat overshadowed, on the one hand by the more fundamental concept of competence, and on the other by a tendency to specify language operations more closely, thus moving towards a more detailed analysis of communicative activities. As useful expressions of proficiency, however, the 'four skills' continue to be important categories in language pedagogy.

At this point a major distinction between two broad types of communication skills should be introduced. It is a distinction which is important to make but which has been almost completely absent from recent discussions on curriculum and objectives, i.e. the distinction between intralingual and crosslingual skills. Language courses normally aim at giving students an intralingual command of skills, meaning that the language activity can be carried out without reference to the student's first language. In reading or listening comprehension the utterances or the printed page are expected to be apprehended directly and their interpretation is not dependent on translation into L1. In speaking, the L2 user is visualized as constructing his utterances without reference to L1, and in writing the aim is to be able to compose in the target language without 'construing' sentences from an L1 base. In short, whether one or more skills are the main objective, an intralingual perspective always assumes that the skill is mastered in such a way that the learner can function in the manner of a native speaker of the target language, even though the extent of target language mastery is not assumed to equal that of a native speaker.

The second set of skills, the crosslingual skills, are collectively referred to as mediating. They are carried out in either the graphic mode ('translating') or the audiolingual mode ('interpreting'). The crosslingual or mediating skills are regarded here as language learning objectives in their own right for those trained professionally to be translators or interpreters. Mediating activities are socially and intellectually justifiable activities. To be able to relate the source language and the target language to one another is valuable and in many circumstances unavoidable. It is furthermore desirable to be able to mediate between native speakers of different languages. As a result of the late nineteenth century reform movement crosslingual activities almost totally disappeared from language teaching theory, and they are rarely considered either as objectives or as legitimate teaching techniques. By now, however, we are far enough removed from the abuses of translation which prompted the reformers that we can reconsider the role of crosslingual activities both as language learning objectives and as teaching strategies.

Unlike the crosslingual skills, the intralingual skills have been much emphasized. Their recognition both as separate skills and in combination with one another was a dominant feature of language teaching in the 1960s, and in spite of the move away from them in language teaching theory since then, in practice the four skills are still widely used concepts which are unquestioned by many teachers. They have been, so to speak, the life-blood of language teaching. But because of their pervasiveness no conceptually clear distinction has been made between the four main intralingual skills as teaching objectives and their use as teaching strategies. Here it should merely be pointed out that they constitute possible proficiency goals which are midway between abstract 'competence' and the more clearly specified inventories of uses of language we will turn to next. The intralingual and crosslingual skills are treated more fully later in our discussion of teaching strategies (see Chapter 10).

Language behaviour

The proficiency objective is specified most closely if we particularize the language behaviour, that is the activities, uses, or functions which the learner is to be able to carry out at the end of the course. Specifications of this objective correspond to the common-sense demands of language learners who are often able to identify their specific wishes:

1 All I need is to be able to skim lists of German titles in mathematical journals so as not to miss any important developments in my field.
2 I have to be able to study historical documents in Italian. I don't have to be able to speak or write the language.

The rationale for expressing objectives in concrete detail and not simply in broad outline as competence or one or other of the four skills is easy enough to explain. As the above examples suggest, many language learners have specific ideas of what they want. Very often there is an immediate need for particular aspects of a new language while other aspects are regarded as less important, for instance in foreign language learning for business and technology, or in the case of second language learning among immigrants and foreign students. Actual examples are special purpose English for flight attendants, language courses for students in the physical sciences or technology, English language courses for immigrant doctors and nurses, and programmes in academic writing for foreign students. Where the variety is clearly defined it has proved possible to prepare detailed inventories of expected language use.

As we have observed, there has been a strong movement in language pedagogy towards such closer specification of language learning objectives. One never teaches or learns the 'whole' language. Selection should, therefore, not be arbitrary but should be made on rational grounds. From educational theory, particularly testing and programmed learning, came the emphasis on specification of objectives; from linguistics and sociolinguistics has come the recognition of language varieties, the concept of register variation, studies of discourse, and the analysis of communication according to topic, setting, language function, and the role relationships among language users.

These different influences culminated in the 1970s in two main attempts to specify objectives in terms of language use: i.e. the Threshold Level Project of the Council of Europe, and the languages for special purposes movement. In order to specify both objectives and content, techniques had to be worked out to determine what a given group of learners or an individual learner needs to learn. This consideration has led to study of the ultimate desired or required outcome: What are the terminal objectives, i.e., what should the learner be able to do at the end of the course? It has also demanded enquiry into the typical initial state or entry behaviour of the learner in question: What is the learner's background and previous language experience that serves as the starting point?[3]

Such an inventory can be stated in the traditional categories of phonology, grammar, and lexis. But due to the influence of developments in linguistics, sociolinguistics, and semantics, recent statements have tended to be expressed in terms of notions, functions, and discourse features. This twofold analysis has given rise to closely specified expressions of objectives and inventories of language content, such as those suggested by Munby (1978). Proficiency is often closely defined in behavioural or performance terms and is offered in the form of lists of ordered language items. The syllabuses prepared under the aegis of the Council of Europe are perhaps the most concrete examples of this type of objective. The advantage of a close specification of proficiency lies in its concreteness and detail as opposed to the much broader and vaguer expression of proficiency as competence or skills. However, the degree of specificity of the inventories has been critically examined, and the difficulty of translating the syllabus specifications into classroom materials and teaching procedures has raised questions about the close specification of language use.[4]

We conclude this examination of proficiency as the first objective of the language course by recognizing that there are advantages and disadvantages in whatever choice we make, whether we conceive of proficiency abstractly and generally, or in concrete and specific terms. What, then, should guide our choice? Where learners know their direction and have specific purposes in mind or where learners' needs can be clearly identified, specificity of course objectives will often be an advantage, especially if the time available for training is short. However, where purposes are less clear or more general, the broader concepts of communicative competence or skills may be more appropriate. The choice may also be partly determined by the level of language instruction. In the early stages of language learning it may be advisable to operate with a broad competence view of language proficiency. As the learner progresses, a greater degree of specialization may suggest a shift towards a skill emphasis and a more detailed specification of proficiency objectives.

Cognitive goals

Language courses do not normally have as a principal aim explicit knowledge, information, conceptual learning, and other cognitive outcomes. As we will see shortly, these are sometimes specifically rejected, because they are regarded as unimportant or irrelevant to the learner's needs. Yet, we will suggest that cognitive outcomes should not be dismissed a priori; on the contrary, in many circumstances they have a valuable role to perform. In the first place, a cognitive goal might consist of knowledge and information about the target language. Second, it could refer to knowledge about the target culture and society. It might further involve the development of certain skills: observing, discriminating, and examining linguistic or sociocultural phenomena; gathering, sorting, and organizing information; storing and retrieving data; making, applying, and revising rules; problem-solving and reasoning; or relating the target language and culture to the source language and culture. The effect of such mental activities can and should be cognitively stimulating. They could have the effect that was claimed in an earlier age for the teaching of Latin, namely, that it would provide 'mind training', an outcome that was later rejected as illusory. Needless to say, in proposing a cognitive goal there is no intention of reviving any notion of empty 'mental gymnastics'. Rather, the expectation is that cognitive goals will add a new and valuable dimension to a language course and strengthen it without being in any way detrimental to proficiency.

Many curriculum subjects, such as the physical sciences, geography, or history, have a mainly cognitive goal, i.e. the acquisition of a body of knowledge, although there has been a shift in education over the last two or three decades from 'storing the mind' with information to acquiring the conceptual skills of finding and handling information, drawing inferences, problem-solving, and so on. The Bloom taxonomy of the cognitive domain represents a major attempt to define the psychological processes to be developed in such content subjects. The two main principles that the Bloom analysis established were: (a) to be serviceable, knowledge items should be placed into an ordered framework, and (b) instead of constituting inert baggage, knowledge should come into active use through a set of mental processes of increasing generality (see Bloom 1956).

When language teaching goals have been formulated they have usually been expressed—at any rate from about the 1960s—as the acquisition or development of proficiency ('competence' or 'communication skills') rather than as the acquisition of explicit knowledge or conceptual skills. Indeed, it has often been said that the goal of language teaching should *not* be explicit knowledge. The student who has diligently learnt many words or studied the grammar has not necessarily acquired a practical command of the language. In the 1960s this scepticism about knowledge was expressed in the slogan of the audiolingual method 'Teach the language, not *about* the language.' In line with this view, Halliday, McIntosh, and Strevens (1964) argued vigorously against intellectualizing language learning:

> The use of a grammar book turns a skill subject into a content subject, one in which the teacher can teach facts instead of imparting skills. But an hour spent in teaching the facts of grammar, of phonology, or of lexis, is not an hour of teaching the language.
> (Halliday, McIntosh, and Strevens 1964: 254)

This kind of argument convinced some language teachers not to treat foreign languages as content. It strengthened their belief in non-thinking, habit-forming ways of teaching through repetition and imitation. Some ten years later, when Krashen's Monitor theory became popular, subconscious acquisition processes were regarded as more important than conscious learning. Although the grounds for rejecting conceptual learning in the language class had shifted, the effect was the same: the cognitive domain was once more treated as irrelevant and, if anything, a hindrance to foreign language proficiency. Against this non-cognitive interpretation, Valette (1969, 1971, 1981) and Valette and Disick (1972) recognized that, in terms of the Bloom taxonomies, language learning could not be explained as psychomotor and affective learning alone. It has a cognitive component. Yet, the categories of the cognitive domain in the Bloom taxonomies, which had been developed for knowledge systems such as the sciences, were not readily applicable to language learning. Consequently, the attempts to apply the Bloom scheme of the cognitive domain directly to language learning have not been altogether satisfactory.

In sorting out the role of the cognitive domain a distinction must be made between knowledge acquisition (and other cognitive activities) as means in the development of proficiency, and knowledge (and other cognitive activities) as ends. In this chapter, our main concern is not how knowledge about the language can be useful as an aid or instrument for the acquisition of proficiency. The question is whether knowledge and other cognitive activities are needed and are worth cultivating. Given the centrality of language proficiency as an objective, we have to ask ourselves: What conceptual knowledge could, in certain situations, constitute a legitimate objective? We will distinguish two aspects.

Linguistic knowledge

In identifying a distinct cognitive objective, we must ask ourselves what we believe is the value of conceptual linguistic knowledge for the language learner beyond any intrinsic cognitive component of proficiency. Knowledge about the language consists of a linguistic analysis in which the language is conceptualized as systematically as possible. In the popular mind, such knowledge is typically equated with 'knowing the grammar' of the language, but it extends beyond syntax and morphology to include knowledge of any systematic aspects of the language as a means of communication. The concern is generally one about grammar teaching as a means to achieving the proficiency objective. The debate hardly ever refers to knowledge about the language as a desirable end in its own right. It is widely believed that such conceptual knowledge need only be discussed as an aid to proficiency. Linguistic knowledge as a goal is rarely mentioned.

Language study is frequently perceived as 'dry' and 'dull'. Such views are no doubt often based on childhood memories of inadequate teaching of grammar in schools where a long-standing tradition in mother tongue teaching has given grammar a bad name. This has often not been rectified through the treatment of language in university language departments where the descriptive study of the contemporary language tends to occupy, even today, a subordinate role in comparison to the scholarly and critical study of literature. On the other hand, linguistics as an autonomous discipline with a bearing on the study of particular languages has begun to change this negative view of linguistic knowledge. It has gradually spread the conviction that the study of language in general and the systematic study of contemporary languages can be an interesting and exciting field of enquiry. To be curious about language and to find out about languages, how they function and why, is a perfectly legitimate goal, perhaps in the first place for the student of linguistics, but beyond that for anyone who is curious about linguistic phenomena. Learning a new language often arouses such curiosity.

For a student of linguistics, it is the proficiency objective that may quite legitimately be subordinate or entirely absent. The study of the linguistic system of language X or Y may be the linguist's sole or major objective. His aim is to find out how certain features of the language can best be described and accounted for in the most economical way, and what this knowledge contributes to general linguistic theory, without ever thinking about acquiring any proficiency in the language under investigation. Even where the proficiency objective is dominant, as it is likely to be in the majority of cases of foreign language learning, it is conceivable that some knowledge about the language is a subsidiary goal. Sweet, in his classic *The Practical Study of Languages* (1899), conveys the idea that languages are worth studying as manifestations of the human capacity for speech, quite apart from their usefulness as media of communication. In a similar spirit, Bodmer and Hogben's *The Loom of Language* (1944), aimed to create in readers a curiosity and excitement about languages and language families. Teachers who have not eradicated this sense of adventure by treating linguistic knowledge as a harsh and unpleasant discipline usually find that learning a second language brings students face to face with fundamental issues about the nature of language which can be of absorbing interest to enquiring minds.

To create linguistic awareness or to respond to the natural curiosity of language students of different ages may, under appropriate circumstances, constitute a worthwhile objective. Naturally this is not always so. We can visualize language learning situations where such linguistic knowledge in its own right would not be appreciated and might even be out of place. Sometimes language learners themselves overtly exclude linguistic knowledge from their objectives:

1 All I want is to be able to read.
2 I want to be able to talk. I'm not interested in grammar.

In such cases a restriction of objectives, excluding linguistic knowledge, may be quite justified. In some content-specific courses there may be little time or inclination for students to acquire knowledge about language in general. In teaching very young children or illiterate adult immigrants it may, for different reasons, be inappropriate to give prominence to the objective of linguistic knowledge. In short, there are teaching situations where cognitive objectives should not be salient. But often the exclusion of linguistic knowledge as a goal is not the result of this kind of rational analysis of the learner's needs or wishes. It is much more likely to reflect negative attitudes based on unfortunate school experiences and the widespread belief that linguistic knowledge is inherently worthless and lacking in interest to the language learner. Where linguistics is not out of place, it is not simply a question of offering information *ex cathedra*. It is much more a matter of responding to the learners' natural curiosity and encouraging accurate linguistic observation and linguistic thinking, helping them to discover regularities, uncover general principles, relate language facts to the social and situational context, and solve language problems; in short, it is a question of creating language awareness or, when it is already there, channelling it in productive directions.

Cultural knowledge

Generally, when knowledge about culture and society has been recognized as a legitimate aspect of language teaching, it has been treated as a cognitive objective in its own right, distinct from the proficiency objective. Yet, the concept of cultural competence implies intuitive sociocultural knowledge on the part of the native speaker which can be regarded as the cultural counterpart to communicative competence (see, for example, Robinson 1985; Damen 1987). Consequently, as in our distinction between proficiency and linguistic knowledge, a distinction should be made between: (a) the control of sociocultural rules and information which are part of the native speaker's intuitive cultural competence; and (b) systematic conceptual knowledge about the L2 culture and society.

Cultural competence. Cultural competence implies implicit mastery of the norms of society, the unspoken rules of conduct, values, and orientations which make up the cultural fabric of a society. It further implies the ability to recognize culturally significant facts, and a knowledge of the parameters within which conduct is acceptable or unacceptable. Cultural competence does not necessarily mean conformity. Even a rebel knows the rules and the range of acceptable behaviours, although he may decide not to conform. Cultural competence merges into communicative competence. What is commonly called communicative competence also implies knowledge of many aspects of society and culture: forms of address, choices of register and style, differences in social and regional dialects, and the social values attached to these differences. Many lexical items refer to characteristic features of the culture. It is not possible to achieve any of the proficiency goals without including certain aspects of sociocultural information.

To a certain extent, however, cultural competence is distinct from communicative competence in that it points to mainly social and cultural behaviour and facts, and less to their linguistic manifestations: for example, what table manners should be observed; whether or not it is expected that a visitor should give a present to the host; whether in greeting it is right, wrong, or unnecessary to bow or shake hands, and so on. While the native speaker has acquired most of these and other cultural features unconsciously, the non-native language learner will have to make a deliberate effort to conceptualize at least some of them, while others may be acquired gradually through life in the target language community.

Conceptual knowledge about the L2 culture. Beyond this inescapable sociocultural component of communicative and cultural competence, the teaching of conceptual knowledge about the target culture and society is more widely recognized than the teaching of linguistic knowledge. It is often suggested that the target culture should be presented contrastively in relation to the source culture. Rather surprisingly, it has sometimes been proposed that cultural knowledge be given priority over language proficiency. The rationale for this proposal is the acknowledgement that in some educational situations cultural understanding appears to be a more important goal than language proficiency. The degree of emphasis on cultural knowledge or language proficiency is an educational decision dependent upon the role of language learning in a given society or for a given group of learners.

What the language teacher has to decide in any given instance is whether knowledge about the language and culture is worth having. For several decades language teaching has strongly reacted against the theory of intellectual training through language learning. It has given priority to proficiency as the main, and often the only, goal. This emphasis on language training as such is undoubtedly justified by the need that many learners have to reach an efficient command of the L2. However, there is no reason why language training cannot at the same time pursue an intellectual goal and provide learners with a conceptual grasp of the language and culture. Proficiency and cognitive goals are not antithetical. As we have seen, proficiency itself has a cognitive component. It is a question, then, of the extent to which a language course should provide, beyond the inherent cognitive element of linguistic and cultural proficiency, a more systematic knowledge of concepts and information on language and culture. Such direct teaching within the cognitive domain need not be uninteresting nor does it have to overload the learner with useless factual information or with empty abstractions. It could give language learning the substantial intellectual content and challenge that is sadly lacking in many courses.

Affective goals

The 'affective domain' has long been accorded an important place in education, in response to developments in psychology and educational theory. Since the early years of the twentieth century psychology has concerned itself more and more with emotional and motivational aspects of the human psyche, which had previously been neglected. During the inter-war years, educators began emphasizing the 'education of the emotions'. Education was to be more than the training of the intellect or the learning of specific skills. The 'progressive' school movement, which gained impetus during that period in the United States and

Britain, was particularly active in drawing attention to questions of mental health and to feelings of personal worth in the child as more significant educational goals than the constant striving for knowledge. Since the 1920s, the concept of attitude has been used to give precision to emotively based educational objectives. By including the affective component among educational goals, Krathwohl *et al.* (1964) gave expression to the view that the education of affect is as legitimate an objective as cognitive or psychomotor learning.

Before considering the affective component as a language teaching objective, we must be clear about what the affective domain is intended to cover. From the literature we can infer that it refers to two related aspects of human psychology. One is the development of positive feelings about activities in which learners are being trained, such as reading, music, or mathematics. The other is the relationship between the individual and the activities concerned: what does the individual do about the objects towards which he has such positive feelings? To what extent can it be said that he is involved, that he cares about them and shows concern for them? In the 1950s, the term 'ego-involvement' came into use as a unifying expression for the related concepts of interest, motivation, participation, engagement, and commitment. As noted earlier the affective domain was conceived by Krathwohl *et al.* (1964) as the growth of such ego-involvement from simple awareness of an activity or field of knowledge to becoming personally involved in the activity or being informed about the field. An even greater degree of involvement would be when the activity or knowledge has become part of the individual's self (that is, a more or less permanent 'interest'). At the highest level of ego-involvement the activity or knowledge has become part of the individual's value system and plays a well-defined and visible role in the person's life. In short, the affective domain covers both emotional response and ego-involvement. It is concerned, in the words of Krathwohl *et al.* (1964: 24), with 'changes in interest, attitudes, and values, and the development of appreciations and adequate adjustment'.

Language teaching theorists have been rather slow to recognize the important part that affect plays in language learning. It was in the early 1970s, as part of the general reaction against audiolingualism, that humanistic language teaching theory, including certain new methods (notably Counseling-Learning, the Dartmouth Method, and Suggestopedia), and the work of a few writers, such as Jakobovits, Schumann, Stevick, Burstall, and Brown, placed affect and personality at the centre of attention. Before that, only Lambert and Gardner (1972), in a series of studies, had paid consistent attention to the role of affect in language learning. Their investigations focused on how the existing attitudes of learners and their previously acquired motivations influence the development of proficiency. In spite of this greater recognition of the importance of affect, little consideration was given to attitudes, interests, or ego-involvement as language teaching objectives. Valette (1969) and Valette and Disick (1972) were among the few who attempted to identify a set of distinct affective goals.

There will probably be general agreement on a number of points. First, we approach language learning with certain positive or negative affective predispositions. Next, the experience of learning is likely to influence our attitudes and involvement, whatever affective goal may have been set by the curriculum. Finally, at the end of the course, the learning experience will leave us, more or less permanently, with certain attitudes. In the present discussion, we are not so much concerned with these affective concomitants of language learning, important though they are, as with the issue of whether affective goals can legitimately be specified for language teaching. Some theorists concede that affect may influence or accompany learning, or that it may be a partial outcome, but argue that it is not an objective that can be operationalized like proficiency and, therefore, not one that can be actively pursued.

This is not our view. We will argue that we can identify certain affective outcomes as desirable and others as undesirable, and that we should find ways and means of moving in a positive rather than a negative direction. These positive outcomes can therefore be regarded as goals, as the taxonomies of Valette and Valette and Disick have recognized. The question is how to define these affective goals. In trying to find an answer we should not tie ourselves to the terms set by the Krathwohl taxonomy; rather we should begin by thinking in terms of affective aspects of language and language teaching and perhaps at a later stage consider to what extent our findings coincide with the Krathwohl concepts. Three major affective goals can be identified: (a) second language competence; (b) sociocultural competence; and (c) language learning.

Second language competence as an affective goal

We recognized earlier that competence has an affective component. What does this mean? The novice language learner is normally conscious of the strangeness of the new language. The combinations of sounds, the formal distinctions, the numerous syntactic rules, and semantic relationships are not only new and in many respects unexpectedly different from L1, but they often arouse an emotional response; they may appear puzzling, arbitrary, frustrating, confusing, sometimes amusing, and occasionally also attractive and pleasing. One affective objective of language teaching must be to overcome any sense of rejection of the language and its features on the part of the learner, to encourage first tolerance and acceptance of the linguistic forms and features, and eventually a feeling of familiarity and liking for them.

The learner should also be encouraged to cultivate not only an intellectual understanding of what is obligatory, possible, or permissible in the new language, but an intuitive sense of 'right' and 'wrong'; in other words, 'Sprachgefühl', or a feeling of being at home in the language. The process of arriving at this feeling can rightly be described as the internalization of the new language in the terms of the Krathwohl taxonomy. An intuitive sensitivity should not only be cultivated in relation to linguistic forms; it applies equally to stylistic, social, and cultural features of language use. Gradually, the learner should acquire the emotional associations of language shared by the speech community. Lastly, it is part of the affective goal that the learner should engage in target language activities, and that he should do so with positive feelings; that is, we should encourage the learner to use the language willingly and even with enjoyment.

Affective outcomes in relation to the second language can be represented by the continuum in Figure 3.3. It is clear that to achieve its goal a language course should be designed to cultivate neutral to positive attitudes on the continuum. In the early stages the characterization of attitudes under 'neutral' seems appropriate and one would expect successful learners to move towards the positive end of the continuum as they progress. A course need not necessarily lead to a very positive evaluation which, in many instances, may be regarded as excessive. On the other hand, a course which leads many students to a negative or very negative evaluation must be considered, on the affective score, a failure. The consequences of such negativism for public attitudes to the language should be considered, sociopolitically, a matter of serious concern.

Sociocultural competence as an affective goal

Culture and society as an affective goal cannot be strictly separated from language as an affective goal. The desire to communicate, identify, or integrate with members of the target speech community is both an important objective in its own right and a concomitant of language learning success. In the first place, it is an important task of language teaching to orient learners towards the speech community whose language is being studied. A language course can cultivate mild or strong interest in one or several speech communities, or it may be conducted as if the people whose language is being learnt did not exist (see Figure 3.4). Possible outcomes in terms of student interest are represented by the continuum in Figure 3.5.

In their attitudes to people in the foreign language community and their ways of living learners are likely to go through different phases

Very positive	Positive	Neutral	Negative	Very negative
Enthusiastic about L2 Enjoys listening to, speaking, reading, and writing L2 Praises L2	Enters into spirit of L2 Feels at home in L2 (Sprachgefühl) Feels good and confident about L2	Recognizes, tolerates, and accepts L2 Acknowledges differences and difficulties Has no marked sense of discomfort or disorientation	Finds it hard to accept L2 L2 strange Feels uncomfortable and disoriented about most aspects of L2	Feels L2 is odd, annoying, confusing, and ugly Rejects L2

Figure 3.3 Range of student attitudes to target language

Positive	Moderate	Negative
Convey and cultivate strong interest in C2	Convey and cultivate moderate interest in C2	Convey and cultivate no interest in C2 C2 not referred to

Figure 3.4 Range of student interest in C2 expressed as teaching goals

Positive	Moderate	Negative
Develops a distinct interest in C2	Develops a moderate interest in C2	Does not develop any interest in C2 Is hardly aware of dealing with a language spoken by people

Figure 3.5 Range of student interest in C2 expressed as learning outcomes

which parallel their affective development in relation to the language. To begin with, students may experience a sense of strangeness, particularly over aspects of life which are different from those they are accustomed to at home. The lifestyle may initially be as puzzling as the language. The goal should be not only to promote an intellectual understanding of the social rules that guide the target society, but to enable students to identify or empathize with that society or individual members of it. This goal is presumably identical with the integrative orientation which Lambert and Gardner have attributed to many successful language learners. Negatively, the opposite would be for the language learner to dissociate himself from the target language community and its members and, at worst, to despise them or laugh at them. Developing a positive outlook towards the culture of a community whose language we are studying does not mean that we should be totally uncritical, nor that we should condone all features or aspects of life in that society. But, to begin with, it is more important to understand and empathize than to sit in judgement, either positively or negatively. Excessive adulation is as much to be avoided as severe condemnation.

Policy decisions on sociocultural attitude development for a course would range over the sets of goals and potential outcomes presented in Figures 3.6 and 3.7.

It would be difficult to learn the language of a speech community one totally rejected. An exclusively negative approach to the speech community and its life (for example, 'francophobia') can hardly be considered an appropriate goal. If it occurs as an outcome of a language programme, it can only be regarded as a regrettable result which should

A **Very positive**	B **Positive**	C **Neutral**	D **Negative**	E **Very negative**
Encourage infatuation with C2 Invite total admiration for C2: 'anglomania', 'francomania'	Encourage students to understand and be sympathetic to C2	Encourage students to know (rather than love) C2, to be neutral and detached, or if need be, critical	Cultivate critical or negative attitude to C2	Convey hostility and prejudice to C2

Figure 3.6 Range of student attitudes to the L2 community expressed as teaching goals

A **Very positive**	B **Positive**	C **Neutral**	D **Negative**	E **Very negative**
Admires and loves C2 without reservation	Feels positive about C2	Is objective or detached with reference to C2	Is rather critical of C2	Is hostile to C2 Holds undisguised 'anglophobia', 'francophobia'

Figure 3.7 Range of student attitudes to the L2 community expressed as learning outcomes

be remedied. At the other end of the continuum, excessive and uncritical adulation of a speech community (for example, 'anglomania') on the part of an over-enthusiastic teacher is not likely to be accompanied by a positive outlook among students; more probably it will backfire, antagonizing students, and perhaps lead to the rejection of the speech community. A neutral, non-judgemental, or positive orientation should be envisaged as the most constructive sociocultural goal to pursue.

Language learning as an affective goal

Finally, bringing the learner to approach the language learning task itself in a positive spirit and with an appreciation of what is involved can also be regarded as an affective goal. The learner should be prepared to take the steps needed to learn the language successfully, to co-operate with the teacher and to overcome difficulties, and eventually to study the language independently and to continue to learn even after the stimulus of an organized course is no longer available. The student's attitudes to second language learning as an affective goal can be described on a positive to negative continuum while the student's attitudes as a learning outcome may fall anywhere between A to E on a second continuum (see Figures 3.8 and 3.9). On the first scale, only positive treatment can be regarded as a desirable goal in the affective domain, and on the second continuum, only A and B can be regarded as successful outcomes. If large numbers of students respond to instruction with C, D, or E on the second continuum, the reaction would indicate failure with possible serious sociopolitical consequences.

The affective goals we have proposed are not in conflict with the taxonomy developed by Valette (1971) and Valette and Disick (1972), but they are more wide-ranging and more differentiated in that they

Positive	**Neutral/detached**	**Negative**
Encourage interest in learning L2 Treat L2 learning as worthwhile Urge students to continue study outside course and after end of course Convey enthusiasm for learning L2	Cultivate no particular attitude to learning L2 Treat L2 learning as a job to be done, with no special love or enthusiasm	Treat L2 learning as a harsh discipline or necessary evil Treat L2 learning as mainly an examination requirement

Figure 3.8 Range of student attitudes to learning the L2 expressed as teaching goals

A **Very positive**	B **Positive**	C **Neutral**	D **Negative**	E **Very negative**
Enthusiastic about learning L2	Tackles L2 learning with confidence and enjoyment Is willing and co-operative Handles difficulties in a positive spirit	Accepts L2 without enthusiasm	Learning L2 treated as unpleasant task Avoids L2 learning is irritated by L2 learning Wants to drop out	Hates having to learn L2 Resists learning L2

Figure 3.9 Range of student attitudes to learning the L2 expressed as learning outcomes

distinguish three affective goals, in each of which we recognize both an emotional component and the notion of ego-involvement. These affective goals can be summarized as the development of three sets of attitudes: language teaching should cultivate positive attitudes to the target language, to the speakers of that language, and to the self as learner.

The transfer objective

The choice of target language is determined by a variety of factors. In the case of immigrants to Canada, Britain, or the United States, learning English is probably the prime objective. But in the case of foreign language instruction in schools and universities, the choice of language and the objectives to be pursued are less clearly defined. Although there are usually good educational and sociopolitical reasons for including French or German in the school curriculum, students may find that in later life they need Russian, Spanish, or Arabic. In other cases, once they have grown up, students make no further use of any of the languages they studied in school. Therefore, especially in school and university settings, foreign language teaching should include among its goals more generalized educational objectives than those we have considered so far. These can be summarized as three 'transfer' objectives: acquiring language learning techniques; obtaining insight into language and culture; and developing positive generalized attitudes to language, culture, and language study.

The term 'transfer' is borrowed from educational psychology where it has served for many years to describe the human tendency to generalize what has been learnt in one situation to other situations. An age-old controversy in educational psychology has been whether transfer can be taken for granted, and psychologists, around the turn of the century, attempted to demonstrate that generalization of learning from one setting to another does not automatically occur. This viewpoint had a particular bearing on the teaching of Latin which was often justified not for its intrinsic value as a language but as a form of generalized training. By denying the occurrence of generalized mind training, the theory of transfer removed one of the main arguments for the teaching of classical languages. The conclusion of the controversy was that if we wish transfer to occur we should not take it for granted but should positively 'teach for transfer'. It is this conclusion that leads us to consider transfer as a language learning objective. If we wish to generalize the lessons of learning the mother tongue to the learning of other languages, such generalizations must become one of our teaching objectives. The three objectives summarized under the transfer concept can be said to reflect, on a more general level, the three language-specific objectives we have just considered: proficiency, cognition, and affect.

A language may be taught in such a way that not only is proficiency acquired in that language but appropriate learning strategies and study techniques are generalized to the learning of other languages. This objective represents an application to foreign language teaching of the general educational principle of 'learning how to learn', or 'teaching for transfer' (see Chapter 9). In practice, relatively little has been done to provide students with appropriate techniques to apply to the learning of other languages. However, a few studies have been designed to provide adult learners with insights into language learning processes and good techniques of language study.

When a particular language is studied in the classroom, learners inevitably confront general language problems. Their assumptions about the nature of language, derived from the unselfconscious use of the native language, are challenged. The study of a second language thus becomes an invitation to gain insight into the nature of language in general and into the functioning of the mother tongue. Even a language learner who has been unsuccessful in reaching a satisfactory proficiency level may at least learn from the experience to appreciate the magnitude and complexity of the task. Insight into the nature of language can, therefore, become a cognitive learning objective in its own right. We have already pointed out that cognitive objectives may include knowledge about culture and society. The study of a particular country may be treated as an example of how to approach other countries, leading to general observations about culture and society.

In the affective domain, language teaching may promote positive attitudes to other cultures and societies, to language and languages, and to language learning in general. In the affective, as much as in the cognitive domain, it is possible to generalize from a particular culture and society to openness towards other countries and cultures in general. It is obvious that such generalized attitudes do not result exclusively from the language class. But since, for many students, the language class is the only prolonged cross-cultural experience they are likely to have, it is an important factor in the development of general cross-cultural attitudes. The foreign language teacher may or may not deliberately cultivate an interest in other countries or cultures (Figure 3.10), and the resulting attitudes to other countries may range from very positive to strongly negative, as represented by Figure 3.11.

Positive	**Negative**
Treat L2 community as exemplar and cultivate interest in other countries and cultures	Do not cultivate interest in other countries and cultures

Figure 3.10 Degree of interest in other countries and cultures expressed as teaching goals

A Very positive	B Positive	C Neutral	D Negative	E Very negative
Interested in other countries and cultures L2 learning has whetted student's appetite for contact with other countries and cultures	Is open to and tolerant of different countries and cultures	Feelings about C2 have not generalized to other countries and cultures	Is guarded and mildly negative with regard to other countries and cultures	Has become prejudiced against foreign countries and speakers of other languages

Figure 3.11 Range of student attitudes to other countries expressed as learning outcomes

Socially undesirable attitudes which already exist may be reinforced through the language course. The goal of a course where the transfer objective is present should be to cultivate attitudes as under A or B in Figure 3.11.

The experience of learning one second language is likely to promote certain attitudes and an emotional set towards language and language learning in general. Such attitudes may be influenced by other experiences such as mother tongue instruction and the prevailing attitudes in society. But the foreign language teacher may deliberately aim at cultivating a positive interest in language and in language learning. This goal and the resulting attitudes may be expressed by two sets of scales, one on attitudes to language and the other on attitudes to language study:

Positive ←	→ **Negative**
Cultivate interest in, and curiosity about, language in general	Show no concern with languages other than L2

Figure 3.12 Degree of interest in language in general expressed as teaching goals

Even if the teacher cultivates an interest in and curiosity about language in general (Figure 3.12), we cannot expect all learners to score A or even B on scales 3.13 and 3.15. It would be alarming, however, if the course evoked an E outcome on these scales ('Student dislikes languages'; 'Student considers language learning hateful or boring, or completely rejects it') among the majority of students. One must of course expect some learners to fall under C or D on scale 3.13 ('Student accepts languages but is not interested in languages as such' or 'Other student interests predominate'), even where a teacher has set out to inspire interest and confidence. On the other hand, as already mentioned, a language learning experience should obviate not only an E on scale 3.15, but also a C or D ('Student approaches language learning task reluctantly or anxiously' 'Student avoids language learning if possible'). Ideally, *any* language course should be conducted in such a way that most students would readily subscribe to B on this scale: 'Students would tackle a new language if need be'.

Concluding comments

Before we leave the topic of language teaching objectives, it should be pointed out that there is continuing opposition to the idea of a model which presents a curriculum in terms of process and product, or means

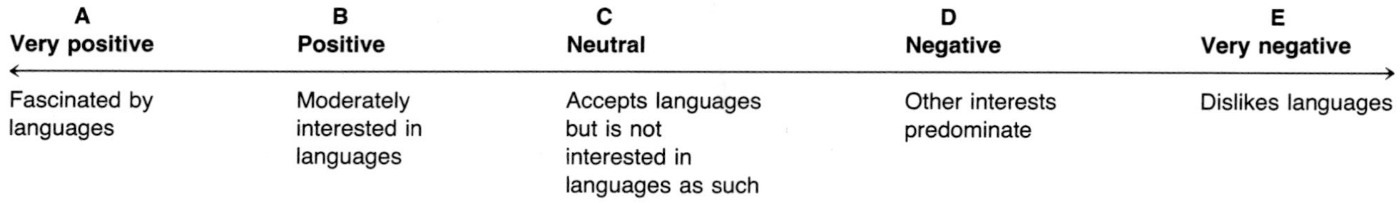

A **Very positive**	B **Positive**	C **Neutral**	D **Negative**	E **Very negative**
Fascinated by languages	Moderately interested in languages	Accepts languages but is not interested in languages as such	Other interests predominate	Dislikes languages

Figure 3.13 Range of student attitudes to language in general expressed as learning outcomes

Positive	**Negative**
⟵	⟶
Cultivate an outlook on language learning and inspire confidence in language learning	Show no concern with the student's attitudes to language learning

Figure 3.14 Range of attitudes to language learning expressed as teaching goals

and ends (see, for example, Tumposky 1984). We believe that the extension of the discussion to cover proficiency, knowledge, affect, and transfer, as suggested in this chapter, will serve to counter the argument that the specification of objectives is too confining. In our view, classroom teaching and teacher education, as well as the evaluation of student performance and any serious discussion of curriculum planning, will benefit greatly from a closer specification of objectives.

Notes

1 See FCLT, pp. 341–59, for a discussion of various aspects of the concept of proficiency in second language education.

2 Note that the targeted norm is often assumed to be that of an educated native speaker of the language, though this norm is typically not precisely defined. Issues frequently arise, for example in an EFL context, as to whether 'American English' or 'British English' is to be the target, such global designations apparently referring mainly to phonology and perhaps also to some vocabulary differences. In some circumstances, as in countries where English serves as a language of wider communication among non-native speakers, there may be good arguments for taking an established regional variety as the norm (cf. Kachru 1982, 1985; Smith 1981, 1983; Strevens 1982; Rampton 1990).

3 The notion of 'learner needs' remains somewhat ambiguous. Brindley (1989), for example, refers to a study in which three different teacher orientations to students' needs were found: a general language proficiency view of needs, a psychological/humanistic view, emphasizing learners' affective and strategic needs, and a specific purposes view emphasizing instrumental needs. Brindley emphasizes the importance in curriculum planning of reconciling, through information sharing 'what learners want and what teachers think they need' (1989: 76).

4 See also the reservations expressed by Widdowson (1987) concerning English for Specific Purposes courses with narrowly specified aims. He argues that such courses risk resulting in a restricted competence that will not be transferable to other contexts of use.

A **Very positive**	B **Positive**	C **Neutral**	D **Negative**	E **Very negative**
Is confident and positive about language learning Is prepared to tackle new language	Would tackle new language if need be	Approaches language learning task reluctantly or anxiously Resists breaking out of L1	Considers other languages strange and forbidding Avoids language learning if possible	Considers language learning hateful or boring Completely rejects language learning

Figure 3.15 Range of student attitudes to language learning expressed as learning outcomes

PART THREE

Content options

Content options

Turning now to syllabus content, we must remind ourselves that the chief principle underlying a multidimensional curriculum is that teaching requires more than the teaching of language as such. As already indicated, we identify four main content areas which will now be looked at more closely:

1 The study of the target language;
2 The study of the target culture;
3 Communicative activities;
4 General language education.

The first two areas imply the systematic study of language and culture, while the third represents a syllabus of global and integrated activities which involve the use of the language in its sociocultural context. These three syllabuses together constitute different but complementary approaches to the target language. The fourth syllabus invites the learners to take a wider and more detached view of their involvement and to reflect in a generalized way about languages, cultures, and learning. In other words, three of the syllabuses—like the three objectives, proficiency, knowledge, and affect—are language-specific. The fourth syllabus—like the fourth objective, transfer—reaches beyond the particular language being learnt.

Each content category requires one syllabus (or several syllabuses), i.e. an inventory of topics and a suggested sequence. We can anticipate that, over time, there will be shifts of emphasis from one syllabus to another or among topics or areas within each syllabus. Moreover, we should envisage different ways of integrating the syllabuses so that they are not seen as separate entities. A particular task or activity may involve reference to more than one syllabus. However, in order to do justice to all the syllabuses we will treat them one by one, although in practice there will be bridges from one to another, and in a single language class the aim should be to integrate thoroughly the contribution of all the participating syllabuses. Each of the four syllabuses is intended to contribute to the objectives we have outlined, and we must, therefore, estimate to what extent they meet these expectations. The different syllabuses require a variety of teaching strategies, and for this reason we will treat strategies in Part Four separately from the syllabuses although, as we will see, certain strategy options are quite closely associated with particular syllabuses.

Of the four syllabuses that have been proposed as constituting a multidimensional curriculum, the language syllabus is probably the least controversial. In principle, it would be questioned only by those who have abandoned their belief in the role of any form of linguistic analysis in language teaching. In our presentation we do allow for a non-analytic approach to language learning through the communicative activities syllabus. But in the view we offer here we balance a non-analytic approach to language learning with an analytic one, which is the function of the language syllabus.

In this section we will discuss the four syllabuses in detail, beginning with various aspects of the language syllabus: pronunciation (Chapter 4), grammar (Chapter 5), and functional analysis (Chapter 6).[1] This will be followed by a discussion of communicative activities (Chapter 7), culture (Chapter 8), and general language education (Chapter 9). In this presentation, we will treat each component as a syllabus in its own right. By calling a component a syllabus, we claim that: (a) it is a teachable entity, (b) it makes a specific contribution to the total language curriculum, and (c) it can be arranged in a sequential order.

Note

1 A chapter on lexis was also envisaged by the author but did not form part of the manuscript. In that he planned to incorporate it as a component of the language syllabus, it is clear that Stern viewed the systematic study of vocabulary as an important element of the curriculum, over and above any incidental exposure to vocabulary use that would occur through the communicative activities syllabus.

In determining objectives and content for a lexical syllabus, he saw as an initial issue the complex question of what is involved in lexical competence (see, for example, Carter 1987; Nation 1990). He was concerned with vocabulary selection and control in the early stages of a language course and recognized the pros and cons of past word frequency studies in this regard (for discussion see Carter and McCarthy 1988: 1–11). The more recent availability of concordances based on large corpora of computerized language data would most certainly have been considered relevant to the lexical syllabus, not only with respect to the need for up-to-date reference materials for both learners and teachers (Ilson 1985; McCarthy 1990: 132–44), but also for the many possibilities such concordances offer for systematic word study (Willis and Willis 1988; Willis 1990).

Stern identified as a major challenge for teachers the question of how to promote retention/recall of L2 vocabulary. In his chapter on the lexical syllabus, he planned to review a wide variety of techniques for strengthening vocabulary retention, ranging from the traditional practice of memorizing lists of isolated words with translations or definitions, to semantically-oriented approaches to vocabulary organization in the form of diagrams, grids, trees, and semantic mappings of related meanings (for example, Gairns and Redman 1986: 13–43; McCarthy 1990: 93–7), to more context-embedded techniques enlisting the support of a combination of learning modes and senses, for example via images, realia, mime, and so on (for example, Morgan and Rinvolucri 1986: 54–68). The review of techniques would also have included a consideration of mnemonics for vocabulary learning (for example, Morgan and Rinvolucri 1986: 118) and of formal word-building activities involving, for example, affixation and compounding in English (for example, Redman and Ellis 1990: 7–9, 68–72). Finally, the importance of personalizing the systematic study of vocabulary was emphasized by Stern with reference to an article describing how university students of German L2 were given individual responsibility for 'collecting' new words of their choice (Kramsch 1979).

4 The language syllabus: pronunciation

Introduction

In learning a foreign language, pronunciation has always been an early obstacle to overcome. According to Kelly (1969), language pedagogy since time immemorial has attempted to come to grips with the pronunciation problem either intuitively or by an analytic approach, and this broad duality of pronunciation teaching method is, in Kelly's view, still the main option today. In spite of this common element across the ages, we can observe marked differences in the treatment of pronunciation at different times. Until the last decades of the nineteenth century, the majority of foreign language courses did not pay too much attention to this problem. They treated it as a preliminary difficulty in the mastery of the alphabet of the new language. The main task was to try to give the letters of the target language the sound values they normally convey to the literate native speaker. Pronunciation teaching, if it played a role at all, was thus only a preparatory task for getting as quickly as possible to the real problem of language teaching: the foreign language grammar. In order to give help to the learner in how to pronounce a French, English, or German text, courses usually provided their own home-made transliteration in which the sound values of the language were reinterpreted in a rough-and-ready manner, using the nearest equivalents offered by the mother tongue spelling system.

The late nineteenth century reform movement led to a radical change in the approach to pronunciation teaching in that it became a central preoccupation for the early stages of second language instruction.[1] The main objective for teaching beginners was to give them a 'correct' pronunciation, and in doing this the newly invented phonetic notations were given a key role.[2] Some reformers insisted on an exclusive use of phonetic script for the first few weeks of the course. Others believed that for an even longer period—for example, for the entire first term, or even for the first one or two years—the language should be offered through a phonetic notation avoiding conventional spelling in order to forestall any 'contamination' of correct pronunciation through misinterpretations of the standard orthography. The presentation of a phonetic notation was often accompanied by the use of sound charts and diagrams, showing the position of different sounds in the oral cavity.

During the early years of the twentieth century, some of the enthusiasm for phonetics was lost. The new practices had been introduced to do justice to the spoken language, to encourage a good pronunciation, and as a means of avoiding spelling confusions. But the use of phonetic script in the early stages did not produce the faultless pronunciation that had been expected. Instead, it tended to confuse and irritate language learners who either mistook the phonetic notation for the spelling system of the new language or who had grown impatient with these prolonged preliminaries and wanted to get on to 'real French' or 'real English'. However, while phonetics declined in school-level language courses, it continued to develop as an academic discipline at university level and also in the phonetic training of advanced language learners and future language teachers. The courses given to these students can be described as courses in 'practical phonetics' which were largely concerned with the systematic study of speech sounds and included intensive exercises in sound discrimination and pronunciation. In many ways, these courses had a remedial character in that they attempted to eliminate ingrained defects of pronuncation. They were often very prescriptive and very demanding, with a great deal of emphasis on the acquisition of a 'good' and 'correct' pronunciation with a 'perfect accent' as the ultimate ideal.[3]

With the development of modern linguistics during the first half of the twentieth century, phonetics and phonology became associated with, and eventually incorporated into, linguistics. Gradually, a more theoretical and empirical research approach to the study of speech sounds evolved, leading to scholarly writing on phonetics and phonology and detailed authoritative studies on the phonology of particular languages.[4] In the 1940s and 1950s, a new systematic approach to phonology, based on the concept of the phoneme, was introduced into structural and audiolingual language teaching. Exercises were devised which drew attention to changes in lexical or grammatical meaning brought about by specific sound contrasts. Such exercises were not so much concerned with accent or pronunciation as such; they showed that phonemic contrast was an important device in making a language work. A variety of minimal-pair drills were used to alert students to those phonemic contrasts which are significant in the vocabulary or grammar of a language.

The contrastive study of speech sounds across languages, which aroused considerable interest in the 1950s and early 1960s, was intended to identify similarities and differences between the sounds of the target language and the language of origin. It was believed that by working on these contrasts, language curriculums would systematically help students to overcome the phonological difficulties that were presented by the new language. It was in this spirit that, in the late 1950s, the newly founded Center for Applied Linguistics in Washington, DC, commissioned a number of contrastive studies of the phonological systems of French, Italian, Spanish, and German, each of which was compared with the phonology of English in order to identify the problem areas in the phonology of various foreign languages for English-speaking students.[5]

Since the 1960s, a practical compromise established itself in the teaching of pronunciation which still prevails today. This compromise is well represented in the pedagogical literature (for example, Rivers 1975, 1981; Allen and Valette 1977; Celce-Murcia 1987). These writings recommend pronunciation teaching as an important aspect of the language syllabus. They pay attention to sound discrimination as well as to the productive aspect of pronunciation training. They lay emphasis on segmental phonemes, phonemic contrast, and contrastive analysis. A variety of practical exercises illustrate this approach. The pedagogy of pronunciation teaching creates an awareness of the sound-symbol interaction and invites movement from sound to written symbol and vice versa, as in dictation or reading aloud. It also recognizes the importance of suprasegmental features and offers practice in stress and intonation. Most of the training takes place relatively early in a course; but the complete concentration on this one aspect of language learning, which was characteristic of the late nineteenth century, is no longer favoured. Pronunciation is introduced more gradually and more unobtrusively, but by and large it still constitutes, in the main, an early phase of teaching and is gradually replaced by attention to global listening and speaking activities, grammar teaching, and the like.

Nevertheless, it is noteworthy that a considerable number of pronunciation materials exist for the remedial training of advanced learners whose pronunciation requires improvement. The fact that there is a need for such remedial practice material indicates that pronunciation frequently deteriorates or fossilizes at a relatively low level. Some of the writings on phonology and pronunciation for advanced learners often go into minute and quite technical detail. The suggestion, therefore, seems to be: (a) that a renewed systematic attack must be made for advanced learners, and (b) that the methodology demands a sophisticated phonetic and phonological type of instruction. In any case, this literature indicates that a wealth of scientific knowledge of phonetics and phonology is available and that it can be transmitted successfully to students who wish to overcome a foreign accent, eradicate major defects of utterance, or improve the overall quality of their pronunciation.[6]

As a rationale for procedures commonly employed in the teaching of pronunciation at any level, Strevens (1977) suggests a three-stage gradation. To begin with, teachers should encourage students to mimic and imitate without wasting much time on explanations, because in many situations straightforward imitation is all that is needed. Where there are difficulties which simple mimicking or imitation do not overcome, instruction should move to 'speech training', that is, specific exercises which attempt to deal with a particular pronunciation problem. The pedagogical literature offers an abundance of techniques for this purpose. But such speech training can be utilized without going into technical detail, except that the exercises may implicitly draw attention to a sound segment, a speech movement, or a point of stress, rhythm, or intonation. If this procedure does not work, instruction would, at the third or final stage, move to 'practical phonetics', that is, more explicit phonetic or phonological explanations. In this way, the technical analysis of the speech production process is minimized. It does not dominate pronunciation training. It is a last resort, and students are not overwhelmed with phonological theory and technicalities where, in the main, simple imitation and perhaps some carefully designed exercises are sufficient.

A different sequence for the teaching of pronunciation has been proposed by Hammerly (1982). To start with, he recommends practice in auditory discrimination so as to make sure that the students learn to hear the differences between the two (occasionally three) sounds (1982: 342). In phase two, awareness and understanding of the underlying phonetic mechanisms are developed. What this amounts to is practical phonetics at an earlier stage than Strevens proposes. Phase three, production, practises the sound features and shifts to practice 'with attention on communication, the result being integration of each new sound into the growing system' (1982: 345). It is in this final phase that imitation is encouraged, short sequences first, then longer ones, finally using the sound feature in a name, a saying, or a mini-dialogue.

To sum up, while in recent years pronunciation teaching has not maintained the central place in the language syllabus that Sweet (1899) thought it should have, it is recognized as an important component of language pedagogy. A number of useful techniques for training pronunciation exist. Against this, it should be pointed out that from about 1980 communicative language teaching has led occasionally to a neglect of pronunciation or a loss of interest in it among certain practitioners. This has, in turn, prompted other teachers to re-emphasize the need for attention to pronunciation in order to enable learners to communicate effectively (see, for example, Callamand and Pedoya 1984). Phonetics and phonology, the two disciplines which have the most direct bearing on pronunciation teaching, have changed considerably during the course of this century under the influence of new developments in linguistics and the growth of sociolinguistics and psycholinguistics. They have become theoretically more complex disciplines, supported by empirical research studies. The relationship between modern phonetics and phonology and pronunciation teaching is more tenuous than it was eighty or a hundred years ago when a relatively simple phonetic science was clearly seen as the parent discipline. We can, however, observe a few general tendencies in the field of linguistic science which affect the modern view of pronunciation teaching.

The distinction between phonetics as the general science of speech sounds and phonology as the study of the sound systems of particular languages has helped to clarify what it is we have to deal with when we teach pronunciation: that is, the physiology of producing speech sounds on the one hand, and on the other, the specific system of distinctive sound features which characterize the target language. Both disciplines have a contribution to make to pronunciation teaching. But the distinction between them has made it clearer that the learning of new sounds requires relearning movements of the vocal tract and that learning a new pronunciation is to a large extent physiological and neuromuscular. In this respect pronunciation teaching is 'more like gymnastics than linguistics' (Strevens 1977: 81). However, because of the fluidity of the speech movements themselves and the different proportions of the vocal tract utilized in different individuals, the movements that create the sounds cannot be described with absolute precision, let alone prescribed in detail. The postures demanded for each segment should be regarded as an idealization of real speech movements which are made differently by different individuals. What we learn in learning the pronunciation of the target language is a system of relationships among different sounds.

The sociolinguistic view of language has brought about several important changes in the definition of objectives in teaching pronunciation. In the first place, the tacit assumption of the acquisition of a native-like pronunciation as the ultimate objective is no longer seen as appropriate in all circumstances. Pronunciation is viewed much more as a vehicle for interacting with native speakers. In deciding on a pronunciation target, it is now customary to take into account the role of the foreign speaker *vis-à-vis* native interlocutors. An important consideration is that the learner's pronunciation should be intelligible to the native speaker (Avery and Ehrlich 1992a; Wong 1987). It is usually not necessary for the learner to acquire a native-like accent. On the contrary, it is often more appropriate for a language learner to signal his status as a foreigner by his non-native accent than to make strenuous efforts to appear indistinguishable from native speakers.

Besides intelligibility, another social criterion that has emerged is the acceptability of pronunciation, that is, it should avoid having features that are offensive, irritating, or absurd in the opinion of the native listener. On this score, a carefully enunciated and neutral way of speaking may be more appropriate for an L2 learner than one which has strictly local characteristics and which may cause native speakers to feel that the learner is poking fun at them. On the other hand, as a listener the learner may have to be alerted to a variety of accents and characteristics of informal speech, such as elisions and contractions, which deviate from the standard and which characterize the speech of regular language users in different situations or in different regional or social settings.[7] Discourse analysis has influenced pronunciation teaching through much greater attention to rhythm, stress, intonation, and changes in pronunciation in larger units of speech than isolated words or sentences spoken out of context.[8] Finally, psycholinguistics has exercised an influence on pronunciation teaching and learning. The widespread belief that young children are always superior to adults in the acquisition of a perfect, native-like pronunciation in a new language can no longer be sustained, because some experimental evidence has clearly contradicted it.[9] Nevertheless, the belief that children are better language learners still prevents some adults from even trying to reach a satisfactory level of pronunciation.[10]

Psycholinguistic research has contributed to questioning other common beliefs about pronunciation learning. Looking at much of the literature on pronunciation teaching, one cannot but be struck by the lack of empirical evidence for many established practices. These may have a certain face validity and may be sanctioned by the judgement of experienced teachers and methodologists, although their efficacy is quite questionable. For example, the interrelationship between sound perception and sound production in a second language and the role of feedback are very complex, and simple recipes of interaction on which many teaching techniques are based have not been supported by research evidence. The need for a more empirical approach to the study of learning a new pronunciation, using the methods of psycholinguistic research, is increasingly being recognized.[11]

Some basic issues in pronunciation teaching

The first issue is how much importance should be attached to phonology, sound discrimination, and pronunciation teaching. As we have seen, most methodologists accept the principle that pronunciation has an important place in language teaching relative to other areas covered by the L2 curriculum. A few writers, however, fear that too much importance has been attributed to it. The York study (Sanderson 1982) used as one of its criteria for successful language teachers the statement that they would be 'vigilant about pronunciation, intonation, and stress' (Sanderson 1982: 126–7). However, the study found that, although this criterion did apply to some of the teachers in the sample, it was by no means universal. Several teachers in the study did not wish to be heavy-handed and weighed up the importance of correct pronunciation against the greater importance of spontaneity and fluency.

Krashen and Terrell (1983) make a powerful case against too much attention to the kind of intensive early pronunciation practice that is reflected in the prevailing approach. They firmly state: 'In the Natural Approach we do not recommend any specific activities for pronunciation, especially in the early stages' (1983: 90). Krashen and Terrell are not convinced that sustained early pronunciation practice has much effect on ultimate pronunciation. They believe that a 'preproduction period' would allow students to develop a feel for the language (ibid.), and they reject as unfounded the fear, frequently expressed by teachers, that bad pronunciation habits will become ingrained and therefore difficult to eradicate. In their view, pronunciation habits are not so firmly established in the first two years that they cannot be changed later.

Another argument for downplaying pronunciation training in language instruction has been advanced by Leather (1983: 199). In his view, too much insistence on correct pronunciation may interfere with the learning of grammar or vocabulary, 'if a learner who is anxious to avoid mispronunciation is therefore reluctant to attempt utterances containing new grammatical or lexical items.' Leather accordingly recommends that pronunciation learning should be considered 'in the context of the whole L2 programme.' Against these warnings about laying too much emphasis on pronunciation training, the more typical view is one that can be illustrated by this quotation from Allen and Valette:

> Most teachers agree that early insistence on correct pronunciation can save many hours of remedial work later on. Bad habits are easily formed and very difficult to change.
> (Allen and Valette 1977: 56)

According to this view, the teacher needs to insist on good pronunciation from the outset. Allen and Valette believe that 'constant practice in listening discrimination, pronunciation, and intonation using a variety of drills and exercises can go far in forming good habits of correct speech' (1977: 56).

There is at present no convincing empirical evidence which could help us sort out the various positions on the merits of pronunciation training. It looks as if the point of view represented by Krashen and Terrell (1983) attributes too little importance to the direct teaching of pronunciation, while the other, illustrated by Allen and Valette (1977), may be too sanguine about the effectiveness of systematic early training. Both of these opposing views appear to underrate the complexity of pronunciation learning. Krashen and Terrell rely too sweepingly on the ability of learners to absorb and reproduce accurate pronunciation without specific instruction. Allen and Valette, on the other hand, make the training techniques appear a simple and foolproof way to successful pronunciation.

It must not be forgotten that many teachers have become disillusioned with pronunciation training. The following quotation reflects this not uncommon pessimism:

> The fact is, minimal pair practice alone sometimes seems to yield minimal results. This may be part of the reason the teaching of pronunciation has fallen into disfavour in so many programmes. Lack of success is discouraging to teachers, and students sometimes feel that pronunciation is an endless succession of unrelated and unmanageable pieces. If the work is so discouraging, shouldn't we just drop it? (Gilbert 1984: 1)

As we shall see shortly, the demand for high levels of pronunciation accuracy does not have to be the same in all types of courses; but regardless of the pedagogic context, there are three universal considerations why pronunciation is important even though it may be difficult to teach and learn. These considerations may be described as: (a) linguistic, (b) communicative, and (c) affective.

As was rightly observed by Sweet (1899) and later again by the structuralists in the 1940s and 1950s, the importance of pronunciation does not lie in 'sounding like a native speaker'; rather, it lies in mastering the grammatical distinctions and the different meanings that are signalled by the phonic features. Consider these English examples:

1 count counted
2 mouse mouth
3 (a) We've often gone up to that lookout
(b) He's got to look out when he talks to his boss.
(Gilbert 1984: 21)

In (1) the distinction is grammatical, in (2) it is lexical, whereas in (3) the difference in stress between *look*out vs. look *out* distinguishes a compound noun from a phrasal verb. In order to master the lexicon and the grammar, the learner must feel at ease with the sound features of the language. If he does not, grammar and vocabulary as well as discourse, all of which make use of sound differences and differences in stress or intonation, become very difficult to learn. In other words, pronunciation learning does not impede the learning of grammar and vocabulary, as Leather (1983) feared. It is an essential prerequisite. It is not so much the perfect mastery of the pronunciation that matters as a sense of familiarity with what the language sounds like, or what Krashen and Terrell (1983) have called the feel for the phonology, that is desirable in almost any type of language course one can think of.

It has been said that the emphasis on communication has brought about a decline of interest in pronunciation.[12] It may well be that in order to encourage learners to get meaning across, the details of pronunciation have been neglected. But if we reflect on what communication involves, namely understanding and being understood, there is no question that serious defects in pronunciation (as well as in the receptive mastery of the sound system) cannot be tolerated. A number of recent writers (Callamand 1981; Celce-Murcia 1987; Naiman 1992) have argued for more effective pronunciation teaching as a way of ensuring better communication, and writers on communicative language teaching (for example, Canale and Swain 1980, and Canale 1983) firmly state that the formal features of a language, including its phonology, must not be neglected if the learner is to achieve some measure of communicative competence.

In Chapter 3 we pointed out that language competence has an affective component. Nowhere is this more relevant than in the learning of pronunciation. The student must come to terms emotionally with individual sounds as well as with the overall sound pattern and intonation contours demanded by the new language. There is plenty of evidence that this is often difficult. For example, it is not uncommon in pronunciation classes to find that students laugh at the sounds they are to make in learning the new language. Moulton (1962), in his masterly contrastive study of German and English sounds, has succeeded in capturing the emotional involvement of students in attempting to learn a new phonology:

> The student may be willing intellectually to accept the fact that the sounds of German are different from those of English. Quite often, however, he is not emotionally able to do this. The sounds of English constitute for him all that is normal in human speech; anything else strikes him as distinctly abnormal. Though reason may tell him otherwise, his emotions tell him that the *ü* of *Tür* is a 'queer' sound which no normal, sensible human being would seriously use. Likewise, the uvular *r* of German strikes him as a quite outlandish rendition of what ought properly to be the familiar constricted *r* of English; and the *ch* of *doch* is to many students an almost indecent sound which ought to be kept outside of language entirely and used only for clearing the mouth of phlegm. These are involuntary reactions, of course; but they can be emotionally very strong. Being told to say such sounds as German *ü*, *r*, and *ch* is a little like being told to wear wrong clothing, to behave in a socially improper way. Anyone who has tried to teach German pronunciation will be familiar with the embarrassed giggles and titters and blushes which the new sounds produce during early stages of instruction.
> (Moulton 1962: 1–2)[13]

Unless the student can overcome the strangeness of the pronunciation demands of the new language, he will have great difficulty in coping with almost any other aspect of the language, its grammar, vocabulary, and writing system. In other words, the value of pronunciation for learning the language is pervasive, and the teaching of pronunciation under any circumstances cannot be regarded as a luxury one can easily dispense with. In our view, then, pronunciation is never unimportant, although the level of accuracy of pronunciation as an objective may well vary considerably for different types of courses.

A syllabus for pronunciation teaching

In view of the importance of pronunciation, both receptively and productively, it is essential for every course designer to develop a rationale for the role of pronunciation in the curriculum. On the basis of this rationale a syllabus should be worked out giving directions on what to aim at and what to teach, when, in what order, and how.

Objectives of pronunciation teaching

To begin with, the curriculum designer must clarify the objectives of pronunciation teaching. The main proficiency goal can be described in general terms as phonological competence, that is: (a) the ability to recognize and discriminate significant sound features, (b) the ability to produce intelligible and acceptable sounds, both segmentally and prosodically, and (c) the ability to interpret written language phonologically, as in reading aloud, and to recreate spoken language graphically, as in writing from dictation and note-taking. In most instances, as we have already pointed out, it is unnecessary to strive for a native-like command of the pronunciation. Many successful language learners will retain an 'accent'. The goal, in most cases, should be intelligibility and acceptability rather than native-like perfection.[14]

While, as a speaker, the learner is likely to be guided towards a single model of clear and careful diction, perhaps with slight variations to distinguish informal and formal ways of speaking, on the receptive side a mastery of a wider range of speech varieties should normally be aimed at. The learner should be able to cope with the spoken language in many different situations, distinguish casual from formal and declamatory speech, and identify and understand slight regional and social variants of the L2. Learners aiming at a high level of phonological competence, such as future language teachers or interpreters, will attempt to meet all these objectives to the full. Others who require only limited phonological competence would scale down the objectives accordingly.

As far as a cognitive objective is concerned, the course designer must consider what knowledge about phonetics and phonology is desirable. In the case of advanced students and language specialists, this knowledge could be wide-ranging, technical, systematic, and detailed. However, for ordinary language learners it is sufficient to gain an understanding of the speech mechanism, to be able to make some comparisons between sound features in L1 and L2, and to acquire a minimum of carefully selected sets of concepts and terms describing the speech mechanism and the sound system.

In view of the profusion of terminologies and concepts, it is important to keep the knowledge component of pronunciation teaching carefully under control, and not to expect language learners to become expert phoneticians within the confines of a practical language course. Affectively, however, it is crucial for all language learners to be given the opportunity to adjust emotionally to the new sound system and to acquire positive feelings about it. More specifically, the learner should come to feel comfortable acoustically with the sound system of the L2 as well as with its psychomotor aspect. The value of a clear and intelligible pronunciation for the purposes of communication should be understood by all learners.

Syllabus design

Until recently little thought has been given to the options in syllabus design for pronunciation teaching (but see Catford 1987; Firth 1992a; Wong 1987). The traditional pattern that has evolved since the nineteenth century reform movement consists of an intensive phase of pronunciation learning at the beginning of the course with an emphasis on segmental phonemes, followed soon after by graphic learning, that is, learning how to transpose sounds into graphic symbols (dictation) or graphic symbols into sounds (reading aloud). The attention to phonology thereafter declines, and generally consists only of sporadic error correction. At a much later stage, it is sometimes taken up again intensively as remedial action for a small number of very advanced learners or future language teachers.

This pattern of an over-intensive start and increasing neglect, followed by another burst of intensive remedial action after several years does not seem well adjusted to what one would expect to be the growth pattern of pronunciation. At the start, it is obviously difficult for language learners to accommodate themselves to the multiplicity of sound features in a new language.[15] This is bound to be a gradual process which should probably be approached gently and slowly and which should be interwoven with other language learning activities. A pronunciation syllabus would, therefore, be best designed in conjunction with a grammatical and lexical syllabus, thus slowly building up over time an increasingly differentiated phonological competence and knowledge.

In the phonological literature, a great deal of detailed information is available, particularly on commonly taught languages such as English and French. The descriptive knowledge of these languages is of inestimable value as a resource base for curriculum developers and teachers. But the wealth of information carries with it the danger of overwhelming students with minute technicalities. Much of the information could not possibly be mastered by students and certainly not in the early stages of a language course. The course designer must be very selective and focus on a few communicatively necessary features of the phonology of the target language, always bearing in mind that learners should not be confused or discouraged by an excessive zeal for details which are not commensurate with their overall level of proficiency.[16]

Order of presentation

Should separate speech sounds (vowels and consonants) be presented before suprasegmentals, or the other way round? The nineteenth-century reformers introduced pronunciation by starting with individual sounds, vowels and consonants, paying little attention to stress and intonation. In this respect they followed the older tradition of pronunciation teaching which was similar to the introduction of the alphabet. This order of presentation remained unchallenged for many years, but recently, it has been called into question. This is due in part to new developments in the more accurate observation of speech sounds in context which has shown that the isolated sound is an abstraction. Speech sounds are produced in a continuous chain in which each individual sound is influenced by preceding as well as subsequent movements. Moreover, the linguistic interest in discourse has recognized as basic the flow and rhythmic pattern of longer speech sequences. All this has prompted a reversal of the traditional order. In more recent pronunciation courses it is not uncommon to find the treatment of vowels and consonants at a later stage in the presentation, while the earlier units deal with intonation, syllables, stress, and rhythm.[17]

Is the older or the newer approach preferable? No order should be considered sacred. In developing a syllabus of sound features, teachers should not feel tied to an unthinking older tradition or to a newer fashion; instead, they should consider whether a particular order has specific pedagogical advantages or disadvantages.[18] At no stage in a pronunciation syllabus should learners lose sight of the overall picture. They cannot deal successfully with particular sound segments without being able to relate them regularly to the way these sounds manifest themselves in the stream of speech. This fact should always be borne in mind in designing a pronunciation syllabus.

Perception and production

It has always been recognized that the teaching of pronunciation involves both perception and production. But earlier procedures of pronunciation teaching tended to lead the learner as quickly as possible to making the new sounds as the main, if not the only, focus for pronunciation training. As present research and experience stand, it appears that the immediate pressure on learners to articulate new sounds may be misguided. There is some evidence to suggest that a lengthy period of listening to authentic speech samples and making observations about them may be a better introduction to the sound system than an early insistence on imitating particular sounds out of context.[19]

According to this view, it is appropriate to give students plenty of opportunity to listen to and watch speakers of all kinds: young and old, male and female, cheerful and angry, articulate and reticent; voices with regional accents, everyday speech, or declamatory styles, and so on. Students should also have the opportunity to observe speakers in real life or on video and to be made aware of speech movements, facial expressions, gestures, body postures, and such paralinguistic features as breathing, pausing, speed of utterance, and degrees of loudness (from whispering to shouting).[20] Much of this will occur in the course of the entire language curriculum, i.e. during regular speaking and listening activities and as a part of ordinary acts of communication. What makes it pronunciation practice specifically is the attention to sound features which in ordinary communication would not be specially focused upon.

There is no firmly established knowledge about the best balance between perception and production. Common sense would seem to suggest that we cannot produce a sound feature which we cannot perceive. On the other hand, we do not automatically produce all the sounds that we are able to perceive. We should recognize that the relationship between auditory sound perception and articulation is intricate, and simple folk wisdom about it may be plausible but not necessarily right. There is, however, no question that language learners need more opportunities to absorb the sound patterns of a new language through observation than they have tended to have in the past, and this principle should be reflected in the pronunciation syllabus.

Techniques of pronunciation teaching

The procedures for pronunciation teaching can be represented as a continuum from implicit to explicit, as shown in Figure 4.1.

In describing the stages on this continuum, we have adopted the three distinctions made by Strevens (1977) to which we have added a fourth: exposure. Exposure stands for the presentation to learners of authentic speech by the teacher, in a recorded form with no guidance, or simply

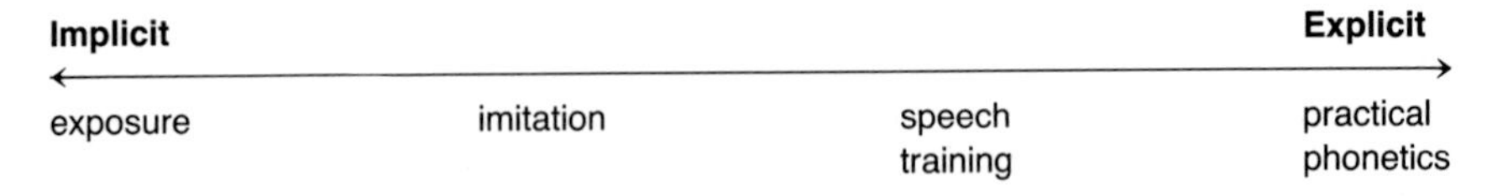

Figure 4.1 Range of procedures for teaching pronunciation

through naturalistic situations of language use. Any of these would provide an opportunity for learners to observe the target language, to accommodate themselves to its sounds, rhythms, and intonation patterns, and to absorb them without any formal instruction. The next three stages move, as previously explained, from direct exhortation to imitate and deliberately designed speech training, that is, pronunciation exercises and drills, to the final stage of practical phonetics. In Strevens' view this progression represents an ascending order of sophistication and intellectualization for teachers and students (Strevens 1977: 85).

Strevens urges us to be optimistic about the effectiveness of these training techniques. He believes that pronunciation can be learnt easily without, on the whole, having to be very technical. Only a few aspects may be difficult, and deliberate training or detailed phonetic explanations should be reserved for them. It is certainly sound advice not to overstate the problems and difficulties of pronunciation learning, and to recognize that the bulk of the sound system can be learnt without too much trouble. In our view, however, the failures and difficulties of pronunciation teaching must not be dismissed too lightly.

In many language teaching manuals, imitation and mimicking are recommended as the simplest devices to ensure an accurate pronunciation. In a rough-and-ready sense this may be right. Imitation, however, is not as simple as it is often made out to be. It is based on the assumption that the learner is able to distinguish accidental performance characteristics from phonologically relevant features of the sounds. This requires a great deal of perceptual and cognitive acuity and discrimination.[21] Moreover, an inability to imitate sound features may not always be neuromuscular, perceptual, or cognitive. It may lie in a deep-seated affective resistance to making sounds which appear to violate a person's language ego. They may stem from an overall resistance to the target language and an unwillingness to empathize with the native speakers who provide the model the learner is supposed to imitate. The approach to pronunciation becomes an indicator of how an individual learner relates to the language he learns or to the speakers of that language, and exhortation to imitate may not be sufficient to overcome this resistance.

Both speech training and practical phonetics to a greater or lesser degree appeal to the cognitive control of the learner in acquiring a foreign pronunciation. As we will see again and again, the distinction between cognitive-analytic and non-analytic global teaching strategies presents us with a dilemma which is fundamental to the whole of language teaching. Speech training and practical phonetics as more or less cognitive strategies have a legitimate place in pronunciation teaching. Nevertheless, the question is to what extent relatively unconscious processes such as voice modulation, breathing, and the neuromuscular actions involved in speech production can be controlled by deliberate exercises and phonetic explanations. The exercises seem to focus in a direct and practical way on sound features and the diagrams, explanations, and neuromuscular experiments of practical phonetics are the only way in which teaching can bring to the learner's attention the mechanisms that control pronunciation.[22]

We have little evidence to indicate what type of explanation or analytic procedures are helpful to learners and which are not. For example, how far are learners helped by diagrams of the head showing the position of the tongue in producing certain sounds? At what stage of language learning does a phonetic or phonemic notation help learners in the mastery of pronunciation? In considering the role of practical phonetics, it must be remembered that explanations should not only be considered as ways of achieving phonological competence; they might also add to the learner's knowledge about the foreign language and about speech in general, thus meeting knowledge and transfer objectives rather than the proficiency objective.

The injunction to imitate is not a simple request to mirror someone else's speech gestures. It requires empathy and identification with target language speakers. Some courses have tried to overcome the learner's inhibitions by asking students to relax physically and to control their breathing, to treat pronunciation practice as playing a part, to pretend that they are a French or English person, to pretend that they have a French or English accent, or even to adopt a specific native speaker role ('You are a Belgian journalist living in Brussels, and your name is Paul'). While these techniques may work up to a point, eventually the student must come to terms with himself as a speaker of the other language and, so to speak, widen his language ego so as to incorporate in it the L2 pronunciation.

Ultimately, the mechanics of pronunciation are not the only aspect to which we have to pay attention. Pronunciation is likely to be influenced by the learner's personal attitude to the target language and to the speakers of that language. Pronunciation should be treated as a symptom reflecting a largely unconscious state of mind. On the whole, we have tended to treat pronunciation too exclusively as a simple case of voluntary control over the speech apparatus. This is no doubt true up to a point, but beyond that we have to deal with the expression of self-image, ethnolinguistic attitudes, and empathy which is not confined to pronunciation, but for which the learner's approach to pronunciation is a sensitive indicator.

Concluding comments

In the literature, pronunciation teaching has tended to be treated as a technical task which can be met by straightforward exhortation to imitate, systematic exercises, or phonetic explanations. Difficulties in coming to grips with pronunciation problems are often treated as rather rare exceptions. In our view, resistance to pronunciation problems are quite common and present a real obstacle to many language learners. In trying to overcome such resistance we may have to attempt to identify the causes. At the surface level, the cause may be perceptual or neuromuscular. In such cases, speech training exercises and practical phonetics are probably the appropriate remedy. At a somewhat deeper level, some adult learners have persuaded themselves that they are 'too old' to learn an L2 pronunciation. There is now fairly conclusive evidence that there is little justification for this self-fulfilling prophecy.[23] Some learners lack an understanding of the role of pronunciation in communication. It has been found that recognizing the importance of a clear (rather than perfect) pronunciation can in itself encourage learners to improve.[24]

Notes

1 See Howatt (1984), especially pp. 171–89.

2 For example, according to Sweet, who divided language teaching into five stages, 'the first stage, the mechanical, begins with a thorough mastery of the pronunciation of the language which is being learnt, which presupposes a general practical knowlege of phonetics based on the sounds of the learner's own language' (1964: 117).

3 A key figure in the development of practical phonetics in Britain was the well-known phonetician Daniel Jones who laid the foundations for the teaching of English and French phonetics at University College, London. His influence on the teaching of phonetics at the university level was widespread through his well-known and widely used writings on phonetics, such as *The Pronunciation of English* (1909) and *An English Pronouncing Dictionary* (1917). In France, Paul Passy (e.g. 1906) exercised a similar influence. (See Howatt (1984) for further references to works by Jones and Passy.) The earlier work on practical phonetics teaching in French is illustrated by Armstrong (1947).

4 For a brief account and references to more detailed studies see FCLT: 130–1. Phonetics and phonology are treated in general textbooks on linguistics.
5 The Contrastive Structure Series (CSS) included studies of the phonology of English and German (Moulton 1962), English and Spanish (Stockwell and Bowen 1965), and English and Italian (Agard and Di Pietro 1965). Sajavaara (1981: 35) rightly points out: 'It is ominous in a sense that to this day the CSS volumes remain the last "complete" contrastive presentations of any two languages and that the studies between English and French and between English and Russian were never published'. But see also Delattre's (1965) comparative study of English, French, German, and Spanish.
6 For English, see for example Bowen (1975), Morley (1979) and for French, Léon and Léon (1964), Léon (1966), and Rivers (1975).
7 The following are illustrative of this literature: Prator and Robinett (1972); Brown (1977); MacCarthy (1975, 1978); Callamand (1981); Pennington and Richards (1986).
8 Pennington and Richards (1986) contrast the traditional phonemic-based approach to pronunciation with a broader, discourse-based approach and suggest that a broader focus on pronunciation in the context of discourse should be emphasized. The writings of Gillian Brown on spoken English (e.g. Brown 1977; Brown and Yule 1983b) have laid particular emphasis on the characteristics of informally spoken English which learners have to acquire. See also Temperley (1983). It is characteristic of this discourse perspective that many recent writings on phonology do not start with segmental phonetics followed towards the end of the course with suprasegmentals. Instead, they frequently start with larger units or prosodic features and gradually break down the larger sequences into smaller segments and deal with particular sounds, vowels, or consonants towards the end of the course. See, for example, Callamand (1981); MacCarthy (1975); and Celce-Murcia (1987).
9 For discussions of this issue see, among others, FCLT: 361; Ellis (1985); and Genesee (1988). For a summary of research findings and an argument supporting maturational constraints in language learning, see Long (1990). According to Fledge (1988), there is no conclusive evidence for the view that adults are less able than children to acquire new features of pronunciation. A study by Neufeld (1988) reveals that adults can achieve native-like proficiency in phonological perception yet be deficient in articulatory production.
10 Gilbert (1984: 45) makes this point very effectively.
11 Since the 1960s, there have been some studies on pronunciation

learning. Some have attempted to demonstrate that discrimination training facilitates pronunciation learning. Trying to make sense of contradictory data, Hammerly (1982: 341), concludes that 'perception facilitates production *and* vice versa. That is, whether the initial act is one of perception or production, each act of perception seems to facilitate production and each act of production seems to facilitate perception, in a sort of gradually closing mutual feedback loop'. Leather (1983: 210), who has also reviewed a number of studies on different forms of training, tries to explain the conflicting and confusing results. He states that there is no reason to assume that perceptions and productions advance in parallel, that the judgements about pronunciation on which the interpretation of these studies hinge show little consistency, and finally that it may be that there is no single technique for facilitating the acquisition of all classes of L2 sounds under all conditions.

12 For example, Callamand and Pedoya (1984) make the point that: 'l'enseignement de la prononciation, qui exige un travail minutieux et souvent systématique, n'a plus sa place dans une classe de langue qui privilégie l'acquisition d'un bagage communicatif diversifié et la spontanéité des échanges' (1984: 56).

13 Gilbert (1984: 52) makes the same point about Asian students learning the 'th' sound in English: 'Tongue-between-the-teeth sounds (interdental "th") are rare in other languages. They may be embarrassing for some students to practise because of the feeling that it is impolite (even disgusting) to show one's tongue'. See also Acton (1984), who discusses ways of dealing with fossilized pronunciation.

14 This point is made convincingly by Gilbert (1984) who calls her pronunciation course *Clear Speech*.

15 Recent writers seem to be divided on the issue of whether pronunciation practice should be introduced at the very beginning of language instruction. Celce-Murcia (1987); Wong (1987); and McCandless and Winitz (1986) favour delaying pronunciation until sufficient communicative listening experiences have been built up, while others argue for the opposite (Naiman 1992; Firth 1992a).

16 Well accepted information is lacking on how the currently available pronunciation course materials assist students in acquiring a better pronunciation. What explanations, diagrams, exercises help or hinder? The answer to such questions lies in empirical research on different approaches to the teaching of pronunciation.

17 Standwell (1973) argues that the phoneme has a psychological reality for native speakers from early childhood (see Leather 1983: 200). However, the preferred order of presentation among

recent writers is suprasegmental features first and then a gradual introduction to segmental aspects (Firth 1992a; McNerney and Mendelsohn 1992; Naiman 1992; Catford 1987).

18 Here again, there is a lack of data based on carefully structured presentations of actual pronunciation teaching.

19 This research is well summarized by Leather (1983). A study by McCandless and Winitz (1986) suggests that extensive auditory input at the beginning stages of instruction results in improved pronunciation compared to traditional procedures.

20 For a description of paralinguistic features see Brown (1977, Chapter 7).

21 Hammerly (1982: 353) points out that imitation is not simple. 'It involves (1) perception of the model, (2) reproduction of the model, (3) perception of one's own production, and (4) evaluation of one's own production in relation to the model'. Leather (1983) draws attention to the lack of research on imitation.

22 Several writers have pointed to the need for self-correction and self-monitoring procedures as a means of making learners aware of their pronunciation problems with the ultimate goal of helping them achieve comprehensibility (Naiman 1992; Browne and Huckin 1987; Firth 1992b).

23 Gilbert (1984: 45) includes among her exercises a short talk on the age issue, partly as an exercise in listening comprehension, but partly also as a pep-talk: 'Most adult language learners believe that pronunciation is a more or less hopeless task at their age. This sense of discouragement keeps some students from making any real effort to improve. This produces a self-fulfilling prophecy; a student who makes no effort does not improve. For this reason it is important to encourage students to believe that they are personally capable of considerable improvement'.

24 Here Gilbert (1984) once more appeals to teachers to believe in the importance of intelligible pronunciation. She bases herself on an interesting study by Suter (1976) in which the belief in the importance of pronunciation was the best predictor of pronunciation success, except for the even more important mother tongue influences.

5 The language syllabus: grammar

Introduction

Traditionally, grammar has been the *sine qua non* of language teaching. Until quite recently, it was simply taken for granted. Today, however, grammar teaching in all its aspects is questioned. Should grammar be taught at all? Is it a hindrance rather than a help? Does grammar offer the best organizing principle for a language curriculum, or are there other principles of organization which are more suitable? If grammar, what kind: traditional, structural, transformational, or any other school of thought? Just as communicative language teaching has cast doubts on the value of pronunciation teaching it has also led, even more forcibly, to similar doubts about grammar teaching.[1]

The term 'grammar' is sometimes used very widely so as to include the entire analysis of a language, including phonology, morphology, syntax, lexicology, semantics, and discourse analysis. In view of the close interrelatedness of these aspects it is not unreasonable to work with a wide definition, in which grammar is synonymous with linguistic analysis. As we are concerned in language teaching with the language in its entirety, boundaries between the sound system, the grammatical system, the lexical system, and the system of discourse are not too important.[2] However, since in this part of the book the different aspects of language analysis are being treated one by one, we will focus particularly on morphology and syntax,[3] although some of the observations made here with regard to grammar in this narrower sense would be equally applicable to other branches of a formal linguistic analysis.

Developing a policy on grammar teaching

In order to arrive at a sound policy on grammar teaching we must avoid over-simplifying the issues and bear in mind that there is no single answer to the question of how to handle grammar in the classroom. According to Celce-Murcia (1985), we have to consider the course objectives together with a number of learner variables such as age, educational background, and learning styles, in order to make 'informed decisions about the role of grammar in language teaching'. The different aspects, including those already mentioned by Celce-Murcia, will now be discussed under the following headings: (a) basic assumptions about language and learning; (b) sources of grammatical information; (c) grammar and language teaching objectives; (d) treatment of grammar in the language class.

Basic assumptions about language and learning

To begin with, a grammar teaching policy reflects views about language and learning. It is important to be clear about them, because they affect our approach to grammar. If we adopt the view expressed by Macnamara (1973) that 'it is impossible to specify the elements and rules of a language' (1973: 253), or that the rules we give to students 'are merely hints' (ibid.), we practically rule out any constructive role for grammar. Once we consider that grammar has a role to perform, we must assume that it is possible to analyse and describe language linguistically. It is extravagant and not very helpful to suggest that all existing grammars of, say, English or French are worthless or totally inadequate. Obviously, these descriptions are not flawless, and grammarians frequently uncover imperfections in the treatment of certain linguistic features. But such criticisms do not alter the fundamental belief in the possibility of describing languages grammatically and of being able to discover valid rules of syntax. We may come to the conclusion that a grammatical syllabus is not the most suitable approach for second language learning and use another principle of syllabus planning, as Wilkins (1976) tried to do; but as long as we isolate formal features of a language, we express a fundamental acceptance of linguistic analysis as a possible source of data for second language learning.

Grammar teaching is particularly liable to be influenced by different views on language learning. In this respect, the main parameter is the ability to learn a language through deliberate study and formal practice as opposed to a subconscious absorption of the language through use. Krashen's insistence on the primacy of acquisition has tended to downplay the value of deliberate study and practice. On the other hand, the learner and the language learning process can be viewed quite differently. Paulston and Bruder (1975) consider that formal practice and grammatical explanation are absolutely essential to induce learning, even for learners who live in a target-language milieu. We interpret interlanguage research, which has studied second language learning phenomena for a period of almost twenty years, as follows: there is no simple choice between the deliberate practice and study of grammatical forms and the intuitive acquisition of these forms through use in real-life contexts. We believe that both processes come into play and should be encouraged in a teaching programme.

The complexity of the development of grammatical accuracy among second language learners has been particularly well illustrated through careful studies of French immersion programmes in Canada. In immersion classes the emphasis is on the use of language for learning other curriculum subjects and therefore the acquisition of grammar in these classes is not the centre of attention for either the learner or the teacher. A study of some of these students' persistent errors, particularly in certain verb forms, at various grade levels has led to the conclusion:

> The simple provision of meaningful input which is comprehensible to the learner . . . while clearly necessary, is not in itself sufficient to promote productive use of a marked formal aspect of the L2 in a classroom setting.
> (Harley and Swain 1984: 309)

The researchers suggest that more attention should be paid by teachers to formal features of the target language, but they add that they are 'in no way advocating a swing towards extensive use of explicit grammar teaching in an immersion program, although we do believe that there is room for some selective grammatical explanation, which is attuned to the maturity level and metalinguistic ability of the students' (ibid.: 310). In this interpretation the problem of the role of grammar teaching in relation to the development of the learner is openly recognized.

Teachers should decide for themselves on the basis of their own experience to what extent conscious learning can be helpful. They should bear in mind Celce-Murcia's distinction between various learner factors according to which focus on grammatical form becomes more or less important, as indicated in the following figure:

Learner factors	**Importance of a focus on form**		
	Less important	Moderately important	More important
Learning style	Holistic	Mixed	Analytic
Age	Children	Adolescents	Adults
Proficiency level	Beginning	Intermediate	Advanced
Educational background	Pre-literate No formal education	Semi-literate Some formal education	Literate Well-educated

Figure 5.1 Learner factors which influence a focus on grammatical form in language teaching (adapted from Celce-Murcia 1985)

Celce-Murcia (1985) recognizes that some learners have a preference for more holistic learning while others are more analytic. To some extent there may be an age factor, with young children tending to the holistic side and adults to the analytic. There may also be differences according to proficiency levels. Grammatical refinements may mean less to a student in the early stages of learning a new language while an advanced learner may want to make subtler grammatical distinctions. Educational background enters into it, too. Students with little formal schooling sometimes have difficulty with grammatical abstractions while the highly educated may look for detailed grammatical explanations.

Sources of grammatical information

As language teachers we must look critically at the quality of the grammatical information at our disposal. If we are native speakers of the language we teach, our most immediate source is the grammatical intuitions which make up our native competence. But these intuitions can be deceptive. We may speak a local variant of the target language which is different from other local variants and from the standard. Moreover, as native speakers we may have never consciously considered what is puzzling for an L2 learner until we notice the difficulties encountered by our students. In other words, native intuition is not enough. We must use other sources of information, such as a textbook or reference grammar. If we are not native speakers of the language we teach, it is even more important that we should have access to trustworthy grammatical information.

If we teach English, French, or one of the other world languages, the availability of reliable reference grammars and good textbooks is treated very much as a matter of course. But this, too, can be deceptive. Once we are off the beaten track of a few widely studied world languages, we find that accurate grammatical information is much more difficult to come by. Moreover, usage in all languages changes over time, and consequently our interpretation of the data constantly needs to be revised. The grammar of the target language is never static. It follows that we must be clear about the nature and sources of information on which our grammatical syllabus and our grammar teaching are based, or should be based.

The development of linguistics and applied linguistics over the past quarter of a century has brought about a better understanding of how we proceed in developing pedagogic grammars. At the outset, it is necessary to be clear about different conceptual levels of grammatical statement.[4] Figure 5.2 symbolizes these relationships.

Starting at level 1, grammatical theory as part of linguistic theory will

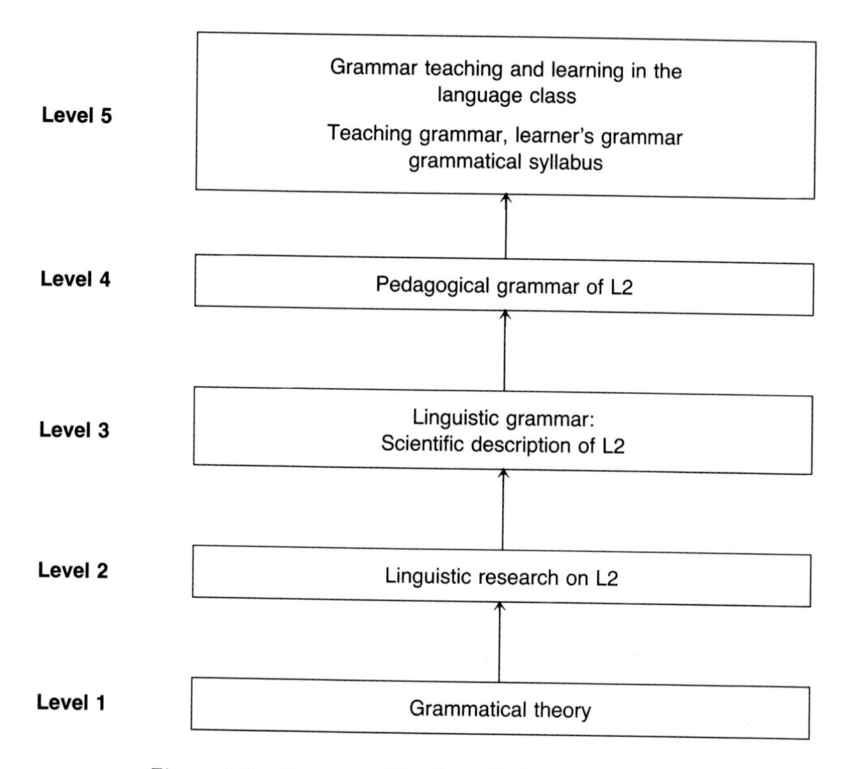

Figure 5.2 Conceptual levels underlying grammar teaching

propose one or several models which provide the categories and procedures for descriptive research on the grammar of any language. These categories and procedures constitute the necessary tools to analyse and describe the grammar of the target language (level 2). Such research has the dual purpose of: (a) testing the theoretical model against the reality of language X or Y, and (b) contributing to the more adequate description of that language. For the practical purposes of language teaching we are probably more interested in (b) than (a). At the next level we find a composite picture of many research studies which comprise as full a description as possible of the language. Such a description constitutes a scientific statement which offers us the best possible analysis of the target language, usually in terms of a particular school of linguistic thought. We refer to it as the linguistic (or scientific) grammar of language X or Y.

The theoretical linguistic controversies of the 1960s led to the conviction that it is unwise to try to apply the results of linguistic analysis directly to syllabus development or language grammar teaching. A 'filter' or 'interface' is needed which will help us to sift the various scientific descriptions and relate them to the practical situations in which the grammatical data are used. This fourth level is often referred to as pedagogic grammar which can be visualized as a teacher's handbook of information. It is the main resource for all the purposes listed at the fifth level.[5] At level 5, we find the grammatical syllabus, teaching grammars, learner grammars, and the actual teaching of grammatical aspects of the second language through explanations, exercises, drills, and so on. Ideally, all these manifestations of grammar should be founded on clearly identifiable sources. But neither the textbook writer, the syllabus developer, nor the classroom teacher should be expected to sift through the mass of theoretical research, to weigh up the merits of this or that theoretical model, or to search for grammatical information. This is the role of the pedagogic grammar. However, practitioners should be aware of what pedagogic grammar they are using as a resource. If challenged, they should be able to produce it as evidence and use it for documentation. They should be able to refer to it as a constant stand-by.

An example of a pedagogic grammar at level 4 is provided by *The Grammar Book: An ESL/EFL Teacher's Course* (Celce-Murcia and Larsen-Freeman 1984). This book does not claim to be a general and comprehensive analysis such as *A Comprehensive Grammar of the English Language* (Quirk, Greenbaum, Leech, and Svartvik 1985). It is written specifically for ESL/EFL teachers and deals with those topics 'most frequently taught in the ESL/EFL classroom' (ibid.: 1). *The Grammar Book* also offers teaching suggestions at the end of most chapters and each topic has a further bibliography of titles, some of which develop the topic in greater detail while others give additional teaching suggestions. *The Grammar Book* also brings in 'facts about language typology (i.e. what goes on in other languages), about second language acquisition (i.e. typical or possible learner errors) and about discourse analysis (i.e. grammar beyond the sentence level) where such information is available to us and useful to you' (ibid.: 7). The authors draw on insights from transformational grammar and traditional grammar, and they sometimes discuss the treatment of grammatical topics from different points of view before explaining why they have adopted a particular type of analysis. Grammar is not treated as an absolute, and the teacher who uses this book as a source of information can gain from it a critical and independent approach to making grammatical judgements.

Some writers on pedagogic grammar recognize that the current state of linguistic science means that 'we cannot aspire to much more than partial knowledge about the language we are teaching,' as Berman (1979: 292) aptly remarks. In this study, Berman examines a number of rules of English grammar and shows that they are usually only 'partial generalizations' (for example, 'The definite article is not used with abstract nouns in English') and sometimes they are downright false (for example, 'When the main verb is in the past tense, all other dependent verbs must also be in the past tense'). Berman recognizes that these rough-and-ready rules of thumb may be quite adequate in the early stages of language learning, but as students progress, they should be introduced to more sophisticated rules which will be 'true to the nature both of the students' target language and of language in general' (ibid.: 300).

Fifty years or so of linguistic research and linguistic theorizing have led to a demand for greater scholarly accuracy and sensitivity in the target language descriptions on which pedagogical grammars (level 4) and syllabuses as well as course materials (level 5) are based. This is reflected in the frequent articles which discuss how to teach grammar more effectively, and which are often critical of the analysis of grammatical facts and their interpretation in textbooks or teaching grammars.[6]

Grammar and language teaching objectives

For the most part, the debate about the usefulness of grammar in language teaching has been a debate about the value of overt grammatical knowledge for the acquisition of proficiency. But as we saw in Chapter 3, grammar may also be an objective in its own right. We must, therefore, distinguish between grammar as a means to the achievement of proficiency, and grammar as an end. Today, there is no single prescribed formula for the attainment of proficiency. It is recognized that how much emphasis we give to grammar depends on the specific proficiency objective that is aimed at. Celce-Murcia (1985: 4) has tabulated some differences in proficiency objectives and corresponding degrees of importance of a focus on grammatical form:

Learner factors	**Importance of a focus on form**		
	Less important	Moderately important	More important
Learning style	Holistic	Mixed	Analytic
Skill	Listening, Reading	Speaking	Writing
Register	Informal	Consultative	Formal
Need/use	Survival	Vocational	Professional

Figure 5.3 Proficiency objectives which influence a focus on grammatical form in language teaching (adapted from Celce-Murcia 1985)

According to this figure, the receptive skills require less grammatical knowledge than the productive ones and, between the two productive skills, writing is more grammatically demanding than speaking. In informal exchanges grammatical lapses are less serious than in a formal letter or speech. For someone who learns the language just to get by and meet day-to-day 'survival' needs, grammatical accuracy is less critical than for another person who needs the L2 for vocational or professional purposes. If proficiency is the goal, the demand for grammatical accuracy is not an absolute, and teachers must use their judgement and adjust their demands to the estimated need in this respect.

However, we must not overstate these distinctions in the demand for grammatical accuracy. Learners must be able to identify essential structural clues when they are listening and reading, even though they may not need to know them so well that they can produce them without being prompted. It would also be misleading to think that in informal talk grammatical errors do not matter at all. The frequently expressed view of some students—'I only want to be able to talk informally, I don't really need any grammar'—ignores the linguistic complexities which are often far greater in the rapid give-and-take of informal conversation (quite apart from the sociolinguistic and pragmatic complexities) than in the more explicit formal use of written language. Although Celce-Murcia's table makes a valid point about the relative importance of grammar, the tabulation must not be interpreted too literally.

Nowadays, it is so much taken for granted that the interest of the learner is directed only to proficiency that the possible teaching of grammar as an objective is entirely overlooked. Admittedly, it is more common to find that students regard grammar purely from the instrumental point of view and would like to have as little as possible of it. But it should not be overlooked that an interesting treatment of grammar can awaken an intellectual curiosity, and change negative attitudes.

The grammatical syllabus

In the early years of this century a grammatical syllabus was a clearly defined set of topics, presented in textbooks in a conventionally accepted order. The first indications that a grammatical syllabus could be modified and selectively adjusted for given groups of learners appeared in the 1920s when the frequency principle, which was first applied to lexis, was recognized as equally applicable to grammar. It was suggested that rarely used syntactic features of a language could with advantage be excluded from a syllabus. Syntax frequency lists began to appear, but they did not make the major impact on course design that lexical frequency lists had done. Grammar—like phonology—was not regarded as an area in which the language teacher had many options. The arrangement of grammatical items was also uncontroversial. It was regarded as a matter of course that teaching should progress from the simple to the more complex. The criteria for what could be called simple or complex—i.e. easy or difficult—was not a matter of great concern. These were regarded as common-sense judgements which did not require any fundamental change in the established grammar teaching tradition.

A more self-conscious approach to the grammatical syllabus did not develop until after World War II. The applied linguists of the 1950s and 1960s were critical of earlier language courses both in the grammar translation and the direct method tradition. These methods, they believed, had paid too little attention to the principle of careful grammatical gradation which at that time was considered indispensable to good language teaching. This view of the grammar syllabus was founded on the firm belief that it was possible to provide a logical and psychological sequencing of grammatical items based on valid descriptions of the target language.

During the period between 1945 and 1965 many applied linguists, particularly in America, regarded contrastive analysis as a key instrument for establishing the grammatical, and other linguistic, content of language programmes. This approach was first advocated by Fries in 1945 when he wrote:

> The most effective materials (for foreign language teaching) are based upon a scientific description of the language to be learned carefully compared with a parallel description of the native language of the learner.
> (Fries 1945: 9)

This principle was taken up and elaborated some twelve years later by Lado in *Linguistics Across Cultures* (1957). Although contrastive analysis was criticized after 1965 and increasingly became a subject of controversy, its use in curriculum development in the preceding period further reinforced the idea that grammar teaching could and should be based on stated principles of content selection.[7]

The discussion of *gradation* in Mackey (1965) and *grading* in Halliday, McIntosh, and Strevens (1964) were the first major modern attempts to conceptualize progression in second language curriculums. Applying gradation to existing curriculum materials, Mackey distinguished 'grouping' and 'sequencing'. Looking at materials from the point of view of grouping will show what grammatical items have been, or could be, placed together, and looking at them from the point of view of sequencing leads to an understanding of consecutive arrangement. The criterion that emerges from grouping is that items should not be placed in a course haphazardly; they should be brought together because they go together linguistically or because they can be associated with one another psychologically. Mackey offers as an example of good grouping in an English course the teaching of such adverbs as *usually*, *often*, or *frequently* together with the simple present. As for sequencing, Mackey was of the opinion that a careful linguistic analysis could lead to a satisfactory arrangement of language items. A few years later curriculum developers worried about whether it is theoretically possible to establish linguistic or psychological principles of sequential arrangement. These concerns are not expressed in Mackey's analysis. However, the fact that he analysed and categorized possible ways of grouping and sequencing focused the attention of course writers on the problems involved in attempting to order grammatical items. Halliday *et al.* (1964) looked at the problem of order and arrangement more from the perspective of a teacher who has to plan a course lasting a number of hours, weeks, months, or years. They distinguished *stage* as a broad division of time segments and *sequence* as an ordering of language items within stages. Unlike Mackey, Halliday *et al.* treat sequencing as a matter which is determined mainly by intuition and experience.

By the early 1960s, the strict selection of language items and careful sequencing were widely regarded not merely as a possibility but as a basic requirement of good language teaching. Descriptive linguistics would provide the necessary linguistic data, and with the help of selection criteria and contrastive analysis, course designers hoped to make an adequate decision about language content and to put the selection into a justifiable sequence. The new audiolingual courses of the period aimed to provide a carefully designed selection and gradation of grammatical material, while older language courses were criticized for their lack of systematic attention to principles of selection and sequencing.

The grammatical scepticism of the early 1970s and the shift of interest to communicative syllabuses eroded the confidence in a grammatical syllabus. Some authorities questioned the belief that it is possible to establish criteria according to which a grammatical syllabus might be organized in a logically, psychologically, and pedagogically satisfactory way. Corder (1973), for example, discussed this issue and concluded:

> The fact is that at the present time we simply do not know to what extent linguistic categories have psychological reality, and therefore to what extent what might be a logical linguistic sequencing of items in a syllabus is psychologically logical, and therefore the optimum ordering from a learning point of view.
> (Corder 1973: 308)

Furthermore, according to Corder, 'when one examines the arguments for a logical sequencing of grammatical forms in a syllabus, they usually boil down to some vague notion of relative ease or difficulty, without foundation in linguistic theory or description' (1973: 311).

Apart from questions concerning the conventional arrangement of grammatical features, the debate about the primacy of grammatical or functional categories has further complicated syllabus design since the 1970s. During this period, an attempt was made to give up grammatical sequencing and to build language courses on a semantic basis with grammar taking second place (cf. Wilkins 1976). Other writers (for example, Brumfit 1980b), have reaffirmed their belief in giving primacy to grammar, arguing that grammar can at least be arranged in a reasonably logical sequence, whereas semantic categories of notions and functions are much more difficult to arrange. Thus, Brumfit proposes

> to use the grammatical system as the core of the syllabus in a ladder-like series of stages and to be prepared to relate all other essential material to this series. Thus notional, functional, and situational specifications can be conceived of as a spiral round a basically grammatical core.
> (Brumfit 1980b: 5)

The belief in the value of some kind of grammatical syllabus has not been lost, except by those who radically reject any kind of analytic and formal approach (for example, Prabhu 1987). However, modern thought on the grammatical syllabus is characterized by selectivity. Grammatical items are not included because they have always been taught, but because they can be justified in relation to the type of course, its length, objectives, and the student population. Valdman (1980a), for example, has advocated for the typical American two-year high school or college course a reduced grammatical content which is more in harmony with the interlanguage competence that can be achieved in the limited time available. Valdman adopts the idea of what George (1972) has called a 'little language', i.e. one

> within which the learner can take the initiative without producing too many errors . . . each item in the little language should be psychologically justified, and should be easy to pronounce and spell, morphological features should be regular, and the items should enter into predictable syntactical relationships.
> (George 1972, quoted in Valdman 1980a: 83)

Without accepting as the ultimate answer the solution proposed by George and recommended by Valdman for these particular circumstances, the principle that items should not be included in a grammatical syllabus unless they can be justified in relation to the length and purpose of the course and the characteristics of the student population would probably be widely accepted.

Recent experience with notions, functions, and speech acts as well as with discourse and other communicative categories (see Chapter 6) has not provided a replacement for the grammatical syllabus. But thinking about grammar now tends to be related to functional–communicative aspects of language teaching. No course developer nowadays would consider a grammatical syllabus as the only valid curriculum principle. The key question is how best to integrate a grammatical syllabus with the demands of a functional or communicative/experiential syllabus. Given that a grammatical syllabus has to be developed, certain simple pedagogical principles are widely accepted, and are rightly emphasized in the literature. All writers on grammar teaching observe that grammar is cumulative (Allen and Valette 1977: 82) or, as Corder (1973: 297) has it, 'not just cumulative, it is an integrative process.' Accordingly, Allen and Valette (1977: 82–3) draw attention to the concept of requisite knowledge or requisite learning. Even if the entire grammar of the L2 cannot be logically built up as a unified and coherent structure, there are many complex items which presuppose previous knowledge, and it is vital for the teacher and course designer to recognize such prerequisites, as illustrated in the following list:

New material	Requisite knowledge
agreement of adjectives	genders of nouns to be used
irregular adjectives	forms of regular adjectives, genders of nouns to be used
direct-object pronouns (accusative)	forms of the direct object (accusative), genders of nouns to be used
position of object pronouns	forms of object pronouns, forms of verbs to be used
French: conditional tense	formation of future stems, imperfect endings or review of imperfect tense
German: prepositions of place	accusative and dative forms of nouns to be used
Spanish: subjective forms	imperative
French and Spanish: imperfect vs. preterite, *passé composé*	forms of the imperfect and the past tense
French: *passé composé with être*	present tense of *être, forms of regular adjectives, past participles of -er verbs*
inverted word order	regular word order, forms of verbs to be used

Figure 5.4 Requisite knowledge in grammar teaching (adapted from Allen and Valette 1977)

Grammatical syllabuses are justifiably criticized if they are purely 'linear', that is, if they introduce grammatical topics one by one in a 'discrete-point' fashion (Martin 1978:152; Rutherford 1987:159). Most language teachers recognize that there is a need for regular revision of grammatical items, but what is more important and less frequently recognized is that items are not merely repeated; ideally, they should be taken up again in a new context and expanded so that the treatment in the syllabus encourages the gradual development of a network of associations. In keeping with this principle, Corder (1973); Howatt (1974); Martin (1978) and others, have recommended a cyclical or spiral treatment of grammatical items. No item in the syllabus that has once been introduced should ever be lost sight of. Each item is periodically reintroduced, and not simply in its original form; instead it is placed into ever new contexts, or associated with additional information. This principle is, of course, applicable not only to grammar but to any other syllabus; however, it is particularly important for grammar teaching. An advantage of the spiral or cyclical approach is that it is unnecessary in designing a syllabus to present a grammatical topic in its entirety at the point where it first appears. What the syllabus designer has to do is to estimate what aspect of an item should be presented first and what should be added later when the item is picked up again. The skill of syllabus design lies in reconciling the need for gradual introduction and recycling with giving the learner a chance of getting an overview and a global picture of a particular grammatical topic.

In one recent interpretation of a grammatical syllabus (Rutherford 1987, Chapter 12), there is to be no prior specification of language content at all, but rather a specification of how any given content (chosen according to non-linguistic criteria) is to be grammatically exploited via 'consciousness-raising' activities (see also Sharwood Smith 1981) that will promote the learner's ability to make his own structural analysis of the target language. Despite his explicit rejection of a prespecified grammatical content, Rutherford sees the second language curriculum as 'grammar-centred' in a broad sense, and he sets three conditions to be met in curriculum planning, of which the first two do, none the less, seem to envisage some linguistic criteria for content selection.[8] Rutherford's emphasis in his grammar-centred approach on teaching the learner how to learn (1987: 153) appears to overlap with our conception of a general language education syllabus (Chapter 9).

The outcome of this discussion on grammatical syllabus design is twofold: in spite of doubts about the feasibility of a sequential arrangement, the grammar of a language cannot be taught all at once. Some sort of selection and sequencing is needed, and therefore a grammatical syllabus must be provided. However, while a grammatical syllabus is in our view indispensable, it should no longer be regarded as the sole organizing principle of curriculum design. In other words, the grammar syllabus does not stand alone; it must be related to other subsystems of language as well as to the non-linguistic syllabuses in the second language curriculum.

Treatment of grammar in the language class

Nowhere is the uncertainty about the role of grammar more clearly revealed than in the decisions we make about grammar teaching in the classroom. Whatever position is taken by a teacher today, it is bound to be influenced by the recent history of grammar teaching and the debate it has given rise to. The 'traditional' approach to grammar teaching, which goes back to the first half of the nineteenth century, was overt and confident. Regardless of the age of the pupils, good classroom practice meant, in the words of the preface to *A Primer of French Grammar* (Somerville 1936) teaching 'in the same systematic, thorough way as Latin grammar is taught'. This, it was hoped, would result in 'a far sounder and more general knowledge' of modern languages (ibid.). The teaching of grammar was quite simple and straightforward and has not really changed a great deal. A principle of language structure is presented in the form of a generalized statement or rule which may or may not involve the use of technical terminology. Thus, in *A Primer of French Grammar*, addressed to pupils aged about seven to twelve, we find the following rule:

> Adjectives and past participles used as adjectives agree in gender and number with the words to which they refer e.g.:
>
> La Mer Noire.
> The Black Sea.
>
> Ces maisons sont bien bâties.
> These houses are well built.
>
> Elle est belle.
> She is beautiful.
>
> (Somerville 1936: 19)

The rule may be presented in the learners' native language or in the target language, and there is no attempt to ensure that the wording of the rule is intelligible to the user of the grammar. The rule is illustrated by examples, accompanied sometimes by further explanations and followed by applications of the rule in the form of exercises or drills. With slight variations, this sequence constitutes one of the most widespread approaches to grammar which has maintained itself over years of conventional language teaching and is still quite common in language classes and many, if not most, course materials. Certain details have changed over the years. Thus, direct method advocates insisted on the use of the target language in explaining grammar rules, and they tended to move from examples to generalization rather than from a general principle to its application. The audiolingual method emphasized rapid oral drills, while cognitive theorists found a new role for grammatical explanation. All of these approaches involved some form of overt grammar teaching.

A much more radical challenge was presented by those who denied the value of any overt grammar teaching or covert selection of grammatical input. This position, which evolved during the 1970s as a result of second language acquisition studies and interlanguage research, received its clearest formulation in the writings of Dulay, Burt, and Krashen.[9] Krashen's views on learning and acquisition were to have a particularly powerful influence on the rejection of overt grammar teaching.

We can recognize various positions on the grammar teaching issue which fall roughly on a continuum, as follows:

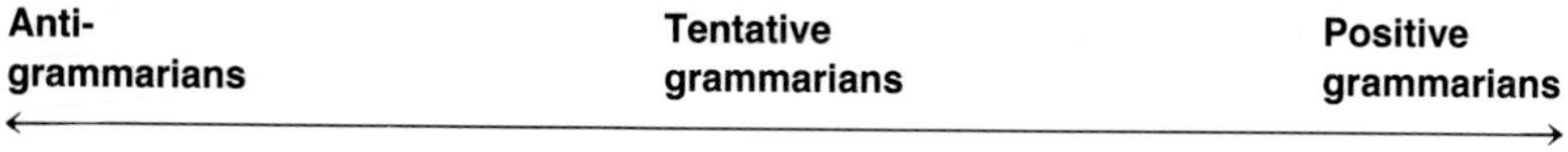

Anti-grammarians	**Tentative grammarians**	**Positive grammarians**

←——————————————————————————————→

Figure 5.5 Positions adopted towards the role of grammar in language teaching

Anti-grammarians answer the question 'Can syntax be taught?' (Ellis 1984) with a clear and unambiguous 'No'. They believe that the analysis of grammatical features has no bearing on the ultimate competence of a second-language acquirer. If we adopt this position, the overt teaching of grammar—or any other formal feature of language such as phonology—is ruled out. While in practice this viewpoint has not been widely adopted in its extreme form, it has strongly influenced the other two positions on the grammar teaching continuum. As Chastain (1976: 341) put it: 'At various times grammar has been almost an unmentionable in second-language education'. At the other extreme, positive grammarians adopt a confident and sometimes an almost aggressively positive stance:

> We believe that old-fashioned grammar rules and practice in applying them in structural drills remain the crucial centre of the process of language learning.
> (Paulston and Bruder 1975: 42)

Between these two extremes we find different gradations of accepting or rejecting the centrality of grammar in the classroom. One point of view, which is not at all uncommon, is that of the tentative grammarians. They acknowledge that there is an important aspect of second language acquisition which cannot be influenced by grammatical analysis. Yet, practical experience suggests to them that one cannot entirely do without overt grammar teaching, and they tend to adopt a cautious, tentative attitude towards grammar. Thus, in their study on the interlanguage of immersion students Harley and Swain recognize the limitations of the anti-grammarian position, and recommend as a remedy 'The provision of more focused L2 input which provides the learners with ample opportunity to observe the formal and semantic contrasts involved in the relevant target subsystem' (1984: 105).

In case teachers take this as a mandate to emphasize the rote memorization of decontextualized grammar rules and parsing of sentences, they hasten to add: 'This does not necessarily involve explicit grammar teaching' (ibid.). However, if students are invited to identify a 'relevant target subsystem' such as the French verb, and to observe 'the formal and semantic contrasts involved', this is in essence, if not in name, what explicit grammar teaching is all about. In deciding on the role of grammar in the classroom, it is important not to equate explicit grammar teaching with 'old-fashioned' or 'inferior' pedagogy. Moreover, recognizing that grammar teaching has its uses does not mean that this is the only strategy available. Harley and Swain (1984), for example, recognize the need for 'simple provision of meaningful input which is comprehensible to the learner' as a necessary avenue to proficiency, but not as a sufficient one by itself.

Naturally, if we adopt the point of view that language analysis has no role to play in second language acquisition, the teaching of grammar is indeed ruled out. Any approach to grammar, however discreet or disguised, must set out from some kind of linguistic analysis. All grammar teaching pays attention to forms and structures whether the analysis is made explicit to the learner or is simply an underlying covert intention on the part of the teacher, expressed in the course design or the emphasis of the teacher's input (for further discussion, see Chapters 11 and 12).

The positive grammarians have tended to present a single-minded point of view suggesting that, once grammar teaching is accepted as legitimate, there is only one 'common-sense approach'. Consequently, the possible options and variations in the treatment of grammar in the classroom have largely been overlooked. Celce-Murcia (1985) has summarized various approaches in Figure 5.6 which distinguishes more effective and less effective ways of grammar teaching.

More effective	Less effective
communicative activities	manipulative drills
context-embedded practice	context-free practice
text-based exercises	sentence-based exercises
cognitively demanding activities	cognitively undemanding activities
authentic materials	contrived materials
interesting and motivating content	dull or neutral content

Figure 5.6 More effective and less effective ways to teach grammar (adapted from Celce-Murcia 1985)

We suggest that a language can (and should) be approached experientially and non-analytically within a language learning curriculum. However, recognizing the importance of the experiential component does not invalidate the possibility of tackling the L2 analytically at other times, through grammar teaching or other forms of linguistic analysis—phonological, lexical, or functional. We therefore adopt a positive view of grammar teaching, just as, in Chapter 4, we adopted a positive view of the teaching of phonology. In the following section we will draw attention to various options we have to bear in mind if we want to develop a sound policy for the treatment of grammar in the language class.

Policy and options in the classroom treatment of grammar

The teacher's attitude to grammar

To begin with, it is important to examine our own view of grammar teaching. Until recently, many teachers were encouraged to feel negative about grammar, to adopt an emotional anti-grammarian stance, and to regard grammar as inherently 'dull' or 'old-fashioned'. From this point of view, the teaching of grammar, if it had to be done at all, should be done surreptitiously. Grammar teaching may be necessary but it is nothing to be proud of. We must make an effort to free ourselves of such prejudices and to re-examine the possibilities and merits of grammar in the language class. This does not mean, of course, that we should accept all grammar teaching without question or condone inappropriate, excessive, or incompetent grammar teaching.

Language learning, besides other things, does involve paying attention to, and eventually mastering, the formal features of the second language. The untutored second language learner tends to miss these features, because they are often inconspicuous aspects of a language involving minor variations in word order, small words like prepositions or conjunctions, and slight inflections of form which it is easy to miss. Grammar teaching, positively looked at, helps learners to become skilled in recognizing, analysing, and eventually mastering these elusive structural features which are an essential aspect of proficiency.

Contextualizing grammatical features

The literature on grammar teaching unanimously urges teachers to put whatever grammatical feature is being taught into a meaningful context of practical use so that the meaning is never in doubt. For example, Allen and Valette suggest:

> The teacher who begins the lesson by saying, 'Today we are going to study interrogatives,' may lose many of the students. If, however, the students are conversing and need to ask questions of their teacher or classmates, they will want to learn the interrogative forms.
> (Allen and Valette 1977: 82)

In the same way, Paulston and Bruder point out that the first step in teaching a structural pattern is to 'introduce it in context, in a piece of extended language' (1975: 28). However, they rightly oppose the 'seeded passage' in which the grammatical feature is introduced to an excessive degree. Valdman (1980a) illustrates this point with an example from Rivers in which the present tense of *aller* is presented:

> Paul: Où vas-tu ce soir?
> Madeleine: Je vais en ville avec ma famille. Nous allons au cinéma.
> Paul: Qu'est-ce que vous allez voir?
> Madeleine: Zazie dans le Métro. Mes cousins vont voir le même film demain.
> (cited in Valdman 1980a: 87 from Rivers 1975: 22)

As Valdman points out, the grammatical seeding is remarkable in this short text because it contains all the forms of the present indicative paradigm of *aller*, except the 3rd person singular *va*. But the outcome is a 'poor example of an authentic speech transaction' (Valdman 1980a: 87).

While the 'today we will study the interrogative' approach may not be particularly inviting, it seems unreasonable to expect learners who have encountered a grammatical feature in a single text to be immediately eager to learn it. Sometimes it may be necessary for a grammatical item to be encountered several times in different situations before the learners become aware of its relevance. A context has the advantage of showing the grammatical feature in use, and this may motivate the students to learn it. But it has the disadvantage that the feature is hidden in the situation and in the flow of discourse. What the language teaching literature fails to emphasize is the skill needed to pick out a relevant grammatical feature from a context or situation. For the teacher the grammatical item to be learnt is obvious. Its place in the context presents no problem. He can also locate the grammar point in the syllabus of which it forms a part. To the learners, on the other hand, the item is unfamiliar, and because it has no salience, they may not understand what they are supposed to look for or why.

In a grammar teaching experiment in England (Ellis 1984: 142), thirteen ESL students aged 11 to 15 were supposed to learn how to ask WH-questions (who, what, where, and when) with 'little in the way of grammatical explanation'. The children were grouped around a wall frieze displaying events taking place in a high street, which was meant to provide a natural and lively context for learning to ask WH-questions. It is, of course, quite possible that the children examined the pictures and the events depicted on the wall frieze without being aware that the point of the exchange was to focus attention on appropriate ways of asking questions. Learners need to be clear about what the formal features are to which they are meant to pay attention.

It is usually not enough to see the formal feature in use although that is one necessary step; it is equally important to be able to abstract the formal element from the different contexts in which it might occur. Learners need practice not only in contextualizing but also in decontextualizing, that is, they need to be able to abstract a formal element from its context. This requires experience in attending to, observing, isolating, and analysing grammatical features and treating them as signals for given meanings or expectancies. This receptive and observational phase, which would help learners to become attuned to particular formal signals or cues, is not sufficiently emphasized in discussions of grammar teaching. In fact, it is often omitted and hardly figures at all in most of the literature.[10]

The grammatical context

Another aspect which is often overlooked is the placing of the grammatical feature to be studied in the context of the total grammatical system. In the section on syllabus design we saw that attention has been paid to the gradual and cyclical development of grammatical competence. But the syllabus design is generally addressed to the teacher. We pointed out in the previous section that the teacher sees the item being taught in the context of the whole grammatical syllabus. It is equally important for learners to see a particular feature which is the subject of a lesson not merely as an isolated item but as part of an evolving system of interrelationships which should become increasingly differentiated as it grows.

The individual item may be all-important while it is being studied. But it must also be looked at in relation to the whole grammatical subsystem of which it forms a part, such as question forms in English, past reference in French, or honorifics in Korean. By seeing a particular item in a grammatical context the student will acquire a better orientation to the grammar as a whole. For this reason it is often a good idea for students to be able to consult a reference grammar. The amount of detail a reference grammar should provide depends on the age, linguistic background, and educational experience of the students. In some cases students may be able to build up their own reference grammars in notebook form. A reference grammar need not be a huge compendium which is frightening and discouraging for the novice or near-novice.

Rules and explanations

Much uncertainty exists about the value of rules and other forms of explanation for the acquisition of grammatical features. As we saw in the example from Somerville's *A Primer of French Grammar*, teachers in the grammar-translation tradition had few inhibitions in this respect. They accepted the necessity of grammar rules as an integral part of language learning. Since then, the debate about 'rules for their own sake' compared with 'language teaching without rules' has shown no signs of coming to an end. In the audiolingual era it was axiomatic 'to teach the language, and not about the language', but the decline of audiolingualism led to a re-evaluation of explanation in language teaching.

In the early 1970s, Cooke (1974) made a comprehensive study of the role of explanation and concluded with a plea for a more differentiated and less sweeping approach. It is true, of course, as Cooke points out, that we should be on our guard against the overuse and misuse of explanation. However, an inadequate application of the explanation principle is hardly a basis for developing a position on the use of analytic strategies in general. The argument for explanation is based on the assumption that it can be an aid for certain students under certain circumstances. In other words, the tendency to generalize about explanation for all conditions of teaching and learning is unrealistic and misleading. Cooke concludes an extensive review of the literature as follows: 'While there are various dangers in the use of explanation, there are many situations in which analysis in some form can conceivably be a help, provided it is adjusted to the demands and abilities of the learners' (1974: 68).

The role of explanation in grammar teaching is a particular instance of a broader issue: the role of analysis and conscious attention to formal features of the target language in the acquisition of proficiency. It is part of the general question of the relative importance of explicit and implicit teaching and learning strategies. It is in the area of grammatical explanation that the controversy about the value of conscious learning and unconscious acquisition has been fought out most vigorously. Grammar rules obviously are not always a help. Learners cannot always cope with the complexities of grammar rules and grammatical generalizations. Often learners do not have the terminology which would enable them to understand a particular grammar rule, let alone apply it. But even if they can handle the terminology, it is still a far cry from understanding a grammar rule intellectually and applying it in deliberately designed exercises, to its intuitive real-life application in ordinary language use.

Grammatical terminology

For the formulation of grammar rules an important first consideration must be the terminology in which they are presented. Berman (1979: 295) distinguishes between technical terms such as 'article', 'adjective', 'case', 'pronoun', and an equally important subtechnical vocabulary which consists of general words used in a particular way, for example, 'derive', 'refer to', 'agree', 'substitute', and so on. Both types of vocabulary are needed as long as learners are expected to have a technical understanding of the second language grammar. But the technical as well as the subtechnical vocabulary should be introduced gradually and with care, always bearing in mind the learners' maturity and background. The aim should be 'to simplify the wording of rules maximally', and 'clarity should be an overriding principle' (ibid.: 296) if explanations or rules are to be a help in the student's acquisition of proficiency.

Grammar practice

Another key aspect of the treatment of grammar is practice of the grammatical features. Language teaching has moved a long way since systematic practice was first introduced some two hundred years ago. For decades it consisted simply of translation exercises. However, the direct method and the audiolingual approach diversified practice techniques considerably. The generic term 'practice' covers what in language courses are usually referred to as exercises and drills. What they have in common is that they are not real communication nor are they intended to be. They involve the application of rules in concrete examples in order to give students the opportunity to rehearse an item or to apply it concretely in a particular grammatical context. If we want to make a distinction between exercises and drills, exercises tend to be more open-ended, while drills are usually constructed so that they allow only a single correct answer.[11]

Both in actual teaching and in the methodological literature a great deal of emphasis is laid on drills and exercises as a way of achieving grammatical competence. For example, in a Canadian observational study on teaching French in a mixed urban-rural school district we read:

> In almost all the lessons, language learning appeared entirely as a set of formal routines.
> (Ullmann *et al.* 1983: 45)

> A number of activities observed in this grade 4 class were formal in nature and included drills to practise vocabulary and spelling.
> (op. cit.: 35)

Sanderson (1982: 85) provides a practical illustration of the dominance of grammar practice in a language class. In this case, one sequence after another was devoted to a single grammatical point. A similar dominance of grammatical practice was noted in the Stirling study:

> Fully half the FL segments fell into the single category of interactive FL manipulation, 'drill/exercise,' and another third was accounted for by the even more tightly constrained categories of 'imitation' and 'transposition'.
> (Mitchell *et al.* 1981: 28)

Some writers oppose a formal grammatical syllabus and with it an emphasis on drills and exercises in the language class on the grounds that 'a grammatical focus invariably distorts any attempt to communicate' (Krashen and Terrell 1983: 72). The deliberate avoidance of specific grammar practice is illustrated by this suggestion to students:

> When you do try to speak in the new language the teacher is interested in what you have to say—not whether you have said it perfectly. Neither you nor the teacher will be overly concerned with grammar errors in your speech while you are a beginner.
> (Krashen and Terrell 1983: 74)

A similar shift away from concern with grammatical correctness and grammar practice in the classroom is illustrated by this description of a beginners' course in Spanish which is built around 'scenarios' and 'the avoidance of elaborate grammar drills and exercises':

> Grammar is introduced through the presentation of topics of relevance to the students' personal interests. The students absorb grammar as the teacher answers their questions in connection with the performance of the scenarios. As the course proceeds, increasingly complex matters of grammar are introduced according to the students' expanding ability to ask about them. The point is that structural matters are introduced not according to the teacher's estimation

> of what is appropriate but as a result of the students' perceived need for grammar.
> (DiLaura 1983: 340)

This approach presupposes that students have had some previous experience of language analysis so that they know what questions to ask, and the use of charts and 'prepared material' (DiLaura 1983: 341) suggests systematic grammar explanations. What is absent from this treatment of teaching, however, is practice through exercises and drills.

It is noteworthy that even among those who do not reject the use of formal exercises and drills the use of drill-type activities is hedged in by provisos. They warn against the boredom and frustration that excessive and indiscriminate use of formal practice can engender; they condemn nonsensical drills, the modern equivalent of 'la plume de ma tante', and drills that are too repetitive, too long, and lacking in real challenge.[12] A second main concern is lack of transfer from the drilling of a structure to its application in natural language use. The expectation of audiolingualism that a well-drilled structure will become habitual and will, therefore, be automatically applied in real-life language use has not been realized. This observation led Rivers (1972) to the distinction between skill-getting and skill-using exercises. According to Rivers, practice should not be confined to the former; it must lead to the latter.

It was on similar grounds that Paulston and Bruder (1975) proposed a division of drills into three kinds: mechanical, meaningful, and communicative. In this classification all three types of drill are seen as legitimate and indeed necessary. Paulston's scheme is based on behaviouristic premises in which mechanical habituation represents the first stage of language learning, a view which would today be endorsed by very few teachers. However, the general concept of gradation suggests that the transition from formal grammar practice to independent language use should be guided by appropriately graded exercises. The recent trend is towards contextualized drills set in a situation which is relevant to learners. The question is whether such drills require learners to make realistic choices, or whether they have the same weaknesses as earlier drills which learners were able to perform effortlessly but with few lasting benefits (Chastain 1987).

The problem of grammatical practice has recently reappeared in the study of immersion-type language programmes. In these programmes the emphasis is on learning the language through communicative use. Yet, it has been found that certain grammatical features such as verb tenses or the order of pronouns are not adequately acquired. The question arises why this should be so, and whether the judicious introduction of exercise material which would provide intensive functional practice of important grammatical features might be 'the missing link' between formal structural practice and the unguided use of language. Recent research carried out in the Modern Language Centre at the Ontario Institute for Studies in Education suggests that learners may indeed benefit if form and function are more closely linked instructionally (Harley 1989).

A third issue is the relationship between explanation and grammatical practice. In the literature this issue is usually discussed in terms of the relative merits of inductive versus deductive approaches to grammar teaching. The distinction has been neatly summarized in Figure 5.7.

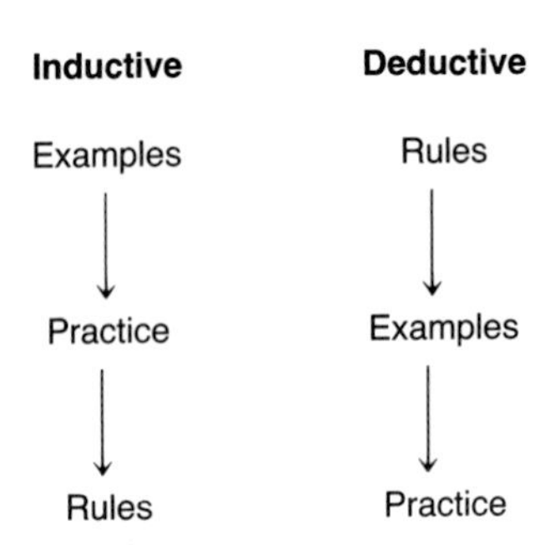

Figure 5.7 The inductive-deductive paradigm (adapted from Berman 1979)

Educationally, the inductive sequence is probably to be preferred, because it encourages language learners to start out from their own observations and to discover the principle or rule for themselves rather than being told in advance what the rule is. However, it may be unrealistic to expect that the L2 grammar can be entirely 'discovered' by the learner. The deductive sequence, therefore, cannot be ruled out altogether. In any case, even if discovery learning is the teacher's goal, the examples are often—quite justifiably—pre-selected, and so the 'discovery' of a grammatical principle is often a carefully guided rediscovery rather than one which is based on natural language behaviour.

If both the inductive and deductive principles are borne in mind, we gain a better perspective on what is practically possible and beneficial for the learner. 'The idea . . . is a constant interplay between example, rule, and practice allowing for maximal flexibility' (Berman 1979: 297). The question for the teacher is how best to balance the different phases of grammar teaching: observation, explanation or rule, examples, practice. The different phases do not come in complete blocks, one after the other. Rather it is a matter of forward and backward motion, a gradual process of familiarization and accommodation.

Error correction

Finally, error correction is also part of the grammar learning process. Pedagogy has fluctuated between meticulous and detailed error correction, which can be counterproductive, and the deliberate withholding of feedback in order to avoid discouraging learners. Celce-Murcia (1985) compares 'more effective' with 'less effective' teacher correction strategies:

More effective	Less effective
teacher elicits information from class	teacher lectures, gives rule, or explains
teacher elicits peer or self-correction	teacher corrects directly
teacher gives focused, specific cues as to what correction is needed and where	teacher gives indirect, diffuse cues on type and location of correction needed
teacher conducts meaningful practice of problematic form	teacher conducts mechanical drill of problematic form
teacher corrects selectively	teacher corrects everything

Figure 5.8 More effective and less effective teacher correction strategies (adapted from Celce-Murcia 1985)

Nearly two decades of error analysis and interlanguage studies have led to the notion of the inevitability of error in second language learning, and this has encouraged a greater tolerance in teachers' attitudes to student performance. On the other hand, an outright refusal to correct can be disorienting and confusing. Ideally, learners should develop the ability to monitor their own performance and to correct themselves. But if the teacher does not provide the corrective, the learner has no yardstick. A complete absence of feedback would only be justified in cases where students have been made thoroughly inhibited by constant and nagging overcorrection. Thus, an element of judicious error correction is required to complete the cycle of classroom treatment of grammar.[13]

Concluding comments

In this chapter we have argued that deliberate study and intuitive acquisition both have an important role to play in a second language programme, and that there is, therefore, a need to develop a sound policy on grammar teaching. Empirical research has not yet made it clear whether teaching/learning approaches that include a focus on grammar have a definite advantage over those that do not (Ellis 1985;

Long 1988). However, there seems to be a general consensus that some attention to consciousness-raising and error correction should be included in any second language programme. The current trend is towards incorporating more focused input in such a way that students can make their own choices within the context of communicative tasks. At the same time, we would argue that there is still a role for selective formal practice that provides the learner with an opportunity to try out the relevant features safely away from the pressure of real communication. In recent writings, we see a tendency to question the specific selection and ordering of grammatical patterns, since language acquisition is seen as a cyclic or 'metamorphic' process (Rutherford 1987), rather than a linear one. It should be remembered that grammar does not normally function as an end in itself but as a means towards successful communication. It is, therefore, important that we do not treat grammar in isolation, but that we take care to relate it to the other, non-linguistic syllabuses.

Notes

1 The following should be consulted for recent and current thoughts on grammar in language teaching: Allen (1973); Allen and Valette (1977, Chapters 5 and 6); Allen *et al.* (1990); Berman (1979); Celce-Murcia (1985); Celce-Murcia and Hilles (1988); McKay (1987); Paulston and Bruder (1975, Chapters 1 and 2); Rivers (1981, Chapter 4); Rutherford and Sharwood Smith (1988); Ur (1988). Most other books on language teaching methodology also discuss the role of grammar, for example, Finocchiaro and Brumfit (1983, pp. 30 and 121–5), and Savignon (1983: 189–90). References to more specific issues will be mentioned at appropriate points in the chapter.

2 Berman (1979) discusses the elasticity of the concept of grammar. She refers to the 'traditional notion of grammar as meaning syntax, with perhaps a little morphology thrown in for good measure' (p. 287). She contrasts this view of grammar with that of Hebrew speakers whose school grammars deal mainly with morphology and morphophonology.

3 Finocchiaro and Brumfit (1983: 30) include under the grammar system: (a) morphology which comprises inflection for plurality, tense, possession, etc., and derivation such as prefixes, suffixes, and infixes, (b) morphophonemics which comprises sound or spelling changes, and (c) syntax.

4 For a more detailed treatment of the interaction between linguistics and language teaching see FCLT, in particular Chapter 9, and especially pp. 175–7, 181, 185–6, and Figure 9.2. Berman (1979,

p. 280 and note 3) also contrasts a linguistic or scientific grammar and a pedagogic grammar.

5 It should be noted that the distinction between levels 4 and 5 is not always clearly made in the literature. Teaching grammars at level 5 have also been called pedagogic (or pedagogical) grammars. In our view, it is important to conceptually distinguish between a pedagogic grammar at level 4 and a teaching grammar at level 5.

6 Good examples of an improved interpretation of a grammatical datum are Richards' (1981) discussion of the progressive in English and Terry's (1981) treatment of the *passé composé* and the imperfect in French. Richards (1981) also deals with the presentation of the progressive in ESL textbooks, but only after having dealt with the nature of tense and aspect in English. A study by Bailey (1989) adds to the literature on the interdependence of form and function by illustrating how similar forms (i.e. progressive -ing) are learnt differently depending on their function.

7 For further details on contrastive analysis during this period see FCLT: 159–60, 168.

8 According to Rutherford (1987: 150–1): '(1) Some kinds of decision must be made as to what aspects of the grammatical system are the major sources for data from which the learner may ascertain the most powerful formal generalizations; (2) choice of language content, notwithstanding whatever *non*-linguistic criteria it needs to meet, must be such as to ensure the sufficiently timely appearance of the grammatical aspects identified in (1); (3) in bringing all this to the attention of the learner (i.e. consciousness-raising), great care and sensitivity must be exercised that the pedagogical instruments for C-R maximize the probabilities for learner receptivity'.

9 For example, Dulay, Burt, and Krashen (1982: 19) write: 'the notion that formal, explicit rule knowledge must precede natural use of the language is not supported by current research findings'. They go on to add that 'despite painstaking efforts on the part of both teacher and students to consciously focus on the structures, rules, and vocabulary of the target language, a minimum ability to communicate through the language still eludes most students who study foreign languages using traditional formal methods' (ibid. 20). They do not, however, adopt a radical no-formal-grammar approach. Their suggestions to teachers contain the following: 'Include some time for formal grammar lessons for adults . . . . Include a regular time or phase in your curriculum for formal grammar lessons. The amount of time allotted should be small in relation to the rest of the curriculum' (ibid.: 267).

10 Rivers (1981: 107), however, stresses the need for observation: 'Students should encounter a certain structural pattern several

times in authentic stretches of foreign-language discourse before practising it in drills. In this way they will be able to observe its relationship to other structural elements in the language system'. Rutherford (1987) and Ur (1988) both recognize the need to present grammar in a way that gets learners to perceive the structures and make meaningful generalizations about them within given contexts.

11 Stevick (1976: 65), in a chapter on drills and exercises, comments: 'At the Foreign Service Institute of the Department of State, we have customarily distinguished between drills and exercises. In a drill, there is at any time only one student response that will be accepted as entirely satisfactory, while an exercise may have two or more acceptable answers'. According to Chastain (1987), drills should not be set up in such a way that learners produce the right answer without making any choice. Rather, drills should simulate to some extent the form, context, choice, and meaning characteristics that are present in real-life situations.

12 The conditions and criteria for grammatical drills and exercises are set out in Rivers (1981: 102–9). Paulston and Bruder (1975: 22–42)) describe the basic procedures of a grammar lesson. Allen and Valette's (1977) chapter on general procedures serves a similar function. Berman (1979) emphasizes the interaction between rules, examples, and practice. The reader might care to compare these different approaches.

13 Dulay *et al.* (1982: 36) have presented a discouraging picture of error correction. Although they conclude that error correction is 'not a very reliable tool,' they go on to state that this does not necessarily mean that 'correction plays no role in language learning'. Allen *et al.* (1990) discuss the role of grammar-based and meaning-based activities in core French and French immersion classes, and conclude that there is a role for error correction within the context of meaningful tasks. 'The concept of error-free does not mean that we have to return to a rigid, authoritarian, transmission mode of teaching. It does mean that we will try to ensure that students are fully committed to whatever communicative task they have set themselves, and that they will not be satisfied until they have conveyed their intended meaning as fully and accurately as possible' (Allen *et al.* 1990: 76). For a review of recent work in error correction see Chaudron (1988).

6 The language syllabus: functional analysis

Introduction

If we look at communication as instructional content or substance, we can distinguish two approaches: one that is more analytic, and another that is global and non-analytic. The first approach handles communication through the study of speech acts, discourse rules, and sociolinguistics, while the second approach encourages the spontaneous use of language without drawing the student's attention to any particular aspect of language structure or function. These two approaches to communication are not in conflict with each other but they are different in character and have contributed in different ways to language pedagogy. In the debate on communicative language teaching, the distinction between analytic and non-analytic approaches has often gone unrecognized. The distinction is an important one, however, and we will treat the two approaches separately. In the present chapter we will consider the analytic approach to communication, and to distinguish it from the non-analytic experiential approach we will refer to it as 'functional analysis', and the syllabus towards which we are working as a 'functional syllabus'.

The functional approach reflects a view of language and language proficiency which has evolved over a period of about two decades. During this time the scientific study of language has expanded into various areas which have in common the fact that they take the social and environmental context of language users much more into account. The disciplines which reflect these changes in language study are semantics, discourse analysis, sociolinguistics, the ethnography of communication, and pragmatics.[1] In recent years, functional analysis has also been influential in the development of language syllabuses, language teaching materials, and teaching methodology. Here we need only remind ourselves of a few landmarks in the developing role of functional analysis in relation to language pedagogy: Wilkins' (1976) concept of a notional syllabus; the work of the Modern Languages Project of the Council of Europe (Trim 1980; van Ek and Trim 1984); Widdowson's (1978) approach to communicative language teaching with its emphasis on 'use' rather than 'usage'; Munby's (1978) model for defining the content of special purpose language programmes; and, finally, the well-known attempt by Canale and Swain (1980), and later Canale (1983), to analyse communicative competence as a basis for test development and the study of proficiency.

In order to understand functional analysis and its role in language teaching, the following diagram may be helpful:

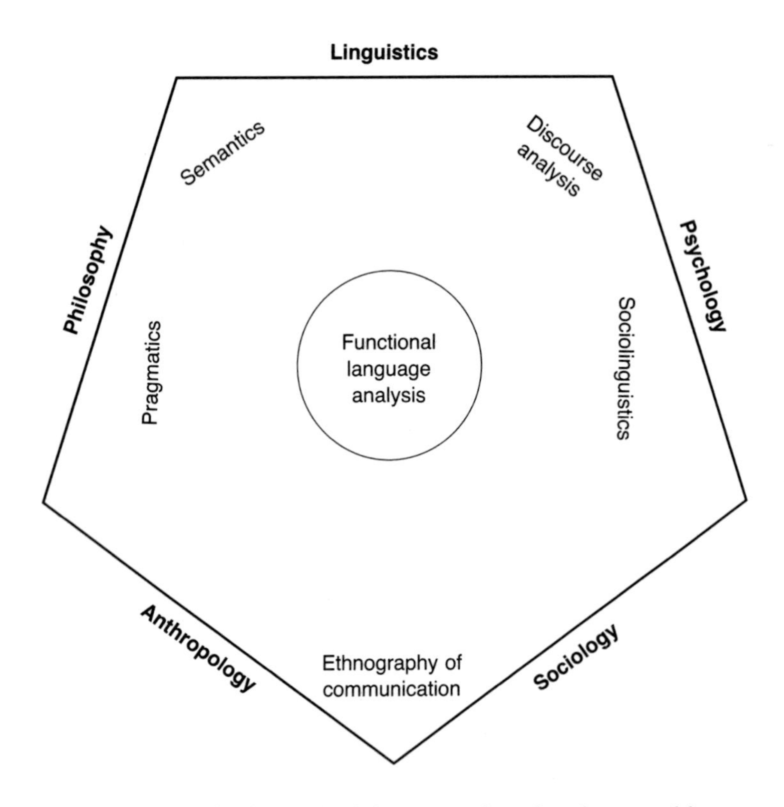

Figure 6.1 The disciplines which have contributed to functional language analysis

As Figure 6.1 indicates, an important aspect of functional analysis is its interdisciplinary nature. The major 'parent' disciplines (philosophy, linguistics, psychology, anthropology, and sociology) are represented on the outer rim of the diagram. Each contributes to the five disciplines directly related to functional analysis which surround the central core. It is in the central core that we find the key concepts of functional analysis itself, including setting, role relationships, speech act characteristics, and rules of language use. It is generally agreed that an account of functional analysis must begin with the five inner disciplines of Figure 6.1. However, these disciplines are not easy to separate from one another. While they share a common concern to place language in context and to enhance our understanding of language in use beyond the sentence level, they differ in their relationship to the major fields of study and consequently tend to represent somewhat different perspectives on the data.

Concepts of functional analysis

In order to examine the influence of functional analysis on applied linguistics and language pedagogy, we can use some of the concepts which Hymes (1967) identified as important in acts of communication. When language teachers say they teach for communication or for communicative competence, their teaching is likely to emphasize some or all of these features.

Setting

Early in the present century Malinowski, and following him Firth, pointed to the need to study language in the 'context of situation'. The speaker and listener operate in some setting which has to be taken into account in interpreting language use. The importance of setting (context, situation, framework) has been increasingly emphasized in discourse analysis and pragmatics. The literature shows convincingly that utterances become meaningful in context, and if we change the context the same utterance can mean something different. Thus, in Levinson's (1983: 280) example, a speaker who at the beginning of a lecture says: 'It's five past twelve' is not giving a time signal like a radio announcer; in the context of a scheduled activity such as a lecture the speaker is indicating that he is justified in beginning the activity, as if to say: 'In view of the fact that the lecture was announced for 12 noon, stragglers will have had time to come by five past twelve. We should therefore start and not wait any longer.' It is a call for action which will be interpreted in this way by the participants. It is the shared context of the participants that gives the utterance its specific communicative value.

What we read and hear in our native language makes sense to us because we can intuitively create a plausible context which in most cases is confirmed. In learning a second language, we do not possess this capacity to construct a reasonable context to the same extent. We tend to assume that the contexts are the same as in the first language. This may be partially so—to some extent our past L1 experience is valid and applicable in the L2 learning situation—but it may also be misleading. Lack of context and wrong contextualization are problems of second language learning. Isolated sentences without context are difficult to handle. Equally, selections of texts, as they are often offered in course-books or on tape, lack points of reference and are difficult to grasp because they are presented 'out of context'. The context, then, provides a time frame, a place frame, and a set of expectancies for interpreting messages. It is not simply a matter of decorative background; context gives meaning to the text, and stands in a dynamic relationship to the participants in the verbal exchange.

Participants

Another feature of functional analysis is that it does not, like a formal analysis, abstract away from the addressor and addressee. Functional analysis looks at language use as a process rather than as a product, usually involving a speaker or writer who wants to say something to a listener or reader who, in turn, actively interprets the message. Functional analysis examines the interaction between the participants, taking account of possible differences in their status and social roles. A language learner brings to the use of the second language his experience of a first language in which, in a similar way, transactions and interactions between participants occur. However, the relationships between interactants in one culture may differ from those of another. Thus, in some societies strangers in the home are treated with formality and deference whereas in another informality is emphasized. These differences are reflected in the language use that is appropriate for a stranger to observe.

Learning a second language involves being conscious of the interactions taking place among other speakers. In this respect the learner is an observer in the target society. But as a second language learner he also becomes involved as a participant. He moves from his own social background into another society as a foreigner or stranger. In turn, the host society approaches the learner with certain attitudes and expectations. The different participant roles which have emerged from functional analysis have also become important in communicative language teaching. There is now a greater awareness of differences in language use that go along with changes in role and status. Language instruction has attempted to capture these differences through role play and simulation.

Ends

In functional analysis, language use is visualized as a purposeful activity with identifiable goals. Thus, we are concerned with the intentions of the speaker or writer, as well as those of the listener or reader who does not receive the message passively, but actively selects and interprets in order to give meaning to what he receives and to make use of it for his own purposes. The question of language use as a goal-directed activity goes to the heart of functional analysis. It has been raised as a broad philosophical issue in relation to the nature of language, and in a more specific sense in enumerating and classifying the functions of different speech events. At a general level Bühler (1934); Jakobson (1960), and Lyons (1977) have distinguished language use as practical and factual on the one hand and personal, emotional, and social on the other, using the following contrasting pairs of terms:

representative and expressive (Bühler)
referential and emotive (Jakobson)
descriptive and social-expressive (Lyons)

In a similar way, Brown and Yule (1983a) distinguish between two main uses of discourse: one is transactional, that is, the use of language for such practical purposes as buying, ordering, and explaining; and the other is interactional where language is used for social purposes, as in a friendly social chat.

More detailed functional analyses have been attempted over the last two decades. They have been largely stimulated by the writings of two philosophers, Austin (1962) and Searle (1969). Austin made the points that there are ways of using language which, contrary to the claim of the logical positivists, cannot be judged as being either true or false. They are performatives such as promising, naming, and so on where language is used to effect a change. These uses of language are really actions achieved through the use of speech or in other words, speech acts. Illustrations of this use of language are utterances such as:

1 I hereby name this ship HMS Flounder.
2 I sentence you to ten years' hard labour.

By themselves these utterances do not constitute effective performatives. They must be uttered by the right person, in the right place, and at the right time. However, as Austin suggests, the concept of performative has a wider application. Underlying most, if not all utterances is an illocutionary force, that is, the intention to perform a speech act. The speaker always wants to do something: he wants to assert, persuade, convince, question, or, if need be, to warn, or threaten. The idea of the speech act has been further elaborated by Searle (1969). Lists of speech acts have been proposed in order to capture the different uses of language. It is also recognized that an utterance can simultaneously represent different speech acts.

It is this view of language use, with an emphasis on what the speaker intends to do by saying something, that has been influential in discourse analysis, pragmatics, and the ethnography of communication, as well as in language pedagogy. It is almost axiomatic nowadays to acknowledge that 'all utterances not only serve to express propositions, but also perform actions' (Levinson 1983: 243). However, while it has been valuable to recognize the varied functions of language use which can be direct and open as well as subtle and indirect, the attempt to classify and enumerate all language functions has run into difficulties. It has been impossible to establish lists of speech acts which are not arbitrary. Moreover, while discourse analysis may be illuminated by considering speech acts, it is clear that speech acts are not always single utterances but may stretch across several utterances.[2]

From the point of view of language pedagogy, speech act theory has been valuable in identifying the multiple purposes of language use. It has also helped to make clear the underlying intentions of the speaker and listener. Although the attempt to enumerate a finite number of speech acts and to base language teaching syllabuses on them has been only partially successful, it makes sense to focus on the speech acts that are realized by discourse. As we shall see shortly, speech act theory has had an enormous influence on syllabus development as well as on materials and teaching methodology.

Speech act characteristics

Here we are concerned with the characteristics of the message transmitted from speaker to listener, and not with grammaticality or any other formal characteristic of the utterance. Within the speech situation as defined by Hymes, for example at a party, there may be a speech event, for example a conversation, and within the conversation a speech act, for example a joke. Hymes' concept of speech act, which appears more elastic than that of Austin or Searle, suggests that speech acts combined into speech events are equivalent to discourse. A speech event belongs to a certain genre, such as a conversation, lecture, prayer, poem, curse, or blessing. It can be in a certain key, i.e. serious or jocular, formal or casual, and it can vary according to the medium in which it is presented, that is, either written or spoken.

In language teaching the concept of a text is of course not new. It has for centuries been customary to present learners with 'texts', that is, not isolated sentences but prose narratives, poems, and since the introduction of the audiolingual method, dialogues. Older textbooks, as the name indicates, contain selections of texts chosen from literary and philosophical writings, sometimes with particular topics or themes in mind, such as descriptions of nature or persons, philosophical discussions, narrations of events, and so on. In French language pedagogy there is a systematic procedure of text study or text analysis, referred to as *analyse de texte* or *lecture expliquée*, a mixed literary and linguistic intensive study of literary texts. This was first introduced as a detailed form of literary analysis in mother tongue education, and then taken over into the advanced study of French as a second language.

While text study as such is well established in language teaching, a systematic scholarly 'analysis of naturally occurring connected spoken or written discourse' (Stubbs 1983: 1) is relatively new. It is important to stress that discourse analysis is not only concerned with literary texts, although these are not excluded. It examines all kinds of naturally occurring discourse: shopping lists, hastily written memoranda, telephone conversations, interviews, classroom talk between teacher and students, business letters, or personal letters. Discourse analysis of formal writings includes not only literary texts but scientific texts, journalistic writings, and other types of texts.

An important distinction, made by Brown and Yule (1983a: 22–5), is that between discourse-as-product and discourse-as-process. In language teaching, traditional work with texts has typically been discourse-as-product. What discourse analysis attempts to do is to study how a speaker or writer with certain purposes in mind proceeds to express his meaning and what the listener or reader does to interpret this meaning. Discourse analysis is thus concerned with the internal structure of written texts and conversations. Investigation has focused on such questions as: What makes a series of utterances hang together so that it has the quality of a text or conversation? What devices are used to open a conversation, to change topics, to interrupt, and to break off contact? In written texts, what are the conventions of introducing a topic, developing an argument, or concluding a presentation? We can see the influence of discourse analysis in course books which teach students how to participate in conversations and discussions. For example, exercises have been devised to provide training in expressing agreement or disagreement, or in qualifying a statement made by another participant. In addition, attention has been drawn to how an argument is set out in writing because conventions differ in different cultures.[3]

Norms and variety

Sociolinguistics and discourse analysis have not only had the effect of adding more rules of a different kind to the description of a language. These disciplines have also shown the degree of variation and variety that is possible within a language. This has led to the study of social and regional variation, and of varieties which ostensibly deviate from the normative standards that societies tend to impose on language use: for example, creoles and pidgins, as well as child language, the 'interlanguage' of language learners, the speech of bilinguals, and social varieties such as Black English. The impact of these studies has been to loosen the concept of norm and of standard. The accepted standard is recognized as a 'variety' among others. It is invested with a certain prestige but it is not necessarily superior to other varieties. Today, we are much more conscious of the complexity of language, and of the arbitrary nature of linguistic norms or 'standards' in pronunciation and grammar. We are much more tolerant of variations within a language, and as a result there is also a much greater tolerance of 'errors' in second language learning.[4]

The communicative orientation in second language teaching has relaxed the tight grip of conformity, standard, and absolute correctness as the main guiding principles. Instead, teachers weigh the purpose of communicating meaning against conformity to grammatical norms, or as Brumfit has frequently put it, the merits of fluency versus those of accuracy. It is sometimes argued that the communicative approach has led to inaccurate and incomprehensible fluency, and this has prompted a reaction, a demand for a renewed emphasis on grammatical accuracy and less tolerance of error. There is no simple answer to this dilemma. We will simply note here that the sociolinguistic study of linguistic variation at different levels of society, including child language acquisition and second language learning, has drawn attention to the complexity of the concept of linguistic norm, language variety, and language error.

Functional analysis in language pedagogy

Since the late 1960s, there has been a constant search for ways in which the new linguistic disciplines of discourse analysis, sociolinguistics, and pragmatics might be brought to bear on language teaching, a movement which has crystallized as the 'communicative approach'. We will now briefly review some of these efforts. Broadly speaking, functional analysis can be said to have been a liberating influence, because it has taken language pedagogy out of a narrow preoccupation with the formal features of language. The new emphasis on meaning, texts, speech functions, and so on is not only exciting, it is also closer to the living reality of language in use.

The different disciplines involved in functional analysis have led to varying emphases. Some writers have given precedence to semantics and have focused on notions, functions, and Austin's and Searle's concept of the speech act. Others have worked out the implications of discourse and conversational analysis, paying attention to aspects of cohesion and coherence in language use, and revising their views of the four skills. Others again have adopted the speech act model derived from Jakobson and Hymes. Functional analysis, therefore, appears in language pedagogy in a variety of guises. It has contributed to the formulation of language teaching goals through the concept of communicative competence; it has had a profound influence on syllabus design; it is reflected in newer approaches to teaching methodology and teaching materials; and it has influenced methods of evaluation.

Communicative competence as a goal of second language teaching

When Hymes (1967) and Campbell and Wales (1970) contrasted communicative and linguistic competence, they did not in the main have second language pedagogy in mind. Their chief concern was to offer a theoretically more adequate scheme for the analysis of the native speaker's intuitive language command, and the point they were making was that the native speaker's knowledge of the language was more than knowledge of its grammar. A knowledge of language enables the speaker to function communicatively in the society to which he belongs. Language teachers were sympathetic to this view of language proficiency and readily adopted the concept of communicative competence as an expression of the goal for second language teaching (see, for example, Jakobovits 1970). As early as 1968, Spolsky suggested that language tests should not merely assess the mastery of grammar and lexicon as evidence of L2 knowledge. Instead,

> A more promising approach might be to work for a functional definition of levels: we should aim not to test how much of a language someone knows, but test his ability to operate in a specified sociolinguistic situation with specified ease or effect. The preparation of proficiency tests like this would not start from a list of language items, but from a statement of language function; after all, it would not be expected to lead to statements like 'He knows sixty percent of English,' but 'He knows enough English to shop in a supermarket'.
> (Spolsky 1968: 93, as quoted by Jakobovits 1970: 86–7)

A few years later, Spolsky (1978) elaborated his definition of what it means to know a language and included concepts of communicative competence. Basing himself on Hymes' model, he argued convincingly that a full description of an individual's communicative competence would need to cover at least five dimensions:

1. Linguistic dimension: lexicon, semantics, grammar, phonology.
2. Channels: oral-aural, speech-writing, gesture.
3. Code dimension: (a) varieties available—languages, regional dialects, social dialects, styles, registers; (b) control of code selection rules.
4. Topic dimension: what can be talked about.
5. Setting dimension: ability to function in various domains (home, school, work, community, etc.)

(Spolsky 1978: 126)

The influence of Hymes' model and of sociolinguistics generally is quite evident in this analysis of communicative competence. At the same time, Spolsky's interpretation of what it means to know a language implies that, while the grammar and lexicon are not enough, they are nevertheless basic to a definition of communicative competence. In Spolsky's view, creativity and redundancy are also essential characteristics of language which should be taken into consideration.

Although communicative competence was not always described in the same way, it soon became the most widely recognized goal of second language teaching. Savignon (1972), in her pioneering experiment on communicative competence in the foreign language classroom, defined it as 'the ability to function in a truly communicative setting—that is, in the dynamic exchange in which linguistic competence must adapt itself to the total informational input, both linguistic and paralinguistic, of one or more interlocutors' (Savignon 1972: 8). While this description of communicative competence is less clearly related to a particular school of thought, we can clearly see that the act of communication is viewed here as a 'dynamic' process in which context and the intentions and roles of the participants have some bearing on the second language learner's use of language.

In the late 1970s, Canale and Swain again came to grips with the question of communicative competence. They did so at the invitation of the Ontario Ministry of Education, which had plans to develop communicatively oriented tests in French as a second language. As a first step, the researchers undertook a thorough and critical review of the theoretical and research underpinnings of the notion of communicative competence. Their study (Canale and Swain 1980) is a comprehensive and well-considered analysis of the many linguistic influences that had to be taken into account in sorting out the somewhat confused scene of communicative language teaching. Their enquiry led the investigators to propose a scheme of communicative competence which was divided into three underlying competencies: (a) grammatical competence, comprising the formal linguistic aspect of language use, phonology, grammar, and lexis; (b) sociolinguistic competence, based mainly on sociolinguistic considerations but including also a less clearly defined discourse component; i.e. 'sociocultural rules of use and rules of discourse'; (c) strategic competence comprising 'verbal and non-verbal communication strategies that may be called into action to compensate for breakdowns in communication due to performance variables or to insufficient competence' (Canale and Swain 1980: 30).

In a later version, Canale (1983) slightly modified this scheme by separating the discourse from the sociolinguistic component and proposing a fourth element, discourse competence. Strategic competence was also somewhat widened to include efforts 'to enhance the effectiveness of communication' (Canale 1983: 11). Apart from these modifications, the analysis by Canale and Swain has remained unchanged. It is widely quoted and used as a clear and convenient statement of communicative competence as a goal of second language teaching. The influence of sociolinguistics and discourse analysis on this expression of the goal of second language learning is once more clearly evident.

Functional analysis and syllabus design

The widespread questioning of grammatical syllabuses which occurred during the 1970s prompted the Council of Europe Modern Languages Project to search for a new and more satisfactory basis for European language courses for adults. A number of ideas were explored, and eventually Wilkins (1976) came up with a firm proposal for a semantically-based syllabus design in his book *Notional Syllabuses*. In this well-known work, Wilkins proposed three sets of organizers: semantico-grammatical categories, categories of modal meaning, and categories of communicative function. Semantico-grammatical categories are basic concepts or propositional meanings which in European languages are often expressed in grammatical form, such as time through the tense system, or quantity through singular and plural. Wilkins' list of such categories include the following concepts: time, quantity, space, relations (agent, object, instrument), and deixis. Categories of modal meaning are modifications of language use through which speakers express degrees of certainty (for example, probability, doubt), or commitment (for example, intention or obligation). Finally, categories of communicative function, the largest of the three sets of categories, list speech acts under six main headings and numerous subheadings.

A few years later, Wilkins (1981) acknowledged that *Notional Syllabuses* had not made clear at what point in syllabus development the semantic categorization should occur. He also expressed the view that the three sets of categories 'need to be integrated into a fuller view of language behaviour and communication' (Wilkins 1981: 86). Paulston (1981) criticized Wilkins' scheme because according to her:

> Language forms are generative while notions are not, and since one cannot in fact divorce function from form in language, it makes more sense to me to organize a syllabus along linguistic forms which can generate infinite meanings and many functions, rather than to organize content along a finite list of functions.
> (Paulston 1981: 93)

Similar objections were raised by Brumfit (1980b, 1981) who argued that grammatical items can be arranged in a logical order but speech acts can only be enumerated, without any grounds for a particular order.

This argument led to Brumfit's proposal that language syllabuses should continue to be mainly grammar-based, with speech acts and other functional categories loosely woven around the grammatical core.

The Council of Europe Threshold Level syllabuses, which were developed between 1971 and 1975, also attempted to incorporate aspects of functional analysis. Wilkins' notional scheme certainly played a part but it was not regarded as sufficient by itself. Eventually, van Ek developed a scheme which used categories suggested by Jakobson and Hymes and was probably also influenced by the sociosemantic views of Halliday. Van Ek specifies the following main components for the definition of language learning objectives:

> The situations in which the foreign language will be used including the topics which will be dealt with.
> The language activities in which the learner will engage.
> The language functions the learner will fulfil.
> What the learner will be able to do with each topic.
> The general notions which the learner will be able to handle.
> The specific (topic-related) notions which the learner will be able to handle.
> The language forms which the learner will be able to use.
> The degree of skill with which the learner will be able to perform.
> (van Ek 1975: 5)

The grammatical system is subsumed in these specifications as a necessary but secondary component. The Threshold Level in effect adopted Wilkins' argument of the primacy of functional categories over grammar in the design of a syllabus. But neither Wilkins nor van Ek was concerned with discourse features or the systematic treatment of sociolinguistic variation.

Several other syllabus designs were proposed between 1976 and 1985. They are alike in giving prominence to functional analysis, but they vary in the emphasis they place on it and the aspect of functional analysis (speech acts, discourse, sociolinguistic variations) which they highlight. Most of them are also concerned with the interrelationship between grammar and functional analysis in the syllabus. Alexander (1979), for example, showed that a language syllabus can be purely functional or it can combine structural and functional features in several ways. It can give priority to function over structure or vice versa, each resulting in a different type of syllabus. It can also be theme or topic-based and pay attention to both the structural and functional features of the theme in question. Yalden's (1983) proportional syllabus also legitimizes structural as well as functional components but varies the proportions as the course progresses. In her scheme, structural teaching predominates and functional aspects are secondary in the early stages; as the course progresses, the functional component expands more and more. In Allen's (1983) three-level curriculum scheme, the functional component is central and forms a bridge between the structural-grammatical component and experiential component which is message-oriented and linguistically uncontrolled. The position of the functional component in Allen's scheme, combining discourse and speech act categories and sociolinguistic features, emphasizes its importance for the language development of the learner.

Functional analysis in the language class

While functional analysis has affected the overall design of language curriculums, it has made its most decisive impact on teaching content, methodology, and materials. This influence is not uniform or easy to pin down. Different authorities have laid emphasis on different aspects, some stressing the analysis of discourse (Coulthard 1985), others the speaker's intentions expressed through speech acts (Finocchiaro and Brumfit 1983), and others again the negotiation of meaning (Hatch 1978; Varonis and Gass 1985; Rulon and McCreary 1986). In view of the fact that different disciplines with different perspectives are involved, it is hardly surprising that functional analysis has not led to a clearly identifiable pedagogical approach. Before indicating the differences, let us begin by pointing out features largely held in common by most interpretations of the role of functional analysis in the classroom. The functional component in the language class complements formal or structural teaching. There are differences in viewpoint as to what extent a structural or functional emphasis should take precedence. There is, however, a general consensus that the formal treatment of a language by itself is not enough. Whatever shape functional analysis takes, it is likely to add something to the treatment of language which was previously missing and which must now be included.

Broadly speaking, communicative analysis is a way of coming closer to the living reality of the language. It draws attention to certain features of language use which were not within the purview of structuralism. The question, of course, is how to convey this living reality of language to the learner without overwhelming or confusing him. Sociolinguistics, discourse analysis, and the ethnography of communication have extended the empirical database of linguistics and have created a heightened awareness of linguistic varieties, of variations of language use in different situations, of differences between spoken and written language, and of the complexities and subtleties of spoken and written discourse. This knowledge has made language pedagogy very sensitive to artificialities in textbooks and in the classroom, leading to new demands for greater authenticity of language use.[5] More specifically, the application of functional analysis has led to the following results:

Demand for contextualization. Whether a course operates with texts or with separate exercises, functional analysis insists on placing utterances in context, or it encourages learners to create a context for themselves. There is still a possibility that certain aspects of language may be taught in decontextualized ways; but on the whole a functional approach demands that the setting is defined and that the interactions between setting, participants, and speech events are taken care of.

The importance of participant roles. In functional analysis, the participants in a language transaction are always stated, whether we are dealing with a written text, a conversation, isolated utterances, exercises, or drills. The same principle applies in communicative language teaching. Learners are encouraged to adopt and exchange roles and to be aware of role differences. This attention to the participants applies at all levels of language teaching whether the message is a short conversational exchange or a full-length book.

Semantic emphasis. Functional analysis adopts a semantic orientation. Its main concern is with meaning and how it is conveyed through verbal interaction. What are the speaker's (or writer's) intentions? What message does the speaker want to get across? How is the message interpreted by the listener (or reader)? It follows that communicative teaching attributes importance to the interaction among the participants and their attempts to develop or negotiate meaning.

Emphasis on speech acts. In accordance with the semantic principle, the identification of speech functions or speech acts has played a crucial role in bringing functional analysis into the language class.

Emphasis on discourse. Functional analysis implies discourse analysis. It treats discourse (written texts and conversation) as the basic unit of language learning, not isolated words, grammatical forms, or sentences.

In the next section we will see how some of these principles have been translated into classroom practice.

Contextualization

Emphasis on the context of speech events is reflected in the contextualization of exercises, thus bringing grammatical practice closer to the reality of language use. Context is necessary not only because it makes an exercise more credible as a language event, but because it is often essential in order for it to make sense. It has already been pointed out that to understand a linguistic message we need a context, and if it is not given, we tend to construct one so as to make sense of the message. This natural tendency to contextualize is exploited in exercises where the situation is not given and the learner is asked to construct a context from the events he hears or reads. Learners need practice in contextualizing. In one ESL course, the student listens to snippets of talk and has to guess the situation; that is, he has to construct the situation and setting from listening to the speakers:

Two speakers: Man/Man
A. Two more beers, please.
B. Sorry, no more, time's up.
A. Oh, go on, Jack, just two more and then we'll go. I promise.

Two speakers: Man/Woman
M. Well, how about it? It'll be a good film.
W. No, no, thanks. I've got to wash my hair tonight.

Elsewhere in the same course, the same utterance (for example, 'It's raining' or 'The door is open') is presented in three or four different settings changing the meaning of the utterance. The exercise is presented in three columns:

Utterance Meaning Context

Sometimes the context is given and the meaning has to be interpreted, and at other times the meaning is given and the context has to be provided. These examples illustrate the greater awareness of context as an important component in a communicative approach to language teaching.

Emphasis on topic or theme

In a strictly linguistic approach to language or language learning, the topic of discourse is relatively unimportant. Anything will do that illustrates the grammatical or phonological point that is to be made. Hence the classic examples of 'La plume de ma tante' and 'Colourless green ideas'. It is characteristic of a communicative approach that topics are not chosen arbitrarily but are meant to reflect the needs of learners, their real or presumed interests, or some other (for example, educational) rationale. A reasoned choice of topics is also essential for an experiential approach to communicative teaching (see Chapter 7). In an experiential approach, the class is concerned with the inherent interest of a topic, whereas in an analytic approach the focus is on the language used to deal with that topic.

The *English in Focus* series initiated by Oxford University Press in the early 1970s illustrates a linguistic approach to a variety of academic subjects, the sciences, medicine, sociology, and so on, in which the texts were intended for study of the discourse characteristics of language use in these different discipline areas. Here the learner's interest in the discipline, for example, physical science or social studies, is taken for granted (Allen and Widdowson 1974; Widdowson 1978). A few years later, a similar approach was used to produce modules on topics which are of importance to ESL learners in Canadian schools, for example, geography or social studies. The emphasis is partly on the inherent interest of the topics but partly on the use of language in talking and writing about the topics in regular school programmes (Allen and Howard 1981). In North America generally, there is increasing interest in a content-based approach which involves the concurrent teaching of academic subject-matter and second language skills (Mohan 1986; Brinton *et al.* 1989). Although the emphasis is on authentic content rather than linguistic analysis, there is a role for activities which focus explicitly on form–meaning relationships, and which help to develop accuracy and precision of language use.

The combination of a linguistic approach with a topical focus is a characteristic development of teaching based on functional analysis. It should be stressed that in this treatment the point of the topic is not merely to have something to talk about in the language class; the topic is of importance to the students, and the analytic treatment is designed to make the topic itself more accessible through deliberate linguistic analysis.

Participant roles

A functional analysis identifies the addressor and addressee and more specifically their role relationship: for example, doctor and patient, parent and child, guest and host, hotel receptionist and traveller, worker and boss. This is done not merely because it is more vivid and more natural, but because the roles imply certain contexts and topics and therefore affect the language being used. Functional analysis has led to the use of roles in language teaching, both in formal dramatizations and as part of a great variety of normal language practice techniques. Thus, in many classes exercises are devised so that students practise in pairs or groups, each adopting a role (for example, parent and child) and then switching roles. Communicative exercises are devised with role-play in mind. They can vary in complexity and may be more or less linguistically demanding.

Littlewood (1981) has distinguished different levels of role-play. At a fairly simple level for beginners or intermediate learners, students and their partners are each given a card with suggestions for what to say in their respective roles. Littlewood's illustration of such cued dialogue is:

Learner A	Learner B
You meet B in the street.	You meet A in the street.
A: Greet B.	A:
B:	B: Greet A.
A: Ask B where he is going.	A:
B:	B: Say you are going for a walk.
(etc.)	(etc.)

At the next level of complexity in Littlewood's scheme role-playing is controlled through cues and information. Again students receive cue cards which describe their role and intended utterance:

> Student A: You arrive at a small hotel one evening. In the foyer you meet the manager and ask if there is a room vacant. Ask the price, including breakfast.
>
> Student B: You are the manager of a small hotel that prides itself on its friendly, homely atmosphere. You have a single and a double room vacant for tonight.

At further levels of complexity, each student receives a card which explains the situation, the student's role, and a goal without suggesting details of expression:

> Student A: You wish to buy a car, etc.
> Student B: You are a car salesman, etc.

As another step Littlewood suggests role-play in the form of a debate or discussion in which the discussants represent different walks of life and different points of view on a public issue, for example the local vicar, the principal of a primary school, and two ladies from a small town discuss fund-raising for a charity. Finally, Littlewood suggests large-scale simulations and improvisations in unusual circumstances (Littlewood 1981: 51–62). It is clear that advanced role-playing activities demand not only a high level of linguistic command, but also a good deal of cultural background, knowledge, and life experience. Note that Littlewood's examples are very English in character. It is beneficial for learners to familiarize themselves through role-play with personalities representing the target culture. It is also often the only way in which the class and the teacher can mentally break away from the conventional teacher-student relationship.

Role-play does not have to be elaborate. By simply ascribing defined roles to the speaker and listener, utterances become more meaningful and usually more interesting even in the simplest repetitive drill. In order to make role-play practical, the classroom learner must be prepared to adopt impersonations not all of which he is likely to perform in a foreign language situation. Thus, in one unit on French wedding ceremonies, the students are invited to be bride, bridegroom, the couple's parents and relatives, and even the priest who performs the marriage ceremony. Students performing these different roles undoubtedly widen their range of language and their capacity for empathy. At the same time it is not uncommon to observe demands for role-play which far outstrip the student's linguistic knowledge and which presuppose unrealistic levels of experience and imagination.

In giving students different roles, we often overlook that the most important role the learner has to perform is that of himself as a foreigner in a new linguistic and cultural environment. This has a bearing on which expressions to learn and which to avoid. In their desire to be realistic and authentic, some course writers indiscriminately teach expressions which may be appropriate for certain kinds of native speakers, but which could cause embarrassment if used by the foreign learner. The recognition of participant roles has consequences for the conduct of a language class, implying a need for pair work or small group activities. These are not the only ways in which participant roles in second language learning can be acknowledged, however. What is more important to keep in mind is that a message in isolation makes little sense. In any given speech event, we have to recognize the role relationship of the interactants.

Linguistic norms and variability

Another effect of functional analysis, derived largely from sociolinguistics, has been the introduction into second language teaching of linguistic variation. Learners are increasingly being made aware of distinctions in language use that reflect social situation, topic, and relationships between participants. The concept of appropriateness has been given a more prominent place in language teaching than previously. There are differences in use between speech and written discourse, and social distinctions—degrees of familiarity and respect—expressed in particular through forms of address. The influence of situation on language use may be demonstrated by drawing the attention of learners to the stylistic differences between an academic paper on a scholarly topic, a seminar discussion on the same topic, and an informal conversation.

For the learner it is particularly important to be sensitized to those uses of language which are considered appropriate for a second language speaker with an imperfect command of the target language. Some course writers introduce slang and trendy expressions which go with certain highly specific settings but are of limited use to the foreigner who lacks a sense of their restricted appropriateness. For example, in Edmondson and House (1981) we find common exclamations in English presented in four groups ranging from 'oh', 'ah', and 'really' in Group A to 'damn', 'bloody hell', 'Jesus Christ', and 'not again!' in Group D. The authors make the point that learners tend to under-use exclamations, except for the polite 'oh' which is often over-used. However, there is no reference, in this otherwise excellent study of talk in English, to the deliberate breaking of social taboos by the use of Group D exclamations which in many circumstances may be quite inappropriate.

Semantic emphasis

For several authorities the emphasis on pragmatic meaning is perhaps the most important feature of communicative language teaching. To some extent, this has simply been a reaction of teachers against the over-concentration of most past teaching methods on phonological and grammatical accuracy. This semantic emphasis has not meant a rejection of linguistic forms, but rather a shift of emphasis towards the expression and interpretation of meaning. Thus, among the first experiments in communicative language teaching (Savignon 1972) were exercises which were designed to give students the experience of conveying meaning to one another on topics of genuine interest, even though their ability to express themselves on these topics was still imperfect. Similarly, the majority of exercises in the Bundesarbeitsgemeinschaft's *Diskursstruktur und Übungstypologie* (1975) require learners to understand the meaning of words in given contexts, to put sentence fragments together so that a meaningful unit is created, to associate text with pictures, to distinguish true from false statements, or to ascribe statements to contexts or individuals. In other words, there is a strong preoccupation with the meaning of words, utterances, and texts.

Another indication of this semantic emphasis is a concern with the intended meaning of utterances as opposed to their propositional meaning. Here Austin's concept of illocutionary force has found its way into language pedagogy. A frequently used example is 'The window is open' which, though ostensibly a statement of fact, may express the speaker's wish to have the window closed because it is cold. For a second language learner it is not always easy to understand the illocutionary force of such an utterance. In some languages, however, it may be customary to use a face-saving indirect formula of this nature rather than to issue a request, express a difference of opinion, or refuse an invitation in a direct manner. Clearly the distinction between propositional and intended meaning can be very important in language learning for the avoidance of misunderstandings and social blunders.

Functions and notions

Among the semantic approaches to communicative language teaching, one of the most influential has probably been Wilkins' emphasis on speech acts or functions as part of a notional syllabus. For many advocates of the communicative approach this has been the central and sometimes the sole component; for others it has formed only a part, but still an important part, of communicative teaching.

In a pedagogical grammar of English by Edmondson and House (1981) a major part of the book is devoted to the description of speech acts or 'illocutions', categorized as follows: requests, suggests, invites, permits, wills, resolves, complains, apologizes, excuses/justifies, forgives, thanks, minimizes, congratulates, sympathizes, remarks, discloses, tells, opines, greets, how-are-yous, okays, extractors, wish-wells, leave-takes. Exercises involving role-play usually require students to carry out speech acts, such as greeting, inviting, refusing, persuading, and accepting. It has become customary in devising exercises to specify the functions involved. For example, in an exercise called 'Guess who's coming to dinner', involving menu cards and discussing menus with a partner, the speech functions practised are described as: 'Inquiring about and sharing personal facts and preferences; discussing foods' (Omaggio 1984: 66). A list of functions relating to situations, topics, and the people involved, is provided by Finocchiaro and Brumfit (1983: 61–70).

Discourse emphasis

The final linguistic contribution to the communicative approach to be examined here is discourse analysis. In some interpretations of communicative language teaching, discourse analysis plays no part and 'discourse' is not even mentioned; in others, it is the key to the approach, comprising most or all of the other aspects we have considered above. Broadly speaking, the influence of discourse analysis has been to facilitate the transition from sentences to larger units of text. Attention has been drawn to discourse features and to the acquisition of 'discourse competence' as part of the overall communicative competence of the second language learner (Hatch 1978; Larsen-Freeman 1980; Carrell 1985).

It is largely as a result of discourse analysis that course materials have appeared which emphasize the rhetorical organization of written and spoken texts. Thus, we find materials on 'gambits', i.e. helpful expressions for those who wish to develop effective conversational strategies.[6] Many learners of English as a second language find that they are schooled in literary expressions and feel handicapped in coping with conversational exchanges. Similarly, foreign students in an English-speaking university often find they lack the skills needed to participate in seminar discussions. Analysis of the characteristics of different kinds of oral discourse has been found useful for developing these skills (Edmondson and House 1981; Boyer, Charbonneau, and Nault 1982).

Concluding comments

Functional analysis can play a major or minor role in a language syllabus. If all the features we have identified are present—contextualization, participant role definition, emphasis on topic, sociolinguistic variation, general semantic emphasis, speech act identification, discourse analysis—then functional analysis plays a major role. Often, however, the syllabus may simply emphasize one or two aspects of functional analysis. For example, the Council of Europe Threshold Level syllabuses have generally stressed contextualization, role definition, and speech act identification, while the *English in Focus* series stresses topic, semantics, and discourse. So far there are few materials which emphasize sociolinguistic variation.

A number of test designers have focused on the analytic characteristics of communicative testing. For example, a communicative French test, prepared for adolescent students in immersion programmes (Swain 1984), is deliberately designed to emphasize tasks to be performed in a given context, i.e. seeking summer employment. The interactive role of the test takers is defined, and their discourse competence is elicited as well as their ability to cope with sociolinguistic variation. In an English as a second language test for Canadian university entrants (Wesche *et al.* 1987) the focus is on different types of academic discourse which the student has to respond to or produce. While the tasks, as in the French example, are intended to be as real as possible and thus to reflect communicative experience, the design of the test is based on functional analysis, particularly discourse analysis.

In short, functional analysis has sparked off a rethinking of the linguistic content of language syllabuses and tests, and has led to a prolonged debate on syllabus design which began in the 1970s and has continued to the present day. There is a widespread consensus that the new linguistic disciplines should be represented in language courses, and that they promise second language programmes which will be more lifelike, more authentic, more realistic, and less abstract than courses based entirely on phonology, lexis, and grammar.

Notes

1 Semantics, dealing with the description of word and sentence meaning, is perhaps closest to the formal core of linguistics. Discourse analysis is concerned with the underlying principles of text structure, and also with the means whereby we produce a coherent piece of writing or manage a conversational interaction. Pragmatics can be broadly defined as the study of intended speaker meaning within a particular context. Ethnographers set out to examine general patterns of communication in society, while sociolinguists typically deal with questions of language attitude, the social implications of varieties of language, and language variability as a result of changes in context or social role. For background discussion, see: Palmer (1976), Lyons (1977), and Allan (1986) on semantics; Brown and Yule (1983a), Stubbs (1983), and Coulthard (1985) on discourse analysis; Leech (1983) and Levinson (1983) on pragmatics; Saville-Troike (1982) on the ethnography of communication; and Hudson (1980) and Wardhaugh (1986) on sociolinguistics.

2 Levinson (1983: 278) concludes a detailed critique of speech acts with the observation 'there are some compelling reasons to think that speech act theory may slowly be superseded by much more complex multi-faceted pragmatic approaches to the functions that utterances perform'.

3 The basic insight is that different languages and language groups (e.g. Semitic, Oriental, Romance) have rhetorical patterns which often differ markedly from the organizational style of written English. See Kaplan (1966, 1988) and the papers in Smith (1987).

4 For a recent discussion of error analysis and transfer, see Odlin (1989).

5 As Widdowson (1983: 30–1) points out, the term 'authenticity' is ambiguous. On the one hand, it can refer to naturalistic textual data, but on the other hand, it can be used to refer to purposeful communicative activity on the part of the language user. Since an authentic stimulus in the first sense does not necessarily lead to an authentic response in the second sense, a central problem of pedagogy is to discover ways of using 'contrived means to achieve a natural end'.

6 Di Pietro (1987) describes a 'strategic interaction' approach based on 'scenarios' which provide practice in the recognition and use of verbal strategies, and allow learners to develop shared information in specific contexts. Roberts (1986: 71), citing work by Di Pietro, proposes to revitalize the dialogue 'as a pedagogical device which may be employed in the teaching of transactional competence'.

7 The communicative activities syllabus

Introduction

With the communicative activities syllabus we change perspective and adopt an entirely different view of the target language. This syllabus, providing for communicative activities in a language course, represents a relatively new concept. Teachers have been familiar with communicative activities for many years; but the idea of making use of them systematically and of developing a distinct syllabus of such activities is certainly not widely known and probably even less widely applied. In our view, this type of syllabus is one of the most important recent developments in the second language curriculum. In order to formulate a coherent language teaching policy, it is essential that we should be clear about the role of communicative activities in the classroom.

What is meant by a 'communicative activity'? We use this term to designate motivated activities, topics, and themes which involve the learner in authentic communication. The essential characteristics of a communicative syllabus may be described as holistic or authentic, and the teaching strategy associated with this syllabus as experiential or non-analytic (see Chapter 11). In a communicative syllabus the main focus is on the activities themselves, the topic or experience, and not on the language as such or any single aspect of it. What, then, could be classified as a communicative activity? Any activity—talk, task, problem, project—that involves learners in 'real' communication. It may be a short episode in a language class; it does not have to be a complex project. An example or two may help. Thus, if in a language class the teacher asks a student to open a window, this exchange becomes a communicative activity if the circumstances genuinely warrant the request. But if the purpose of the utterance is to practise making requests using the imperative form, it is a linguistic exercise within the language syllabus and not a communicative activity in our sense. Again, if the teacher asks a student whether he has any brothers or sisters and adds 'Answer in the negative', the question is designed to provide practice of a point of grammar. It is not a question of any communicative value, since the teacher did not ask out of interest in the student's family background.

Communicative activities in the language class are not confined to the subtle distinctions in classroom talk we have just illustrated. They may be major enterprises including activities beyond the classroom. For instance, if in the context of a language course arrangements are made for a class trip or exchange visit to the target community, the preparations and the trip itself involve many quite substantial communicative activities. Although they may be intended to provide opportunities for language practice, they demand 'real' language use in the joint planning of the journey, gathering information about places to visit, dealing with the finances of the trip, contacting families and schools, and arranging for somewhere to stay. Students may visit families in the target community, or participate in classes in the school with which the exchange has been arranged. In short, the students will find themselves in various real-life situations where the target language must be used. These are communicative activities *par excellence*. The focus is not on learning specific language features but on putting the language to use as the circumstances require. In this chapter, our concern is with questions such as: What do such real-life experiences contribute to language learning? Can they be incorporated in any significant way in the language class? How can they be planned to constitute a 'communicative syllabus'?

Some theoretical assumptions

What are the assumptions underlying the kind of communicative activities advocated in the literature? The crucial one is the distinction between message-oriented and medium-oriented activities (Dodson 1976). In normal language use—that is, when we talk to someone, read a newspaper, listen to a news broadcast, take part in a discussion, write a letter or report—our attention is focused mainly on the message, not on its formal linguistic properties. When we communicate in our first language, we pay little, if any, attention to the linguistic forms or the 'code' in which we communicate. This intuitive use of language for communication is characteristic of an expert user of the language. Indeed, for a native speaker it may be quite difficult to isolate formal features of the code being used.

Learning to read and write and other aspects of schooling force us to focus on the code to a certain extent; literacy, therefore, represents an initial kind of training in language analysis, that is, in paying attention to formal linguistic features. Nevertheless, to focus on the code and to communicate at the same time is difficult, if not impossible. One of the central problems in language teaching is this code-communication dilemma.[1] When we talk or write we can of course pause and quickly switch from communication to code, as for example, when we search for a word, decide on the correct spelling, or choose an adequate formulation of a thought, but if we dwell on the code for too long, the flow of communication is lost and the meaning of the message escapes us.

Children learn their first language in the process of communication without focusing on the code. If they are exposed to more than one language in their natural environment, they become bilingual and even multilingual. By contrast, the experience of learning a second language by first learning the code, as is commonly the case in formal schooling, has been far less successful. This is why empirical research since the early 1970s has aimed primarily at understanding the conditions and processes of 'natural', untutored first and second language learning. There are three main problems in formal code teaching:

(a) The Humpty Dumpty effect. It is difficult to make the structures studied one by one in the language class coalesce into a serviceable instrument (i.e. it is easier to break a language apart than to put it together again).[2]
(b) The complexity of the linguistic system. According to Macnamara (1973) and Prabhu (1987), language is too complex to be handled at a conscious level.[3]
(c) The transfer problem. What is learnt analytically in the classroom is not automatically applied under conditions of real language use.

These shortcomings of formal instruction have been known for a long time and pedagogical practice has always tried to compensate for them. Exposing learners to the reality of language use through contact with native speakers has been widely recognized as necessary for an advanced command of a second language. The direct method of the late nineteenth century was partly an attempt to introduce communicative activities into the language class, so that the meaning of utterances would have to be apprehended by the learner immediately and directly. What is relatively new in recent pedagogical experimentation is communicative activities which are systematically built into the curriculum from a very early stage of language learning. According to this point of view, communication is not a late phase that follows language instruction; it is an integral part of instruction from the beginning.

A number of writers have argued that informal learning through communication and attention to meaning has certain necessary qualities which formal learning lacks (Newmark 1971; Savignon 1972; Krashen 1982). Communicative activities are believed to encourage subconscious learning of the second language. Since in acts of communication the learner's attention is mainly on the meaning of the message and not on the code, whatever learning occurs during such language use must be largely subconscious. Even if we do not accept the 'strong' version of Krashen's language acquisition theory according to which conscious learning cannot become subconscious acquisition (Krashen 1985), we can adopt the view that there must be opportunities for subconscious assimilation, and these cannot be provided if exposure to the language is rigidly controlled and confined to what can be handled by the learner at the conscious level. Besides the need for subconscious learning, there are further arguments in favour of a communicative syllabus:

(a) To be effective, the move from formal study to language use has to occur repeatedly during the learning process. Hence the need for a communicative syllabus, not just for an occasional communicative activity.
(b) If the language is only presented as a code through formal exercises, vocabulary study, rehearsal of specific functions and the like, the learner is never confronted with the totality of language which is needed as a kind of constant reality test.
(c) Communicative activities offer the opportunity to develop coping techniques that are needed when the learner is on his own in the natural language environment. Such coping techniques require regular exposure to real-life language situations.
(d) Communicative activities give the learner an opportunity to develop a personal relationship with the target community through direct contact with individual speakers and thus to experience and define his status as a 'foreigner' *vis-à-vis* the new language, its culture, and community.

For all these reasons, it is nowadays acknowledged that communicative activities must not be too strictly separated from formal learning. The point of view taken in this book is that communicative activities are an essential component of a language curriculum, but that there is still a place for an analytic language syllabus. At different phases of the learning process the emphasis may shift from the linguistic to the communicative component or vice versa, but within the curriculum as a whole both are needed; they complement each other and blend together. With reference to learning objectives, the assumption is that both the linguistic and the communicative syllabuses contribute to increased second language proficiency. There is, however, another reason why a communicative component is important. If we ask ourselves why we want to be proficient in the second language the typical answer is that we will thus be in a better position to make contact with members of the target language community. A communicative component assists in realizing this possibility. It opens channels of communication to the target community at a personal level of contact and provides life experiences mediated through the second language.

Principles of a communicative activities syllabus

Whatever differences there may be between the various approaches, all theorists agree that a natural setting provides the best possible conditions for learning the target language 'communicatively'. In order to have a prototype for communication in a second language classroom, we will begin by pointing out four key features of communication in a natural setting. The classroom cannot, and indeed should not, offer everything the natural setting does but it can approximate it in several respects. Once we have isolated the essentials of natural communication we will see more clearly where language classrooms fall short of the ideal, and what a communicative syllabus might do to rectify these shortcomings. As an example, let us consider a young woman who is a university student spending a year of residence in France. In what way does this constitute a particularly favourable situation for learning French?

Contact with a variety of target language speakers

One of the shortcomings of a language class is that the teacher is usually the only second language contact person. In a natural target language setting our student is immediately face to face with a number of native speakers. If she lives with a family, there are usually several individuals with whom she must communicate. In the most favourable situation there would be one person in particular, such as an exchange partner, who would act as a guide and friend, but she would also be in contact with other people who have different ways of speaking the target language. During an exchange visit, there is usually an opportunity for close contact with a few native speakers and for superficial contact with a variety of others. The reality of contact with native speakers is an essential experience for a second language learner.

Access to various target language settings

An obvious limitation of textbooks is that the settings are often stereotyped and usually very carefully controlled. In contrast, a visit or exchange has the merit of placing the learner immediately in a natural environment for language use. During her visit to France, from the moment of arrival to the time of departure, our young student finds herself in many different situations: in the street, at the university, at the home of her exchange partner, on a sports ground, or at a concert. Some of these situations may be fairly predictable, but others are not; they may even involve stress, through illness, accident, or personal relations. The language contacts are largely informal and mostly unrehearsed. The wealth and variety of situations that the target environment offers cannot be matched in a classroom. But this wealth and variety can also be daunting, and it may be more than the student can cope with.

Opportunity for authentic language use

While in a language class attention is usually mainly on the code, in a natural setting it is almost entirely on the message, on getting meaning across and on making sense of what one hears and reads. Usually there is no time to dwell on the formal features of the language. When she is in France our university student is exposed to the target language in a completely uncontrived way, and she uses the language as circumstances demand. The second language comes to her in day-to-day events in the home or in the street. The language contacts are even more productive if her visit is not simply as a tourist but involves study or work in the target environment. This legitimizes her presence, intensifies her participation, and increases her opportunities for target language use. The demands on her communicative skills are likely to be considerable: for example, she will have to cope with routine chit-chat and politeness formulas, make enquiries, listen to explanations, understand directions, use the telephone, take part in conversations, understand lectures, write essays, and provide information about herself and her home country.

Capacity for personal involvement

Whether or not this immersion in the second language environment is a positive experience leading to greater language proficiency and to closer personal contacts with native speakers depends not only on the opportunities described above, but also on the learner's background, motivation, and capability. For example, if she has an inadequate second language background, she may be completely overwhelmed and unable to cope with the opportunities offered. Instead of viewing the situation as a golden opportunity she may be confused, embarrassed, and disoriented, and she may shut herself off from any contact with native speakers. Even if she has had a year or two of instruction, she is likely to find that a natural target language environment is very different from a conventional language class. The student must attune herself to learning 'on the spot', and to coping with informal language learning; she must develop strategies of communication to help herself cope, and strategies for learning the language informally in a natural setting.

A classification of communicative activities

The classroom cannot recreate the full impact of life in a natural environment but it can provide some of its characteristics—and this is just what the communicative syllabus is designed to do. We can arrange communicative activities in descending order, ranging from those that are closest to the communicative reality of the target language milieu to those which are furthest removed from that reality but still retain certain characteristics of genuine communication:

1 Field experiences

1.1 Natural communication
- short-term visit to target language community
- study abroad
- student exchanges
- correspondence/pen-pal schemes
- video/cassette tape exchanges

1.2 Contrived arrangements
- L2 school
- total or partial immersion programmes
- other subject taught through L2 (sheltered classes)
- L2 'house'
- L2 day or lunch meeting
- L2 camp

2 Classroom activities

2.1 Classroom management
- student-teacher interaction (e.g. apologizing for being late)

2.2 Other routines
- instructions (e.g. ouvrez vos livres)
- rubrics for exercises
- explanations and verbal exchanges arising from other syllabuses

2.3 Invited native guest speakers

2.4 Topics and activities arising from learner's personal life
- self, personal background
- daily life events
- schooling
- family
- personal interests and activities
- professional activities
- beliefs, opinions, values

2.5 Substantive topics
- total or partial immersion
- subject matter content taught through L2 (e.g. sheltered psychology classes)
- study of literature

(continued overleaf)

2.6 Classroom exercises
- giving and following instructions
- information transfer
- information gap (techniques)
- jigsaw (techniques)
- problem solving
- informal talk tasks
- role-play, drama techniques, and scenarios

Figure 7.1 A classification of communicative activities according to their approximation to genuine communication

Communicative activities within a language programme are not necessarily in-class activities. As indicated in Figure 7.1, field experiences can be arranged which fulfil three main criteria of natural communication: contact with native speakers, experience of the milieu, and opportunity for natural language use (1.1). Field experiences can also be made available through contrived arrangements (1.2). While these do not provide an exact replica of the natural setting, they do represent close approximations. Contact with native speakers is arranged and the speaking situations are quite varied and natural, for example, second language days at school or a second language camp.

Within the language class it is also possible to arrange for communicative situations which can be roughly ordered on a scale, ranging from those that involve natural communication to those which are more contrived. Thus, classroom management and other routines (2.1 and 2.2) are real communication involving at least one native or quasi-native speaker (the teacher) interacting with the students. Another possibility is for a native speaker to be invited to the language class as a guest (2.3). The activities listed under 2.4, 2.5, and 2.6 would in most cases be carried out without native speakers. Nevertheless, 2.4 and 2.5 involve a motivated use of language and the transfer of real information, and therefore resemble natural communication even if the native-like milieu is missing. Finally, we find under 2.6 activities which may lack the motivated interest of 2.4 and 2.5, but which still have certain communicative features such as unpredictability of discourse, or information gap.[4] These classroom activities will be discussed in detail below. First, however, we will review the four characteristics of natural L2 communication from the point of view of language learning in the classroom.

Contact with native speakers

One of the most difficult problems in making classroom learning communicative is the absence of native speakers. In many parts of the world students have to learn English with little likelihood of seeing or hearing, let alone making personal contact with, a native speaker. In other countries the teacher is likely to be a native speaker. This has the obvious advantage of providing at least one contact person. But the presence of a single native speaker may have the disadvantage of distorting the varied reality of the native speech community. Any form of field experience, such as a short trip across the Channel for French or English children, gives at least an impression of the reality and diversity of target language speakers, and these short-term visits are invaluable (1.1). The need to provide a range of L2 contacts underlines the importance of inviting native speakers into the language class as guests (2.3). Other useful devices from this point of view are correspondence schemes, and exchanges of videotapes or cassettes.

While nothing quite replaces face-to-face contact with native speakers, there are other ways in which contact can be created vicariously, i.e. through well-chosen readings, sound recordings, or films. Literary texts (novels, short stories, essays, and poems as well as drama) can give insight into authors and their fictional characters, leading to greater understanding of the country concerned. Films can do the same, perhaps even more vividly than books. But the characters in a play, film, or book need interpreting. Do they correspond to real people or are they stereotypes or inventions which may distort the image of the native speaker? The students may not be in a position to judge; such interpretation needs the guidance of the teacher. Ideally, a communicative syllabus creates some kind of personal relationship between the learner and individuals in the second language environment. If by the end of the programme, students have had the opportunity for some kind of live contact with target language speakers, these experiences will usually fulfil one important purpose of a language course.

Access to a target language milieu

The advantages of direct access to a target milieu are obvious and wherever possible opportunities for such access should be an integral part of the course. This is sometimes difficult in foreign language settings where no target milieu is immediately accessible. In a second language situation, where the learner is surrounded by the target language community outside the classroom, it seems less important at first sight. But contacts with that community are often very restricted, and a second language class can make accessible a wider range of situations which in the ordinary course of events are not so easily experienced.

If access is not available on a regular basis, the next best thing is the creation of a special environment that recreates some of the characteristics of the target language milieu, i.e. 'contrived arrangements' (cf. 1.2

in Figure 7.1). They include: (a) the choice of a second language school, (b) the creation of a second language environment in which the L2 is used for instruction either all the time of part of the time, (c) another curriculum subject or substantive content taught via the second language, (d) a special 'house' or regular lunch meeting that creates the conditions of second language living within the school context, (e) a second language camp with social activities and sports that involve the use of the language, and (f) any of the above introduced on a reduced scale as activities in the second language class. The need to create a second language environment also justifies carrying out classroom management, routine exchanges and other communications in the second language (2.1). By creating a target language milieu within the language class the teacher sets up conditions for communicative events. To be successful this requires the co-operation of the students.

Each of these arrangements offers useful situations of language use. However, they all have their limitations, being much less varied, more routinized, and therefore more predictable than situations in the natural environment. Some of these deficiencies can be compensated for by deliberate measures. For example, in an immersion class the school subjects taught in the second language are normally covered comprehensively but students lack the opportunity to talk about their everyday lives beyond the school setting. This essential element of informal language use will, therefore, have to be deliberately introduced. With good will on the part of the students and the teacher's awareness of the limitations of such contrived arrangements, they can provide a very useful introduction to the target language milieu and to target language use in real-life situations.

Opportunities for language use with emphasis on the message

The use of the language for authentic discourse is the central condition for establishing a communicative activities syllabus. If neither direct field experience nor contrived arrangements are possible, we are left with this feature as the basic minimum requirement. Under normal field conditions, opportunities for target language use are constantly present. They range from language use for survival (finding an address, buying food, asking for accommodation in a hostel or hotel, ordering a meal, buying a plane or train ticket, using the telephone to make enquiries or appointments) to the use of the language in personal ways or for business or study, including attending a lecture course, taking part in professional discussions, or reading journal articles in one's special field. These are natural and diverse language uses all of which involve personal contacts with native speakers. Even under contrived arrangements, very favourable conditions can be set up for language use. Thus, as we have already noted, immersion and sheltered classes focus on the subjects being taught, while the 'mini-immersion' of weekends in a target language camp can offer useful short-term experiences which complement regular class activities.

Within the language class, topics and activities arising from the personal interests of students or those offered by the teacher—social, historical, or cultural activities, drama, arts and crafts, or other subject matter content—can be useful vehicles for motivated language use (cf. 2.4 and 2.5 in Figure 7.1). These should not be arbitrary activities chosen at random; ideally, they should be carefully selected to fit into an overall framework. If, for example, a literary text is chosen with a view to the age, maturity, and interests of the class it should engage them personally as readers. Texts are not only to be read, they can also be talked about for their aesthetic or human qualities, they often serve as historical or cultural documents, and episodes from literature can be re-enacted and re-created by the students.

The final category in Figure 7.1, classroom exercises (2.6), is perhaps the most widely used group of communicative activities. These activities commonly consist of tasks designed to have certain characteristics of natural discourse. They emphasize meaning and usually involve information transfer or information gap; they display a degree of unpredictability; and they require initiative on the part of the student in establishing communication. Many of the activities discussed in the literature fall into this category. There is no hard and fast distinction between these communicative tasks and those discussed in the previous section. They are simply less motivated by any particular personal interest. To that extent they can be regarded as less communicative in the sense in which the term is used here. But all of them provide some opportunity for authentic language use with primary attention to meaning.

The learner's personal involvement

Whether or not an activity is experienced communicatively by the students depends largely on the attitudes they adopt as learners. We have previously described communicative activities as participatory in character. That is, they invite the personal involvement of the students. Teachers can provide the necessary conditions, that is, they can arrange for native speakers to visit the class, they can create access to the target language milieu, or they can offer other opportunites for language use. But it is ultimately up to the learners whether they participate willingly, reluctantly, or not at all. We have already seen that although immigrants may have optimal opportunities for communication they may not be mentally prepared to seize the opportunity. Learners in the language class may react in a similar manner even to the most carefully prepared activities. On the other hand, a task which meets only one of the four communicative criteria may 'catch on' and create an excellent vehicle for learning.

The teacher has to exercise skill in overcoming resistance among the students, and in helping them to cultivate an interest in the target country. This interest manifests itself in their willingness to make contact with members of the L2 speech community through using the language either receptively or productively for some worthwhile purpose. One way of entering into contact is through the sharing of personal experiences. The most vital cross-cultural links are often created by people who have strong interests in common, for example, in music, sports, medicine, or science. Among the communicative activities listed in Figure 7.1, those under 2.4 offer a useful point of entry. If students are enabled to choose projects or activities which build upon their personal interests, this will enable them to communicate first with their teacher and members of their class and ultimately, when the occasion arises, with those in the target language community who share their interests.

To sum up, the prototype for communicative activities for second language learning involves four conditions: contact with native speakers, access to a second language environment, opportunities for authentic language use, and the personal involvement of the learner. A communicative activities syllabus attempts to recreate some or all of these prototype conditions.

Communicative activities in the language class

In this section the potential range of communicative activities in the classroom will be discussed. The literature provides many helpful suggestions (for example, Johnson 1982; Guntermann and Phillips 1981; Kramsch 1984) but it rarely considers the full range of possible activities and does not distinguish clearly enough between communicative activities and the functional analysis of communication (see Chapter 6). We will consider in a later section the relationship between these two aspects. Our main focus here is on topics and activities that lend themselves to introduction in the language class.

Communicative activities fall into four broad categories: (a) the conduct of the language class; (b) topics arising from and relevant to the learner's personal life; (c) substantive topics which are educationally or professionally significant; (d) communicative classroom exercises, i.e. small-scale activities that enable students to practise characteristic features of second language discourse. In much of the literature on communicative language teaching it is only the fourth category that is widely recognized and discussed, although some authors (for example, Krashen 1984; Krashen and Terrell 1983) also recognize categories (a), (b), and (c) as part of a communicative syllabus.

The conduct of the language class

Since the early days of the direct method it has been recognized that the conduct of the class itself forms an excellent opportunity for communication. In a typical direct method class the instructions given by the teacher ('Ouvrez vos livres à la page 15') and the rubrics of exercises ('Complétez les phrases suivantes') were always in the target language. It was recognized that these instructions and general classroom management helped to create a second language ambiance in the classroom and an opportunity for authentic communication. Since the direct method reforms it has been axiomatic for many teachers that the 'language of instruction' should be the second language. In some systems this is rigorously adhered to, in others there is a more tolerant compromise between use of the first and second languages. For example, the guidelines for the State of Hesse in Germany point out the usefulness of second language communication in the classroom, such as apologizing for being late, expressing wishes, making suggestions, and offering criticisms. They refer to the classroom as the primary communicative setting ('Primäre Kommunikationssituationen'). At the same time, these guidelines do not regard the second language as an absolute must and indicate situations where use of the mother tongue is quite appropriate and even to be preferred (Rahmenrichtlinien, 1980: 36 and 40).

In second language (as distinguished from foreign language) instruction, for example in language classes for Canadian immigrants, it is often inevitable that the target language is also the language of instruction, either because the students come from different countries or because the teacher has no knowledge of the students' native language. Where much of the classroom management takes place in the second language, this undoubtedly offers the student a regular opportunity for communicating in the target language. What has been lacking—in spite of the long history of this approach—is a systematic study of classroom language and its effective exploitation for second language learning. Studies of classroom discourse are useful, but on the whole they have not been undertaken as a source of guidance for classroom management in second language classes. More research in this area is needed.[5] It is likely that discourse analyses will reveal that school conventions in different countries vary, hence studies of this kind would not only offer examples of authentic communication but would also serve as an introduction to the culture of the school in the target community.

It is useful to look upon the other syllabuses—those that are not specifically labelled as communicative—as offering the most directly relevant topics for discussion in the second language class. The language syllabus requires talk about language, and the culture syllabus demands discussion of cultural topics. Similarly, the general language education syllabus will introduce questions about language and culture in general, and about language learning and how best to study. If many or all of the explanations and verbal exchanges arising from these syllabuses are carried out in the second language, they offer a rich field of relevant and purposeful discourse. It is a major policy issue for language teachers to determine the extent to which the other syllabuses should be used as vehicles for communication. If all classroom interactions are to be in the second language, it obviously limits what can be talked about. It is a challenge to the ingenuity of teachers to present complex topics, for example in culture and society, in a way that is comprehensible to the second language learner without distorting the information. Some teachers argue that in the early stages one should not limit classroom content to what can be presented in the second language but rather widen the scope of the discussion through the different syllabuses. This might be justified even though some of the information would have to be presented through the medium of the students' native language, or bilingually.

In short, the language class in itself—especially if it has a diversified curriculum—offers a good basis for communicative activity. The teacher can recreate in a controlled fashion and, therefore, in a manageable form certain of the characteristics of real-life communication. Classroom management, different topics and fields of discourse, and tasks implicit in the various syllabuses can present the learner with a rich variety of communicative events to react to, approximating the potential diversity of life in the target language community. In real life a person is constantly giving and receiving information, and an information-rich curriculum can recreate some of these conditions within the limits of the language class. We must recognize that a language is not normally used to talk about language but about other things, and these things must also have their place in the second language curriculum. The communicative syllabus is intended to take care of this relatively open category which we have divided into three topic areas. These topics will now be dealt with one by one.

Topics arising from the learner's personal life

For most learners it is important to recreate their own identity in the second language. A person's life-style, daily activities, interests, thoughts, in short his whole person, is bound up with his first language.

Any contact with native speakers of the target language requires that at least some experiences should be expressed in that language. Two prototype situations can be envisaged: the student as host entertaining a second language speaker, and the student as guest in the second language environment. These relationships can be rehearsed in the language class when students interact with each other in pairs, small groups, or with the teacher. Such classroom interactions do not have the same degree of authenticity and communicative force as real-life communication, but they can approximate to it if they are treated seriously. Interactions of this kind in the language class are not only a rehearsal; they become 'real' communication if the participants are encouraged to get to know each other and to treat the simulated situations as authentic.

There is no single inventory of topics that can be offered as universally applicable. The topics depend largely on the learners' personal situation, their dominant interests, and the relationships envisaged with the target community. Typically, learners provide information about themselves and enquire or receive information about the target language interlocutor on the following topics:

Self, personal background, and daily life: name and address, home town/village, country or place of origin, personal status, occupation. Customs vary as to how acceptable it is to talk about oneself or enquire into the circumstances of one's interlocutor ('How old are you?' 'How much do you earn?').

Daily life: normal routines, the main events of the year (festivals, special days), one's personal calendar.

Schooling: factual information about school and attitudes to it. The student's own status, interests, and aspirations. Comparison with the interlocutor's experience.

Family: in the case of young students talk is likely to be about parents, grandparents, brothers, and sisters. In the case of older students it would also include talk about one's marital status or children. Personal and family history and biographical reminiscences can bring individuals closer to one another. However, one may also touch sensitive areas of personal life and it is important to avoid lack of discretion in a language class.

Personal interests and activities: artistic, musical, literary, dramatic, sports and games, hobbies and leisure interests, such as stamp collecting, care of pets, sewing, carpentry, computers, gardening.

Professional activities: job, place of work, professional training, vocational skills, major interests, and aspirations.

Personal beliefs: opinions, values, convictions, and philosophy, including political and religious interests and activities. These may be areas which are particularly valuable for communication; they may also be sensitive and may not lend themselves to open classroom discussion.

In most situations of second language use, it is appropriate to show interest in the life of the target community and at the same time to be forthcoming about oneself. Often, where there are similar interests across the language barrier, such communalities create a bond of understanding. At the same time, it must be recognized that social customs vary in the extent to which it is acceptable to probe into personal matters. That which in one culture may be regarded as showing friendly interest may be condemned in another as unpardonable curiosity and infringement of privacy.[6]

Substantive topics

This set of topics is distinguished from the two previous ones in that they do not arise directly from the communicative demands of learning the language or from the immediate needs of the learner. Substantive topics are seen as being of educational relevance and as having merit in their own right. Although they derive from various approaches to second language teaching over a number of decades, most recently it has been Canadian immersion education which exemplifies this type of content-oriented approach most vividly. Years of research on immersion education have demonstrated, as Krashen has put it, that subject learning *is* language learning (cf. Krashen 1984). By learning a subject in the second language the subject matter is mastered and progress is made in the second language. This principle holds true whether all school subjects are taught in the second language, or one or two subjects only are offered in the second language in addition to formal language instruction. The so-called 'sheltered' psychology course offered experimentally in the University of Ottawa (Wesche 1984; Brinton *et al.* 1989) represents another application of the same principle. Several of the other contrived arrangements referred to in Figure 7.1 are further applications. In all these instances the learners become involved in some activity of inherent interest, a subject they wish to learn or a skill they wish to perfect. The activity is offered in the second language; thus the language is learnt through use in a significant situation and the activity is developed at the same time.

However, Krashen (1984) has pointed out that certain conditions have to be met both for the subject to be learnt and for language proficiency to be advanced. It is not simply indiscriminate exposure to the subject matter through the medium of the second language that is required. The delivery—lecture, readings, explanations, tasks expected of the student—must be adjusted to the students' level of proficiency. In Krashen's terminology, success depends on 'comprehensible input'. Therefore, the course designer and the teacher have to be conscious of the students' ability to cope with the new subject matter in an imperfectly known language. Teachers usually make these adjustments intuitively. For example, they explain terminology more carefully, they use more visuals and diagrams, their delivery is somewhat slower and more distinct, and the tasks assigned to students are appropriately scaled down. Students who have been exposed to this type of programme report that the use of the language for some other purpose helped them to gain confidence and advanced their proficiency (Edwards *et al.* 1984; Wesche 1984, 1985). It should, therefore, be regarded as a reasonable extension of a language curriculum to introduce subject matter—entire courses, themes from educational programmes, or other worthwhile topics—into the language course as one possible type of communicative activity. Any such substantive component would involve purposeful listening and reading, carrying out educational tasks involving the use of the L2, acquiring a technical vocabulary, and learning to be at home in a subject area through the medium of the second language (Brinton *et al.* 1989; Mohan 1986).

Combinations of subject matter and language teaching are of particular value to university students who are studying abroad and who find that they have difficulty in coping with courses designed for native speakers. Equally, immigrant children who have difficulty in coping with the regular school programme can be helped by special sheltered courses which combine subject matter and language teaching. This approach is also useful for language learners with special research or professional interests. When a language is being studied within a broader educational programme, it is appropriate to decide which topics within the other subjects can be taken up in the second language class. The aim should be to create a link which will enhance both the study of the language and the student's general education. In none of these cases, however, is it a question of arbitrarily picking topics from other school subjects. The choice of such topics should be clearly motivated and should make sense within the programme, and the justification should be equally clear to the student.

We have already observed that literary texts meet our criteria for a communicative activity remarkably well. In the first place, a literary text provides contact with a native speaker who has something to say. Second, a good text creates its own milieu and places the reader vividly in a particular target language setting. Third, literature is an example of authentic language use which conveys a significant message. The reading of a literary text demonstrates its truly communicative character when we find that our students insist on continuing to read a story because they are intrigued by the plot and wonder about the ending, when they laugh spontaneously at an amusing episode, or when a human problem, depicted through the story or fable, captures their imagination and arouses empathy. On these occasions students become directly involved in an issue through the literary message. Whether or not reading a literary text is a communicative activity depends very much on the way the text is treated in the classroom. The treatment might well include literary analysis or criticism that creates an awareness of the aesthetic structure of a play, the philosophical thought of a poem, or the human interest of a novel. In fact, anything that heightens the reader's awareness, including discussions or dramatizations which follow from the study of the text, makes reading a communicative activity within the concept of this syllabus.[7]

On the other hand, we would not regard as a communicative activity exercises which merely use the text for widening the reader's vocabulary or for the purely formal practice of unrelated linguistic items. The criterion for deciding what is not a communicative approach is any form of study or practice which treats the text as a linguistic specimen and, therefore, ignores its specific literary or human qualities. On the same grounds, we would also exclude from the communicative activities syllabus texts which are broken up and interrupted by grammatical exercises. As we have emphasized before, formal exercises do have their place in a language syllabus. But literary readings will lose their specific experiential contribution if they are simply treated as linguistic exercise material without regard for their literary quality.

Because teachers often find it difficult or lack the time to prepare projects which engage students in communicative activities, the OISE Modern Language Centre for many years prepared teaching units for French as a second language under the auspices of its Modules Project. Many of the modules or teaching units which this project produced consist of suggestions for substantive communicative activities. Some of these modules are addressed to younger children with relatively little French, others have been designed with older and more advanced students in mind. The focus of these units is on games (for example, *Le hockey*), general information, such as a unit on French newspapers in Canada (*Le journal: une introduction*), the making of maple syrup (*Le temps des sucres*), career possibilities for older students (*Le monde des affaires: carrières bilingues*), or literary-artistic interests (for example, *Chansons et chansonniers*, or *Gilles Vigneault: l'homme et l'oeuvre*). Some modules deal with such topics as the political careers of Pierre Trudeau and René Lévesque, together with their views on the Canadian political issues of federalism and separatism. The activities in these units involve the use of language which is directed to the treatment of the topic in question, not to providing vocabulary or grammar practice *per se*.[8]

For Canadian students aged between 11 and 14 who are learning French in school, it is an appropriate part of their curriculum to begin to think about planning trips to French-speaking parts of Canada. A grade 8 teaching unit prepared in the context of a national study of the French curriculum (see the Conclusion) is intended to capitalize on the students' own life experience, i.e. their knowledge about travel and activity planning (Duplantie, LeBlanc, and Tremblay 1986). The purpose of the unit is to give precise shape to such planning; for example, it draws attention to the principle that as travellers we should prepare ourselves mentally, read about the places we intend to visit, think about the time available and the costs involved, and ask ourselves what our interests and priorities are. The teaching unit is based on a visit to a largely French-speaking city, Quebec. In the course of the unit, the students examine brochures and are invited to make choices among the various attractions the city offers. The unit gives them the opportunity to consult written texts in French and listen to radio announcements, as well as gather information from an interview with youngsters of their own age. The students are further encouraged to apply what they have learnt to planning a visit to another city, or to work out plans for a French-speaking visitor coming to their home town. In short, the teaching unit focuses on travel planning and gathering information for a trip—not on any specific language items. The unit does include a language skills component in that it provides some training in 'skimming' a written text and in listening for the essentials in radio announcements. However, these skills are not treated abstractly and out of context; they are integrated into the activities involved in the preparation for a journey.

Communicative exercises

The activities we have discussed so far were based on 'motivated' topics. That is, they were not chosen at random, but arose logically and naturally from clearly defined situational, personal, or academic needs. Either they were class management transactions, or they arose naturally from the life experience of the learners, or they had an educational rationale and were based on substantive issues. This would not be the case for the present category of communicative activities, however. The topics themselves may be of no special interest, and therefore they are relatively weak from the communicative point of view. As we saw in Figure 7.1, they are the furthest removed from the prototype of communicative authenticity (2.6). What distinguishes communicative exercises from linguistic practice is that the teacher's intention is to provide opportunities for relatively realistic language use, focusing the learner's attention on a task, problem, activity, or topic, and not on a particular language point. If the intention is to practise a linguistic item or rule the activity would belong to the language syllabus. We want to emphasize this distinction so that both the linguistic and the communicative activity approach to language teaching are clearly identified.[9]

Guntermann and Phillips (1981) have proposed numerous exercises under the rubric of 'communicative course design' which according to our criteria fall more appropriately under language practice. This is because the critical factors are points of grammar, and it is these that form the basis for communicative practice. In each case, Guntermann and Phillips start from an important grammar point which manifests itself in certain communicative functions, and this leads to what they describe as 'real' activities and practice. For example, they suggest that the distinction between the imperfect and the present perfect in German (or between similar verb oppositions in French and Spanish) comes into use in recounting events. They therefore propose as an exercise that 'students pretend to be arriving home . . . and each tells a family member the main occurrence of his/her day' (1981: 335). In this role play the students must talk about past events. The focus is on the practice of the past tense and not so much on the interaction between parents and children. This type of exercise may be skillfully designed to embed practice in a natural context, but nevertheless the motivation is to practise a point of grammar.[10] In a communicative activity, as understood in this syllabus, grammar is not the organizing criterion. The focus is on the activity or topic, and not on a specific aspect of the code.

At least seven approaches to communicative exercise design can be identified in the literature: giving and following instructions, information transfer, information gap, the jigsaw principle, problem solving, informal talk tasks, and role-play and drama techniques.

Giving and following instructions

This is a simple but valuable communicative activity. It represents an important aspect of communicative teaching which Johnson (1982) has called the principle of task dependency. The use of the language is task-oriented, and learners experience the language at work. As a communicative activity the focus is not on the use of any particular grammatical form or speech function. The point is to experience the relationship between language use and task fulfilment. The action or task need not be complicated. In fact, in the early stages it is quite acceptable, and indeed very satisfying, for the learner to carry out very simple actions and tasks in response to an L2 command.[11]

Information transfer
According to Johnson, 'A central characteristic of communicative language teaching is that it focuses attention on the ability to understand and convey information content' (Johnson 1982: 164). In ordinary language use we often have to do such things as gather information from a timetable, relate a table or map to a text, or extract information from a diagram. This skill is obviously more advanced than giving and receiving instructions as in our first type of communicative exercise. In one of Johnson's examples, the information in a letter of application to a club has to be transferred to an official form (ibid.: 165). In order to perform this task one must have a sufficient command of the L2 to read and interpret the letter. At the same time the form helps direct the reader's attention to important items of information, thus facilitating the reading process. The skill developed by this classroom exercise will also be useful during a stay in the target country when one is likely to have to complete forms which require the handling of similar kinds of information.

Information gap
Among recent concepts for making communicative language teaching a reality, that of information gap has perhaps been the most widely employed. If A talks to B, A must assume that B does not already know in advance what A is going to say; otherwise there would be no point in talking. One of the criticisms that is often made of the question-and-answer routines of language teaching is that no information is passed between questioner and respondent. The teacher who asks the question already knows the answer, and the student answers in expected ways. Real questions and answers have an element of doubt and unpredictability, demanding choice and decision-making among the interactants. This element of unpredictability can be introduced in a number of ways. The simplest technique is to give the respondent an option so that the first speaker does not know in advance what the answer is going to be. For example, A gives B an invitation, which B either accepts or declines. By introducing an information gap, the first speaker has to adjust his response in a realistic way to the information he has received. Exercises involving an information gap thus create conditions which closely parallel real-life situations where the reaction of a speech partner is never perfectly predictable.[12]

The jigsaw principle
In a further development of the information gap principle, instructions or separate bits of information are given to two, three, or more groups of students. These groups must then communicate with each other and the co-operation among them leads to some sort of closure: making up a story or solving a murder mystery. In this arrangement, the members of

each group have first to communicate with each other and then the spokespersons for all the groups have to collaborate in the solution of the problem. Each group, so to speak, represents one piece of the jigsaw puzzle (for an example, see Klippel 1984: 49).

Problem solving
Some activities are designed to present students with problems, riddles, or puzzles which arouse their curiosity. To find the solution, pairs, groups, or the class as a whole are asked to think and talk about the problem. This kind of task involves use of the target language with a focus on the problem rather than on the language, and this is precisely why some teachers have found it a useful communicative activity.

Informal talk tasks
In her pioneering experiment on communicative language teaching, Savignon (1972) introduced a variety of informal talk tasks which, for many teachers, have remained the prototype of communicative language teaching. These tasks 'ranged from short (1–2 minute) exchanges between a student and a fluent speaker of French in a simulated situation to whole group discussions on topics of current interest' (Savignon 1972: 25). The emphasis in these activities was on getting meaning across, on the *what* of communication rather than the *how*. Some of the tasks had a certain affinity with the kinds of notions and functions which were at that time being evolved by the Council of Europe Project, for example, greetings, leave-taking, information-getting and receiving. To the extent that their focus is on the content of what is being said rather than on the practice of specific functions, they belong to this syllabus rather than to the functional analysis component of the language syllabus (see Chapter 6). The tasks were presented as short scenarios: 'An American in Chantilly wants directions to the museum'; 'A new French student needs directions to the library'; 'Tell the French student about yourself' (Savignon 1972: 28). Group discussions were popular 'because the participants were expressing their own ideas rather than performing in a hypothetical situation' (ibid.: 30).

Role-play and drama techniques
A final way of widening the communicative possibilities of the language class is by role-play, scenarios, and other drama techniques. The main interest of these techniques lies in the global use of language in lifelike situations. In many cases, these techniques approximate real-life language use to a remarkable degree (Livingstone 1983; Maley and Duff 1978; McRae 1985; Di Pietro 1987). The settings that can be imagined and simulated and the specific situations which can be described provide a context and a stimulus for realistic language use. The advantage of role-play lies in the fact that the use of language in a dramatic situation

is likely to include the full complexity of language use: emotional overtones, posture, gesture, and appropriate actions. The more closely the learner can identify with the role or task the more it provides a natural language experience.[13]

Levels of difficulty in communicative activities

Our discussion so far has made it clear that there are a great variety of communicative activities available for use in the language classroom. Such activities provide what has often been lacking in conventional language classes, i.e. opportunities to use the language in lifelike situations which are meaningful, non-trivial, of direct interest to students, and of educational value. In principle, such activities compensate for the limitations of the classroom. At the same time, they have the advantage that they can be selected in keeping with learner proficiency and experience and are, therefore, likely to be less overwhelming than the direct, constant, and unregulated exposure to language use in a natural environment which can be unmanageable and exhausting for the L2 learner.

One major problem that remains to be considered is how to allow for the limitations of the learner in planning communicative activities.[14] It is clear that many of the activities we have described presuppose an advanced level of proficiency. If it is assumed, as it is here, that communicative activities have a role to play in language learning at all levels, it is important to develop criteria by which to assess the difficulty of a communicative activity for learners of different degrees of proficiency. These criteria, supported by empirical data, could then be used in the development of a communicative syllabus. The following criteria are suggested:

The predictability-unpredictability dimension. Language teaching techniques have often been criticized on the grounds that much of the talk is predictable, and new information is rarely transmitted from the speaker to the listener. But authentic discourse outside the classroom also varies in its predictability. Many conversational routines in ordinary life—greetings, leave-takings, enquiries, requests, and politeness formulas in general—are fairly stereotyped. On the assumption that standard expressions are easier to learn it seems reasonable to introduce them fairly early in a teaching programme and to leave the more unpredictable uses of language for a later stage. In some contexts the teaching of such expressions could be regarded as a linguistic activity; but their use in the classroom is communicative and belongs to our area of communicative activities.

The receptive-productive dimension. Communication in its natural form does not make the clear distinctions between audiolingual-graphic skills or receptive-productive skills which are often made in language pedagogy. Whatever skills are needed in a given situation will be used. Nevertheless, there are activities in which the receptive skills predominate, and it can be assumed that in the early stages preference would be given to those activities in which the demand for productive skills is minimal. For example, in our discussion of communicative exercises we placed the carrying out of commands first because, at least to begin with, they do not involve production. In the Ottawa sheltered class experiment (Wesche 1984), productive demands (i.e. essay writing) were scaled down for the same reason and the emphasis was placed on learners' receptive skills.

Length of utterance. Brown and Yule (1983a: 16) in their analysis of conversational English make a simple distinction between 'short turns' and 'long turns': 'A short turn consists of only one or two utterances, a long turn consists of a string of utterances which may last as long as an hour's lecture'. It is obvious that long turns are more demanding than short turns in comprehension as well as production. This suggests that in the early stages of language learning preference should be given to activities involving short turns so as not to make too heavy a demand on the learner.

Contextual support. Communicative activities which are embedded in practical activities, for example, cooking while listening to instructions or doing art work under verbal guidance are easier to handle than, say, following an hour's lecture on philosophy. In school settings, subject matter drawn from history, which makes use of abstractions and relies mainly on speech or written text, is more demanding linguistically than art or physical education, both of which are visual and involve movement.

Linguistic complexity of content. If the subject matter is expressed with unfamiliar vocabulary or if the discourse structure is complicated, it may tax the learner unduly. If rapid exchanges among many participants are involved, as for example in an open discussion, the less experienced learner may quickly lose track of the argument. If the text is not straightforward but demands 'reading between the lines' or awareness of innuendo and irony, such high degrees of subtlety may also be lost on a reader or listener with a low level of proficiency.

Familiarity of content. Subject matter with which the L2 learner is familiar is easier to handle than topics which are entirely novel. For example, professional people—engineers, physicians, or educationists—can often establish rapport across language boundaries and deal with complex texts, simply because the subject matter is familiar to them. The less familiar we are with the issues involved or the theoretical concepts with which target language speakers are operating, the more difficult it is to understand L2 discourse.

Clarity and familiarity of delivery. If voices are clear or a text is legibly written they are more manageable for the L2 learner. Familiarity with the style of delivery or the format of the text is also helpful. For example, in some countries it is usual to print the table of contents at the end of a book while in others it is customary to have it at the beginning. Awareness of these external criteria of clarity and familiarity can help in deciding where to place a communicative activity.

Stress. Communicative activities are likely to be more difficult to engage in for a second language learner under conditions of stress, discomfort, fatigue, physical danger, emotional distress, or hostility than in a calm and positively toned situation. Affective considerations should also be borne in mind in the placing of communicative activities.

This discussion of levels of difficulty raises the question of whether an element of language control means that the activity is no longer 'communicative'. It is true that in the prototypical situation of communication in a natural environment there is no linguistic control in the sense that the learner is exposed to the language in the way the situation demands. In other words, the choice of language in a natural setting is not specifically directed to the needs of the second language learner. However, it does happen in native speaker discourse that the flow of speech is interrupted to clarify a point of grammar or to correct a mispronunciation. And a native speaker in a target language setting might well ask what a word means or check the spelling in a dictionary, so that code considerations momentarily interrupt the communicative flow.

Similarly, in a communicative syllabus the language aspect is subsidiary to the demands of the topic or situation. Even if the teacher pays attention to specific language items (grammatical structure, vocabulary, style, or intonation), the activity is communicative so long as the intention is to transmit meaning, rather than to focus on the code. It is, therefore, quite within the scope of the communicative syllabus to exercise a certain degree of linguistic control, which can best be visualized as a continuum.

At one extreme, there is no linguistic control; at the other, there is a great deal of control, i.e. the freedom of expression is hedged in by linguistic considerations. Nevertheless, the emphasis is still on the activity. A sheltered class at the University of Ottawa is quite rightly considered communicative because the emphasis is on learning the subject matter, psychology. In spite of the concern for content in this setting, language considerations also determine the rate of delivery, the use of visuals, and the type of assignments. Such a course falls approximately halfway between the extremes on our continuum.

Concluding comments

As we saw in the Introduction to this book, it is possible to distinguish two main trends in the ongoing debate on communicative language teaching. The first trend, which gave rise to the concept of a functional syllabus, is to base teaching on the insights of sociolinguistics and pragmatics and to develop a curriculum in terms of situations, social roles, and language functions. The second approach is to interpret the curriculum in terms of activities, topics, or tasks with the aim of involving the learner in authentic acts of communication without emphasizing the structural or functional aspects of the code. We have argued that these two approaches are not in conflict with one another but that they have contributed to language pedagogy in different ways. In order to formulate a coherent teaching policy, we must also distinguish between tasks in which the organizing principle is grammatical and those in which the focus is on the topic, message, or theme. A task stops being communicative only if the choice of activity has been prompted by purely linguistic considerations. As we have already indicated, the exercises devised by Guntermann and Phillips (1981) are linguistic in nature according to this criterion, even though the authors have worked out the communicative implications of the language points involved. Such exercises are of course valuable, but they fulfil a different function in the language programme. We believe that by recognizing the different contributions of grammatical analysis, functional analysis, and communicative activities, we will cover the range of approaches more adequately than if we fail to make these important distinctions.

Notes

1 See FCLT, pp. 405, 473, and 505–6 for a discussion of the code-communication dilemma.
2 On the Humpty Dumpty effect, see FCLT, pp. 183–4.
3 Prabhu (1987: 21), for example, writes: 'Perhaps the most important implication of generative grammar for second language pedagogy is that the grammatical descriptions used for constructing syllabuses or practice materials are hopelessly inadequate as descriptions of the internal system which learners have to develop in order to achieve grammatical accuracy in their language use. It is therefore unlikely that any planned progression in a grammatical syllabus would actually reflect or regulate the development of the internal grammatical system being aimed at'.

4 For example, the tasks devised by the Regional Institute of English in South India (Prabhu 1987) involve gaining information from maps and timetables. But the maps are not introduced as a means of working with maps in geography and the timetables are not presented with an eye to logical or mathematical thinking. These tasks are merely convenient vehicles of language use and as such are deemed suitable for use in the language class. Likewise, anecdotes and stories are not introduced for their literary or cultural interest; they are simply ways of challenging the students to think about a problem in English and thus use English for some purpose.
5 See Chaudron (1988) for a comprehensive review of studies on L2 classroom discourse and further references.
6 Stern (1980c) suggests an inventory for Canadian anglophone and francophone students at the high school level who are preparing for exchange visits, while Krashen and Terrell (1983) provide an inventory of topics which reflect the personal interests of American university students. It is easy to see that inventories of this kind can be treated quite non-communicatively. One can, for example, talk about jobs in general in order to extend one's vocabulary. Such talk becomes communicative to the extent that it is treated personally by the learners and applied to themselves or to a real or potential interlocutor.
7 For a discussion of literary reading in the communicatively oriented classroom see papers from a symposium of the Goethe House New York (Heid 1984). The book includes contributions in both English and German.
8 The French as a second language modules were prepared by a team of writers including Rebecca Ullmann (project director), Valerie Argue, Martha Balchunas, Joan Howard, and Joyce Scane, and were published by the Ontario Institute for Studies in Education between 1972 and 1982. For more details and a discussion of the Modules Project see Stern *et al.* (1980) and Ullmann (1987, 1990).
9 Clarke (1989) provides a synthesis of the issues in materials development relevant to communicative exercises and provides an extensive bibliography. Two books by Nunan (1988b, 1989) provide helpful suggestions for communicative exercises. Recent work on task-based language teaching is also relevant here. For the theoretical background, readers may refer to Long (1985) and Foley (1991). Candlin and Murphy (1987) provide further information on language learning tasks.
10 See also a collection of grammar games (Rinvolucri 1984) which are challenging and lively, but since their main purpose is the practice of grammatical features, for example, phrasal verbs, prefixes and suffixes, and the past and the present tense, they are

legitimately language activities rather than 'communicative' ones in the sense in which we have interpreted that term in this chapter.

11 An easy communicative exercise is the 'Sit down' and 'Stand up' of the classical direct method. It has been exploited as a language learning technique in various programmes, and has been most systematically developed as a distinct 'method' by Asher (1977). The method is known as Total Physical Response (TPR) because Asher attributes importance to the vigorous motor action carried out in response to the second language command. Krashen and Terrell (1983) regard TPR as useful at an early receptive stage of instruction when students are expected to respond by action rather than by verbalizations. For an account of TPR see Asher, Kusudo, and de la Torre (1983), and Richards and Rodgers (1986: 87–98).

12 A good many ingenious exercises have been developed along these lines, recreating in the second language some of the conditions of natural discourse. In order to apply these techniques, it is usually necessary to arrange the language class for pair work or in small groups (see Littlewood 1981). Allwright (1979) used the information-gap principle in an experimental remedial ESL course at university level. Part of the course was designed to provide information about the university and its programme, thus helping students to become acclimatized to their new environment. Information-gap tasks are also discussed by Nunan (1989).

13 It should be noted that drama techniques can be used for various purposes, not necessarily only as communicative exercises. They might, for example, have linguistic objectives, such as the improvement of pronunciation, learning of words through miming vocabulary items, or to practise a grammatical form. For example, Caré and Debyser (1978: 68–9) illustrate the practice of the conditional in French (tu devrais, tu aurais pu, tu n'aurais pas dû, etc.) with the following role play: husband and wife—the wife having been away for a time comes home and finds her flat in a deplorable state, dirty and untidy, beds not made, dishes not washed up, bills unpaid, and so on. The wife reproaches her husband: 'You could have . . . You should have . . .' creating endless opportunities for the use of the conditional.

14 Chapters 5 and 6 of Nunan's (1989) book deal respectively with the grading and sequencing of communicative language learning tasks.

8 The cultural syllabus

Introduction

Turning to culture, we deliberately shift focus away from language as such towards the people who use the language: where and how they live, what they think, feel, and do. It is nowadays a commonplace in language pedagogy to stress the importance of culture teaching and to say that language and culture are intertwined, that it is not possible to teach a language without culture, and that culture is the necessary context for language use.[1] It should be stated at the outset that we will not recommend a single and universal policy for culture. The policy is likely to vary depending on circumstances, types of students, and goals. What we will concern ourselves with are the grounds on which such a policy can be justified, and how we can best develop arguments for deciding what policy to adopt in a given situation.

Culture teaching derives from social and cultural anthropology, which aim to provide a comprehensive description of the way of life of a society. There is no question that culture, at least on paper, forms part of most language curriculums. In Britain it is called 'background studies',[2] which immediately defines its position as subordinate to language. In France it is often referred to as 'civilization'.[3] In Germany, where the concept probably originated, it is more usual nowadays to describe culture teaching as 'Landeskunde' (area study) rather than 'Kulturkunde'.[4] Whatever it is called, there has been a continuing history of this aspect of language teaching dating back at least to the early 1950s and even further to the beginning of the century.[5] An early expression of a broader perspective—not yet in terms of anthropological 'culture'—was a seminal British report *Modern Studies* (1918), which emphasized the need for a better knowledge of a country and its people as part of second language education. The concept of 'modern studies' was intended to convey this wider perspective more adequately than the traditional term 'modern languages'.

In the wake of World War II, under the growing influence of the social sciences, there was an increasing emphasis on the study of history, geography, and institutions as a necessary part of language learning. Nelson Brooks, the leading language teaching theorist of the 1960s, was one of the main advocates of a strong cultural component in second language curriculums. His major work, *Language and Language Learning* (Brooks 1964), contained a chapter on 'Language and culture' which emphasized an anthropological approach to the study of culture. In addition, in his speeches and articles Brooks argued eloquently for a consideration of the cultural aspect, outlining a wide-ranging concept of culture in the anthropological sense.[6]

A number of American language teachers have continued to make a case for culture.[7] The Northeast Conference on the Teaching of Foreign Languages has had a long-standing interest in this subject, going back to its beginnings in the 1950s. Since then, the publications of the Northeast Conference have regularly drawn attention to the importance of the cultural aspect in language teaching.[8] A wealth of suggestions on the classroom treatment of cultural aspects has been offered by Allen and Valette (1977); Lafayette (1978b); Rivers (1981); Hammerly (1982); Seelye (1984); Robinson (1987); and Damen (1987). On policy, content, objectives, and methodology there is a good deal of consensus among the writers. No major controversy has emerged, and there have been few changes in treatment over the last two decades. However, in spite of this strong endorsement by the theorists, the cultural component has remained difficult to accommodate in practice. It does not play a major role in most language curriculums, and there are only a few language courses where the cultural component is systematically treated.

Culture teaching in language classes has remained quite limited. For example, recent classroom observation studies carried out in Britain indicate that 'there is little emphasis on developing pupils' knowledge about the foreign culture' (Sanderson 1982: 131).[9] In the United States the President's Commission on Foreign Language and International Studies, which deliberated in the late 1970s, was prompted by similar concerns. The terms of reference coupled together foreign language studies and international studies, the latter covering approximately what is treated in this chapter under the term culture. The report of this commission criticized the inadequacies of both:

> The problem extends from our elementary schools, where instruction in foreign languages and cultures has virtually disappeared, to the threatened imminent loss of some of the world's leading centers for advanced training and research on foreign areas.
> (USA 1979: 1)

In order to develop a policy on culture teaching we must try to explain the gap between the broad theoretical consensus we have noted and the lack of impact of the culture concept on language classes. We will suggest that the reasons for this discrepancy lie in certain difficulties presented by culture teaching which have tended to be glossed over in the literature. The writers have no doubt done this in good faith because they wished to show that culture teaching is not only valuable but also feasible. A sound policy on culture depends on our willingness to recognize the difficulties and problems it has presented; and it is only if we make efforts to overcome these impediments that culture teaching will take its legitimate place in second language education.

In our view, the following four issues have to be dealt with: (a) the vastness of the culture concept; (b) the problem of goal determination and the lack of accessible information; (c) questions of syllabus design and the difficulty of according an appropriate place to culture in a predominantly language-oriented curriculum; (d) questions of teaching procedures and the difficulty of handling substantive subject-matter in a mainly skill-oriented language programme.

The concept of culture

The concept of culture, which has to be understood before we can attempt to determine the topics and goals of culture teaching, is notoriously difficult to define. Looked at historically, we can identify two stages. Before World War I and in the inter-war years it was beginning to be recognized that in order to make sense of a particular language and literature some systematic understanding of the country and its people was needed. The study of the history, geography, and institutions of the country was regarded as a useful background and complement to language and literary studies. Such cultural teaching also included the great accomplishments of the target community in the arts, music, and drama, as well as in scientific discovery, sports, and whatever other achievements the people take pride in. In France, courses on 'civilization' often dealt with these broad areas of national heritage, which began to form part of a language teacher's background knowledge. After World War II the growth of social science, in particular anthropology and sociology, led to a different emphasis. Based on the application to modern western societies of a concept of culture which derived from anthropological studies of tribal societies in the inter-war years, social science laid emphasis on what is often referred to as the 'way of life' or 'life-style' of a community. This concept is hard to define but it refers to typical behaviour in daily situations, i.e. personal relationships, family life, value systems, philosophies, in fact the whole of the shared social fabric that makes up a society.[10]

Since the 1950s, it has been increasingly recognized that knowledge of a country as a component of language teaching should emphasize this way-of-life culture. It received particular emphasis because the earlier concept of humanistic or 'Olympian' culture—the great achievements of a nation—was already recognized, whereas this newer and less clearly defined but powerful notion had to establish itself in the minds of language teachers. The theorists recognized both concepts as legitimate, and since the 1960s various labels have been used to indicate the two approaches. The traditional concept of culture as great achievements, refinement and artistic endeavour, or in Brooks' terms 'formal culture', is widely referred to as 'Culture with a capital C'. This contrasts with way-of-life culture, or in Brooks' terms 'deep culture', which is referred to as 'culture with a small c'. The combination of these two very wide and diverse approaches has led some writers to abandon the attempt to define culture. For example, Seelye, refusing to offer a precise definition, simply describes it as 'a broad concept that embraces all aspects of the life of man' (1984: 26).

Some writers, faced with the problem of such an encyclopedic definition, have tried to reduce the vast and amorphous nature of the culture concept to manageable proportions by preparing lists of items or by indicating a few broad categories. In Brooks' view, for example, 'culture is best imparted as a corollary or an obbligato to the business of language learning' (1964: 89). Accordingly, he lists some sixty topics and questions which will provide an informal introduction to the daily life of the country whose language is being learnt. The following are examples from Brooks' list:

> *Childhood literature.* What lyrics, rhymes, songs, and jingles of distinct aesthetic merit are learned by all young children?
>
> *Discipline.* What are the norms of discipline in the home, in school, in public places, in the military, in pastimes, and in ceremonies?
>
> *Pets.* What animals are habitually received into the home as pets? What is their role in the household?
>
> *Yards, lawns and sidewalks.* What are the equivalents of American back yards, front lawns, and sidewalks in residential and business areas? What is their importance in the activities of young people?
> (Brooks 1964: 91, 94)

The list offered by Brooks focuses particularly on the everyday culture of young Americans who approach a foreign culture with their own interests and values in mind. Chastain (1976: 389–92) offers a similar list of forty-four topics ranging from typical student activities and education to the social and economic systems, the press, good manners, women's liberation, and other general topics. Chastain (1988: 304) presents a revised and shortened list of topics. Both Brooks and Chastain emphasize that their lists are not exhaustive. They focus on topics which are likely to be of interest to language learners at the secondary school level or in undergraduate courses at university. There is no indication where the information on these topics is to come from. It is probably assumed that the teacher is knowledgeable enough to be able to supply the data. Nor is there any suggestion that the cultural data should be more than isolated gobbets of information which are seen as being 'interesting' and 'stimulating'. There is no attempt to provide a unified concept of the country which will have a specific function in the treatment of the target language.

To overcome the fragmentation resulting from the presentation of cultural titbits, Nostrand (1978) developed a scheme referred to as the Emergent Model which classifies observations under a few broad headings:

1 **Culture:** value systems, habits of thought, assumptions about reality, verifiable knowledge, art forms, language, paralanguage and kinesics
2 **Society:** organized under institutions: familial, religious, economic and occupational, political and judicial, educational, interactional, intellectual and aesthetic, and recreational; the mass media; stratification and mobility; social proprieties (*le savoir-vivre*); status by group and sex; ethnic, religious and other minorities
3 **Conflicts:** interpersonal and intergroup conflict, intrapersonal conflict
4 **Ecology and technology:** exploitation of physical resources, exploitation of plants and animals, demographic control, health care and accident prevention, settlement and territorial organization, travel and transportation
5 **Individual:** integration at the organismic level, intrapersonal variability, and interpersonal variation
6 **Cross-cultural environment:** attitudes toward other cultures and toward international and supranational organizations

Figure 8.1 Nostrand's (1978) Emergent Model of cultural analysis (adapted from Seelye 1984)

As can be seen from Nostrand's classification, these headings demand a comprehensive as well as a detailed scholarly approach to the country in question. Nostrand does not suggest that the information under all six headings must be complete in order to understand a culture. The headings simply help the observer to place his observations in a context. From observations under these six headings Nostrand tries to derive a few basic themes which characterize a society and give it unity and a specific character. He argues that it is through evolving a few major themes that we come to understand a culture.[11]

As we have seen, Seelye (1984) refuses to define culture. In order to avoid getting lost through using too broad a concept he proposes that human beings in any society have to meet certain basic physical and psychological needs, and that the conventional way they meet these needs provides an entry to an understanding of their culture.[12] This approach is less structured than Nostrand's classification, but it provides a useful basis for deciding what human beings in different societies have in common and what distinguishes these societies from each other:

> People everywhere are impelled to satisfy certain basic needs such as for food and shelter, for love and affection, and for self-pride. Man has banded together to meet these needs. Predictably different bands of people have developed different ways of doing so.
> (Seelye 1984: 28)

None of the schemes we have reviewed so far is easy to apply. Brooks and Chastain require a factual information base which one cannot expect the classroom teacher to have without a resource guide. Moreover, because of their vastness and diversity, the inventories lack coherence. In contrast to these two examples, Nostrand's scheme has greater unity and makes an attempt to discover underlying patterns in the observed cultural phenomena. But it is not so much a framework for a cultural syllabus as an ambitious research tool which could be used to develop portrayals of different cultures. Seelye's approach via basic psychological and physical needs has the same weaknesses as Nostrand's. It merely provides an approach to the study of culture from a particular perspective. It suggests a research approach rather than offering the basis for a teaching syllabus.

A simple and useful threefold classification has been suggested by Hammerly (1982) which combines traditional and anthropological concepts. This scheme is much more clearly geared to the demands of learning a second language than any of those we have so far considered. Hammerly distinguishes between: (a) information (or factual) culture, (b) behavioural culture, and (c) achievement (or accomplishment) culture.

> *Information (or factual) culture.* 'This refers to the information or facts that the average educated native knows about his society, the geography and history of his country, its heroes and villains, and so on' (1982: 513). 'The second-language learner who wants to communicate with native speakers must somehow get a sense of the world view native speakers have of themselves and their own country' (1982: 514). This criterion gives informational culture a definite direction and at the same time limits it to manageable proportions.

> *Behavioural culture.* This is Hammerly's (1982: 515) interpretation of anthropological, way-of-life culture which he claims to take largely from Nostrand and from Seelye's principle of physical and psychological needs. It is defined as typical 'actual behaviour plus attitudes, values, etc.' Hammerly regards this as the most important aspect of

culture for second language learning: 'Behavioural culture—especially conversational formulas and kinesics—is the form of culture most important to successful communication' (ibid.). The problem of lack of definition and vastness in the interpretation of culture is not resolved in this formulation.[13]

Achievement (or accomplishment) culture. This is the traditional concept of 'artistic and literary accomplishments' (ibid.) which Hammerly recognizes but regards as less important than behavioural culture for second language learning.

While Hammerly's classification does not solve the problem of the range of cultural topics, the threefold distinction is useful in that it brings together humanistic and anthropological concepts and introduces a helpful division into a number of categories which are particularly well adjusted to the needs of the second language classroom.[14]

In trying to define the area to be covered by culture in second language teaching, we have to be clear about the relationship between language and culture, or language and society. In the 1960s when the study of culture was vigorously advocated, the emphasis was not only on culture in the anthropological sense; it was also an emphasis on the relationship between linguistic phenomena and social events, social structure, social stratification, and cultural referents. At that time—in North America at least—linguistics was distinctly asocial and even asemantic, and language was studied mainly in terms of its formal characteristics. One powerful argument for the teaching of culture was that it provided the necessary contact between language on the one side and society, culture, and real life on the other. Since the late 1960s, language has begun to be viewed increasingly in social, pragmatic, and semantic terms. Sociolinguistics as a discipline has established itself. Discourse analysis has related language to interpersonal realities. In other words, a whole area which in the past had been one of the main justifications for a cultural emphasis is now part of the treatment of language itself.

The question we have to ask is whether there is a place for cultural studies in which the emphasis is not so much on sociolinguistics but rather on aspects of culture 'beyond language', such as human relations, way of life, social organization, and the factual and accomplishment cultures to which reference is made in the literature on culture teaching. There is no question in our mind that a foreign language must be studied sociolinguistically. But in addition, a language course demands that the learner should come as close as possible to the people who use the language, the way they live, what they do, think, and dream. We believe that the reality of people and places constitutes the specific contribution of a culture syllabus. Although the central focus of culture teaching is not language but people, places, and actions, this reality manifests itself also in language, and therefore the linguistic manifestations of culture cannot be ignored. However, in the language syllabus the linguistic phenomena are central and the sociocultural aspects peripheral, while in the culture syllabus it is the other way round. In this way the role of a culture syllabus is clearly defined and complementary to a language syllabus.

Cultural goals

The theory of culture teaching which evolved during the 1960s and 1970s was influenced by a simultaneous emphasis on behavioural objectives in education. Writers on culture were eager to show that, even if the concept of culture was somewhat vague, cultural goals could be expressed in clear and unambiguous terms. The writings of Seelye, and also Valette's work on testing, have been prominent in the attempts to demonstrate that cultural goals can be made operational in the classroom (Seelye 1970b, 1984; Valette 1977).

In specifying objectives, most authors have adopted Nostrand's simple formulation that the overall goals of cultural teaching are cross-cultural understanding and cross-cultural communication. The first of these is a highly cognitive goal for which Nostrand devised the Emergent Model. This demands a detailed analysis of a culture and an attempt at a subsequent synthesis through the discovery of the main themes of the culture. Nostrand had thus set the stage for a cognitive approach to cultural objectives. However, in Nostrand's theory understanding by itself would not be enough if the student kept the foreign culture at arm's length. The teaching of culture should lead him to experience the culture directly through contact with native speakers and through developing some sort of personal relationship with the target language community. In other words, Nostrand recognized that culture teaching involves, besides the cognitive, a social and affective component.

Nostrand's formula of the goals of culture teaching as cross-cultural understanding and cross-cultural communication has been basic to the more operationally expressed objectives, for example, in the writings of Valette (1977); Lafayette (1978b); Hammerly (1982); and Seelye (1984). Thus, Seelye describes the goals of culture teaching as seven skills to be developed in the learner:

1. *The sense, or functionality, of culturally conditioned behaviour.* The student should demonstrate an understanding that people generally act the way they do because they are using options the society allows for satisfying basic physical and psychological needs.
2. *Interaction of language and social variables.* The student should

demonstrate an understanding that social variables such as age, sex, social class, and place of residence affect the way people speak and behave.

3. *Conventional behavior in common situations.* The student should indicate an understanding of the role convention plays in shaping behavior by demonstrating how people act in common mundane and crisis situations in the target culture.
4. *Cultural connotations of words and phrases.* The student should indicate an awareness that culturally conditioned images are associated with even the most common target words and phrases.
5. *Evaluating statements about a culture.* The student should demonstrate the ability to make, evaluate, and refine generalities concerning the target culture.
6. *Researching another culture.* The student should show that she has developed the skills needed to locate and organize information about the target culture from the library, the mass media, people, and personal observation.
7. *Attitudes toward other societies.* The student should demonstrate intellectual curiosity about the target culture and empathy towards its people.

(Seelye 1984: 9)

Seelye's goals, except for goal 3 which is behavioural and goal 7 which is affective, are strongly cognitive in their orientation. The same applies to Valette (1977), who summarizes the goals of culture teaching in five categories:

1. *Cultural awareness*, comprising geographical knowledge, knowledge about the contributions of the target culture to world civilization, knowledge about differences in the way of life as well as an understanding of values and attitudes in the second language community.
2. *Command of etiquette*, i.e., polite behaviour.
3. *Understanding of daily life*, including unfamiliar conventions, such as writing a cheque or reading a timetable.
4. *Understanding of cultural values*, requiring the interpretation of the target culture and the learner's own culture.
5. *Analysis of the target culture*, based on theories of cultural analysis such as the Emergent Model or Basic Needs.

Except for category 2 and in certain respects 3, which are behavioural, Valette's list implies an informational and analytic approach to culture teaching.

Hammerly (1982), basing himself partly on his threefold analysis of culture into factual, behavioural, and achievement culture, and partly on Nostrand and Seelye, comes up with the following list of ten goals in an approximate order of difficulty for second language learners:

1. Knowledge of the cultural connotations of words and phrases.
2. Knowledge of how to behave in common situations.
3. The development of interest and understanding toward the second culture.
4. Understanding of crosscultural differences.
5. Understanding of intracultural institutions and differences.
6. Research-like projects.
7. Development of an integrated view of the second culture.
8. Ability to evaluate statements about the second culture.
9. Development of empathy toward a second culture and its people.
10. Academic research on second cultures.

(Hammerly 1982: 522–24)

In spite of differences in terminology and emphasis, there is consensus between these and other lists of objectives. All of them stress, above all, the cognitive goals of culture learning: knowledge about the target culture, awareness of its characteristics and of differences between the target culture and the learner's own culture; and a research-minded outlook, i.e. willingness to find out, to analyse, synthesize, and generalize. Also included in this cognitive set of objectives is an emphasis on understanding the sociocultural implications of language and language use. At the same time, nearly all of these lists recognize the affective goals of culture teaching: interest, intellectual curiosity, and empathy. Finally, they all acknowledge a behavioural component, both receptively in that students should be able to interpret culturally relevant behaviour, and expressively in that they should have the ability to conduct themselves in culturally appropriate ways. Hammerly makes the point that 'behavioural culture should be emphasized throughout the second language program, at the beginning and intermediate levels in particular' (1982: 515), and Robinson (1985: 99) emphasizes the development of 'cultural versatility', i.e. 'modifying one's own cultural repertoire'. On the whole, however, the behavioural aspect, sociocultural proficiency, receives far less attention than linguistic proficiency in the approach to language.[15]

The attempt to define goals of culture teaching, in comparison with the teaching of language, suggests a marked shift from an emphasis on competence or proficiency, that is an intuitive mastery of language, to a strongly cognitive orientation in the teaching of culture. As we saw earlier (Chapter 3), it is legitimate for different syllabuses to have different objectives, because each syllabus makes its own demands and pursues its characteristic goals. Culture, according to the theorists we have considered, is more akin to social studies or literature and therefore adds a new dimension to language teaching. Culture teaching, according to this conception, is less skill-oriented than it is problem-oriented, fact-finding, and evaluative. Although these qualities are known to be useful in the treatment of the language syllabus, many teachers have not been schooled in the corresponding techniques for the treatment of culture. The literature has, on the whole, failed to point out the difference in emphasis between the approach to culture and the approach to language. This difference in goals between language and culture has added another difficulty to overcome in the treatment of culture in second language education. In order to discuss some of the problems, we propose to distinguish the following aspects: (a) the second language learner's perspective, the native speaker's perspective, and the perspective of scholarship; (b) the goals of culture teaching; (c) the areas that make up the content of culture teaching; (d) the current lack of resources.

Three perspectives on culture

The second language learner's perspective. A weakness in the treatment of culture has been that the different perspectives under which it can be studied have not been clearly distinguished. While the aim of an anthropologist is to pursue a particular hypothesis or to develop as full a description of a society as possible, for the language learner the culture has a different significance. Where the language is learnt as a foreign language the target community is usually physically and psychologically distant, for example when English is learnt in Argentina or French in Australia. In these cases culture teaching is a guarantee that real people in real places use the target language as a normal means of communication. Culture teaching provides the context without which the language remains an empty code and lacks credibility from the learner's perspective. For immigrants or foreign students learning the language in the host community the reality of the culture is not in question, but culture teaching offers the opportunity for a carefully planned introduction to the new environment.

Both groups of learners approach the target language community and its culture with certain presuppositions and expectations. The literature has pointed out that culture teaching should help to overcome prejudice and stereotypes which can prevent learners from coming to terms with the reality of the target culture. There is a tendency among novice learners to generalize from limited experience and, as it were, to sit in judgement on the new culture. New cultural experiences—for example, food habits, sleeping conventions, customs of greeting and farewell—almost inevitably provoke comparisons with the learner's home culture.

Most writers on culture teaching have drawn attention to the different ways in which learners come to terms with a new culture and how their approach to it changes over time. The process of 'acculturation' has been described by Schumann (1978); Brown (1980), and others. Acculturation is likely to be different in the following situations: a foreign language learner on a short visit to another country; a learner living in the host community as an immigrant; or a learner in a bilingual country learning the language of the other speech community.

Hammerly (1982: 524–5) states categorically that we can become bilingual but not bicultural. Schumann (1978), however, shows that a target language and culture can be approached in different ways depending on how we view our own culture in relation to the other culture. He distinguishes three typical strategies: assimilation, preservation, and adaptation. In the case of assimilation, language learners give up their own life-style and values and adopt those of the target group. Preservation involves maintenance of the native life-style and values and rejection of the target language group. Adaptation is an attempt to preserve one's own life-style, while also adopting and incorporating elements of the target language culture. In other words, adaptation is an attempt to become bicultural. These distinctions are particularly applicable to immigrants, but there are parallels in the attitudes of foreign language learners.

Besides these fundamental differences in outlook towards the target language community, Schumann, Brown, and others have drawn attention to different phases in cultural adjustment. After the initial excitement, an individual suffers culture shock. Gradually he recovers and comes to terms with many features of the new culture while others continue to disturb him. This is a prolonged phase of culture stress. It gradually merges into the final stage when the learner accepts the new culture depending on his overall assessment of himself in relation to the new culture and the country of origin. At this fourth stage the learner displays one of the three strategies we have already described: assimilation, preservation, or adaptation. These stages and strategies cannot be fully controlled by teaching, but sensitive teaching can influence them. A teacher must make some kind of assessment of the situation of the students, and the purpose of language and culture learning, and on this basis help students to approach the new culture in the most constructive way.

The native speaker's perspective.[16] One of the most important aims of culture teaching is to help the learner gain an understanding of the native speaker's perspective. Nostrand and others have drawn attention to the development of empathy, that is, the ability to look at different aspects of life the way they appear to members of the target language community. This perspective gives culture teaching a definite direction, and makes it much more manageable, relevant, and appropriate. For example, culture teaching schemes usually refer to the geography and history of the target community as a broad topic area for the cultural syllabus. If we did not adopt the native speaker's perspective, these two subjects could become quite unmanageable within a second language course; a comprehensive and detailed study of the geography or history of the target community is out of the question. What matters from this point of view is to sensitize the learner to the way places, persons, and historical events are perceived by ordinary members of the speech community. This means that the geography or history aspect of culture teaching is not necessarily that which a geographer or historian would present. The question we are asking is how native speakers view their own country and their own history. What qualities do native speakers commonly associate with the capital city, the seaside, the mountains, a resort, a port, an industrial centre, the countryside, and so on? What historical personalities do they know, and what do they mean to them? What symbols of nationality have significance?[17]

Of course, native speakers are not a homogeneous group. It is, therefore, also important to gain an understanding of the range of common knowledge, to note differences in viewpoints and opinions, and even to discover conflicting views on the same subjects. These personal perceptions, attitudes, items of information, or opinions can be learnt by talking to native speakers, asking questions and expressing an interest in what is said, by listening attentively, by watching what people do, and by reading newspapers, advertisements, announcements in magazines, and fictional or non-fictional literature. It is a matter of becoming sensitive to the state of mind of individuals and groups within the target language community. The research skills that some culture teaching schemes include (for example, Seelye's goals 6 and 7, and Hammerly's goal 4) are intended to cultivate this awareness and empathy, which in essence make up a large part of Nostrand's concept of cross-cultural understanding.

The scholarly perspective. While the first and second perspectives focus on the subjective views of the learner and members of the target community, there is also an important place for scholarly enquiries which provide a more detached and objective view of the target culture. Such enquiries would use the normal research and study techniques of the relevant disciplines: geography, history, and the social sciences, as well as the humanistic studies of literature, history of art, or musicology. In a later section we will have more to say about research data for culture teaching. Here we merely wish to point out that the scholarship of the social sciences and humanities provides a more objective, systematic counterweight to the subjective and informal approach of the two previous perspectives. The three perspectives complement each other and can be considered equally valid but distinct. The literature on culture teaching has too readily assumed that the approach to culture is either that of the humanities or that of social science. The informal and subjective perspective has never been completely left out but it has not been assessed for what its specific contribution might be.

Summary of cultural goals

The goals of culture teaching have already been expressed as proficiency, cognitive, and affective objectives. The transfer objective, which takes us beyond the teaching of the particular culture, will be treated separately later. Parallel to the teaching of language, the teaching of culture can be regarded as leading to a generalized sociocultural competence, to certain sociocultural skills, or to specific socioculturally appropriate behaviour. For a westerner learning another western language and culture, the cultural competence demanded is often very similar to the behaviour he can derive from his native cultural experience. The two cultures, say, of Italy and English-speaking Canada, may not be alike in every respect, but they are likely to have much in common, and it is only where they are different that sociocultural competence has to be acquired, or particular skills or behaviour patterns have to be learnt.

Unfamiliar conventions, such as how to write a cheque (Valette 1977: 274) or how to read a railway timetable (Valette 1977: 272), are relatively simple behavioural items which it is important for the learner to master. Other conventions and practices may be part of a group of skills, such as eating behaviour, which reflect certain prevailing attitudes in the society or which relate to a whole set of understandings. Culture teaching is to a large extent behavioural and should lead to cultural proficiency; that is, the learner is acquiring the skills to conduct himself in socioculturally appropriate ways. Valette has described this aspect as etiquette, others have called it manners, others again have referred to it as customs. There is usually a range of options within which individuals can exercise their choice. On the other hand, customary conduct as well as other features of the culture express certain principles, relationships, or thoughts which the learner needs to be guided to perceive and understand. The literature has made amply clear that these involve cognitive learning in that they invite observation, analysis, problem solving, and comparison.

Cultural events of any importance also imply affective states of mind. Most foreigners react emotionally to the food conventions of the new culture with feelings of pleasure or displeasure which, according to cultural expectations, may be expressed or covered up. Expressions of emotion, such as the joy of greeting, the sadness of farewell, or attitudes displayed at a wedding or a funeral, are deep-seated psychological events in response to fundamental human needs, as Seelye has reminded us. But the way emotion is expressed on these occasions is to some extent conventionalized and may differ among different language groups. In some societies, for example, it is customary to play down the emotions of greeting or farewell or the act of congratulating; in others, individuals or groups are expected to 'let go'. For learners it is not only a question of understanding the affective characteristics of a cultural event, they must come to terms internally with the values and emotions expressed in the new culture. Learning a new culture implies affective learning.

The content of culture teaching

The various schemes of cultural description we have examined have been devised to give as comprehensive an account as possible of a given culture. They are based on a combination of humanistic and anthropological categories. The tendency has been to make them too encyclopedic and not to gear them to the specific needs of the second language learner. If we try to remember the second language perspective we can keep the areas for a cultural syllabus to manageable proportions. We will now discuss six topics covering those aspects of culture teaching which the average language learner is most likely to require.

Six aspects of culture teaching

Places. The learner needs some sense of physical location to which to relate the target language. In the case of immigrants, it is obvious that the places they must get to know are those where they have taken up residence. But the immigrant learner still needs an orientation to the geography of the country as a whole. If we are designing a syllabus for a foreign language learned at a distance, a choice has to be made of a particular country or region to be considered as the main target area, ranking other possible areas in an order of priority. In choosing a target area, our principal concern will be to describe how the geography is perceived by native speakers. In Canada, for example, it is the narrow fringe closest to the United States which is the most inhabited. 'Going up north', as might be said by a person living in Toronto, suggests not only travel in a northerly direction but a trip to less inhabited parts of the country where it is customary to go on vacation. Therefore, 'going up north' calls up mental associations in native speakers of 'getting away from it all', relaxing, and having a holiday. 'Up north' is also 'cottage country', or it might also be expressed as 'going to the cottage'; that is, in the less inhabited north there is vacation property, and those living and working in the south, in an industrialized urban area, sometimes have or dream of having a cottage or hideaway, which is often more primitive than an apartment in the city, but which is one's own and close to nature. An ESL learner in Canada, therefore, must understand that the native speaker's 'cottage', 'going to the cottage', or 'going up north' have a specific meaning that would not necessarily be the same in London or Sydney. It is part of the psychological geography of Canada which a language learner who wants to familiarize himself with the social setting needs to know about. To acquire this personal native speaker's geography does not preclude a more objective approach. But for language learning, this affectively tinged view of the physical environment is often as important as the objective study of street plans or maps.[18]

Individual persons and way of life. In culture teaching, as we have emphasized, the focus is primarily on people, how they live, and what they think, value, and do. Consequently, this second topic area is perhaps in many ways the most important. Personal contact with a native speaker, a family, or a small group of friends will help to make the language a living reality. Through personal contacts, visits, or residence in the community, the learner can become familiar with the local life-style. By making contact with everyday life, by observing it, and asking questions about it, the learner can get attuned to the customs of the community. Beyond that he can gradually explore the prevailing thoughts, values, expectations, antagonisms, fears, and problems of the individuals concerned. Of course, we cannot generalize from one person or a small group to an entire country or region. But getting to know one individual can give the learner an entry into this aspect of a culture. Coming to terms with the way of life of a community is partly cognitive. We have to observe and interpret what we see and hear. But it is also strongly behavioural in that a foreigner will be expected to conform to certain customs and expectations, such as the etiquette of removing shoes on entering a house, or eating behaviour at a meal.[19]

People and society in general. The learner should be led to identify significant groups indicative of social, professional, economic, and age differences, as well as those which reflect regional characteristics. Once again, it is not necessary to undertake an 'objective' enquiry in the manner of a sociologist or social anthropologist. If we adopt the native speaker's perspective, it is much more a matter of finding out how people view themselves in relation to various groups in society or in relation to society as a whole. Do they think of themselves as upper, middle, or working class? How do they look upon other people in their society? Do they have strong, weak, or no religious affiliations? Are there social, racial, or regional prejudices in their community? Are people peaceful and friendly with each other, or afraid, hostile, or suspicious? Do they help each other, compete, fight, or gossip? Do they take an interest in neighbours or are they out of touch with people in their vicinity? What picture of life in the society arises from these observations? What picture of life arises from literary writings on the society in question?[20]

History. The learner needs an opportunity to get to know the significant historical developments of the country or region, including the history of minorities. He should get to know the historically significant symbols, notable events and trends, and the main historical personalities as well as critical issues, past and present. All this can be studied objectively in a scholarly fashion as in the historical or political science literature. But it needs, above all, to be looked at from the point of view of native speakers whose historical perceptions, values, political knowledge, preferences, and antagonisms provide the main basis for the historical understanding and empathy that are needed in a language learning context.[21]

Institutions. These include the system of government—central, regional, and local—the educational system, social welfare, economic institutions, the military and the police, religious institutions, political parties, and the media including television, radio, and the press. The learners should familiarize themselves with these to an extent that corresponds to the level of knowledge they have of similar institutions in their home country, or that corresponds to the knowledge that native speakers normally possess on the basis of their own experience. Here again, we are looking for an optimal mix of the learner's own interests and needs, the concepts and perceptions of ordinary members of the speech community, and accurate and documented information based on knowledge of the legal, administrative, or economic system.[22]

Art, music, literature, and other major achievements. The learners should be able to acquire knowledge about and an appreciation of artists, musicians, and writers and their works, and know of other great figures and their achievements to the extent that these are common knowledge in the speech community and constitute a heritage of 'common literacy'. This does not preclude a more scholarly study, but what matters most of all is to provide the learner with the knowledge and values that are commonly accepted in the speech community. Beyond that, the second language student may have special interests in literature, fine art, drama, or the cinema. These would then have special importance and encourage learning from a particular cultural perspective.[23]

To summarize, the six topic areas and the approach we have proposed distinguish the teaching of culture within a language course from a fully-fledged study of cultures and societies. We can meet the problem of the vastness of the culture concept by adopting a more selective and differentiated approach to the six main areas of culture teaching. There are, of course, other factors which further limit the teaching of culture: the learners' age, their level of maturity, and their previous language learning experience, as well as their general educational background and their specific goals. All these factors taken together make it clear that the content of a cultural syllabus cannot be the same as that of a conventional anthropological or humanistic survey.

The current lack of resources

Besides the unwieldiness of the culture concept, a further problem is the absence of resources, the lack of cultural research, the patchiness of documentation, and the overall shortage of systematic descriptive accounts of cultural data. Language teachers who do not want to neglect the cultural component need accessible and reliable information. We take for granted the existence of grammars and dictionaries. Even literary knowledge is well-documented thanks to extensive research in the universities. But no equivalent resources exist for the major cultures whose languages we teach. The everyday life of target cultures is poorly documented. It has not yet formed the subject of sustained and systematic research. So far this area of research lacks an academic home. Research on culture should probably be located in the language departments of universities. However, the main preoccupations of these departments are linguistic or literary, and while there is a certain recognition of the study of 'civilization', there is no clear awareness of an interdisciplinary area between linguistics and literature on the one hand, and sociocultural and anthropological studies on the other, which would establish a knowledge base for culture teaching. The admonition to avoid stereotyping is difficult to observe as long as scholarship in cultural studies is not more widely developed.

We have made it clear that culture teaching must not be confused with a formal course in social and cultural anthropology and that a more informal and personal entry into a foreign culture is possible and appropriate. But such a subjective approach does need a more objective input as a corrective and as a source of systematic information. We should, therefore, aim to develop teachers' guides which provide well-substantiated cultural knowledge.[24] A few such studies on the United States have been produced, but they are in short supply and the research is usually not ongoing. The lack of information is a deficiency which is difficult to overcome, and it certainly has some bearing on the scantiness of culture teaching. Until this lack has been remedied, teachers and course writers have to help themselves as best they can with the currently available resources. By failing to draw attention to this gap in our knowledge the literature has done a disservice to the cause of culture teaching.[25]

Techniques of culture teaching

The interest in culture teaching over the last twenty-five years has given rise to a great variety of techniques. Some go back much further, and were first employed in the early decades of this century. Nostrand (1974) lists twenty different techniques and divides them into eleven experiential and nine cognitive activities. Chastain (1988) distinguishes between several in-class and some out-of-class modes of presenting culture. Hammerly (1982) has listed and briefly sketched some thirty techniques which he has arranged in an approximate order of difficulty for second language learners.[26]

A broad distinction among techniques of culture teaching should differentiate between teaching in three situations. The first is culture teaching in foreign language courses in which the student is physically and often psychologically far removed from the reality of life in the target speech community. Here culture teaching provides background and context which brings the speech community to life, and helps the student to visualize and vicariously experience that reality. The second situation is one in which students may be physically far away from the target language environment but psychologically it is much more real to them because they are preparing to visit the country for a holiday or to work there. Some of the techniques developed in the United States, such as the 'culture assimilator' (see below), were originally designed for preparing Peace Corps volunteers or workers involved in technical assistance for life in a foreign environment. The third situation to consider is that of students, immigrants, or personnel already in the target language milieu. In this situation, we do not have to invent the cultural setting. It is much more a question of helping students to come to terms with the environment as they find it, offering guidance, explaining puzzling features, and correcting errors of conduct or misunderstandings.

Besides the learner's situation, *vis-à-vis* the cultural milieu, other factors that have a bearing on the choice of techniques include the age, maturity, and educational level of the students. Writers on the methodology of culture teaching have been eager to show that it is possible to present culture in ways which are not confined to lectures or formal readings on the geography, history, and institutions of the target society. The literature offers a varied array of techniques that promise to bring culture to the language class in vivid, practical, and personally relevant ways. In the following analysis, we make a distinction between eight different approaches.

Creating an authentic classroom environment

Classroom decorations and displays of all kinds, posters, cartoons, maps, newspaper cuttings, and exhibitions of realia, including such trivia as theatre tickets and programmes, bus and train tickets, railway and airline timetables, restaurant menus, and so on create a visual and tangible presence of the target community. This is particularly important in a foreign language setting where the reality of language use in the speech community is geographically and psychologically far removed from the classroom.[27]

Providing cultural information

Several techniques have been developed with the intention of informing the language class of cultural facts or drawing their attention to cultural comparisons in compact, interesting, and readily accessible ways without taking too much time away from the 'regular' language learning business. *Cultural asides* are items of cultural information offered by the teacher as they present themselves in the course of language work. They are important because they help create a cultural context for language items and help the learner to create a network of mental associations similar to those which the items evoke in the native speaker.[28] The 'slice of life' technique (Taylor 1970) consists of a short attention-getting input, for example a recording of a popular song as the class settles down to a Spanish lesson or a short tape-recording of Spanish news items in the last two or three minutes.[29]

One of the most influential devices for culture teaching is the *culture capsule*, based on a suggestion by Taylor and Sorenson (1961). This, as the name indicates, is an isolated item of information on the target culture. The originators thought of it as a small self-contained unit with a script prepared by the teacher. The verbal presentation was to be combined with realia, visuals, and other aids. The substance was to be presented by the teacher with the help of a prepared script and various supplementary resources. The presentation could be followed by discussion or role-play. The treatment of a capsule was not to take up more than about ten minutes of a lesson period. A weekly culture capsule in a year's course, so Taylor and Sorenson argued, might amount to as many as thirty-six cultural exposures. They suggested that the resources for each capsule could be conveniently stored in a shoe box so as to be readily available when needed. Although each capsule was designed as a self-contained unit, the originators had a broad scheme of eight sociocultural headings under which to classify the capsules. Therefore, the fact that each capsule was independent did not make the use of the capsules incoherent, so long as they were seen to be pieces in a broader pattern.[30]

The concept of *culture clusters*, which has been developed by Meade and Morain (1973), is an elaboration of culture capsules. Culture clusters are combinations of conceptually related culture capsules or they are a major set of activities broken up into its constituent parts. Two or more capsules which belong together can form a cluster. According to the originators, the cluster should be concluded by some sort of activity, for example a dramatization in which the set of capsules is integrated into a single sequence. Seelye offers the example of a family meal in France consisting of three capsules: (a) how to set the table; (b) how to behave at table, and (c) the family together at the table. Allen and Valette (1977) use the example, offered by Meade and Morain in their original article, of a French country wedding, divided into four capsules described as *La cérémonie civile*, *La cérémonie religieuse*, *Le repas de noces*, *Les différences entre un mariage mondain et un mariage campagnard*. The four capsules together culminate in a re-enactment of a wedding ceremony or a verbal account and explanation of a French country wedding. In Seelye's capsule on how to behave during a family meal a visual shows the set table and chairs, and a narrative is presented by the teacher or acted out by students:

> When soup is eaten, the large cuillère à soupe is used. However, the French spoon the soup toward themselves and eat from the end of the spoon, not the side. While eating, it is proper to keep your free hand on the table, not in your lap. Also, the bread is quite handily used to scoop up vegetables or sauces and clean up the plate at the end of the meal. To cut food, the knife is used in the right hand and the fork in the left. Food is then put directly into the mouth with the left hand and the fork. The knife is held in the right hand while chewing or returned to the porte-couteau while not being used. . . . When whole fruits (such as apples or pears) are served, they are not eaten with the hands. The fork is again used in the left hand to hold the fruit and the knife is used to cut and peel the fruit. The pieces of fruit are then eaten with the fork in the left hand. It is important that the plate be empty at the end of the meal since this shows you have enjoyed the meal. At the end of the meal, in some French families, children thank their mother for the food she prepared.
> (Seelye 1984: 136)

After the practice, it is suggested that students demonstrate the correct way to eat bread or soup, and how to cut up and eat fruit, meat, and vegetables.

As a teaching device, this capsule introduces students to an aspect of way-of-life culture that lends itself well to behavioural training. At the same time, it suggests certain meanings and values: cleaning the plate indicates appreciation of a meal; it does not mean greediness. The usefulness of the capsule depends largely on the validity of the information.[31] Is the described behaviour generally applicable in a French home environment, or does it reflect only the customs of an urban middle class family? Is it a useful guide to the type of behaviour expected of a foreigner? For a traveller or worker living in the host community it is important to know what aspects of behaviour are tolerated from a foreigner and which would be regarded as embarrassing, unacceptable, or even rude and ludicrous. Even in a foreign language setting where the language is learnt for educational purposes and not for immediate application, it is valuable for school-aged students to be made aware of the meanings attributed to eating behaviour in different societies.

Cultural problem solving

In this approach, the learner is not simply presented with information, but is confronted with a culturally significant situation which may present a problem to a foreigner visiting the country. These are usually questions of manners or customs, for example, what to say or what not to say in a given social situation. The class is invited to solve the problem. This approach has been developed systematically for use as a self-instructional programme by Fiedler, Mitchell, and Triandis (1971), through a device called the *culture assimilator*.[32] The student is provided with a series of episodes of target culture behaviour. Each episode describes a critical incident in which an American and a host national interact. The situation is puzzling to the American; it may even offend his sense of values. The student is provided with four plausible explanations, in a multiple-choice format, of which only one is considered correct. The feedback tells the students why one explanation is right and the others are wrong in the cultural context. The explanation of the correct solution as well as the reason why the three distractors were wrong provides vivid and challenging lessons on the way of life of the target society. Consequently, a series of these episodes constitutes a course in cultural adjustment.

Behavioural and affective aspects

The audio-motor unit. This time the cultural information is presented in the form of a set of commands which constitute an action sequence. The audio-motor unit is an application of Total Physical Response to a culturally significant series of actions.[33] Lafayette (1978b) illustrates the audio-motor unit with appropriate behaviour in a restaurant: entering, sitting down, ordering a meal, eating it, paying the bill, and leaving. It also involves carrying out actions in ways which are accepted as correct and in keeping with local customs. The student learns the etiquette of the culture, for example, bowing correctly or taking one's shoes off when expected to do so.

Dramatization has been widely used in culture teaching.[34] It may be no more than a different format of presentation comparable to exposition or narration. But dramatization does something that the previous techniques do not do. It can involve the learner in role-play and simulation. In this way the learner is encouraged to put himself into the position of being a member of the target culture, and role-play thus becomes a training in empathic behaviour. Several of the techniques under this heading are designed to make cultural phenomena accessible to very young learners through dramatizations or the use of masks or puppets (Rivers 1981: 327), or to older learners who might be willing to read a systematic account of the target society and culture. These techniques involve presentations of scenes of daily life in dramatized form, either as a narrative or a short film or as a scene presented to the students or acted out by the students themselves. The scene would be designed to illustrate a cultural fact, value, or problem. The presentation would then be followed by an explanation or discussion. Such dramatizations make cultural differences vivid and memorable, and are useful devices particularly for students with little or no experience in a foreign culture.

Mini-drama, like the culture assimilator, was developed by social scientists for cross-cultural education and was then applied to foreign language instruction. It consists of a series of skits or scenes of everyday life illustrating culturally significant behaviour. The skit is read, viewed on a video, or acted out. Actions are interrupted and discussed by the teacher and the students. Mini-dramas are designed not only to present a problem situation but also to involve students emotionally by identifying them with one or another character in the episode. Thus, in one scene two American students misinterpret a situation out of ignorance and behave in socially inappropriate ways:

> In a street market in Cannes, the two young Americans, Cindy and Debbie, decide to buy peaches from a street vendor, and start picking out the peaches they want to buy, thus offending the rule of the street market to let the vendor pick out the fruit and not to interfere with her display.
>
> *Vendor:* (sarcastically) Eh bien, mesdemoiselles, you're planning to buy the whole tableful?

Debbie: (whispers to Cindy) Is she ever rude! I wonder what her problem is! Probably had a fight with her husband this morning.

At this point the scene is interrupted for class discussion.

Role-play and simulation have also been used to make points about culturally appropriate or inappropriate behaviour. Since they involve the student in improvising actions and verbal exchanges between the simulated characters, they require a high level of language command and are, therefore, suitable for advanced learners. The conduct or language of the characters may or may not be culturally convincing. The evaluation of the simulation is, therefore, as much part of the learning experience as the simulation itself. The different techniques discussed so far make use of episodes, either in narrative form or dramatized, or short exposés followed by discussion. Whether these techniques are sound depends mainly on the content they illustrate. Is the episode or the exposé a valid presentation of the cultural facts? Do the solutions sensitize the learners to true cultural features? Do they sharpen the student's cultural perceptions? There is always a danger that such episodes will overdraw and caricature the cultural feature and assume a fixity of cultural conduct where often a range of behaviour is possible. The lists of techniques are useful in that they draw our attention to various ways in which culture can be presented. They indicate that the teaching of culture does not necessarily depend on a sophisticated knowledge among students. There are ways of teaching culture which can be adjusted to different age levels and to different educational backgrounds.

Cognitive approaches

While the majority of the techniques we have described so far can be regarded as experiential rather than academic or systematic in nature, it is important to remember that there are students in certain situations who may wish to cope with an academic study of the target culture and society through readings, lectures, discussions, and debates.[35] Often the paucity of reliable data requires that students should approach a culture not as a given to be acquired from books but rather as a topic for exploration. In this case, they will need techniques of enquiry rather than facts about the target culture. We made the point earlier that second language learners are not social scientists. Their interest in the target culture and society is not primarily abstract, theoretical, and scientific. Nevertheless, some students do take an intellectual interest in a country and its culture, and they are willing to approach the new society as critical observers and to adopt objective techniques of systematic enquiry. The literature has recognized this and Nostrand (1974), as well as Seelye (1984), and Robinson (1987) have emphasized the importance of research techniques as a way of enabling students to find out for themselves, and to approach the new society with an open mind.[36]

The role of literature and the humanities

Although the techniques we have described so far have been influenced by developments in social science and largely reflect a social science approach, it is also widely recognized that contact with the humanistic culture—the Olympian culture, in Brooks' terms—should also be cultivated. Contact with the arts and humanities can be at an experiential level and, therefore, can involve learners in personal participation, for example, through singing in a choir, watching a play or film, seeing works of art or architecture, or getting to know the folklore.[37] Historically literature was the main avenue to the target culture, but during the course of this century, as a result of the growing interest in a social and scientific approach to culture, the role of literature has declined and has been almost entirely crowded out. The question to ask today is whether this neglect of literature is justified or whether it should be reconsidered for its specific role in culture teaching.

As we have already observed, the principal authorities on culture teaching—Brooks, Nostrand, and Seelye—have insisted on an integration of the humanistic and social science approaches. They, therefore, implicitly accord a place to literature and differ only in the degree of emphasis they place on the literary component. Seelye (1984) can be said to lay less stress on the literary component than Nostrand (1974) or Marckwardt (1981), who both make a strong case for literature as a source for culture teaching. In their view, the different literary genres have the power to evoke a quality of empathy and to develop the kind of understanding that is needed if we want to enter into the thoughts, motives, and feelings of L2 speakers. With a knowledge of literature no less than the cinema or theatre a teacher could select writings, as well as films or plays, which help in understanding specific aspects of the target culture.

Hammerly (1982: 532–3) illustrates a much more guarded approach to literary readings as a resource for culture teaching. In his view, 'literature is very restricted as a source of information about second cultures' (1982: 532). He warns against the stereotyping of characters in works of literature and the tendency of writers to reflect their own idiosyncratic point of view which is not necessarily representative of the way of life of a society. Moreover, literary writings of the past cannot be used as safe sources for interpreting contemporary society. Dickens' *Oliver Twist* or Galsworthy's *Forsyte Saga* cannot be treated as images of contemporary England. In Hammerly's view literature is not a source of culture teaching; rather, the understanding of a literary work presupposes an understanding of the culture. Hammerly's caution is justified, and would be acknowledged by Nostrand and others. Having said this, we conclude that literary readings have a place in culture teaching. In many cultures, particularly those whose languages are widely taught, literature performs an important role in society, particularly if we include folk tales, nursery rhymes, children's literature, and other widely read books which constitute a common heritage of literacy. Literary works sometimes epitomize the thoughts, feelings, and values of the target culture in memorable ways. The literary message may be superior to a formal exposition and can provide an excellent entry into a new world of thought and feeling.[38]

Real-life exposure to the target culture

This usually involves either bringing a native speaker into the language class or taking students into the second language environment. Such contact experiences have several purposes which are broader and often less clearly defined than simply culture learning. We have, therefore, treated them as part of the communicative syllabus. We can think of exposure to the target culture as informal learning or as systematic enquiry, a field study or project in which the learner acquires and uses various research techniques. Treating direct contact experiences as part of culture learning emphasizes that exposure to a new culture and a new language in its natural setting requires skills of intercultural behaviour as learner and informant, as guest and host. It also requires skills of observation, asking the right questions, learning how to be a foreigner, and tact and openness to the lives and concerns of others. Several communicative activities offer opportunities for this type of cultural learning.

Nothing serves better to make the second language a reality than to have the experience of meeting and talking to members of the target speech community. The value of building these contacts systematically into language learning activities has been recognized in Europe since before World War I. It has formed part of European foreign language learning since then and has gradually spread to language teaching in North America and other parts of the world. The distinction we introduced earlier between the three situations in which second languages are learnt is important for these real-life techniques: the foreign language situation with no direct contact with the second language community; the preparatory situation where direct contact is anticipated; and language learning in the second language milieu. The real-life contacts may take various forms:

Pen-pals and tape-pals. The exchange of letters is one of the simplest techniques by which a foreign language learner can gain a sense of reality. Correspondence ranges over any aspect of personal concern and, therefore, the cultural interest is more indirect. However, pen-pals can compare notes on various aspects of their lives and in this way build up a picture of life in the target community as it appears to the students and their friends.[39]

Visits to the language class by native speakers. In a foreign language situation, it is often possible to arrange visits from native speakers to the class and thereby strengthen the student's understanding of the thoughts and feelings of members of the target speech community. The native speaker provides a sense of authenticity. It may come as a surprise to many students to find that people from that faraway country can talk about themselves and their lives and thus move the foreign language from the textbook page into concrete reality. In a second language situation, it is often equally useful for learners to meet people from different walks of life, although for different reasons. In a foreign milieu, it is often doubly difficult to meet and make contact with people in a non-threatening situation. The language class offers that opportunity and can, therefore, provide occasions for getting to know people from different walks of life, who have different approaches to current issues, and who represent a variety of interests.[40]

Visits to other countries and regions. Such visits may be undertaken for various reasons, but one is to give learners first-hand experience of the second language culture and society.[41] It is often possible to set up exchange schemes in which individual students or entire classes visit each other. Individual students and classes may be 'twinned'. Such visits enable guests and hosts to learn a great deal about all aspects of culture from the dual perspective of the foreigner and native speaker. Although the exchanges have a variety of purposes, they invariably constitute an informal introduction to the second culture.[42] If exchanges of the kind suggested above are undertaken on a regular basis, a permanent link between classes and schools can be formed, and a permanent channel of cultural exchange and cultural insight is created.

Making use of cultural community resources

Thanks to immigration one is likely to find native speakers of different languages in most urban communities. Some countries encourage the development of multiculturalism. In this case, the presence of native speakers constitutes a resource for the cultural aspect of second language learning in a foreign language situation.[43] When a second language is learnt in the target-language milieu, the everyday environment constitutes a vast resource which is readily available for culture teaching. It offers many opportunities for visits and projects, enabling learners to come into direct contact with a great many aspects of the target culture.

Cultural syllabus design

One factor which has impeded progress in the teaching of culture is the problem of syllabus design. Very little attention has been paid to the sequencing of a cultural programme in language courses. The main approach has been to regard culture teaching as incidental and to rely on isolated items, offered in the form of small units, cultural asides, culture capsules, cultural assimilators, mini-dramas, and the like, and not to be over-concerned with a coherent and sequential programme. Another question that has been left largely unresolved is the relationship between a cultural syllabus within a second language programme and the other curriculum areas with which such teaching might overlap, for example, history, geography, social studies, literature, fine art, or music. A third issue is the weighting of the cultural component within a language course. How much importance should be attributed to cultural topics relative to other matters? In language courses, the emphasis is generally on language proficiency, and therefore other interests such as culture teaching tend to remain in the background.[44]

All the writers whose work we have reviewed recognize the cultural embeddedness of language and insist that L2 instruction is not possible without placing language items into a sociocultural context. We have already pointed out that this principle merely confirms the sociosemantic and pragmatic view of language. Given this view, the question of weighting means whether, beyond the essential association of language with culture and society, there is a place in second language teaching for the six topics that we have sketched earlier in this chapter (see The content of culture teaching), and what part they should play in instruction. Presumably no universally valid answer can be given to this question. We should envisage that the weighting scale might range from a predominantly cultural emphasis down to a minimal one in which cultural topics are given little or no attention.

Although a strong case has been made for an increase in cultural emphasis, the general assumption seems to be that culture should still be secondary to language. An exception is a suggestion offered by Crawford-Lange and Lange (1984: 141) who note that culture has remained 'peripheral in the foreign-language classroom even when teachers recognize its importance in relation to language'. Their response to this anomalous situation is that language and culture should become integrated by shifting the weight of language teaching towards culture and by allowing themes of daily life treated in a comparative way to be dominant, while language would be subordinated to the substantive interest of the theme.

In our view it is a matter of policy to decide whether culture or language should predominate. In general education courses, culture has indeed been understated, and the literature has been right in trying to redress the balance. There are situations where a predominance of culture teaching would seem to be justified. Jakobovits and Gordon (1974), for example, have made a case for this shift of emphasis in Japanese courses for adults wishing to visit Japan. In the teaching of English as an international language, on the other hand, there would be no particular culture to which the second language could be related. The weighting of the cultural relative to the linguistic emphasis must be decided from case to case depending on the teaching situation for which the curriculum is designed.

While very little attention has been paid to levels and standards of culture teaching and the ordering of such teaching into some kind of sequential syllabus, mention should be made of a few outline sketches which have been proposed. Brooks (1971) distinguishes four levels:

1. Treatment of the family table, schoolroom, playground, homework, chores, letters, games, parties, parades, and holidays.
2. Treatment of 'close-ups of thought and action', as manifested in proverbs, sayings, pictures, and photographs typifying the culture.
3. Treatment of the 'regrettable' and the 'tragic' in the target culture.
4. Attempt at a cultural synthesis.

This division clearly moves from the more concrete behavioural aspects of culture to more abstract and problematical concepts, with hopes of achieving a final integration. Brooks has American high school settings in mind.

Nostrand (1968) also sketches a four-level sequence, designed for adolescent beginners, which is described by Seelye (1972). At level 1, students learn how to conduct themselves in everyday situations, including greeting, leave-taking, and eating, and acquire a knowledge of leisure-time activities characteristic of their peer group. At level 2 students gain 'insights into literature, the family, education, cultural themes, etc.' and some understanding of 'socially similar people in the foreign society' (Seelye 1972: 25). At level 3 the social structure 'belatedly receives more direct attention' (Seelye 1972: 26). Level 4 of Nostrand's scheme, according to Seelye, 'outlines more balanced expectations but it is very briefly developed' (Seelye 1972: 26). In this sketch Nostrand, like Brooks, moves from simple behavioural items to a broader understanding of the culture, which makes sense but is too sketchy to give adequate guidance.

Finally, Hammerly (1982: 522–4) arranges his list of culture teaching objectives in a sequence which parallels progression in the second language, and therefore distinguishes early, intermediate, and advanced stages. According to Hammerly, the cultural connotation of words, culturally appropriate behaviour, and an interest in and understanding of culture can be developed in the first stages of language learning (i.e. goals 1–3). An understanding of cross-cultural differences and the study of cross-cultural institutions is more likely to occur at an intermediate level, while the development of an integrated view of the second culture, a critical appraisal of statements about it, and serious research on the culture are activities for advanced learners.

We should remember that these sequences are plausible but speculative and so far have not been supported by empirical research into actual teaching and learning. In the absence of systematic observation to confirm particular sequences, a policy of cultural sequencing should take into account the criteria which have been used in preparing these speculative lists. First, younger learners should engage in simple activities which will enable them to experience the target culture directly, while older learners can read about the culture in their mother tongue. Second, if culture teaching is to be in step with language learning and also to enhance it, the activities should be in keeping with the expected language proficiency, as Hammerly has rightly emphasized. Third, culture teaching, as Brooks and Nostrand have suggested, should progress from relatively simple and concrete events to generalized cultural themes and a broader appreciation of the whole society.

In many school systems, it is recognized that the second language class should be more closely integrated with other curriculum subjects, and that areas of overlap should be explored systematically at the curriculum-design level. The literature on culture teaching makes hardly any reference to this aspect of culture in second language education. If we take the six topic areas as main themes of a cultural syllabus, it is clear that 'places' relate to geography, 'institutions' to history, 'art, music, and literature' to the humanities, and 'way of life' to sociology and anthropology, which in school settings might be encountered under the heading of social studies. 'Other achievements', such as exploration, scientific discovery, engineering, and so on, can be related to studies in almost any area. Many of the topics are also reflected in the student's native language and literature. However, in recognizing these affinities with other curriculum subjects, we have to remind ourselves that real overlap is likely to occur only if the topics are treated as systematic academic disciplines. The treatment of a topic from the perspective of a second language learner is specific to the second language curriculum.

Concluding comments

While the cultural syllabus deliberately sets out to shift the focus of attention towards the people and culture of the target language, its contribution to second language pedagogy should not be underestimated. A sound policy on culture teaching will recognize the difficulties inherent in presenting the target culture, but will also affirm its legitimate place in second language education. As with the other syllabuses, the cultural syllabus may be developed and manifested in different ways in various contexts. The list of suggested techniques for culture teaching is at first sight large and impressive. However, in some ways the vast array is misleading. There is little evidence of regular use of these techniques in the actual practice of language teaching and we know next to nothing about their comparative effectiveness. The most serious obstacle to using many of these techniques effectively lies in the lack of data and resources for the cultural content to be taught. It should also be added that language teachers are frequently not familiar with techniques of handling substantive content such as those which we find in history, social studies, geography, or natural science. The fact that such teaching has to be done in a second language which is imperfectly known by the students adds another dimension to a complex and challenging task.

Notes

1 Excellent chapters on culture teaching are found in Brooks (1964); Chastain (1988); Allen and Valette (1977); Rivers (1981); and Hammerly (1982). See also Bickley (1989); Steele (1989); Berns (1990); Harrison (1990); Buttjes and Byram (1991); and Byrnes (1991) for further discussion of these issues.

2 It is listed under this heading in the abstracting journal *Language Teaching*.

3 Mounin (1984) makes the point that the meaning of the term 'civilisation' has expanded in France as has the concept of 'culture' in the anglophone world so that they are now practically synonymous. French writers have used the two terms interchangeably in some of the special issues of *Le français dans le monde* dealing with this subject.

4 For some historical observations on 'Kulturkunde' see FCLT: 247–9.

5 The historical development of culture in language teaching since the beginning of the twentieth century is described in FCLT: 246–56.

6 In addition to the eloquent chapter in his book (Brooks 1964),

Brooks frequently wrote and spoke as an advocate of the teaching of culture (e.g. 1968 and 1969). In a guest editorial in *Foreign Language Annals*, Brooks (1971: 54) wrote 'In the second half of the present century there has been a growing awareness of an additional dimension in foreign language study . . . There opens up before us a wholly new way of understanding and appreciating the view of life held by another nation, and, along with this, a deeper insight into our own'.

7 Best known among these are Nostrand, who for over two decades has dominated the culture teaching scene in US language education (e.g. Nostrand 1966, 1973, 1974, and 1978), and Seelye who has written the major American monograph on culture teaching (1984) and numerous articles (e.g. Seelye 1968b and 1970b), which are listed in Seelye 1984. Other well known American writers on culture include Morain (e.g. 1971); Lafayette (1978b); Robinson (1987); and Damen (1987).

8 Northeast Conference publications include Brée (1955); Bishop (1960); Dodge (1972); Born (1976), and several articles on contemporary cultures in more recent reports (for example, Mead 1983). Seelye (1984: 12–3) scathingly criticizes the 1960 Northeast Conference report (Bishop 1960) as 'one such characteristically unsuccessful attempt to coordinate the teaching of language and culture' where 'livid professors, acting as though their basic value system were under attack from imperfectly socialized upstarts, defended with righteous indignation the appropriateness of a literary approach to cultural matters'. While he concedes that a later Northeast Conference (Dodge 1972) 'was characterized by greater acceptance of the legitimacy of culture in language classes', he still finds 'little sign of progress in integrating it into the classroom' (Seelye 1984: 13). A steady recognition of culture in American language education is also reflected in the periodically appearing papers on culture in the influential ACTFL Foreign Language Education Series: Seelye (1969); Morain (1971); Nostrand (1974); and Crawford-Lange and Lange (1984).

9 This observation is particularly interesting in that Sanderson conducted a study of outstanding teachers in Britain. The same point is made in another observational study in Britain on teaching French in secondary schools in Scotland which notes 'the high incidence of segments dealing with course book situations and "fragmented/ non-contextualized" topics on the one hand, and the relatively low occurrence of segments dealing with civilizations, with linguistic material, and with real life' (Mitchell *et al.* 1981: 27).

10 For the bases of the modern culture concept in anthropology, sociology, and social psychology see FCLT, Chapter 10, and Chapter 12: 246–56.

11 Nostrand's Emergent Model is a cultural inventory which has gone through several modifications. It was published in its most recent form in *Contemporary French Civilization* (Nostrand 1978). According to its author, it is based on the combination of a comprehensive model for the study of society, proposed by a Harvard sociologist Talcott Parsons and a 'themal' description of societies, developed by a Cornell anthropologist, Morris Opler. While the two social scientists in fact did not agree that these two ways of representing a society are compatible, in Nostrand's view they support each other. It is worth noting that in a published conversation with Georges Mounin (1984) in the review *Le français dans le monde*, Mounin opposes the search for generalizations about a society, because in his view it leads to clichés.

12 This conceptualization is based on the work of Maslow (1970) who identifies five basic needs which are universally applicable. These are: comfort and survival, safety, belongingness and love, self-esteem and the esteem of others, self-actualization. (Taken from Valette 1977: 281.)

13 It seems reasonable for Hammerly (1982) to base his concept of behavioural culture on Seelye. Nostrand, however, is much more sociological and philosophical than is suggested by Hammerly's way-of-life culture. In our view, Hammerly's division is not as well defined as those of Seelye and Nostrand.

14 Among other classification schemes, mention should be made of one proposed by Lafayette and Strasheim (1980) who adopted five categories from Pfister and Borzilleri (1977): (1) The family unit and the personal sphere: family relationships, eating and shopping, housing; (2) The social sphere: class, structure, work, leisure, attitudes towards sex, population; (3) Political systems and institutions: government, education, law and justice; (4) The environmental sphere: geography (physical and political), economic development, urban vs. rural, natural resources/environment, weather; (5) Religion, the arts and the humanities: the role of churches, folklore and history, literature, music, creative arts.

Taylor and Sorenson (1961) developed another elaborate scheme of categories which consists of seven main headings: technology, economic organization, social organization, political organization, world view (religion and philosophy), esthetics, and education. Their subheadings consist of an application of this scheme to Latin America. Their scheme also includes an eighth subcultural category which identifies biological, geological, geographical, and historical factors.

15 To our mind, the literature on culture does not make the distinction between a sociolinguistic-semantic-functional treatment of language and the specific contribution of a cultural syllabus. For

example, Seelye's (1984) goal 2 'interaction of language and social variables' and goal 4 'cultural connotations of words and phrases' are more adequately part of a language syllabus. There is obviously no clear boundary between language and culture; it is more a matter of agreeing under which heading the sociocultural aspects of language should be treated. In practice they should be integrated as much as possible. The main problems of culture teaching do not lie in sociolinguistics but in the treatment of other aspects of culture beyond language.

16 We use the term 'native speaker' loosely: a member of the target speech community is a native speaker. It does not depend on his birth certificate. A similar point is made in a Forum commentary in *TESOL Quarterly* by Paikeday (1985) which is significantly entitled 'May I kill the native speaker?' Although this commentary refers to pronunciation standards more than cultural membership, the commentary makes the point that 'native speaker' is a fuzzy notion and the term, as used by linguists, merely means 'competent user', with no essential connection with parentage, place of birth, first language, and other circumstantial differences in language acquisition' (Paikeday 1985: 393). We have this rather loose definition in mind when we use the term 'native speaker' in this chapter.

17 Seelye (1984), for example, devotes an entire chapter to 'asking the right questions'. Crawford-Lange and Lange (1984: 145) criticize most current presentations of culture as offering product rather than process approaches: 'Students are taught about culture; they are not taught how to interact with culture'.

18 Most inventories include a geographical-geological category. Nostrand (1978) has a section on ecology and technology, in which ecology includes the exploitation of physical resources as well as of plants and animals. Hammerly (1982) includes this category under informational culture, Lafayette and Strasheim (1980) under the environmental sphere. In all of these, however, it is understood that we are dealing with a scholarly discipline, not with the perceptions of native speakers and language learners. Seelye (1984) does not specifically identify this aspect.

19 The way of life aspect is clearly recognized in most schemes. Hammerly (1982) characterizes it as behavioural culture. For Seelye (1984) it is covered by goal 3 'conventional behaviour in common situations'. Nostrand's (1978) scheme is less concerned with the conventions of daily life than with more abstract categories which cover the underlying ideologies and philosophies of a society. Most of the questions raised in Brooks' (1964) inventory fall into this category, as do headings 1 to 16 and 18 (typical student activities, money, leisure activities, and friends) on Chastain's list

(1976: 389–91). Chastain (1988) presents a revised version of this scheme. If these lists are to be treated as objective scholarship they would present the teacher with an impossible task. On the other hand, if they are considered the result of informal observations during visits, in the home of friends or exchange partners, the lists offer useful signposts for enquiries and personal observations.

20 Under the influence of sociology, several schemes probe social stratifications and divisions. 'Society' is one of the main headings in Nostrand's (1978) scheme (see Figure 8.1). Lafayette and Strasheim (1980) similarly include 'The social sphere' as one of their main headings (see note 14 above). Several of Chastain's (1976, 1988) topics also point to a sociological analysis. For Hammerly (1982: 514), it is part of informational culture. However, he restricts this area to 'whatever the members of the second culture cherish or consider very important'. What matters is how the learner relates to the society and how native speakers view it. A detached study of society has its place of course, but it is not as central to the majority of language courses as are the native speaker's social perceptions.

21 Under the heading 'culture', Nostrand (1978) refers to the people's self-concept as well as foreign views of the culture (see Figure 8.1). This includes their world-picture and subsumes a view of history. For Hammerly (1982), this category falls once more into the rather broad category of informational culture.

22 For Nostrand (1978), the institutions are subsumed under 'society', while Lafayette and Strasheim (1980) include a separate category, 'political systems and institutions'.

23 Nostrand (1978) lists art forms under his first category, 'culture', and intellectual and aesthetic institutions, such as the *Académie française*, under 'society'. Lafayette and Strasheim (1980) have a category which they name 'religion, the arts and the humanities'. Allen and Valette (1977: 336–8) subsume under the arts: music, painting, sculpture, and dance, and also include folksongs and folkdances.

24 In FCLT: 254, we present a proposal to establish ethnographic guides for the languages we teach, based on research and descriptions of the target culture. The same chapter also proposes a model for the relationship between fundamental studies, research on particular cultures, descriptions, guides for the teacher and, ultimately, syllabuses, and teaching materials. Elaborate schemes, such as those by Nostrand (1978); Brooks (1964); Chastain (1976, 1988); and Lafayette and Strasheim (1980), must remain programmatic unless they are sustained by systematic research.

25 It is a curious omission that, in spite of the elaboration of cultural

inventories and ingenious suggestions for teaching methodology, the basis of information has been disregarded. Seelye (1984: 150–1), in his detailed and carefully written monograph, sees the question of a research basis purely as a problem of 'finding information' and dismisses the issue in a page and a half as an exercise in bibliographical resource work. In the final chapter, promisingly entitled 'What are the sources?', the issue is again treated too lightly. Referring to an article on data retrieval, Seelye (ibid.: 245) continues: 'Articles and books are not, of course, the only source of information. Magazines, newspapers, radio, TV, movies, LP records, and comic books offer much up-to-date data for cultural analysis'.

26 See also Allen and Valette (1977: Chapter 12) and Rivers (1981: 324–37).

27 For more detailed suggestions, see Allen and Valette (1977: 332–3) and Rivers (1981: 332–3).

28 Most writers draw attention to the 'cultural aside'. See, for example, Hammerly (1982: 526–7) and Chastain (1988: 309). Nostrand (1974: 298) refers to it as one of his cognitive techniques under the name of 'incidental comment', Rivers (1981: 326) talks about it as 'experiencing the culture through language use', and Allen and Valette (1977: 334–5) similarly make suggestions for incorporating culture in language learning activities.

29 The 'slice of life' technique is also referred to by Chastain (1988: 309–10) and Hammerly (1982: 527).

30 Most writers include 'culture capsules' in their inventory of techniques. The name itself suggests a compactness and a practical manageable quality which goes well with a clearly defined but restricted role for culture teaching. See, for example, Chastain (1988: 310); Rivers (1981: 329); and Hammerly (1982: 528). Allen and Valette (1977: 353–6) give French and Spanish examples, and Seelye (1984: 130–2) offers a French example.

31 Seelye (1984: 244) writes: 'Some teachers play the game of "Filling Freddie Farkle Full of Fickle Facts". This is commonly accomplished through superficial units on art, food, the market place, the War of Independence, and above all, on the principal navigable rivers and their seamy ports.'

32 The literature is misleading on the culture assimilator. It treats it alongside capsules and clusters (e.g. Seelye 1984: Chapter 7). Hammerly (1982: 527) wrongly describes the cultural assimilator as presenting a single cross-cultural situation. But, unlike culture capsules, each culture assimilator is an entire programmed course in cultural sensitization, consisting of many small cross-cultural episodes. Authors also seem to overlook the fact that culture assimi-

lators were developed and applied outside a context of second language teaching. This is, of course, no reason why they should not also be useful in second language learning situations.

33 The audio-motor unit was described in a key article by Kalivoda *et al.* (1971: 400) as providing practical listening comprehension activities 'which increase knowledge of lexical and structural items, add dimension to cultural understanding, and enliven the learning situation with zest and humour'. Its role is not specific to culture teaching. In a second article, the same authors elaborate on the application of the audio-motor unit to culture teaching (Elkins, Kalivoda, and Morain 1972). See also Chastain (1988: 311).

34 Most writers suggest dramatization in various forms as a series of techniques for the presentation of culture and its incorporation in personal behaviour. Allen and Valette (1977:340–6) draw attention to role-playing as a way to learn the use of language in important everyday situations: greetings, table manners, buying a train ticket, and so on. Rivers (1981:326–30) refers to dialogues, skits, and mini-dramas, as well as masks, puppets, and various forms of role-play. Seelye (1984:chapter 6) describes mini-drama as a 'survival kit for culture shock'. In other words, he emphasizes it as a training in emotional adjustment. The importance of dramatization for the affective learning of culture is also pointed out by many writers.

35 For possible advantages and dangers of describing and explaining culture in the classroom through exposition and explanation see Rivers (1981:325–6). Nostrand (1974:299) includes systematic exposition as one of nine cognitive techniques.

36 Nostrand (1974) dwells at length on observation and inference and treats bibliographical work, analysis and synthesis as distinct techniques of culture teaching. As already pointed out, Seelye (1984:Chapter 8) devotes an entire chapter to 'asking the right questions' including finding information, and interviewing informants. Hammerly (1982) includes 'research-like projects' and academic research rather anomalously among the goals of culture teaching and not among the techniques and activities; by making it a goal he acknowledges the importance for the learner of finding out for himself. For Crawford-Lange and Lange (1984) the systematic inclusion of 'culture-as-process' (and not as product) is the essence of culture teaching. As pointed out in FCLT:256, this self-help may be useful, but it is no substitute for systematic research and resource development.

37 Morain (1968,1969) has made a strong case for folklore as an entry into culture, including under this concept rhymes, folktales, sayings and proverbs. Nostrand (1974) treats literature, cinema, and the

theatre as a way of cultural learning. Rivers (1981) recommends songs, dances, and pictures. Allen and Valette (1977) include the arts—music, painting, sculpture and dance—and make special mention of folk dances and folk music as well as cooking as art forms.

38 Nostrand (1974) writes: 'Literature, including the cinema, can illustrate unforgettably any regularity of a culture, once the regularity has been carefully derived from the widest possible range of sociocultural manifestations' (p. 287). Rivers (1981) plays down the role of literature for culture teaching. Although she does not dismiss it entirely, she warns that even at the advanced level, 'students need to be aware that what they read in fiction does not necessarily depict in faithful detail the reality of life for every individual in the foreign country. The ordinary life of an average citizen rarely provides the specific elements sought by the writer of a novel, play, or short story' (pp. 336–7).

39 See also Nostrand (1974:291), Chastain (1988:314), and Allen and Valette (1977:339).

40 In spite of the obvious usefulness of a native informant, some writers have rightly drawn attention to its drawbacks. Nostrand (1974:290) points out that it is difficult for someone to comment on a native informant's remarks in his presence. The need for preparation for the classroom visit of a native informant is stressed by Allen and Valette (1977:364–5) and Seelye (1984:157–61). The literature only envisages informants in the foreign language situation. The value of informants in language classes in the target language environment is somewhat neglected in the literature.

41 Nostrand (1974:293–5) writes about experience-based projects and includes study abroad schemes. Allen and Valette (1977:347–8) talk about preparations for travel abroad. Chastain (1988:315) briefly discusses summer camps, student exchange, and travel abroad.

42 For a study of student exchanges see Hanna, Smith, McLean, and Stern (1980).

43 'Community resources' are carefully described in Chastain (1988:314–5). See also Hammerly (1982:531). While both these writers only refer to the foreign language situation, Allen and Valette (1977:348–9) include 'field trips' in a target language milieu.

44 LeBlanc and Courtel (1990:91) suggest that culture should be dealt with 25 per cent of the time in a Canadian core French programme, in a context where integration will involve overlap and simultaneous realization of the different syllabuses.

9 The general language education syllabus[1]

Introduction

With this syllabus, we change perspective once more. While all three previous syllabuses involve the learner with the specific L2 they are learning, the general language education syllabus steps back from a preoccupation with the target language alone and invites the learner to consider general questions of language, culture, and learning. Of the four syllabuses, this is the most neglected. A number of language teachers may indeed question its usefulness. We need to remember that we are not concerned in this book with any single type of language teaching situation. All syllabuses are not equally applicable in all circumstances. In particular instances we have to weigh up the importance or emphasis of each of the four syllabuses. But in developing a policy we should consider the full range of possibilities and only after that appraise the choices open to us. In our view, there are very few situations in which the general language education syllabus is totally inapplicable, and there are many in which it could make a valuable if not the most important contribution to a second language curriculum. In order to arrive at a policy on this issue we will consider: (a) the rationale for a general language education syllabus, (b) some recent developments in the area, (c) different types of general language syllabuses, and (d) the scope of content and teaching approaches for this kind of syllabus.

Rationale for the general language education syllabus

There are several considerations which should prompt us to consider a general language education syllabus. The first arises directly from the objectives of a language course. Among these we previously considered the possibility of transfer, and identified specifically three transfer objectives: acquisition of language learning techniques, insight into language and culture, and positive generalized attitudes to language, culture, and language study.[2] The general language education syllabus is intended to develop these qualities in the learners and thereby help them to generalize from their experience of the second language to the learning of other languages, and to language education in general. This syllabus should also contribute to a better understanding of the three other syllabuses and thereby help the learner to approach the specific L2 with insight into the nature of language and language learning. This deeper understanding should make the learning of a specific language all the more valuable and effective. General language education can be an introduction to a language course and help to put second language learning in perspective.

The argument for a general language education syllabus links up with another consideration in language pedagogy which arises from our view of language learning. Learners should not be treated simply as passive recipients of a set of seemingly unconnected tasks but should take an active part in planning learning activities and in assessing their effectiveness. This view has found expression in the concept of learner autonomy (Dickinson 1987). A teacher and a course designer can only do so much. Ultimately the students must learn to function independently and to stand on their own feet. The more they know about language, culture, and language learning, the better they should be able to control the learning process and be responsible for their own development.[3]

A psychological argument for this syllabus can be found in the common human characteristic that people not only use language but are also conscious of language and reflect and comment on it. Such metalinguistic awareness can already be observed in rudimentary form in early childhood.[4] It is stimulated through the various forms of language education in school, learning to read and write and the use of language across the curriculum. Second language learning further develops such metalinguistic awareness. Examples are children's questions to a language teacher: 'How many words are there in Spanish?' or 'How long will it take me till I can speak French properly?' A young pupil went to the teacher after he was first told about irregular verbs in French and commented indignantly: 'Hasn't anyone ever told them that that's not right?' The question for the language teacher is whether to treat such questions as unimportant, even frivolous, or whether to build upon them and to regard the learner's metalinguistic awareness as a psychological basis for a general language syllabus.

We should assume that all language learners, whatever their age, have an implicit view of language and language learning which characterizes their approach to the second language, a view which may be at variance with that of the teacher and of the language course in question. The rationale underlying the teaching procedures may not be accepted by the students if these procedures clash with their views of learning, teaching, language, and society. It is useful for a teacher to observe what these views are and to estimate the difference between the assumptions underlying the language course and the students' perceptions. Teachers may have an intuitive understanding of the discrepancies between their explicit view of language and learning and the tacit views held by their students. Few systematic studies of these perceptions have been made.[5] However, a good start with a general language syllabus can be made by setting out from the natural metalinguistic perceptions and assumptions entertained by the students.

Through a general language education syllabus, the second language course is linked to the rest of the curriculum, particularly to mother tongue education, but also to social studies, and potentially to many other curriculum areas. Indirectly, this syllabus is of importance to the treatment of language in child care, and more generally to many language-related social issues, such as the treatment of language questions in society, linguistic and cultural prejudices, and attitudes to ethnic minorities.[6]

Recent developments in general language education

In recent times, second language courses have tended to be almost exclusively 'proficiency specific'. They seem to be designed to avoid becoming side-tracked into educational generalities for fear of not meeting the primary objective of a language programme. This concentation on proficiency has probably been a reaction against earlier expressions of goals in language teaching, particularly the teaching of classics in the nineteenth century, which focused mainly on grammatical and lexical knowledge. Underlying this objective was the ambitious goal of training the mind and the memory, or treating language as a preparation for coming to grips with literature. The late nineteenth century reform movement made the first major attempt to counteract these ambitious but somewhat impractical goals and to lay emphasis on the practical mastery of foreign languages. Simultaneously, the growing science of psychology questioned the mind training objective which had been one of the mainstays of the classical approach to language teaching. Consequently, in the first half of the twentieth century, the emphasis was mainly on language skills, and increasingly so after World War II as audiolingualism gained ground. Although the teaching of culture was also envisaged, the primacy of practical language training allowed little time for looking upon language in broader educational terms.

In many ways this emphasis on practical proficiency was a sound development, and any return to the philosophy of the pre-reform era is out of the question. Nevertheless, the broader contexts of language learning have never been quite forgotten. Many teachers have misgivings about plunging novices completely unprepared into a demanding language training programme or restricting courses completely to the proficiency objective. In the recent history of language teaching it has often been felt that there is need for some kind of preparation, and for a broader educational goal beyond, or in addition to, proficiency in the four skills.

In the early 1970s, Wilga Rivers (1972) proposed a division of language courses into two stages. It is stage one in this plan which has the character of a general language education component. Rivers' idea was to offer a well-rounded introduction to a language and a people without demanding the learning of the language as a skill, which would be the function of stage two. The stage one course would consist of four elements: (a) an introduction to language through the contrastive study of L1 and L2; (b) an introduction to another people through their language; (c) the experience of 'being another people' through 'authentic interaction'; (d) the experience of communicating with another people, for example, through visits, correspondence, and exchanges. The two-stage approach makes good sense, particularly for relatively mature beginners.

A number of educational systems have experimented with 'exploratory courses' or 'foundation courses' which aim to offer students a more gradual introductory orientation to language study in general. Such an introduction would place the learning of a particular language into a broader context of cultural and social contact with other countries. For example, an independent Los Angeles high school offers a one-year course, 'The phenomenon of language', at the grade 7 level. The first part of the course consists of a seventeen-week introduction to Latin followed by exploratory sessions on French, Spanish, and Russian, and the course ends with an 'informal examination of comparative linguistics . . . . The staff is convinced that this introductory language course has succeeded in creating the broad linguistic foundation upon which a genuinely successful language curriculum must be based' (Sims and Hammond 1981: 107).[7]

Similarly, David Cross, a teacher at the Archbishop Michael Ramsey School in central London, has introduced several changes as an alternative to the conventional language programme for students aged 11 to 15. The first two years are designed as a foundation course in language which involves contact with various languages and a comparison with English. Years 3 and 4 are conducted as intensive language courses—three double periods a week in year 3 (approximately 280 hours) and four double periods in year 4 (410 hours). The foundation course is divided into successive components on German, Spanish, general linguistics, and European studies. This general introduction to language provides a sound basis for language learning for two reasons. First, the chosen second language can be taught in a more concentrated fashion after the varied experiences enjoyed by the students in their two foundation years. Second, a more intensive form of language instruction is more effective than a course offered in small doses over a period of many years. The research that documented the central London programme showed that students who were taught French intensively for only two years achieved comparable results to students who had been in the regular four-year course. However, it is not possible to deduce from the information available whether the result is due to the more concentrated form of language teaching or to the effect of the foundation course on the learners' approach to learning a second language.[8]

In Australia (Quinn and Trounce 1985), the concept of an introductory course dealing with several languages, linguistics, and concepts of culture, became popular in the mid-1970s against the background of rethinking foreign language teaching. However, after a promising start and a spread of this movement between 1974 and 1976, it declined, because it did not live up to its promises. Teachers apparently had difficulty in making the somewhat abstract concepts of linguistics and cultural anthropology accessible to their students. In the opinion of Quinn and Trounce (1985: 140–1) the lesson is threefold: (a) it is difficult for a general language component to be both a subject in its own right and to contribute to the first and second language development of pupils; (b) the general language component requires a breaking down of conventional subject barriers, which is always problematic; (c) it is difficult and perhaps wrong, in the view of these Australian observers, to introduce the abstractions of a general language course too early, since it demands a maturity of mind which is not often found in younger learners.

In Britain, a systematic effort to develop a higher level of language awareness in schools began to take shape in the early 1980s. The interest in language awareness largely resulted from two sources. One was the Bullock Report, *A Language for Life* (1975), which advocated the concept of 'language across the curriculum'. Another important influence was that of the well-known language educator Eric Hawkins who, more than anyone else, has been a strong advocate of the concept of language awareness. Hawkins' advocacy made up for an anomaly in the Bullock Report: in spite of its policy of language across the curriculum, the report made no reference either to foreign languages or to the minority languages of immigrants in the school system. Hawkins saw language awareness as a unifying concept which could provide a common basis for mother tongue education, foreign languages, minority languages, and the language component of all curriculum subjects. In his book *Modern Languages in the Curriculum* (1981), Hawkins outlined the main components of courses on language awareness. A few years later, he continued this particular advocacy, in conjunction with Cambridge University Press, by editing and writing, together with several other authors, a series of six attractive and informative booklets on various aspects of language. These booklets, addressed to pupils aged approximately 11 to

14, were designed to encourage thinking about language. Hawkins also wrote a monograph on language awareness (Hawkins 1984) which presented some of the background to this movement in Britain and simultaneously served as a teachers' guide to the six language awareness booklets.[9]

In 1982, the National Congress on Languages in Education, a body established in 1976 and consisting of British professional associations concerned with language teaching, set up a working party on language awareness. This group investigated current developments in schools throughout Britain, and produced a report (Donmall 1985). According to this report, considerable efforts are already being made in many schools to include language awareness as a distinct activity. This is taking four different forms: (a) courses for 11–13 year olds to create awareness of language and an interest in language as a preparation for language learning—these courses are similar to the foreign language exploratory courses in the United States; (b) a language awareness or linguistics element in humanities or English classes for 11–13 year olds; (c) a course in the language development of children as part of preparation for parenthood or social studies courses in the fourth or fifth year of the secondary curriculum; (d) an introducton to linguistics possibly as part of a general studies course at the senior level of high school education (Donmall 1985: 257).

The survey indicated that well over 200 schools across Britain are involved in one or more of these activities. In addition, a few local education authorities (Leeds, Lothian, Norfolk) have projects on language awareness in groups of schools, and a number of authorities and individual schools interested in initiating language awareness work. It is too early to say whether this movement will have the same fate as its Australian counterpart. However, the likelihood is that it will be more lasting, since it is supported by a sizeable group of specialists and has at its disposal a considerable literature of accessible materials. Moreover, the teachers involved are well prepared through pre-service and in-service courses.

Finally, we should take note of yet another approach which is being evolved in Canada. Although it has not yet been systematically put to the test, it is of interest as a further option. In this case, the language awareness component is not treated as a separate course but as a component of long-term (six to nine year) French courses at the primary and secondary levels. The intention is to integrate it with the more language-specific syllabuses and to design it in such a way that it fosters language awareness and at the same time enhances the learning of the second language. This approach to general language education, which is in harmony with the conception advocated here, has been incorporated in a national project.[10]

Formats of general language education

The above overview has shown that a number of formats have been developed for incorporating a general language awareness component into the curriculum. Of these we will describe three in greater detail.

The preparatory course

The first is the preparatory or exploratory course which has a dual purpose. One of these purposes is to enable students to explore and sample different foreign languages which would help them to decide whether to pursue more prolonged and systematic studies in a second language, and if so which language to choose. A second purpose of this kind of preliminary course is to offer an intellectual preparation by giving students an idea of the nature of language and of the issues involved in language learning. Such courses vary in length; they range from a brief set of introductory lessons of a week or two, to a course lasting a term, a year, or even two years. In the British survey, approximately a third of the courses on language awareness were of this preparatory nature.

In a state secondary school in Melbourne, Australia, a one-year general language course is compulsory in the first year of secondary education. It is followed by a compulsory French course in year 2; for the remaining years, French is optional. However, the number of students opting for French remains high, a fact which is attributed to the success of the general language course. The content of this course centres on four topics: how language began, the development of the alphabet, language families, and parts of speech. Each core topic 'is illustrated with concepts and . . . examples from a wide variety of languages, and each topic is followed by a series of lessons applying the concepts of the French language' (Quinn and Trounce 1985: 139).

The North Westminster Community School, a large multicultural school in central London, offers a language foundation course for the first two years at the secondary level. Three languages, Spanish, French, and German, are offered for one term in each of these two years, except for the last two weeks of each term which are devoted to a more general theme, the World Languages Project. This consists of six units on the following topics: the development of speech; the history of writing; language families and language map activities; language borrowings; language invention and change; the Hebrew and Russian alphabets; Arabic, Bahasa Indonesia, Bengali, and Chinese. In this way, over a two-year period students become acquainted with three European languages, and learn something about six others, including some oriental languages.[11] Foreign language exploratory courses (FLEX) in the United States are similar in design and have a similar preparatory purpose.[12]

The question arises as to whether such general courses, which are in principle attractive, are effective as a preparation for second language study. Do they help students in their approach to learning a second language? Do they help them to decide which language to study? How useful is it to sample different languages?

The independent course

A second type of format is the independent general language course which can be related to mother tongue education, foreign language courses, and to the language development of the individual and society. Independent language awareness courses are being tried in Britain where they tend to be viewed as an educationally advanced activity in general secondary education at the sixth form level. Such courses deal with concepts and techniques of linguistics and serve 'to consolidate what has been learned about language in an unsystematic way in the course of studying English and other languages (modern and classical)' (Donmall 1985: 8). For example, a course on principles of language devised as a sixth form course for an independent school near Reading has the following objectives: to develop the student's awareness of what language is and how it functions, to make him more sensitive to his own and other people's use of language, and to provide an introduction to the basic principles of linguistic study (ibid.: 146). The course is based as much as possible on the student's knowledge of his mother tongue, and it is divided into three sections: the first deals with the nature of language and communication in general; the second consists of an analysis of English phonology, morphology, and syntax; and the third deals with change and variety in the use of English including the student's own variety.[13]

According to the British survey of language awareness courses (ibid.: 257–66) similar introductions to linguistics at the sixth-form level were found in 40 out of approximately 200 schools included in the survey. Evaluations of the Reading course have been positive on the whole, although it is difficult to assess how far 'the students' response to and use of language has benefited' (ibid.: 169). If the general language component comes at the end of a course of study we cannot expect it to have any influence on the language education that preceded it. What it might do is to round off what has gone before, to draw it together in some way and help students make sense retrospectively of their earlier experiences and thus create a heightened awareness of language and language learning.

An integral component of language education

Finally, a language awareness syllabus can be devised as an integral component of language education. This view of language awareness is implicit in some of the British experiences described above. It also underlies the approach to second language teaching which is advocated in this book. For example, the British Report of the Working Party of the National Congress on Languages in Education advocates that language awareness courses should make explicit the pupils' intuitive knowledge of their mother tongue; strengthen study skills for the learning of the mother tongue, foreign languages, and other curricular subjects; improve the reading skills of the verbally less able; and impart an understanding of the value of language as part of human life (cf. Donmall 1985: 7–8). Although this report of the working party advocates the establishment of distinct language awareness courses, its emphasis on language across the curriculum and on the value of language awareness to child development and parental care implicitly suggest an integrated approach.

The content of the general language education syllabus

In thinking about the content of a general language education syllabus in the context of a second language curriculum, we can be somewhat more specific than the British language awareness courses which are broadly related to many different aspects of language education and to the use of language in society. The syllabus we envisage should be closely linked with the other three syllabuses we have considered and with corresponding learners' activities in relation to the target language. The goals of the syllabus should be threefold: it should enhance the learning of the target language; it should provide the student with a set of techniques and a body of knowledge as well as with the outlook needed for learning other languages; and it should enable the student to relate the target language to other educational and social activities. In the following sections we will consider: (a) the general language component, (b) the culture element, (c) knowledge about first language acquisition, and (d) learning how to learn a language.

The general language component

Depending on their age, maturity, and previous experience, students are likely to approach the learning of a second language with preconceived notions about language in general, about the target language itself, and about language learning. If a general language syllabus is designed to guide the learners' understanding of the nature of language, it must take their preconceptions into account. The views of language learners have not been very systematically investigated. The few studies that have been done show that learners of all ages—except perhaps the very young—are able, willing, and sometimes very eager to share their observations on language and on their own learning experience. We can also gain glimpses of learners' views by making casual observations of what students say during the language class.[14]

The problem is that we can easily get lost in the minutiae of the target language. On the other hand, if we ignore the details, our knowledge of the language remains vague and uncertain. It is also difficult for a learner to obtain a feeling for the totality of a language and all too easy to be overwhelmed by isolated aspects, for example a difficult feature of pronunciation or some puzzling grammatical item. The naive language learner often expresses this preoccupation in such remarks as 'I will never learn language X because I'm not musical enough to master the pronunciation.' In this instance phonology seems to loom large and to be the insurmountable hurdle. Other learners may view the vocabulary as a daunting obstacle, others again have irregular verbs on their mind. The fact that the main emphasis of textbooks is usually placed on grammar gives the learner the mistaken impression that learning a language means learning only its grammar. Few courses attempt to give learners a sense of proportion so that they can relate one aspect of the language, such as the tense system, irregular verbs, or the order of pronouns, to the language as a whole.

A general language education component which is based on a linguistic view of language should be able to conteract these misconceptions. It can bring to bear a broader view derived from linguistic geography or historical linguistics, and different aspects of linguistic analysis including phonology, grammar, sociolinguistics, the study of kinesics, and paralinguistics. Recent British experience with various language awareness projects as well as some FLEX programmes in the United States show what is involved in devising an inventory of useful and illuminating general language topics. The series of linguistic topic books, edited by Hawkins, illustrate a well-thought-out approach. These booklets, which are addressed to English native speakers, provide interesting glimpses of different aspects of language, using the students' own intuitive knowledge as the main basis of instruction, but providing a comparison with similar features in other languages.[15]

For the design of a general language education syllabus, the linguistic subdisciplines represent the essential resources to draw upon in order to give the learner the overview, the essential knowledge and categories of analysis, and the appropriate techniques which are relevant for language learning. Naturally, in designing such a syllabus the key questions would always have to be what particular topics are helpful from a language learner's perspective. These topics would have to be distinguished from what is likely to be too difficult or too confusing and, therefore, an added burden rather than a help. In developing an inventory of topics we should bear the following points in mind:

(a) In order to give the learner a broad orientation to the language to be studied we should attempt to put it into a social, political, historical, and geographical context. For example, Pomphrey's language topic booklet *Language Varieties and Change* (1985) includes a world map, a discussion on languages of the world, and exercises about different languages and speakers.
(b) It is often helpful to understand the historical evolution of the target language and the concept of language change over time. Pomphrey (1985) illustrates this with a chapter in her booklet about language families, language change and borrowing, and inventions of new words.
(c) In many instances it is helpful to understand the concepts of standard, dialect, and social varieties of language. Pomphrey (1985: 31–2) illustrates this with varieties of English from Wales, South Africa, North America, Jamaica, Ireland, Australia, and Scotland.
(d) The learner needs to understand the relationship between different aspects of the target language: phonology, grammar, lexis, discourse, and sociosemantic functions. Jones (1984) attempts to do this in his booklet *How Language Works* in the Cambridge series under such headings as 'All sorts of sounds', and 'Words as labels'. The bulk of the book, however, deals with grammatical topics under the headings 'Words together', 'Nuts and bolts of language', 'Doing things with words', 'Gender and what it does', and 'Talking about the past and future'. Another booklet in the same series has a chapter on functional analysis under the heading 'A day in the life of a language user' (Astley and Hawkins 1985).
(e) The learner needs to acquire a feeling for the systematicity of the language: its rules, regularities, and patterns of predictability. 'Grammar, approached as a voyage of discovery into patterns of the language rather than the learning of prescriptive rules, is no longer a bogey word' (Hawkins 1984: 150–1).
(f) The learner needs to understand the writing system of the second language, the relationship between the spoken and the written language, and the specific characteristics of speech and writing (Hawkins 1983; 1984: 113–37).
(g) The learner should be encouraged to explore the similarities and differences between the target language and any other languages he knows. The Cambridge Language Awareness series constantly

invites comparison between different languages and English. In this way the course draws on the learners' intuitive experience of their mother tongue and invites them to compare it with the second language.

The above topics could be summarized in a few lessons. They could also be developed into an independent course, as suggested by the Hawkins series, or they could be spread over several years as an integral part of a language programme (Marland 1987, Hawkins 1987). Obviously, the intellectual maturity of students and their level of linguistic sophistication have a bearing on the kinds and number of tasks to be tackled. Some tasks are more appropriate for older and more experienced language learners, others are suitable for young children just beginning the conscious study of a new language.

Culture in general language education

A generalized concept of culture and related concepts, such as 'speech community' and 'society', can be treated in the same way as language. Just as the general study of language is intended to lead to a heightened language awareness, the generalized treatment of culture can be expected to contribute to a cultural awareness extending beyond the target culture. It can be associated with studies on language awareness or it can be integrated into the cultural component of a language course. Although the syllabus proposed by Hawkins (1981, 1984) does not identify culture as a distinct area of study, some of the British language awareness programmes do in fact include a cultural element.

The Cambridge Language Awareness series includes a number of sections in different booklets which are clearly sociocultural in character. For example, Jones (1984) refers to the theory of linguistic relativity which links language to different cultural perceptions, and talks in fairly simple terms about 'labelling the world another way.' Pomphrey (1985) refers to greetings, important festivals, dress and food. For example, the French word *pain* suggests a 'crusty long French loaf . . . which is very different from the factory packed sliced bread you find in Britain' (Pomphrey 1985: 24). The following principles might guide the development of culture teaching in a general language education syllabus:

(a) Identify the speech community or communities using the target language as its normal means of communication. If there are several, such as those which use English, Spanish, Portuguese, or French, we should decide which community should serve as the principal reference for a given language course. The students should be made aware of why this choice has been made.
(b) In the treatment of the culture component of the general language

education syllabus we should use the same system of classification to make reference to different cultures. We should distinguish the different perspectives of ordinary L1 and L2 speakers, and both of these from the professional viewpoint of the anthropologist or sociologist.

(c) Particular emphasis should be laid on the relationship between cultural features of linguistic phenomena. For example, what sociocultural features, such as social class or professional status, are realized through modes of address, vocabulary, grammar, style, intonation, or gesture? Jones (1984) points out that in one Indian language of Northern California, Yana, the form of words changes according to the sex of the speaker. Thus, a male speaker refers to a deer as *bana*, while a female speaker calls the same animal *ba*. The male and female terms for a grizzly bear are *t'en'na* and *t'et* respectively.

(d) Since a speech community is not necessarily a homogeneous entity, learners should be made aware of group differences (for example, those based on geographic location, social class, and age), and they should learn to recognize the linguistic manifestations of these distinctions. Since most societies are multifaceted and increasingly multicultural, it would be a mistake to present the foreign country as if it had a uniform population and culture.

(e) In order to generalize from the target culture to other cultures it is helpful to compare the home culture to the target one, and to identify the similarities and differences.

Knowledge about first language acquisition

First language acquisition is a topic with a strong claim to be included in a general language syllabus. It covers the acquisition of the mother tongue in infancy as well as the language development of children who are brought up in bilingual or multilingual environments. It also covers the informal acquisition of a second language by children who, as a result of travel or migration, have to adapt themselves to life in another country. All these informal and 'natural' ways of first and second language acquisition are of interest because they stand in contrast to the deliberate study of a second language which forms part of a typical school curriculum.

First and second language acquisition has been extensively studied by developmental psychologists, psycholinguists, and applied linguists over many years. Earlier studies go back to the nineteenth century, but the field has become an area of great scholarly interest only during the last twenty years or so. Since the 1950s, the question of the optimal age for second language learning and the role of nature and nurture in first language acquisition has led to a spate of theoretical and empirical studies. Most of the issues that have been raised are still unresolved, but a good deal of information has been accumulated, forming a rich, although confusing, scholarly resource for syllabus development.[16]

The main question in the present context is what this topic contributes to second language learning. It is inevitable that classroom learning of a second language should give rise to questions about first language acquisition, childhood bilingualism, and informal second language learning by children. The classic example is the observation by Gouin (1880) who tells us that he had tried vainly to learn German by all kinds of methods, marvelling at his young nephew's simultaneous and seemingly effortless progress in his native language, French. Comparing this mastery of a language in a young child with his own miserable failure as an adult, Gouin based his own language teaching reform proposals on what he believed natural language learning had taught him.[17] The value of observations on first language acquisition lies in the fact that they vividly demonstrate many of the problems the second language learner has to face: difficulties of pronunciation, learning new words, interpreting word meanings, and acquiring a knowledge of grammar as well as the rules of contextualized language use. Language acquisition as a topic for a general language syllabus has the advantage of encouraging learners to make personal observations. Children as second language students can often observe the language development of a younger sibling; these observations, which are often remarkably acute, can be reported by them in the second language class. Adults as language learners can make similar observations of their own children or grandchildren.

Simply by making such observations and comparing them with second language learning, we can come to grips with some of the difficulties and see them in a fresh and reassuring perspective. A young child's difficulties in pronunciation, his eagerness to communicate, his ability to express himself with gestures, his determination to find out the meaning of new words, his intuitive understanding of grammar rules—these and many other observations invite comparison with the classroom learning of a new language and contribute to a better understanding of the nature of language. In making such observations and comparisons, we would of course draw attention to the differences no less than the similarities between the two situations. Thus, it has frequently been pointed out that the L1 is acquired over many years and usually in a favourable setting, while L2 learning often takes place in circumstances which do not encourage target language use. Another difference is that L1 acquisition is interwoven with the child's cognitive, conceptual, and social growth.[18] For example, a child learning the English word *dog* grapples with the concept 'dog': what does it include and what does it exclude? The L2 learner as a previous L1 acquirer already possesses a large stock of concepts on which to draw in trying to learn the second language.

The advantage of being able to use L1 acquisition as a topic does not only lie in the fact that it is part of most learners' common experience. There is, today, a mass of empirical data as well as theories about the factors which enter into L1 and L2 development. However, while this body of information is a valuable resource its interpretation is controversial, and conclusions on what our knowledge about L1 acquisition 'means' for L2 learning must be offered with caution. The danger lies in drawing unwarranted conclusions for L2 learning from what appear to be obvious and uncontroversial observations. It must be clearly stated that knowledge about L1 acquisition does not lead to firm and undisputed principles of L2 learning. It may suggest, hint, and indicate, but the data rarely speak with absolute assurance. We should, therefore, be suspicious of the dogmatic nature of some interpretations. In syllabus development on this topic we should be guided by what appears to be the most up-to-date information and the most reliable knowledge, and we must use a great deal of discretion in trying to interpret the findings for L2 learners.

A booklet of 32 pages by Dunlea (1985) in the Cambridge Language Awareness series, is addressed to pupils aged 10 to 15. It describes, through text and illustrations, how a young child acquires language in infancy and early childhood and simultaneously invites comparisons with foreign language learning. It points out that children always learn the language of their environment and it illustrates the role of parents in the process by focusing on the way they help the child to attribute meaning to speech sounds. It indicates how word meanings are gradually established and how we can tell that grammar rules are being acquired. Throughout this booklet, wherever possible, the account of L1 acquisition is interspersed with observations and questions about L2 learning. For example, Dunlea talks about the difficulty children have in making the correct sounds and sound combinations in L1 and then asks: 'Have you met any group of sounds in a foreign language that are difficult to say? Which ones? Which sounds in English do speakers of other languages find difficult?' Similarities and differences between L1 and L2 learning are finally brought together in the concluding chapter. What this text illustrates well is that, through observations about language acquisition and comparisons with L2 learning, the learner can gain new insights into language and see his efforts from a new perspective.

Learning how to learn a language

Of the four topic areas of a general language education syllabus, learning how to learn is perhaps the most important for a second language curriculum. It has a direct bearing on the learning of the target language and may well have the highest transfer value. It is closely linked with the three topic areas we have already described, because the way we attempt to tackle the language learning task is largely dependent on our view of language, culture, and language acquisition. The idea of learning how to learn is not entirely new, nor is it confined to language learning. In other areas of education, its value has been widely advocated at least since Bruner wrote his seminal *Beyond the Information Given*. Educators have argued convincingly that schooling cannot prepare students for all contingencies in a constantly changing world. Therefore, the best curriculum is not one that is based on a static body of knowledge but one which teaches students to cope with change; i.e. one which focuses on the process of learning rather than its product.[19]

Applying this idea to second language education, the investment of time involved in learning an L2 should not only lead to a certain level of proficiency, it should enable the learners to go beyond that level on their own. It should help the students to develop their 'autonomy', that is, give them the ability to help themselves, and to continue to learn independently. At the same time, it should give them the confidence and necessary know-how to tackle other languages efficiently if they are called upon to do so. The idea of a self-reliant L2 learner who is capable of tackling language learning tasks intelligently, selectively, and efficiently has a long history; but the suggestion that it should be an integral part of the normal curriculum of ordinary language courses is still in its infancy. It began to evolve during the 1970s as an offshoot of research on language learning.

Learning how to learn languages builds on a long-standing tradition. Sweet in his classic *The Practical Study of Languages* (1899) appealed to the intelligent student to tackle the study of a language not as a mindless chore, but as an interesting, worthwhile activity. Towards the end of World War II, Frederick Bodmer in collaboration with a scientist, Lancelot Hogben, published 'a guide to foreign languages for the home student', entitled *The Loom of Language* (1944). This work which was described as the 'third of the primers for the age of plenty' followed two other popular books, *Mathematics for the Million* and *Science for the Citizen*. These three books were intended to offer adult learners, whose formal education had been wanting during the inter-war years, an opportunity to approach broad areas of knowledge such as mathematics, science, and language through intelligent and mature self-study. In *The Loom of Language* an attempt is made to introduce the reader to the grammar, vocabulary, and writing systems of several Germanic and Romance languages simultaneously. The aim is to take away the fear of foreign languages, and to convince the reader that language learning is a fascinating adventure and at the same time a manageable task.

Since World War II various linguists have taken an interest in questions of language learning. A well-known pamphlet by Bloomfield (1942) on the 'practical study of foreign languages' led the way.[20] Since then, techniques of language learning, based on linguistic experience, have been suggested in numerous books addressed to missionaries, linguists, anthropologists, and social workers. Since regular courses of instruction were often not available, the languages had to be learned informally through observation and personal contacts with native speakers. A few books or pamphlets on language learning techniques were also produced with the general reader in mind, i.e. those who were planning to take a language course and to learn from a textbook to begin with. All these works reflect interpretations of language and language learning characteristic of the period in which they were written. But this does not mean they are dated and have nothing to say to the present generation. Most of them contain extremely good advice which reflects the skills of able and highly experienced linguists who have grappled with the task of learning languages in the field under very difficult circumstances.[21]

In the early 1970s, it was suggested that second language learning in classrooms should be investigated in order to distinguish more efficient from less efficient language learners. This work was pioneered by Rubin (1975) and a research group at The Ontario Institute for Studies in Education (Stern 1975; Fröhlich 1976; Naiman *et al.* 1978). These investigators and others who continued studies in this area into the 1980s were conscious of the many complex factors that entered into language learning, such as the learner's personality, age, maturity, previous language learning experience, and his view of the nature of language and language learning. But what interested these researchers above all was the learners' strategies in tackling a second language. It was thought that if one could find out what strategies are employed by successful language learners these could perhaps be taught to learners with learning difficulties (Stern 1975). In this way less efficient learners could perhaps be helped to become more effective in their approach. It might also be possible to help good learners with a talent for languages to make the best possible use of their natural abilities.

During the same period Holec and his colleagues at CRAPEL (Centre de recherches et d'application pédagogiques en langues) started training adult language students to become actively involved in their own language learning. The tutors at this centre encourage the learners to work out what they want to achieve, what subject matter they would like to deal with, what skills they wish to acquire, what techniques they would find most appropriate, how much time and effort they can devote to language learning, and so on. Through discussions of this kind the students determine their own programme, report to their tutor from time to time and modify their study plans in the light of their experience (Holec 1987).[22]

Since language learning involves the learner as a person, one component of the general language education syllabus focuses on the learner's background, self-perception, and learning style. Through the work of Curran, Stevick, and others, there has been an increasing recognition of this aspect of language learning.[23] There is a need for the teacher to consider the learner as a person, but equally a need for the learner to come to terms with himself, and to try to understand his own strengths and weaknesses. It should be remembered that the schemes devised by the Council of Europe on language needs also include the background of the learner and as much information as one can gather on the context in which learning takes place. Factors to take into account include the learner's age, maturity, and previous language learning experience. As we have seen in the discussion on phonology, many adults accept it as given that they cannot acquire an authentic pronunciation 'because they are too old'; i.e. the myth about the relationship between age and language learning prevents them from trying. It is, therefore, valuable to discuss what students believe about themselves as learners or what they believe about language learning in general.

With regard to learning preferences, it has been found that some learners with a strong background in formal schooling have a preference for a cognitive-intellectual approach, while students with a negative experience of previous learning are often afraid of formal teaching. Some students express a preference for visual learning, while others prefer programmes with an audiolingual emphasis.[24] Learning styles and preferences should be handled with caution, since sometimes students rationalize difficulties by imagining that they suffer from innate disabilities. It is useful, however, to bring these self-perceptions into the open if only to try to persuade students to widen their range of experience. Learner training schemes rightly focus their attention on the reasons for learning. By giving learners the chance to discuss what they expect to achieve, they can be encouraged to set themselves realistic objectives and not to approach the learning task with illusions about instant proficiency. In this respect, schemes of graded objectives or proficiency standards are useful in that they give learners a realistic idea of what is expected as a result of a given period of language training. It is important for the learner to define his own short-term and long-term expectations and to relate these to what the language course actually offers.[25]

While adults under conditions of voluntary language learning have the opportunity to define their needs and objectives, students in schools and universities frequently take a prescribed course of study. Even in these circumstances, however, it is possible to 'let students into the know' and to discuss with them what expectations the programme implies and what is being looked for at an intermediate stage or as an ultimate outcome. The concept of graded objectives in British schools has not only provided teachers with more manageable course goals, it has also helped students to formulate goals which can be reached in the reasonably foreseeable future.

Central to the training of the learner is the concept of the strategies at the learner's disposal. As Wenden and Rubin (1987) have shown, the interest in trying to improve our understanding of learner strategies is undiminished; so are the efforts being made in learner training, that is, to teach students the strategies or techniques of language learning. In the section below, we examine the concept of learning strategy and outline five main strategies of relevance for learner training.

Learning strategies

The concept of learning strategy is based on the assumption that learners consciously engage in activities to achieve certain goals, that they exercise a choice of procedures, and that they undertake some form of long-term planning.[26] Strategy, as used in this book, expresses the intentionality of language learning. It refers to broadly conceived directions the learner more or less consciously chooses in trying to achieve his objectives. In applying these strategies, the learner engages in certain activities, uses particular procedures, or employes specific techniques. Thus, an awareness of learning strategy options and choices is valuable to the learner, and making him aware of these options forms part of the learner training we have in mind. Learning 'strategies' we define in a way that is parallel to teaching strategies, understood as broadly conceived intentional directions, and learning 'techniques' parallel our definition of teaching techniques (activities or procedures) as the behavioural manifestations of the strategies. These two sets of terms, then, are complementary.

In making the above distinction between strategies and techniques, our use of the term 'strategy' is somewhat at variance with the way it is used in the literature. Rubin, for example, who has pioneered a great deal of this work, uses a very wide definition, and regards strategies as 'what learners do to learn and do to regulate their learning' (1987: 19). Rubin's co-worker, Wenden (1987a: 7), treats strategies as equivalent to what other writers have called 'techniques', 'tactics', 'consciously employed operations', 'learning skills', and so on. Several lists of learning strategies have been compiled which vary in length, scope, and terminology. Some are quite short, listing as few as four (Stern 1983a). Others are longer; for example, Stern (1975) identified ten strategies of good language learners and Rubin (1975) twelve. Rubin and Thompson (1982) list fourteen, summarized in these brief slogans:

Find your own way.
Organize.
Be creative.
Make your own opportunities.
Learn to live with uncertainty.
Use mnemonics.
Make errors work.
Use your linguistic knowledge.
Let context help you.
Learn to make intelligent guesses.
Learn some lines as wholes.
Learn formalized routines.
Learn production techniques.
Use different styles of speech.

If we use a very broad definition and include all language learning techniques, we could come up with even longer lists. In spite of these superficial differences and what appears to be a certain arbitrariness in the classification of learning strategies, there is broadly speaking a consensus on the main strategies.

Whatever scope we give to the concept of strategy, we believe that for learner training it is useful to focus both on broad strategies and on more specific techniques. In preparing a list of learning strategies for this purpose it is advisable to make two initial assumptions about the applicability of strategies to given groups of learners: (a) learner training is meant to raise the learner's consciousness of strategies and techniques available for more effective learning; (b) there is no single foolproof and universally applicable list of strategies or techniques. Age, maturity, level of language proficiency, learners' goals, and personality factors are likely to have a bearing on the combinations of strategies that suit particular individuals in specific language learning situations. On this basis we will now identify five main strategies.[27]

Management and planning strategies

These strategies express the learner's intention to direct his own learning. As Holec (1987) has shown, a learner can take charge of the development of his own programme, helped by a teacher whose role becomes that of an adviser and resource person. This means that we must: (a) decide what commitment to make to language learning, (b) set ourselves reasonable goals, (c) decide on an appropriate methodology, select appropriate resources, and monitor progress, and (d) evaluate our achievement in the light of previously determined goals and expectations. In some situations learners are left entirely to themselves and have to organize the entire programme of study independently. In other cases, many decisions have already been made by the syllabus designer or the teacher. Even so, the programme may need modification, for example, because the students' background knowledge is better or worse than had been assumed. Adjustments have to be made in almost all preplanned programmes, and it is in these situations that negotiations between the teacher and the class are essential.[28]

Rubin and Thompson suggest that students should organize their own programmes of study (1982: 54) and they illustrate this with the suggestions: 'Establish a regular schedule' and 'Learn something new every day.' Several authors have made a distinction between metacognitive and cognitive strategies. What we have called managing and planning strategies fall under the heading of metacognitive strategies: planning, monitoring, and evaluation. In all these the learner seems to stand away from his own learning activities and examines them critically. That is, the learner plans his learning, sets objectives, assesses progress as the learning proceeds, and eventually evaluates achievement in relation to previously set goals. These are all typical techniques which are included under the management and planning strategy.[29]

Cognitive strategies

The techniques which fall under this heading are at the heart of strategy training.[30] These are the techniques learners make use of in the deliberate and formal study and practice of the second language. In the literature they are sometimes referred to as cognitive learning strategies, as opposed to metacognitive or planning strategies. Rubin (1987: 23) has identified six such cognitive techniques 'which contribute to the development of the language system which the learner constructs and affect learning directly', and further defines them as 'steps or operations used in learning or problem-solving that require direct analysis, transformation, or synthesis of learning materials' (ibid.):

1. Clarification/verification
2. Guessing/inductive inferencing
3. Deductive reasoning
4. Practice
5. Memorization
6. Monitoring

(Rubin 1987: 23)

The first technique, clarification/verification, indicates that learners do not completely trust themselves and check comprehension or the way the language functions by consulting a grammar or a dictionary, or by asking an informant or the teacher. For the same reason, good learners tend to be vigilant about their performance in the language and monitor themselves critically. At first such monitoring must be done by someone else who, through error correction and feedback, acts as an external monitor. However, it is important for students to learn to monitor themselves, in other words, to internalize the monitoring function. In the literature on language learning and in teachers' guides, a great deal is made of the distinction between inductive inferencing and deductive reasoning.[31] The important point about both of these techniques is that they treat the language learning task as a problem-solving activity in which learners can either apply principles and rules (deductive reasoning) or attempt to discover for themselves what these principles or rules might be (inductive inferencing).

Under practice Rubin refers to such techniques as repetition, rehearsal, experimentation, application of rules, imitation, and attention to detail; in short, practice is mainly concerned with the development of accuracy (1987: 24). This technique, like the previous two reasoning techniques, is based on the assumption that a language is largely learnt by conscious, deliberate, and focused techniques of study. They involve cognitive processes of identifying, classifying, inferencing, and relational thinking generally. Finally, language learning always presents problems of memory, and efficient memorization is indeed a necessary part of deliberate language learning.

A list of techniques of this kind captures important procedures for good language learning which have much in common with the strategies in conceptual learning generally. However, they are not uncontroversial. Some methodologies do not attribute as much importance to the conscious learning of language items and the deliberate study of the linguistic system. They rely more on unconscious absorption and intuitive processes. Learners may well differ individually as to what extent the use of cognitive strategies is important in their mastery of the language. Even if we accept the view that cognitive strategies are important, it is questionable whether the list we have cited (Rubin 1987) really comprises all the essential techniques and whether the divisions between them (for example, between inductive inferencing and deductive reasoning) are sufficiently clear to justify separation into distinct categories. At least one important cognitive technique of good language learners, observation—that is, careful listening, watching, and reading—is not even mentioned. We cannot claim, therefore, that the list is exhaustive and captures all and only the essentials of a deliberate learning strategy. It is best treated as a useful but tentative list of suggestions which should be verified through empirical studies on techniques used by different groups of learners.

Communicative–experiential strategies

There is ample evidence that language learning cannot be accomplished through formal study and practice alone. The learner must seek opportunities for language use in real-life situations. Whether he reads whatever interests him, listens to the radio, watches films, or engages other people in conversation the important thing is that he must seek opportunities for unrehearsed, authentic use of the language. The point here is that the learner focuses deliberately on content, topic, or activity and uses the language instrumentally. What are commonly referred to as communication strategies, such as circumlocution, gesturing, paraphrase, or asking for repetition and explanation, are techniques which learners use in order to keep a conversation going. These techniques are not employed in order to learn specific points of language; their purpose is to avoid interrupting the flow of communication.[32] The cognitive and communicative–experiential strategies complement each other, and ideally the learner should be prepared to employ both.

Interpersonal strategies

Language learning presents certain social problems, and success in learning is largely dependent on how a learner handles these problems, in other words, on his interpersonal strategy. It is, to begin with, essential to come to terms with the loss of status that an inadequate command of a language imposes upon us and to accept what has been described as infantilization and satellization.[33] As learners, especially in the early stages, we are dependent on help. In this sense we are 'satellites' to someone who provides support and guidance. Because of our comparative helplessness and dependence, our social status as learners is similar to that of a child in the family: it is an infantile status. For this reason Larson and Smalley (1972) have advised language learners to find a family who will 'adopt' them for language learning. Eventually, of course, our aim must be to emancipate ourselves and to cut ourselves loose from the constant need for help, to 'desatellize', and to deal with second language issues independently, for example, to monitor our own progress and to evaluate our own performance. The ability to learn from correction and from monitoring by a teacher, a sympathetic family, or a friend is, however, a necessary stage in the development towards independence.

The experiential strategy is also interpersonal in that it requires us to seek contact with native speakers and co-operate with them.[34] In the target language community we have to come to terms with our status as outsiders, and learn through a process of familiarization to become acquainted with the target culture. As learners, in other words, we face a range of interpersonal and status problems and an ever-changing situation of linguistic emancipation and acculturation. It requires a good deal of interpersonal skill to deal effectively with this constantly changing human aspect of language learning.

Affective strategies

It is widely recognized in the literature that language learning involves affect, and that if favourable affective conditions prevail, learning is likely to be more successful. To a certain extent, affective conditions are subject to control by the learner. A good language learner will attempt to create favourable conditions and to overcome the inevitable problems of negative affect. In other words, good language learners employ distinct affective strategies.[35] A few of the problems for which such strategies are needed should be pointed out.

First, language learning is challenging, but it can also be frustrating. This sense of frustration is often caused by the sheer magnitude of the learning task. It presents problems of memory, attention, co-ordination of the many elements involved, and cognitive control. To learn to accept these inevitable difficulties with equanimity and not to be overwhelmed by them is an important skill a good learner needs to develop. A second problem is the feeling of strangeness evoked by the second language. Many of its features, whether in vocabulary, phonology, or grammar, appear at first sight to be arbitrary and unnecessary. A third emotional inhibitor is the existence of negative feelings about native speakers of the L2. Good language learners are more or less conscious of these emotional problems. Even if they do not conceptualize them as we have here, they are sufficiently aware of them not to build up high affective barriers which would prevent them from learning the target language. They try to create associations of positive affect towards the second language and its speakers as well as towards the learning activities involved. By drawing attention to the potential frustrations or pointing them out as they arise, learner training can help students to face up to these emotional difficulties and to overcome them.

Concluding comments

In this chapter we have discussed the rationale for a general language education syllabus, which until recently has been a relatively neglected aspect of second language curriculum. As we have seen, an important aspect of this syllabus is to teach students the strategies and techniques of language learning. Generally speaking, the approach to learner training in the classroom is likely to be one of information, questioning, and discussion. The goal is consciousness-raising, reflection, and creating an awareness of different possibilities. Learners should be encouraged to think about their reasons for learning the language, their past experience of language learning or schooling generally, the strategies they employ and what specific techniques they have found helpful. Discussions with the teacher and other students are likely to help them to tackle language learning problems in a more conscious manner. Students should also be encouraged to experiment and to develop their own procedures. The literature on learner training suggests that many learners fail to consider all the alternatives and tend to rely on too narrow a range of techniques.

Planning strategies are most highly developed through programmes that are organized so as to invite self-management, such as the ESL and FSL courses of CRAPEL. Here, the students are expected to plan their own programmes and review their procedures as they progress. In school settings, where the second language curriculum is determined by an external authority and is often dominated by a published textbook, students can be encouraged to interpret and understand the objectives, methodology, and overall design of the course. Where the prescribed course has weaknesses, consultation with students can lead to adjustments and improvements. The handling of homework assignments can also become a means of training in self-management. Even under fairly rigid conditions of language instruction, it is possible for students to develop their own planning strategies. Doing this has the added advantage that the students will become conscious of the overall design of the course, with the result that they are less likely to be overwhelmed by the accumulation of isolated details.

The strategy that is most amenable to training is the cognitive learning strategy. For example, the reading of texts or memorization can be done more efficiently if it is divided into certain steps which have been jointly decided upon. Also, vocabulary note-taking can be more or less efficient, depending on how systematically it is tackled. Much of this training is likely to occur as an integral part of working with students on second language materials. It often amounts to little more than drawing a general lesson from suggestions made by the teacher in a particular situation. Training for the communicative–experiential strategy forms an effective counterpoint to the cognitive learning strategy. The students must learn to 'switch off' their analytical apparatus and focus on the task or activity currently being undertaken, or on the development of a conversational exchange.

Although the interpersonal and affective strategies are more elusive, they can also be tackled by drawing attention to questions of status loss, dependence, and feelings of frustration. When students are given choices in what and how to learn, they do more than develop self-management techniques; they begin to take responsibility for their own learning. Affective problems can be tackled by talking about them and sharing perceptions and ideas. It is important for a teacher to be alert for signs of frustration or prejudice against the target language and its speakers, and to decide whether talking about these feelings will help students to overcome them. It would be facile, however, to expect that we can change deep-seated negative attitudes by a single talk or a simple rational explanation.

We have to look upon learner training as part of the purpose of a general language education syllabus. It should help students to understand better the nature of the task they are engaged in, and thus to have a clearer perception of what they are doing when they undertake the many diverse activities that make up a language course. At the same time, it should help them to put the learning of the second language into a wider context, thus contributing to their general education, and, in particular, to their understanding of the nature of language and of themselves as language learners.

Notes

1 We use as equivalent terms: general language education syllabus and general language syllabus. In Britain, the most widely used term for the activities dealt with in this chapter has been language awareness (e.g. Hawkins 1981, 1984).
2 See Chapter 10 for a discussion of language transfer.
3 The concept of learner autonomy was strongly advocated in Council of Europe (1981). A recent Council of Europe publication (1986) reaffirms the principle of autonomy and advocates its promotion through active negotiation between teacher and pupil concerning all learning decisions.
4 For the concept and development of metalinguistic awareness in children, see for example, Birdsong (1988); Clark (1978); Hakes (1980); and Smith and Tager-Flusberg (1982).
5 Wenden (1986) points out that students implicitly indicate what they believe about the nature of language and language learning. However, very few studies have attempted to explore students' explicitly expressed beliefs in any systematic way. Students' views on language and language learning were explored by Naiman *et al.* (1978) as part of a study on good language learners. More recently, Wenden (1986, 1987b) and Horwitz (1987) have attempted to obtain empirical data on students' beliefs. Wenden (1987b: 110) has been able to show that, in their attempts to come to grips with the second language, some learners act noticeably in accordance

with these beliefs, for example, 'learners who emphasized the importance of using the language attended primarily . . . to the meaning and social purpose of the interaction. Learners who stressed the importance of learning about the language were much more conscious of language form'. Horwitz (1987) has developed a Beliefs About Language Learning Inventory (BALLI) consisting of 34 statements on the nature of language learning (e.g. 'The most important part of learning a foreign language is learning vocabulary words'), language aptitude ('Women are better than men at learning foreign languages'), difficulty of language learning ('Some languages are easier to learn than others'), and so on. The inventory was designed partly to find out what beliefs students entertain and partly as a teaching device through which teachers can modify students' misconceptions.

6 Hawkins (e.g. 1981, 1984) has repeatedly emphasized the educational, psychological, and social significance of language awareness courses. He has summarized these objectives as follows: (a) to provide a 'bridge' between English and foreign language learning and between English and the mother tongues of immigrant pupils, encouraging the use of common terminology by teachers and fruitful 'feedback' from one aspect of language study to another; (b) to give pupils insight into the role of language as a distinctive aspect of human behaviour and its importance in learning in the home and in school, and to give them an understanding of and sympathy for linguistic diversity; (c) to give all pupils the necessary background on which to build a lifelong interest in language, emphasizing especially the responsibility of parents for the language development of children in the pre-school years (1981: 305–6). The importance of developing cross-cultural awareness, empathy for other people and global awareness through foreign language instruction is discussed by Curtain and Pesola (1988) and the inclusion of these aspects within an elementary context in the United States is described by both Lipton (1988) and Curtain and Pesola (1988).

7 For an overview of foreign language exploratory courses in the United States see the report on secondary schools by Omaggio *et al.* (1983). Several such courses are also described in Sims and Hammond (1981) from which the account of the Los Angeles school has been taken. See Lipton (1988) and Curtain and Pesola (1988) for recent accounts of the development of various FLES and FLEX programmes in the United States.

8 The experimental courses and an empirical study of their effectiveness are described in a series of articles in *Modern Languages* (Cross 1977a, 1977b, 1978, 1979, 1980, and 1981).

9 This monograph (Hawkins 1984), which is intended to serve as an introduction to the language awareness concept, is divided into two parts. Part 1 discusses general arguments for language awareness education and places the movement in the context of the needs of British education. Part 2 serves as a teacher's guide to six language awareness topic booklets which have been published by Cambridge University Press. These booklets deal with the nature of communication (Astley 1983), the analysis of language (Jones 1984), sociolinguistic approaches to language (Astley and Hawkins 1985, Pomphrey 1985), language acquisition (Dunlea 1985), and the distinction between speech and writing (Hawkins 1983). Hawkins (1987) describes a two-level approach to language teaching and the development of programmes. Level one concentrates on the structure of languages, explaining how they work and on a general awareness of the functions of language and its cultural aspects, while level two focuses on using a language in meaningful contexts.

10 For an account of the project and a discussion of some of the issues involved, see Stern (1982); LeBlanc (1990); and the concluding chapter to this volume.

11 This account is based on a case study of the language foundation course at this school described in Donmall (1985).

12 See note 7 for references on FLEX programmes in the United States.

13 This account is based on the detailed description in the Report on Language Awareness (Donmall 1985) of the programme offered by the Oratory School, Reading. The description includes details of the examination based on this course and evaluative comments by two observers. The Report contains several other accounts of language awareness work in schools.

14 See note 5 above for references to studies of students' views on language and language learning.

15 See note 9 above for a brief description of the Cambridge series edited by Hawkins.

16 For a review of recent trends of thought on first and second language acquisition, see FCLT: Part V, especially pp. 337–412. Among recent writings on what by now has become a vast literature on second language acquisition, mention should be made of Brown (1987); Ellis (1985, 1990); McLaughlin (1987); and Larsen-Freeman and Long (1991). The optimal age issue is discussed by Harley (1986); Singleton (1989); and Long (1990).

17 See FCLT: 152 and Howatt (1984: 166) for Gouin's views on the meaning of child language development for language teaching.

18 Research by Wells and his colleagues in Bristol (Wells 1981a, 1986) underlines the role of interaction between parents and children in children's language and cognitive development.

19 For a discussion of the general concept of learning strategies see Nisbet and Shucksmith (1986) and Oxford (1990). Research on teaching learning strategies is reviewed in Wittrock (1986).
20 For a discussion of Bloomfield's (1942) pamphlet see FCLT: 157–8.
21 The relevance of these books for the teaching of learning strategies is discussed by Stern (1975). Among the books in question, mention should be made of Nida (1957); Moulton (1966); Gudschinsky (1967); Samarin (1967); Yorkey (1970); and Larson and Smalley (1972).
22 Several publications, mainly by Holec, give accounts of the work of the Nancy centre, CRAPEL, on the concept of learner autonomy and on its application to second language teaching (e.g. Holec 1980a, 1980b, 1981, 1985, and 1987).
23 Since the 1970s, several language teaching methodologists have drawn attention to the human aspect of language learning and have urged learners to take their personal situation into account. The main advocates of this orientation are Curran (1976) and Stevick (1980). For an introduction to some of these writings, see Oller and Richard-Amato (1983: Part III). But the learner's self-knowledge is not only that of his emotional characteristics and personality. It also relates to his assessment of his cognitive status: his schooling, mental abilities, language aptitude, and the perception of his learning needs. A guide written by Rubin and Thompson (1982) discusses the results of recent studies on language acquisition for the benefit of adult language learners. One of the recommendations of this guide is that we should reflect on ourselves as learners, so that we will understand our own background, psychological make-up, and preferred ways of learning.
24 For example, the language training programme of the Canadian civil service has attempted to accommodate differences in educational background, aptitude, and learning style by allocating students to three different types of programme: an audio-visual course, an analytical-traditional course, and a functional-situational course were the most widely used options. The students' own perceptions, expressed through interviews, entered into the individual case studies of each student participating in this programme. See Wesche (1981) for more details. See also Skehan (1986, 1989) for recent accounts of learner differences and preferences.
25 Several schemes exist which express mastery levels and which can help students not only to assess what stage they have reached but also what level of proficiency they would like to reach. Graded objectives in Britain (Harding, Page, and Rowell 1980) or the ACTFL Proficiency Guidelines (Hiple 1987) enable students to

indicate what expectations they entertain for their own progress and ultimate achievement.

26 For background information on learning strategies see FCLT: 405–12. Further discussions of learning strategies can be found in Chamot and Kupper (1989); Cohen (1990); Oxford (1990); Oxford and Crookall (1989).

27 In FCLT: 411–2, we identified four learning strategies. We have divided the social learning strategy described in FCLT into two, distinguishing a social or interpersonal strategy from a communicative–experiential strategy. Some recent lists of strategies are provided by Rubin (1987) and Oxford (1989).

28 The involvement of learners in their own syllabus design has been strongly advocated by Candlin (1984); Breen (1984); Breen, Candlin, Dam, and Gabrielsen (1989) and Nunan (1988a).

29 In FCLT: 411, this strategy is referred to as the active planning strategy. Rubin (1987), following Wenden (1986) and O'Malley, Chamot, Stewner-Manzanares, Pusso, and Küpper (1985), subsumes under the broad category 'metacognitive learning strategies', such activities as choosing what to learn and how to do it, prioritizing as part of goal definition, and planning appropriate learning strategies.

30 What we have called cognitive strategies were referred to in FCLT: 411 as 'academic (explicit) learning strategies'. Rubin (1987) refers to them simply as learning strategies. However, because in our view all the strategies we are discussing are learning strategies it is confusing to give the same name to all the strategies jointly as well as to one specific one.

31 As Howatt (1984: 173) points out, the inductive teaching of grammar was a mainstay of the reform movement of the 1880s, in which 'the language of the text provided the data for grammatical rules rather than being used to exemplify rules previously learnt out of context'.

32 For reviews of communication strategies see Ellis (1985); Willems (1987); and Bialystock (1990). In our view, and according to the definition of strategy adopted in this book, the so-called communication strategies are not learning strategies. Although they play a role in the communicative/experiential strategy, they do not fulfil the central learning function of this strategy.

33 These concepts are discussed in FCLT: 382 and 411.

34 Collaboration with native speakers as a good way of language learning has been recommended by Nida (1957), and it has been studied in small children by Wong-Fillmore (1976) and again by Strong (1983: 255), who concluded that his study supported previous research 'which has found a relationship between aspects

of sociability or outgoingness and natural communicative language skills'.

35 For a fuller discussion of affective factors in second language learning see FCLT: 375–86. The affective strategy which is listed in FCLT: 411–2 is not specifically mentioned in other works on language strategies although several scholars attribute a great deal of importance to the affective factor in second language learning.

PART FOUR

Teaching strategies

Teaching strategies

In Parts Two and Three we have deliberately adopted a wide view of objectives and of the possible content categories. This enables us to develop policies which take into account the full range of possibilities when we deal with a wide range of language teaching situations. Turning now to teaching strategies or categories of instruction it is even more important to pursue the same approach, that is, we need to develop a framework which can do justice to different aspects and variations of instruction in a variety of circumstances. In the terminology we adopt we reserve the term 'strategy' for broad intentional action, and the term 'technique' for more specific behaviours, operations, procedures, and activities. Therefore, we view teaching strategies as part of the policy level in our framework (Figure I.2). Techniques which describe concrete action are best viewed as belonging to the practical action level.

The strategies we analyse in Part Four are not simply another term for what used to be called 'methods'. As previously explained, pedagogy has moved away from the concept of fixed methods. It is particularly important that in the development of a policy for teaching procedures we learn to operate with flexible sets of concepts which embody any useful lessons we can draw from the history of language teaching but which do not perpetuate the rigidities and dogmatic narrowness of the earlier methods concept. Accordingly, we will examine the strategies in pairs, each of which can be arranged along a continuum. None of the strategies is new, in the sense that there are no antecedents in the history of pedagogy. All of them are defensible responses to the psycholinguistic problems language learners have to cope with. The methods of the recent and less recent past reflect preoccupations with the issues of language learning which the strategies are also intended to meet. In each case, we will describe a number of techniques which illustrate classroom application of the strategy, and we will refer to research as far as it is available.

What we are aiming to do is to examine the strategies in as detached a manner as possible, in order to overcome the deep-seated prejudices that the treatment variables have encountered in language pedagogy. In presenting them, we will follow an approximately historical sequence. The history of methods reveals how language pedagogy over the past

150 years has attempted to come to grips with the problems of language learning, and the method controversies can be seen as an ever-shifting response to these problems. The instructional options to be considered can be represented as three groups of techniques: (a) intralingual–crosslingual; (b) analytic–experiential; (c) explicit–implicit. In Chapter 10 we will examine the intralingual–crosslingual dimension; the other two strategy pairs will be dealt with in Chapters 11 and 12 respectively.

It should be noted that while there is a natural affinity between certain strategies and content syllabuses, the range of strategy options constitutes a separate dimension which is not coextensive with the content options considered in Part Three. Further comments on the relationship between strategy and content options will be provided at the appropriate points in the following chapters.

10 The intralingual–crosslingual dimension

Introduction

This strategy pair has resulted from one of the most long-standing controversies in the history of language pedagogy: the role of L1 in L2 teaching. However, during the last decade or two it has hardly been an active area of debate. For many teachers, the crosslingual strategy is no longer considered a point for discussion; in theory language teaching today is entirely intralingual. We suggest in this chapter that it may be time to reconsider the use of a crosslingual strategy. At least, we should not dismiss it a priori. The intralingual–crosslingual dimension can be represented as follows:

Intralingual ←	→ **Crosslingual**
Intracultural	**Crosscultural**
L2 used as reference system	L1 used as reference system
Immersion in L2/C2	Comparison between L1/L2, C1/C2
Keeping L2 apart from L1	
No translation from and into L2	Practice through translation from and into L2
Direct method	Grammar translation method
Co-ordinate bilingualism	Compound bilingualism

Figure 10.1 Intralingual and crosslingual teaching strategies

In the above figure, intralingual and intracultural refer to those teaching techniques which remain within L2 and use it as the sole frame of reference. Crosslingual and cross-cultural describe the group of techniques which use L1 or another language as points of comparison or reference. Translation is a principal technique of the crosslingual strategy, while the absence of translation is a criterial feature of an intralingual strategy. However, as we shall see later, both strategies are broadly defined and should not be understood as referring simply to the presence or absence of translation.

Crosslingual techniques have been employed for centuries in language instruction in an unselfconscious manner. A widespread custom was to provide texts with interlinear translations. Grammar books also explained features of the target language in the L1 and freely used the L1 as a reference system. The use of more deliberate and refined cross-lingual practice techniques in the form of sentence translation exercises is said to have been an invention of language teachers in Germany towards the end of the eighteenth century (Howatt 1984: 131). Systematic teaching through sentence translation exercises illustrating and practising particular points of grammar also developed at that time, and became a distinct and widely used method of instruction in Germany in the nineteenth century. It is a technique which has maintained itself in language teaching to the present day.

However, the nineteenth century reformers' battle was first and foremost against this technique, and one of the central principles of reform became the teaching of foreign languages *in* the foreign language. The abandonment of translation as the mainstay of L2 pedagogy encouraged the development of intralingual techniques. One of the main debating points of the reform movement was to what extent the non-use of L1 was a practical proposition. The majority of language teachers had been so accustomed to teaching through translation that a complete ban on L1 in the classroom seemed to many a totally unrealistic demand. The extreme reformers insisted that the exclusive use of L2 could and should be adopted. However, the majority of practitioners favoured a compromise which was expressed in a much quoted phrase of the 1930s: 'If we are teaching German, let us teach as Germanly as possible' (Collins 1934: 419). That is, while it was acknowledged that crosslingual techniques could not be avoided altogether, the emphasis should be intralingual, and it was assumed that the best techniques would be intralingual.

Until the mid-1960s, the opposition to crosslingual techniques steadily increased among theorists, and with a few exceptions, eventually became almost universal. For example, Ervin and Osgood (1954), as part of an overview of psycholinguistics, discussed bilingualism and second language learning and introduced the distinction between co-ordinate and compound bilingualism. According to these authors, in co-ordinate bilingualism the two language systems are kept completely separate from each other, while in compound bilingualism the second language is acquired and known through the L1. Ervin and Osgood regard the co-ordinate command of an L2 as the only serviceable goal and attribute the less desirable compound bilingualism to the inefficient (crosslingual) techniques of conventional school instruction. Here is how they contrast the two:

> This development (a compound command) is typical of learning foreign languages in the school situation. It is obviously fostered by learning vocabulary lists which associate a sign from language B with its sign and its meaning in language A.
> (Ervin and Osgood 1954: 140)

On the other hand, co-ordinate language learning 'can also characterize the second language learner, who, relying as little as possible on translation and immersing himself in the living culture of another language community, comes to speak a second tongue well' (Ervin and Osgood 1954). In the early 1960s co-ordinate bilingualism as an ideal form of acquiring and knowing a second language was advocated by Brooks (1964), the leading methodologist of the time:

> What the learner must not do may be summarized as follows: (a) he must not speak English, (b) he must not learn lists of English-foreign-language equivalents, and (c) he must not translate from the foreign language into English. All these activities will nullify his efforts to establish within himself a co-ordinate system of two languages, and will instead only collapse the structure into a compound system with English dominant.
> (Brooks 1964: 52)

The pre-eminent position of an intralingual strategy is also implicit in many subsequent expressions of policy which are almost universally opposed to a crosslingual strategy. Many writers do not even consider crosslingual objectives.

A few exceptions to this broad trend should be mentioned. The rejection in principle of the crosslingual strategy has from time to time been questioned. Widdowson, for example, has regularly cautioned against the thoughtless abandonment of translation as a technique of instruction:

> The use of translation as a teaching technique has long been viewed with suspicion by language teachers and many, of course, proscribe it altogether as a matter of principle. I want to argue that translation . . . can be a very useful pedagogic device and indeed in some circumstances . . . translation of a kind may provide the most effective means of learning.
> (Widdowson 1979: 101)

Moreover, teachers have rarely applied a rigidly intralingual strategy; indeed, as we shall see shortly, many teachers at all levels do not rely exclusively on intralingual techniques, although they often seem to regard this as a lapse from the ideal.

Here and there, however, we find evidence of an open recognition of the merit of some use of crosslingual techniques. For example, audio-lingual programmes in the 1960s contained dialogue presentations with

L1 equivalents as well as a small number of translation drills. Under the name of 'the bilingual method', Dodson (1962, 1967) has for many years advocated a mixed intralingual and crosslingual strategy which includes a systematic use of L1 in establishing meaning and in practising structures. Dodson makes no apologies for this use of crosslingual techniques. He justifies them on the grounds that, far from needing to operate independently, the L2 learner frequently has to switch from L1 to L2: 'the sign of true bilingualism is not merely the possession of two languages, but also the ability to jump easily from one to the other' (Dodson 1967: 90). More recently, Duff (1989) has provided a wealth of suggestions for interesting activities for translating from the L2 to the mother tongue, involving class discussion and oral pair and group work with brief and varied texts, rather than the traditional focus on written translation of larger texts by individuals in isolation. Duff argues that translation is a useful language-learning activity, because it 'invites speculation and discussion', develops accuracy, clarity, and flexibility, and can be used to work through particular L2 problems that learners are struggling with (Duff 1989: 7). Apart from Dodson and Duff, a small number of experimental studies, to be mentioned below, have reopened the question whether crosslingual techniques might not, after all, have some merit.

In spite of these occasional concessions to a crosslingual strategy, the overwhelming preference for many years has remained unquestioningly on the side of an intralingual strategy. Very little thought has been given to the possibility that a case could be made for a crosslingual strategy. Occasionally, arguments flare up because there are teachers who staunchly defend a strictly intralingual policy, while others who argue that such a policy is impracticable and even not particularly useful plead for a more tolerant compromise. It is, therefore, appropriate to look for more principled underpinnings of the two strategies which can be found in psychological considerations and in contrastive linguistics.

Theoretical issues

When we learn a second language we always set out from a language we already know, i.e. our first language. Thus, whether we like it or not, the new language is learnt on the basis of a previously acquired language. The L1–L2 connection is an indisputable fact of life. In the early stages of language learning, it presents itself as an obvious discrepancy between a high level of proficiency in L1 and zero or close to zero proficiency in L2. Throughout the learning stage that discrepancy continues, although it is reduced as our L2 proficiency increases.

Another characteristic of this connection is that we tend to approach the second language on the tacit assumption that we can use the L1 as a reference system for L2. It is in the nature of linguistic and communicative competence that we behave as if the L1 (or a second language previously learnt) is the yardstick and guide to our new L2. To some extent this is justified. We recognize the existence of language universals, that is features which all or most languages have in common. But we cannot safely predict where the new language we learn is like our L1, where it behaves like all other languages, or where it is different. In the same way we approach a new society with certain cultural presuppositions, and it is only gradually that we begin to realize that customs, conventions, and values in the target culture may be different from the native culture.

There is a third consideration. When we face a new language, it is a challenge to us as individuals. Our first language and the corresponding culture are deeply bound up with our personal lives. A new language and culture demand a personal adjustment. Existing values are challenged. We approach the new language with certain preconceived ideas which may have to be modified. Somehow, therefore, in learning a new language we have to think of ways in which we will personally deal with the L1–L2 connection. Schumann (1978) has described this process as it affects immigrants who must come to terms with a new environment linguistically as well as culturally. But a similar process of adjustment occurs also in classroom second language learning. Every learner has to come to terms with the linguistic and cultural demands of the second language and this process involves the learner cognitively, socially, and affectively.

Linguistic and psycholinguistic theory and research have examined the way individuals and groups deal with the transition from L1 to L2 through interlanguage studies and contrastive analysis. Selinker's concept of interlanguage (Selinker 1972) recognized the systematic nature of the learner's language. It was assumed that to a certain extent the learner develops his own interlanguage system on the basis of his L1, and that in certain ways L1 and L2 fuse. Such transfer or interference phenomena have been attested by research. On the other hand, the characteristics of the learner's language cannot be entirely predicted or explained by transfer from L1 or other languages previously learnt. Certain characteristics of the learner's interlanguage suggest that it is 'created' independently of L1 influences. What is uncertain is whether the learner's language represents a gradual progression from L1-based rules to L2-based rules (the claim of the so-called restructuring hypothesis) or whether it is mainly an independent creation (the claim of the creative construction hypothesis). The restructuring hypothesis assumes the learner's L1 as an initial basis for L2, and it is therefore a crosslingual theory of L2 learning. The creative construction theory offers an intralingual interpretation of L2 learning.[1]

The rationale for a crosslingual strategy is as follows: Let us set out from our deeply ingrained knowledge of the L1, and the inevitable existence of transfer and interference, and use them as a psychological given. We need not deny the fact that the learner uses the L1 for a reference; on this basis we can help learners gradually develop a new L2 reference system, pointing out where the two languages are alike and where they are different. Since in the crosslingual strategy we acknowledge the transfer/interference phenomenon and deliberately move forwards and backwards between L2 and L1, we use techniques which involve comparing the two phonological, lexical, and grammatical systems and help learners to build up the new L2 reference system by making a gradual and deliberate transition from L1 to L2. The same applies to the treatment of sociolinguistic and cultural phenomena.

For the intralingual strategy, we argue that the new system has to be taken on its own and gradually built up from within so that all its parts are interrelated. Intralingual techniques of teaching and learning are designed on the assumption that they help the learner establish verbal connections in the L2, enabling the learner to move about within the system without reference to L1. Equally, it is claimed that through an intralingual strategy verbal expressions become associated directly with objects and situations without the help of L1. This argument was the main platform of the direct method. It has been equally plausibly argued, however, that crosslingual techniques are more direct than intralingual ones because the crosslingual strategy builds on the L1 as the learner's deeply anchored verbal reference system. This system inevitably asserts itself, and it is unwise to pretend that by ignoring it we can set it aside. On the contrary, it is a better policy to make use of it and to build on the presence and strength of the L1 as a basis for L2 learning. An individual learning an L2 tends to transfer rules, habits, and meanings from his mother tongue. This has positive results wherever L1 and L2 coincide but it acts as negative transfer or interference where there are differences. In these cases the learner must make a conscious effort to inhibit the use of L1 as a reference system and deliberately learn new rules or develop new habits unrelated to L1.

A good case can be made on theoretical grounds for either a mainly crosslingual or a mainly intralingual policy. For example, the two strategies may assist learners at different stages of the language learning process. In the novice stage, it may be useful to fall back on comparisons between L1 and L2 and explanations of L2 in L1 terms. But as we progress, it may be more and more important to break the connection with L1 and to remain within L2 for longer and longer periods. This does not mean that intralingual techniques are inappropriate for novices. On the contrary, direct method classes, immersion, or total physical response activities suggest that it is possible, from a very early stage, to handle the L2 'from within' and thus to give the learner some experience of communication without reference to L1. These psychological considerations suggest that neither the crosslingual nor the intralingual strategy is theoretically superior. Since each responds to different characteristics or phases of the learning process, they have complementary merits, and it is much more a question of appropriateness for different stages or purposes of L2 learning whether preference should be given to one or the other.

An important consideration in deciding on a mainly intralingual or a mainly crosslingual strategy concerns the objectives and content emphasis we give to a language course. In discussions on methodology, this consideration is often overlooked and is rarely clearly focused. When the goals of language teaching are defined, we tend to think of proficiency as the main goal and to define it as an ability to master the four skills of listening, speaking, reading, and writing, or as communicative competence. Proficiency in these terms is usually understood to be as close as possible to that of a native speaker. This means that an intralingual command of the language is assumed, and rightly so. If we want to use the L2 to take part in conversation, listen to a lecture, read a newspaper, or write a letter or report, it is better if we can do that without translating from or into L1. Most language learners would like to see themselves arriving at a stage where they can use the second language without inhibition and frustration, and without reference to another language system. It stands to reason that if we aim at proficiency, understood as an intralingual command of L2, the procedures employed in teaching the language must provide intralingual opportunities for language use. For example, if all our reading is through translation from L2 into L1, we train ourselves to read through translation. The main criticism of the grammar translation method by direct method advocates was that the learner was trained to function in the translation mode. In other words, learners in courses of this kind were simply not exposed to the immediate apprehension and use of the L2. One can state axiomatically: if any degree of L2 proficiency is to be attained, an intralingual strategy must be used.

However, this does not mean to say that all crosslingual procedures at all times are unhelpful in the pursuit of an intralingual proficiency objective. As we shall see shortly, crosslingual techniques are more diverse than simply translation. If we bear in mind that the learner inevitably works from an L1 reference base, it can be helpful for him to orient himself in the L2 through the L1 medium or by relating L2 phenomena to their equivalents in L1. The learner must obviously be given the opportunity to use the target language intralingually. But provided that opportunity is given, the use of L1 and other crosslingual techniques in the L2 class can be justified, not as a compromise or a lapse from a unilingual ideal, but because a crosslingual strategy corresponds to natural psychological processes in second language development.

Another important consideration is that as learners we may pursue cross-cultural objectives; that is, translating and interpreting may be skills which we wish to master. The need for exercising these skills arises regularly as soon as we have a reasonable command of an L2. Being able to translate or interpret is a social skill we should cultivate in order to be able to mediate between speakers of different languages. Clearly, a crosslingual strategy would gain greater prominence in situations where L2 learners include any form of translation or interpreting among their objectives.

The content of language courses, too, may indicate a preference for either a crosslingual or an intralingual strategy. All four syllabuses we considered in Chapters 4 to 9 offer subject matter which can be handled intralingually, provided the student's proficiency level is sufficiently advanced. If we want to emphasize the intralingual strategy we may have to sacrifice content and confine ourselves to those topics which students are capable of handling. In a class of native speakers of different languages an intralingual strategy is the only one that is normally possible. However, in a class where students and teacher share a common L1, crosslingual strategies can be employed, and can extend the scope of the L2 programme. In this situation, many portions of the curriculum would be strictly intralingual in order to compensate for the absence of a natural environment. Thus, a syllabus of communicative activities is designed to be offered intralingually, but the language syllabus, the cultural syllabus, and the general language education syllabus might benefit from a partly crosslingual/cross-cultural treatment. To sum up, the emphasis on an intralingual or a crosslingual strategy should be decided in relation to the goals of the learners, their previous experience in the L2, the context in which the programme takes place, and the ability of the teacher to function intralingually or crosslingually.

Research findings

In spite of persistent controversy on the relative advantages and drawbacks of the intralingual versus the crosslingual strategy, very little empirical research has been undertaken to explore the effects of using one or the other strategy or to determine what would constitute an appropriate mixture. There is little dependable information on the degree to which teachers rely on an intralingual or a crosslingual strategy. We do not have any well documented knowledge about the reactions of learners to, or their preferences for, the two strategies; nor is there any clear indication of the conditions which would promote the effective use of a crosslingual or an intralingual learning strategy.

We can glean some information from a few studies. Classroom observation studies usually report the use of L1 or L2 by the teacher or the students in the language class. For example, in one British study (Mitchell *et al.* 1981) most classroom activities were in the foreign language. Nevertheless, out of 1656 observed segments, 10.6 per cent (n=176) involved translation and 21.3 per cent were in L1, so that approximately 32 per cent or roughly one third of the segments involved the use of L1. Another British study used an observation scheme to study the classroom behaviour of outstanding language teachers (Sanderson 1982). One of the observation categories referred to the predominant or exclusive use of L2 in the language class. The study found that the teachers observed varied a great deal on this criterion. None used the L2 exclusively. One teacher used it predominantly, another promoted the use of L2 by the students, while a third expressed awareness of the dilemma:

> You can explain to the children much better, and they can understand you, and there is no question of them not having understood, if you're explaining to them in English. On the other hand, they hear so little of the foreign language. I feel that the more they hear of it just being used normally, perhaps the better.
> (quoted from an interview in Sanderson 1982: 95)

An international study on the teaching of French as a second language in eight countries (Carroll 1975: 267) concluded that many of the data tables show that 'high proficiency in French . . . is associated with a condition where the students report frequent use of French and relatively less use of the mother tongue.' This finding, which is confirmed by other studies, points towards the advantage of a predominantly intralingual strategy where proficiency as a goal has high priority.[2]

The British report on primary French (Burstall *et al.* 1974) came to similar conclusions. Basing themselves on observations of primary classes by school inspectors and their ratings the authors found that:

> Pupils in classes where little or no use was made of English by the teacher were also rated as more fluent and accurate in their spoken French and as having a better standard of pronunciation in French than pupils in classes where English was frequently used. . . . Classes where the pupils made little or no use of English, their fluency, pronunciation and accuracy in French were rated more highly than in classes where frequent use was made of English.
> (Burstall *et al.* 1974: 199)

Burstall *et al.* (1974: 207) summarized the results in these terms: 'the oral fluency of primary school pupils taught exclusively in French was rated significantly more highly than that of pupils who depended more on translation or explanation in English.'

While these results clearly favour an intralingual teaching strategy, the same report quotes the opinions of some students on the predominant use of French which would lead to quite different conclusions:

> French is harder because the teacher does not tell us in English what the word in French means, but does it by action and we don't always understand them. If the word means 'jump' and we don't know, she jumps—like that. In some cases it is not an action word. So we speak words in French that we don't understand.
>
> I can't understand the teacher. She never tells us what she is on about.
>
> Our teacher explains in French and when he has finished, I still don't understand a word.
>
> The teacher blurts out a lot of French words I haven't heard before and expects me to understand them.
>
> I would like, after the teacher has said something, that she repeats it in English. We would be able to understand better, I'm sure.

These examples of children's views indicate that most of the pupils 'feel that their failure to understand French is due to insufficient explanation being given in English' (Burstall *et al.* 1974: 139). It is clear that the children's views are far less positive about the intralingual techniques to which they have been exposed than the observations made by the inspectors. They do not seem to understand the rationale for the intralingual strategy and implicitly express a plea for crosslingual techniques.

Since for most theorists and practitioners crosslingual techniques have recently not been considered valid options, it is not surprising to find that there is hardly any experimental research on this issue. One or two exceptions are worth mentioning. Parent and Belasco (1970) found the use of bilingual texts advantageous in the training for L2 reading comprehension, and Oskarsson (1975) in a carefully designed experiment on vocabulary learning noted that a bilingual glossary is more effective than unilingual word explanations in the L2 and that the adult students in the experiment had a preference for the crosslingual technique of vocabulary presentation.

It seems that research results on this dimension are not substantial enough to provide much guidance. The most widely cited finding is that the predominant use of L2 in the language class (i.e. intralingual techniques) is associated with higher levels of proficiency. But because of the bias against crosslingual techniques, it may well be that competent teachers use intralingual techniques and do not consider the possibility of more efficient crosslingual options. So long as we are comparing inadequate crosslingual techniques and efficient intralingual ones, we obviously have no choice. But once we recognize that crosslingual techniques have a theoretical justification and can also be efficient, helpful to the learner, and interesting, it will become more worthwhile to undertake experimental studies which would explore the particular merits and problems of both strategies. Such studies should also make it possible to suggest in what circumstances intralingual or crosslingual techniques are preferable.

The scope of the intralingual strategy

When the direct method was first advocated in the nineteenth century, the demand for the 'monolingual principle' (Howatt 1984: 208) was very much an act of faith on the part of the reformers; few techniques had been developed which would enable teachers to put this principle into practice. Gradually, however, teachers evolved techniques which were entirely or largely intralingual. Most of the methodological innovations of the past decades have contributed to the intralingual repertoire. Today, inventories of classroom techniques exist of which only a handful are not intralingual. Rivers (1975), in over three hundred pages of techniques for teaching French, devotes no more than about twenty pages to crosslingual procedures. Other writings on teaching approaches, such as Allen and Valette's (1977) inventory of classroom techniques, and books on grammar games (Rinvolucri 1984), proficiency practice (Omaggio 1986), and communicative techniques (Bundesarbeitsgemeinschaft 1977, Klippel 1984) show an exclusively intralingual orientation. Crosslingual techniques as a possible alternative are hardly broached and in most instances not mentioned at all.

Intralingual techniques occur at all stages of language learning. Activities for novice and intermediate learners are more restricted in their scope, rely more on visual support or action, emphasize comprehension, and tend to be repetitive. Advanced learners are given greater freedom of expression, have access to a wider range of texts, including unedited texts, and are allowed more room for individuality and diversity of activities. Intralingual techniques can be illustrated by the following examples which have been arranged in an approximate order of increasing complexity:

Repetition of sounds, words, phrases, and sentences singly by students or in chorus, following the teacher or a recorded stimulus. Copying of written and printed L2 material.

Relating verbal utterances to real objects or pictorial representations: chalkboard drawings, diagrams, wall charts, cartoons, flashcards, posters, pictures, filmstrips, films, including audiovisual courses and materials on video cassettes.

Relating verbal utterances to actions. Action series, 'total physical response', pantomime, miming, charades.

Drills and exercises. Pattern drills: mechanical, meaningful, and communicative (Paulston and Bruder 1975). Language laboratory drills, fill in the blank drills, substitution drills, transformation drills.

Treatment of an L2 text: narrative, descriptive, expository, dialogue, poem, song. The text may be spoken or written, may be from a coursebook or an authentic document (e.g. a newscast or newspaper article). It may be short (a brief exchange or dialogue, a street sign, or advertisement) or long (a story, novel, or play). The treatment may include listening to a narrative, reading detailed text through question and answer, vocabulary study, and reworking the text from various perspectives and expanding on it.

Memorizing a narrative, dialogue, poem, and reciting the memorized text.

Dictation.

Question and answer (teacher-class, class-teacher, student-student).

Composition, guided composition, note taking, free composition, letter writing.

Conversation, interview, discussion, debate.

Role play/dramatization, improvised or prepared, including stage directions in L2.

Games, other play activities, rules of games, and talk involved in games conducted in L2.

Explanations and other discourse in L2 on aspects of language or culture, derived from the different syllabuses discussed in previous chapters. Use of the L2 as the language of instruction so as to offer increased and diversified exposure to the target language.

Activities chosen from the communicative activities syllabus, which inherently demand the use of L2.

Language-class related activities such as meals, trips, weekends, camping, exchanges, and associated activities in L2.

Class management and classroom discourse in L2 between teachers and students and among students.

Other curriculum subjects taught in L2; hobby interests, sporting activities pursued in L2.

Total or partial immersion.

Residence in an L2 environment.

These examples are sufficient to show that the intralingual principle is applicable across the entire spectrum of content and is also implicit in the use of the other strategies we will discuss later. Intralingual techniques may be 'analytic' or 'experiential'; they may be used for the teaching of linguistic features, such as phonology, grammar, or lexis, or for teaching substantive content. They may be designed to practise a particular communication skill, for example, listening comprehension, reading or speaking, a combination of skills, or transposing from one skill to another. The principal negative criterion for intralingual techniques is that they do not use L1 or other languages as a point of reference. Instead, they remain entirely within the framework of L2. As a corollary to this, of course, they do not use translation and other crosslingual activities and comparisons as a means of instruction.

From the positive point of view, intralingual techniques are meant to establish a new language system with its own internal links and connections and encourage the learner to move about within that system in the same way an expert user of the language does. Intralingual techniques are intended to help create intralingual verbal associations. They are also meant to help the learner to link L2 with concrete objects, situational contexts, and the external world in general. They encourage thinking in the second language. In short, they are supposed to provide what Brooks has characterized as a co-ordinate command of the L2. Intralingual techniques provide exposure of the language class to the L2. It is argued that, unless the learner has the opportunity to hear and read as well as to speak and write the L2, there is no chance of developing any practical proficiency. All intralingual techniques are intended to provide these opportunities. In this way the intralingual activities of the language classroom create or simulate an L2 environment. That this is a prerequisite of effective language teaching has been increasingly recognized and is now almost universally accepted.

The unanswered question is whether an exclusive reliance on the intralingual strategy is in fact practicable, and whether it helps learners to achieve the kind of internalized L2 competence they and their teachers strive for. The practicality and usefulness of intralingual techniques are rarely questioned, and specific problems and difficulties which arise in the case of some of the procedures are hardly ever pointed out in the current literature. There is little or no research which critically examines the effectiveness of particular procedures, or weighs up the advantages and disadvantages of one intralingual technique against another.

The chief problem for the teacher in employing intralingual techniques is to make meaning evident, that is, to ensure that the language input to the student is comprehensible and is in fact comprehended. Explanations and definitions in L2 do not necessarily lead to understanding. Real objects, pictures, filmstrips, drawings, miming, actions, and diagrams are essential components of the strategy and not mere adjuncts. They are needed to create verbal links to reality and to situational contexts. But they are open to misinterpretation. Misunderstandings are possible and do occur, and teachers and students have to be constantly on guard against them. Outside the classroom, in situations of normal L2 use, the context often provides clues which help the L2 user; moreover, if the language demands are beyond us, we can abandon our efforts to participate. In the language class, however, language learners are a captive audience, and they cannot give up even if they are totally disoriented.

From the British primary French study we have seen that the well-intentioned use of an intralingual strategy can alienate students because they do not understand the point being taught. Similar findings have been reported by Hosenfeld which show that the intention of intralingual drills can be bypassed by students. There is nothing to stop them from employing a crosslingual learning strategy on intralingually presented materials, as in this instance:

> *Interviewer:* Would you 'think aloud' as you complete this exercise?
>
> *Student:* Avez-vous une voiture? Pourquoi? Do you have a car? Why? No, I'm too young. Non, Je suis trop jeune. Etes vous resté à la maison hier soir? Pourquoi? Did you stay home last night? Why? Yes, I did because I did my homework. Oui, parce que j'ai fait mes devoirs.
>
> *Interviewer:* Did you translate each sentence?
>
> *Student:* I always translate this kind.
>
> *Interviewer:* Why do you translate?
>
> *Student:* To be sure I've got the meaning. Otherwise I can't answer them.
> (Hosenfeld 1975: 161)

Hosenfeld (1975: 162) rightly concludes: 'Analysis of students' reading reveals an area that is much in need of research: the translating strategies of second language learners. The perennial dispute about whether foreign language students do or do not translate is anachronistic. Many do.' The questions we should be asking, according to Hosenfeld, are:

'Who translates, how often, under what conditions, why, and what is the effect of translating upon learning a second language?' (ibid.).

Intralingual techniques clearly provide opportunities for proficiency development. Whether in fact they do promote proficiency depends to some extent on the learning strategies of the students, but also on the skill with which these strategies are employed by the teacher. A serious handicap in a skillful use of the intralingual strategy is a failure to understand how best to relate it to the application of a crosslingual strategy. Too many teachers consider the use of a crosslingual strategy as a 'fall from grace', a practical compromise and not as a legitimate and theoretically justifiable procedure. We would like to suggest that an intralingual strategy would be more effective if its crosslingual counterpart were more clearly recognized as a strategy in its own right complementing an intralingual strategy.

The scope of the crosslingual strategy

As noted above, crosslingual techniques derive from the grammar-translation method. Translation is an important crosslingual technique, but in the past it was used to excess. The resulting negative reaction has been so extreme that the possible value of translation is often dismissed a priori. It has, from time to time, been given reluctant and apologetic houseroom by a few methodologists, but the range and potential of crosslingual techniques has only very recently been reconsidered in the pedagogical literature (Duff 1989). In our view, the scope of a crosslingual strategy deserves further exploration and systematic exploitation.

Crosslingual techniques are based on natural language behaviour which occurs when A does not know the language spoken by B, and vice versa, and A and B wish to communicate. In this situation we look for an interpreter so that we can talk to one another. Similarly, if we need translations of written documents, we welcome the services of someone who through explanations and comments can mediate between us as speakers of two languages. As pedagogical techniques these procedures can be divided into the following categories: (a) mediating from L2 to L1; (b) mediating from L1 to L2; (c) comparative and contrastive techniques; (d) using L1 as a medium of communication and instruction in the L2 class. A crosslingual strategy can be applied more easily in a classroom where second language learners and their teacher share a common L1. Where students come from different language backgrounds, crosslingual techniques are not entirely ruled out, but their range is more limited and they are more difficult to apply. Comparisons across languages add interest to language teaching and may give learners fresh insights into a variety of languages. Moreover, where students already have another L2 to fall back on this language can be treated as an additional resource to which the target language can be related.

Crosslingual mediation from L2 to L1

In this use of crosslingual techniques the learner receives input in L2, and L1 is used to clarify meaning, to check on understanding, and to interpret the new and strange in terms of what is familiar, thus preventing students from feeling lost and disoriented. The techniques available are of two kinds: (a) translation from L2 into L1; (b) the interpretive treatment of texts.

L2–L1 translation. Translation as a set of crosslingual techniques ranges from providing minimal lexical help through glossaries, to the full and detailed translation of texts. Intermediate strategies include the use of translation of isolated words in a text, marginal glosses, or notes accompanying printed or spoken texts. Vocabularies preceding text passages in specially edited editions, or provided at the end of a text in alphabetical order, are common.[3]

Use of L2-to-L1 dictionary. If we use them indiscriminately, without understanding the nature of words and their translation equivalents, dictionaries can be misleading. But if used appropriately, they can lead to insight into the meaning and use of words and they can be a great help in the study of spoken and written texts. The proper use of L2-to-L1 dictionaries is one of the skills a learner should acquire.

L2 text translated into L1 by teacher or class. This procedure has been widely used in classical and modern language teaching. It can help learners to examine a foreign language text closely, to discuss its meaning, and to explore the use of linguistic expressions in comparison with L1. Translation of L2 sentences into L1 equivalents was once standard procedure, but has largely been superseded by intralingual practice techniques which are less cumbersome. Translation may be useful for some aspects of grammar and less so for others. For example, grammatical phenomena which are subject to interference from L1 might lend themselves well to translation exercises in order to prevent the development of undesirable language habits. However, an exclusive reliance on translation may prevent learners from reading without reference to L1 and may impose severe limitations on the comprehension of L2 texts. The systematic use of this technique implies a sophisticated understanding of the nature of translation which has not generally been provided in the pedagogic literature.

Consecutive and simultaneous interpreting. This technique involves the recreation of L2 messages in L1. This can be done as an advanced exercise within a general language programme or as a preparation for learning to interpret. It is subject to the same caveats as the translation of written texts. If this technique is applied routinely to all spoken texts, it is likely to lead a student to rely on the recreation of texts in L1 as a means of understanding, instead of learning to apprehend meaning intralingually.

Interpretive treatment of texts. To aid understanding of L2 texts the teacher can use various devices in the L1, such as: providing a title in L1; introducing or summarizing an L2 text in L1; explaining the context of a text in L1; explaining the meaning of a text by brief commentaries including occasional prompts or glosses; asking L1 questions about an L2 text; discussing in L1 the significance of an L2 text; providing a detailed analysis in L1 of an L2 text.

These interpretive or 'hermeneutic' techniques provide the learner with support and comment on L2 texts of all kinds. It is particularly important that the texts with which the learner is confronted are explained and put into a context. When texts present special problems, explanatory comments and prompts in L1 can often help learners deal with difficulties which might otherwise prove to be insuperable. It is possible to provide detailed explanations and interpretations of L2 texts, for example, speeches, poetry, dramatic works, political statements, and thus provide useful insights into the literature and culture of the target community.

In summary, mediating from L2 to L1 helps the learner to come to grips with the L2 against the background of a familiar medium. The main objective in applying these techniques is to give support to learners in their attempts to achieve comprehension. A negative argument is that they may encourage learners to rely too heavily on L1 support instead of taking the plunge and developing a new independent network of L2 verbal connections.

Crosslingual mediation from L1 to L2

Examples of crosslingual mediation from L1 to L2 include: using an L1 word, phrase, or sentence as a cue for L2 speaking or writing; translation of sentences or texts from L1 to L2; creating a context in L1 for L2 speech acts; simultaneous or consecutive interpreting from L1 to L2. Sentence translation was introduced in the late eighteenth century as a practical and demanding technique for the deliberate study of second language grammar. The translation of texts into the L2, in France referred to as *thème* and in Britain as 'prose translation' (in contrast to an earlier practice of translation into L2 verse!) has been held in high regard as a technique for advanced learners. In many universities and in some schools following the older British tradition and the French tradition of *thème* (translation into L2) and *version* (translation into L1), it is still customary to offer prose translation as an important component of teaching and testing advanced students in some second languages.

Translation of sentences into the L2 is also still widely practised in many countries as a device for teaching grammar. Of all crosslingual techniques, translation into L2 is probably the most problematic. Its advocates regard it as a 'solid' and intellectually demanding way of teaching a language which forces the learner to transpose his own verbal repertoire into the L2, to apply the rules of the L2 grammar and to acquire an active L2 vocabulary. It has been criticized on several grounds. First, translation presupposes a knowledge of the language into which one is to translate, and this is precisely the knowledge the L2 learner lacks. Translation in the opposite direction is much more defensible. By translating from L2 to L1 the learner recreates in a familiar language what is new and difficult and thereby creates mental links between the two languages. In translation into L2, on the other hand, the learner lacks a model or standard. He is forced to construct ('construe') the L2 text from grammar rules and vocabulary, basing himself entirely on his knowledge of L1 without any means of knowing whether the L2 has the same semantic or discourse characteristics as L1. Isolated sentence translation practice may not be subject to the same criticism, since these sentences often act as cues for the practice of previously learned L2 features. But a text cannot be constructed merely from the application of grammar rules and a knowledge of words. The translation technique is based on the false assumption that an L2 can be acquired by applying rules of grammar and a bilingual dictionary to L1 texts. This represents a simplistic view of language. The learner lacks the frame of reference which he must already possess in order to be able to translate into the L2.

The technique of 'packing' L1 texts with linguistic difficulties was introduced in the eighteenth century in the misguided belief that it would provide a mental discipline if the learner had to struggle with demanding language problems. The imposition of translation tasks which are well above the learner's competence level artificially adds to the natural difficulties of language learning. The criticism of this practice is directed not at translation in general as a learning technique but at translation which is not properly geared to the learner's level of competence.

A second argument against L1–L2 translation is that it results in an uneconomical use of learning time. In the same amount of time in which a student struggles vainly with a translation, he can have a more fruitful exposure to the L2 by the use of intralingual techniques. These valid objections to translation into L2 as a major or sole technique do not rule out the possibility that *some* L1–L2 translation techniques could be used with advantage during certain phases of the learning process. For example, they might well be used judiciously for confirmation and reinforcement of previous intralingual learning. They could also be challenging for advanced learners who have built up a diversified L2 framework and who can deal with the semantic and discoursal complexities of the L2. These techniques could also play an important part in the advanced training of interpreters and translators.

Comparative and contrastive techniques

Contrastive linguistics has been defined as 'a subdiscipline of linguistics concerned with comparison of two or more languages or subsystems of languages in order to determine both the differences and similarities between them' (Fisiak 1981: 1). As such, it is certainly relevant to language teaching, particularly to the design of courses, but in itself it does not necessarily constitute a teaching technique or a group of such techniques. However, contrastive linguistics and the crosslingual strategy are both based on the assumption that the linguist or the learner will not treat a new language independently but in relation to other previously known languages. Therefore, it is possible to use the principles of contrastive linguistics to develop a number of classroom activities. These techniques are specifically intended to encourage learners to relate L2 to L1, to discover the similarities and differences between them and to make use of such comparisons for better language learning. The following illustrate these techniques:

Juxtaposition of L2 text and its translation into L1 on opposite pages or interlinearly.

Reading text in L2, simultaneously listening to text spoken in L1 on tape.

Listening to text spoken in L2, reading text in L1.

Practising L2 speech sounds in contrast to equivalent L1 sounds.

Pronouncing L1 with L2 pronunciation or vice versa.

Studying and practising grammatical features of L2 in comparison with L1, and drawing attention to similarities and differences.

Comparing lexical items in L1 and L2.

Comparing semantic or discourse features in L1 and L2.

Comparing sociolinguistic and cultural features in the home and target cultures.

To this we might add the comparative study of L2 texts with functionally equivalent L1 texts: for example, the everyday language of greeting and farewell, letters of congratulation or condolence, newspaper features, road signs, nursery rhymes, applications for a driving licence, and texts on topics of special interest such as sports commentaries, political news reports on the radio, cookery books, or engineering manuals.

Concluding comments

Even in a classroom setting which uses a predominantly intralingual strategy, it is advisable to allow certain well-defined periods in which the use of the L1 is allowed so that questions can be asked, meanings can be verified, uncertainties can be removed, and explanations given which would not be accessible to the learner in L2.[4] The two strategies we have reviewed in this chapter undoubtedy do different things for the language learner. What they accomplish does not entirely depend on how the teacher uses the strategies but also on how the learners respond to them. The two strategies relate directly to the language learning objectives. Intralingual techniques are intended to build up the L2 as a relatively independent system. Thus, if proficiency in L2 communication skills is the principal objective the intralingual strategy will be dominant. However, if the mediating skills (translation and interpreting) are the goal, a crosslingual strategy will also have an important part to play.

Whatever the dominant objective, it is likely that at certain stages during the teaching/learning process both strategies will be productive. In the case of young students in the early stages of a language course it may be more appropriate to use a crosslingual or mixed strategy in a very controlled fashion, and gradually expand the use of intralingual techniques as the course proceeds. In the training of interpreters and translators, it may be more effective to establish the L2 first as a relatively independent system through the use of intralingual techniques before offering a more directly relevant crosslingual training.

The chief problem of the intralingual strategy is that it may leave the learner uncertain about meanings even with the aid of situational or visual clues. However, the problem can be offset by using minor crosslingual techniques as support. The problem of a crosslingual strategy is that it may leave the learner without an independent reference system in the L2, and therefore the essential condition for proficiency is seriously jeopardized. Crosslingual techniques, on theoretical grounds alone, cannot lead to an efficient L2 competence. On the other hand, if L2 learners do not wish to abandon their 'L1 ego' they must somehow reconcile their new L2 competence with an established L1. In such cases, crosslingual techniques, especially those that confront and compare L2 and

L1, can be helpful in coming to terms with this inevitable issue of second language learning.

Finally, on theoretical grounds too, the least defensible techniques are those that move from L1 to L2, as the reformers in the nineteenth century had already recognized: the act of construing an L2 text on the basis of L1 is not only a laborious way of language learning, it is also linguistically the least satisfactory. However, the rejection of one crosslingual technique does not invalidate the entire crosslingual strategy. Ultimately, the solution seems to lie in a carefully controlled use of the strategy. What mixture of intralingual and crosslingual techniques is actually employed by teachers and their students has not been systematically investigated. Nor do we know with certainty what mixture is most effective for different conditions of language learning.

Notes

1 Corder's (1978: 90) view that the language learning process involves an 'interlanguage continuum intermediate between the restructuring and the recreation hypothesis', parallels a pedagogic compromise between an intralingual and a crosslingual strategy.

2 An earlier study by Carroll (1967) on the language attainments of university and college students reported a similar finding.

3 Widdowson (1978: 82–8) introduced the distinction between priming and prompting glossaries. A priming glossary provides dictionary explanations, while a prompting glossary gives the word's meaning in that particular text. Widdowson's examples are intralingual glosses on the lexical items, but the same principle can be applied crosslingually by providing an L1 dictionary translation of words occurring in the text (priming translations) or by offering an L1 translation which fits the context of the text precisely (prompting translation).

4 In Canadian immersion classes it is customary for the teacher to speak French at all times but the young students are not discouraged from speaking English to the teacher. Therefore, in this situation the communication is bilingual, thus allowing students to be gradually eased into the use of the L2 over a period of weeks or months.

11 The analytic–experiential dimension

Introduction

A clear distinction between the analytic and experiential strategies has emerged only gradually since the mid-1960s; today, however, it constitutes one of the key issues in second language pedagogy. As we have already seen, theorists have increasingly opposed the kind of teaching which rigidly controls the content and progression of language courses and imposes on the learner a specific sequence of mechanical exercises and drills. A number of important facts have been drawn to our attention: (a) it is difficult to take a language to pieces without sacrificing some of its essential qualities; (b) the lawfulness of language is not fully understood and therefore any systematic treatment can only be partial; (c) young children acquire their first language in a natural environment without any formal tuition; and (d) the same is true of many adult immigrants. These observations led to a growing appreciation of informal, untutored, and natural approaches to language learning, which finally crystallized in the communicative approach during the late 1970s.

The experiential strategy is global and non-analytic. It invites the learner to use the language for a purpose, and to focus on the message rather than any specific aspect of the code. It is as if we said to the student: 'Take care of the message—the medium will take care of itself.' The student becomes involved in language use, in getting meaning across. Through the experiential strategy students are prompted to become language users and participants in social interaction or practical transactions. This teaching strategy is an essential feature of the communicative activities syllabus, but it is by no means limited to this syllabus alone.

The analytic strategy has come to be defined in contrast to the experiential strategy. An analytic approach is based on techniques of study and practice. It treats the second language and culture as objects to be studied or examined and is thus closely associated with the content of the language and cultural syllabuses. The language learner is placed in the role of an observer who looks at the language and culture from outside and pays attention to formal or functional features which are deliberately abstracted at least to some degree from the living context. In the experiential approach the language learner is subjectively involved in language use. He is accorded the role of an active participant focusing on a message which is presented in an authentic context. In the analytic mode, on the other hand, the language is presented in a relatively decontextualized form. The analytic approach is characterized by an absence of genuine communicative intent. When exercises are being done in the language class the teacher and the students are fully aware that they are not really involved in communication. They are conscious of the fact that they are rehearsing or practising language use, or simply displaying their command of the code.

During the past few years the analytic–experiential distinction has captured the interest of many language educators. It has been variously expressed in the following contrasting terms:

Analytic	**Experiential**
objective	subjective
focus on code	focus on communication
non-communicative	communicative
medium centred	message centered
observation	participation
usage	use
focus on language	focus on topic/purpose
formal	informal
abstract	concrete/realistic
decontextualized	contextualized
skill-getting	skill-using
language practice	language use
predictability of response	information gap
reaction to code	reaction to message
isolated utterances	incorporation of preceding utterances
controlled/restricted language forms	unrestricted/natural language forms
emphasis on accuracy	emphasis on fluency
linguistic interaction	interpersonal interaction
deliberate/systematic/structured	realistic/authentic/genuine

Figure 11.1 Characteristics associated with analytic and experiential teaching strategies

We call one strategy experiential because it involves learners in authentic communication and in genuine experiences which have value, importance, or significance for them. The other strategy is referred to as analytic because it is based on analytic procedures. In some previous work (for example, Stern 1978) these two strategies were referred to as 'formal' and 'functional' respectively. While this is in principle a perfectly good designation, it has led to some confusion. 'Formal' also contrasts with 'informal', but informal language learning can be analytic. The term 'functional' has been used by some applied linguists to designate the analysis of language along functional lines, as in notions and functions. Allen (1983), for example, has used the term 'functional', first in contrast to 'structural', both of which fall into the wider category of 'analytic', and then has contrasted both with 'experiential'. In conformity to this usage, we have abandoned the term 'functional' as a synonym for 'experiential', and use functional only to describe the functional analysis of language.

Most language teaching over the centuries has employed some kind of analytic strategy. This was done openly and unquestioningly in the grammar-translation method. The direct method introduced an experiential element by its insistence on the use of the second language in the classroom; but, in spite of this, the bulk of the classroom treatment dealt with the formal features of language and was just as analytic as grammar-translation. The audiolingual approach, too, clearly embodies an analytic strategy. Its theorists attributed the shortcomings of the direct method to a lack of attention to the proper sequencing and grading of linguistic forms in the language curriculum. They laid stress on the systematic arrangement of structures and the practice of structural aspects through pattern drills which were based on linguistic and behaviouristic principles. The cognitive approach, with its emphasis on the presentation of language as a system, was no less analytic in its teaching strategy. More recent approaches, such as the treatment of notions and functions or discourse features, extend the analytic framework to semantics, pragmatics, and sociolinguistics. But as long as they focus on specific linguistic features, whether these are phonological, lexical, grammatical, discoursal, or sociolinguistic, they offer an analytic approach to language learning in the classroom.

The attack on analysis as the only approach to language teaching and its replacement by an experiential emphasis has evolved gradually since the mid-1960s. The attack was directed not only at the classroom treatment of language but also at syllabus design and the substantive content of language programmes. A number of writers, including Newmark and Reibel (1968); Jakobovits (1968, 1972); Macnamara (1973); Krashen and Terrell (1983); and Krashen (1984), pointed out the shortcomings of analytic approaches and set against them the success of first-language acquisition in the home, bilingualism acquired 'in the street', and informal second language learning in the natural target language environment. What these situations have in common is that language is acquired in the context of real communication without any formal instruction. The weaknesses and failures of second language learning in an analytic classroom, it was argued, can be explained by the absence of any genuine motive to communicate. If situations of real language use could be created in the language class, the language would be learnt more quickly and more effectively just as it is in the natural environment. This, in short, is the case for an experiential strategy and against an analytic one which has been made by the critics of formal classroom teaching since the early 1970s.

From that time on there has been a marked shift of opinion in the direction of an experiential approach. To teach 'communicatively' was beginning to be regarded as essential or at least as very desirable. A pioneer experiment by Savignon (1972) pointed to the value of training in communicative skills in a second language programme. About the same time Rivers made the point that it was not good enough merely to be concerned with 'skill-getting'; it was necessary to ensure that this was followed by a further phase of 'skill-using' (Rivers 1972). On the theoretical side, experiential teaching was enormously strengthened through the development of Krashen's second language acquisition theory, particularly by the low value it attributed to code-focused instruction, and by its confident assertion that such instruction was of minimal value for the central process of acquisition. Such a theory would obviously relegate a language syllabus and an analytic strategy to second place.

In recent years, the claims of experiential language teaching have received welcome empirical support from a series of Canadian immersion experiments (Swain and Lapkin 1982, Genesee 1987). French immersion in Canada is based on the principle that the students receive the same type of education as they would in the regular English programme, except that the language through which other school subjects are presented and discussed is French. The aim of this content-based programme, then, is to teach the regular school subjects while offering the second language through its constant use as a medium of instruction. To begin with, when these experiments started in the mid-1960s, immersion was simply considered a practical way of overcoming language barriers in the education of young children, and relatively little thought was given to the underlying theory. But the success of the experiment and the increasing numbers of schools involved drew widespread attention. Since the mid-1970s immersion has been increasingly recognized as a prime example of experiential language teaching. Although a certain amount of analytic teaching does in fact also take place, Krashen (1984) saw in the immersion experiment a perfect illustration of successful language acquisition which dispenses almost entirely with conscious 'learning' and an analytic teaching strategy.

Other writers, however, pointed to weaknesses in the immersion pupils' French proficiency, and claimed that superficial and uncertain fluency had been bought at the price of accuracy. In other words, the effectiveness of a predominantly experiential strategy was being questioned (Spilke 1976, Bibeau 1984). Even those observers who recognized the strengths of the immersion experiment acknowledged that the interlanguage of immersion students after several years did not automatically develop into an entirely satisfactory level of proficiency (Harley 1984). In line with this criticism, Higgs and Clifford (1982) were warning against a premature 'push toward communication' which, in their view, could only lead to an unsatisfactory, uncertain, and low level of grammatical proficiency. Opposition to Krashen's second language acquisition theory has led a number of other theorists, too, to reassert the positive contribution of analytic techniques to communicative language use.[1]

In view of this controversy, a few researchers since the early 1980s have begun to investigate the respective claims of experiential and analytic forms of language teaching. To begin with, it was necessary to find out to what extent language classrooms had in fact become experiential and how general communicative principles had been realized in actual classroom practice. In order to document 'true communication' in the second language class, Mitchell *et al.* (1981) undertook a number of observational studies in Scottish high schools. These investigators found that even in classes taught by teachers who claimed to be committed to a communicative approach, this approach to the foreign language constituted only short episodes, for example, one per class or less than two per cent of the language activities taking place (Mitchell *et al.* 1981: 28). On the other hand, in a further study, Mitchell was able to show that in the course of a lesson many small incidents occur which allow for the communicative use of the foreign language either as 'pedagogic moves', for example, to explain language points, or as 'managerial/organizational moves', in order to discipline inattentive pupils (cf. Mitchell 1988).

The point which has gradually emerged is that in the language classroom there must be some kind of mix between experiential and analytic techniques. Some of the questions that arise were recently investigated over a five-year period in a series of studies undertaken by a group of researchers in the Modern Language Centre at the Ontario Institute for Studies in Education in Toronto (Harley *et al.* 1990). These enquiries have examined different language learning situations in order to come to grips with different combinations of analytic and experiential teaching. In one of these studies (Fröhlich *et al.* 1985), 13 school classes were observed. They included classes in French immersion because in this type of programme there is a presumption of regular and frequent communicative use of the second language. They further included classes from regular school FSL programmes ('core French') in which French is taught as a subject, raising the question whether under these conditions the prevailing strategy is analytic rather than experiential. The investigators also looked at so-called extended French classes which consist of regular French instruction combined with the teaching of one other subject through the medium of French, i.e. a kind of half-way programme between core French and French immersion. Finally, ESL classes were included in the comparison. Since English is the main language of the wider community in Toronto, learners in these English classes, mainly immigrants to Canada, would have opportunities to use the second language outside the classroom. It was, therefore, interesting to see whether in these different circumstances the language classes would be primarily experiential or analytic.

Based on an observation scheme which was designed to capture the chief characteristics of experiential teaching (see Chapter 2), the study found that the differences between the various language learning situations could be captured with the help of the observation instrument. The classes were differentiated, as expected, on an analytic–experiential scale so that immersion and extended classes were the most experiential, core French was the most analytic, and English as a second language was somewhere in between the two extremes.

In another 'process–product' study the OISE team compared several core French classes in the expectation that teachers would differ in their classroom treatment: some would use a more experiential approach and others would be more analytic. This was indeed found to be the case. The question to be investigated was whether the more experiential classes offer a richer linguistic environment and whether on most scores, except perhaps grammatical accuracy, the experientially taught pupils would out-perform the analytic classes. A problem in this investigation was that the classes were not markedly differentiated from each other—i.e. none of them were clearly at the extreme ends of an experiential–analytic scale—and perhaps for this reason there was relatively little difference in the proficiency levels reached which could clearly be attributed to differences in teaching methodology (Allen and Carroll 1987).

The issue of the relative effectiveness of experiential and analytic approaches is still unresolved, although as a result of recent work cited above it is becoming much clearer that the question is more one of how to balance the two than of selecting one over the other. In attempting to develop a policy on this strategy option, it is important for us to take full cognizance of the positive and negative characteristics of both strategies. As with the implicit and explicit strategy option (see Chapter 12), we find in the literature a kind of natural bias towards one or other end of the scale. The position we would like to start from is that both options have merit but also certain limitations which can only be overcome by combining the two, thus creating a mix of analytic and experiential procedures.

The scope of the analytic strategy

The analytic strategy covers a very wide range of teaching-learning techniques which are all designed to promote the learning of the second language outside a situation of actual use. The learner stands away from the language and examines it or rehearses and practises it in some way. A language item presented and practised through the analytic technique makes no pretence of being real communication. Analytic techniques point to, identify, explain, compare, illustrate, and practise a language feature or an aspect of language use. The training of any of the four skills can also be subsumed under the analytic strategy. Through the analytic strategy the learner is enabled to focus on the code.

Most exercises in coursebooks, and materials for the language laboratory or computer-assisted instruction, as well as many classroom activities, are applications of the analytic strategy. The majority of the techniques described in the handbook of language teaching techniques by Allen and Valette (1977) belong in this category. For example, the following procedure is suggested for the study of the partitive in French:

> Students bring to class as many magazine cutouts of foods as they can find. When called on, they offer them to their neighbours:
> *Student 1:* Voulez-vous de la viande?
> *Student 2:* Merci, je n'ai plus faim.
> *Student 3:* Voulez-vous des haricots?
> *Student 4:* Oui, s'il vous plait.
> (Allen and Valette 1977: 224)

The purpose of this exercise is twofold: it is intended as a speaking exercise (offering food) and it focuses on an aspect of French grammar (using the partitive). Each exchange is a separate little scene between host and guest. The magazine cutouts are merely reminders of what food is being offered, as if the students in their role as host or guest were sitting at a table with a dish containing meat or beans. It is important that the students choosing the cutouts select food items to which it is reasonable to apply the partitive, such as meat, vegetables, sugar, wine, or salt.[2]

A stimulating volume by Gilbert (1984) focuses on one aspect of code learning in ESL, training in English pronunciation and listening comprehension, and illustrates the application of analytic techniques to this area. For example, Gilbert points out that the stress pattern in English is part of a word's proper pronunciation. 'If you place a stress on the wrong syllable, it may be hard for other people to understand you. Knowing the stress pattern is part of knowing the word' (1984: 24). This important item of information and guidance is followed by several exercises in which the change of stress is practised in such word pairs as:

register	registration
examine	examination
geology	geological

In this example the techniques used are linguistic explanation followed by demonstration and practice. Such information should be accurate, appropriate, and clear, and the examples should be both appropriate and useful—as they are in this case. It is no argument against the principle of an analytic strategy that sometimes such information is inaccurate, inappropriate for the target group of students, or unclear, or that the exercises may be pointless and unhelpful.

Analytic techniques presuppose an analysis of the language—not necessarily by the learner but certainly by the teacher, curriculum developer, or course writer. They are designed to teach particular features of the language (including culture) singly or in combination. Consequently, an analytic strategy reflects the state of linguistic theory, and draws upon current descriptions, including those of the target language culture.[3] The range of analytic techniques can be applied to various levels or categories of linguistic analysis: phonology, morphology, syntax, lexis, semantics, discourse analysis, sociolinguistics. Needless to say, formal techniques are not equally developed across all these categories. Generally speaking, at the present time techniques for teaching grammar and phonology are more in evidence than techniques for the teaching of vocabulary (but see Gairns and Redman 1986; Carter and McCarthy 1988; McCarthy 1990). Recently there has been an increasing growth of interest in the teaching of semantic aspects of language, such as notions, functions, and discourse and, to a lesser extent, social variation in language use.

Analytic techniques can be arranged in two cross-classifications. First, they can be classified according to the linguistic features to be focused on and the communication skill or skills used to practise them, as in Figure 11.2. An aspect of grammar, for example, may be presented and practised in one skill or across several skills, and indeed variations in use can be taught by comparing different modes of expression, for example, speech and writing. In Allen and Valette's example the French partitive was practised through a speaking and listening task. An exercise on a sound feature may involve listening only, or listening and speaking in combination, listening and reading, or listening and writing (as in dictation). In Gilbert's example the exercises involve reading the contrasting words, listening to the words spoken on a tape recording, and speaking them. From one point of view, the technique practises a linguistic feature (for example, a stress pattern), from another it practises a communication skill (listening and speaking), and both are designed to contribute to overall proficiency.

Linguistic features focused on	**Linguistic skills involved**			
	Listening	Speaking	Reading	Writing
Phonology				
Morphology				
Syntax				
Lexis				
Semantics				
Discourse analysis				
Sociolinguistics				

Figure 11.2 A cross-classification of the various linguistic features and skills which can be focused on in analytic teaching strategies

Second, we can look at the skills as both ends and means in language training, as in the cross-classification below:

Linguistic skills as means	**Language skills as ends**			
	Listening	Speaking	Reading	Writing
Listening				
Speaking				
Reading				
Writing				

Figure 11.3 A cross-classification of the four language skills expressed as means and ends in analytic teaching strategies

Training in any one skill can aim at that skill alone rather than at a specific aspect of language. For example, if a listening comprehension exercise is intended to provide practice in listening comprehension alone, ends and means are indistinguishable. On the other hand psychological research as well as pedagogical experience have both attributed a great deal of importance to the mutual support of modes of expression across different sense modalities. Inventories of teaching techniques appropriately classify analytic techniques in terms of linguistic features as well as in terms of the four skills. For example, Allen and Valette (1977) describe in one section techniques designed to teach the sound system, the grammar and vocabulary, and in another section techniques which develop the four skills. Rivers (1975, 1981) and Omaggio (1986), on the other hand, use the four skills as the main organizing principle for the presentation of learning activities, some of which are analytic while others are experiential.

As we have seen, the pedagogical debate in recent years has tended to be critical of analysis as a teaching strategy and has pointed out its weaknesses and shortcomings rather than its merits. This has made it difficult to obtain a balanced view of the analytic strategy.[4] In trying to develop a policy on this strategy, it is therefore important to recognize its advantages as well as its limitations. At this point it may be useful to discuss some characteristic features of an analytic teaching approach.

Focus on the code

The analytic strategy focuses on the code. This gives the learner a chance to pause and examine the language gradually, deliberately, and in easy stages. Admittedly, many language courses focus on nothing but the code. Endless hours are spent on minute details of formal linguistic features. Consequently, it may seem almost perverse to remind ourselves that a focus on code is a valuable and indeed necessary part of language teaching. Yet, there is no reason why the analytic approach should not be a valuable, enjoyable, and interesting part of a language course.[5]

Decontextualization

Another positive characteristic of the analytic strategy is that it abstracts, decontextualizes, and isolates language phenomena or skill aspects for scrutiny, diagnosis, and practice. Present-day theory often demands just the opposite, namely, that we should place language items in a context. According to Omaggio:

> Most educators would agree that students must eventually know how to use the language forms they have learned in authentic communication situations. Some would agree that this goal can best be achieved if the forms are presented and practised in communicative contexts. (Omaggio 1986: 91)

While it is important to emphasize context and background for language use, it is equally important to abstract from context and to recognize formal features in different contexts. An ability to focus on one thing at a time can make the language learning task reassuring and manageable. In this way, important aspects of a language (for example, liaison, plural markers, order of pronouns, interrogative constructions, cohesion devices) are made salient for the learner. This is exactly what an analytic strategy can contribute to language learning. The ability to identify particular language features in different contexts gives the learner a useful expertise.

Fragmentation

An obvious danger of dealing with linguistic phenomena in isolation and focusing on them one by one is fragmentation. Language classes often deal with minute points of detail—a single speech sound, a plural ending, or word order—out of context. While paying attention to it, the students have difficulty in storing the information and making use of it because they lack a frame of reference. Items or rules are learned one after another in isolation but items learnt earlier are not incorporated and are quickly forgotten. When theorists talk about context, as Omaggio (1986) does, they usually refer to the context of situation in which a formal feature is found. The importance of this kind of context is unquestioned; but what the learner also needs is some sort of reference system which will provide a *linguistic* context into which to fit new information. A reference grammar or a reference card which displays all the information required may help to overcome what has been called 'the Humpty Dumpty effect' of language learning, that is, the fragmentation that an analytic treatment of language may bring about if we do not take steps to order and systematize the information presented to the learner.[6]

Complexity of the rule system

It has been argued against an analytic strategy that languages are too complex for the rule system ever to be learnt by techniques of study and practice; moreover, the complexity of language makes it impossible to arrange the rules in a simple, logical, and progressive order without violating the intricate interactions among different parts of the system. Finally, there are many aspects of the rule system which are not yet understood. These arguments merely draw attention to limitations of studying a language by analytic methods alone, and suggest that an experiential strategy should complement the analytic approach because it deals with the language more globally. However, these limitations are no reason why one should not make best use of the insights which can be achieved by learners and which may be useful for their proficiency development. An analytic approach to language teaching does not mean that all learners will be presented with the full complexity of the rule system. The main purpose of analysis is to make language learning more manageable. If the analytic strategy does not ease the learner's entry into the language, it has missed the point. What teachers always have to bear in mind is the capacity of a class to cope with language analysis. The age, maturity, and educational background of the individuals concerned have to be considered in deciding on the use of an analytic strategy for a given group of students.

Opportunity for practice

It has been widely acknowledged for well over a century that the mere presentation of facts about the language is not enough. Therefore, an analytic strategy must offer opportunities for practice and repetition. Grammar translation was the first method to introduce practice systematically by offering practice sentences to translate from and into the foreign language. The direct method continued the same principle but eliminated translation and replaced it by intralingual techniques. The audiolingual method developed relatively simple drills on a massive scale in order to encourage habit formation and conditioning. Practice in the form of exercises and drills, involving repetition, substitution, and translation, is still the mainstay of an analytic strategy in language teaching. But how useful are these exercises and drills? Disappointment with the results of massive practice has led to a questioning of analytic procedures and a shift of emphasis to experiential techniques.

Lack of transfer

The most severe criticism that has been levelled against the analytic strategy is the common observation that what has been learnt in the language class through conventional practice techniques does not automatically transfer to language use in real-life settings. For example, the practice of speech sounds in a drill does not necessarily lead to correct use of the same sounds in everyday speech. The British psychologist C. W. Valentine (1950) offers an apt illustration of the failure to apply heavily drilled items in a communicative context:

> In Northern Ireland a common dialectal form is to say 'putten' for 'put'. In a school examination students were once asked to say what was wrong in the sentence 'He has putten his feet on the table'. One youngster wrote: 'He's gone and putten putten and he should have putten put'. The standard form was known, yet the habitual one was used.[7]
> (Valentine 1950: 291)

The frequent failure to apply in use what has been learned formally has called into question the value of analytic practice techniques. Critics of the analytic strategy have pointed out the limitations of conventional practice tasks and this has led to a critical reassessment of drills, the notion of mechanical training, habit formation by methods of repetition, and other types of practice as the mainstay in language training. However, rejecting the massive use of drills does not mean a total rejection of the analytic strategy or even the rejection of all exercises, drills, and other practice tasks. It merely means questioning the undue prominence and indiscriminate use of one aspect of the analytic strategy. While an experiential approach would compensate for some of these limitations it is equally important to recognize how the analytic strategy itself can be improved by taking note of these limitations and compensating for them.

Summary

It is necessary, then, to affirm that the analytic strategy has definite merits and an important part to play. In the past it may have been excessively used and in fact misused. A great deal of time has been wasted on routine exercises which have little purpose and which do not translate into real proficiency and application in language use. But once we recognize the limitations and possible shortcomings of the analytic strategy, there seems to be no reason why this strategy cannot be improved and employed more effectively, especially if it is complemented by experiential procedures. We cannot arrive at a reasonable policy on analytic techniques without considering the role of the experiential strategy, which is the subject of the next section. We will, therefore, return to the analytic strategy after we have discussed the role of experiential techniques, and then consider a combination of these two strategies.

The scope of the experiential strategy

While the analytic strategy is in many ways thoroughly familiar territory to most language teachers, this is not so for the experiential strategy. There is uncertainty about what it is and how it should be put into effect. First, we will discuss the essential features of an experiential teaching approach. Then we will follow up with a number of exercises which have been evolved in recent years and which can be used as a means of bringing experience into the classroom. The main point about experience as a teaching strategy is that we attempt to create conditions in the language class in which the language is not examined, analysed, or practised as an object but is used for a purpose in as realistic a manner as possible. When we employ an experiential strategy, the focus of attention is not the language itself but the messages conveyed by it.

In defining the criteria for this strategy, we will be guided by a number of recent studies, and we will refer in particular to the OISE Modern Language Centre study with its COLT observation scheme which was specially designed to capture communicative characteristics of language classes (Allen *et al.* 1984). Our aim is to identify a number of features which characterize the experiential strategy and distinguish it from the analytic strategy. While the COLT scheme will be helpful in our analysis we are not adopting it in its entirety, because its purpose is different from ours. COLT is based on the tacit assumption that a communicative-experiential orientation is an advance on an analytic strategy which it seems to equate with somewhat dated audiolingual techniques. We would like to view analytic and experiential strategies as equivalent and valid approaches to language learning which are different and which complement each other.

Focus on the topic

The first feature we will use as a criterion for an experiential orientation is that the focus of classroom activities is not on the second language itself but on a substantive topic or theme. We have already established an inventory of topics to be used in the communicative activities syllabus (see Chapter 7). Among these were: (a) classroom topics, (b) personal topics, and (c) educational and professional topics. The activities in all three categories were 'motivated'. That is, the topics were not chosen at random merely to provide language practice. They arose logically and naturally from clearly defined situational, personal, or academic needs.

Under (a) we include, first of all, those necessary communications which have to do with classroom management. The treatment of the culture and general language education syllabuses in particular involves didactic communication, for example narration, explanations, and suggestions on the part of the teacher, and enquiries, questions, or observations on the part of the students. If there is plenty of give-and-take or 'negotiation' between the teacher and the students on the business of the lesson, it follows that there will be communication. While the analytic strategy is central to the content of the language syllabus, the delivery of this syllabus, too, provides opportunities for explanations, feedback, and other verbal exchanges which involve real communication, i.e. an experiential approach.

For topic area (b), subject matter arises naturally from the life experiences of individual learners or groups of learners. Category (c) is based on an educational rationale. A variety of substantive themes, derived from other areas of the school curriculum, may form the basis for communicative activities under this heading. If a student asks: Why should we read this book? Why should we listen to this talk? Why should we solve this problem? the teacher should be in a position to explain the purpose of the activity with reference to a well-thought-out syllabus. Ideally, as we shall see below, the students should play a part in the choice and treatment of topics so that both teachers and students are personally involved in the subject matter. In other words, the activities should be thoroughly motivated. The more this is so, the more the topic area will become a living authentic experience and the subject of genuine communication.

Purposeful activities

Another feature which clearly distinguishes the experiential from the analytic teaching strategy is the nature of the classroom activities. While, broadly speaking, the analytic strategy operates through study and practice of the language with full attention on the language itself, experiential activities are arranged so as to engage the learner in some purposeful enterprise: projects, enquiries, games, or problem solving, in which the focus of attention is planning the task, carrying the plan into effect through different stages, and finally completing it satisfactorily. All such tasks involve communication at the planning and decision-making stage as well as in the actual execution. Consequently, purposeful language use is involved; for example, reading the rules of a game, studying a set of instructions, taking part in discussions on different modes of action, writing a report, planning the layout of a class newspaper, working on a scenario, and so on. The four skills are used in context as demanded by the task, not just practised in the abstract. This approach to tasks—going through a process leading to a product—requires a different mind set from the usual language learning exercises.

If an experiential strategy is applied, the classroom language will have the characteristics of authentic communication as it occurs in ordinary conversation. As we have already noted in Chapter 2, the COLT observation scheme identifies seven characteristics of communication to look for in the experiential classroom: use of target language, information gap, sustained speech, reaction to message, incorporation of preceding utterances, discourse initiation, and relatively unrestricted use of linguistic forms (adapted from Allen, Fröhlich, and Spada 1984: 30). We will now comment briefly on each of these seven discourse characteristics, and then go on to consider the priority of meaning over error avoidance and accuracy, the communicative use of the four skills, and the importance of establishing an appropriate social climate in the classroom.

Use of the target language

At first sight this appears to be an obvious requirement if we wish to create a situation of real language use in the classroom. However, use of the target language is not a distinguishing criterion for experiential teaching, because it could apply equally well to the analytic strategy. It should also be remembered that ease of communication can be helped by crosslingual interventions, i.e. interpretation and explanations in the mother tongue (see Chapter 10). In some classrooms, the use of the mother tongue by students is accepted so as to ease them slowly into the second language. Some language teaching systems also deliberately encourage mixing the two languages so as to encourage the flow of meaning from speaker to listener and comparison between the two languages, rather than insisting on a rigid use of the second language which may inhibit communication. In short, this first criterion cannot be applied mechanically. The use of the second language is obviously needed. As the Stirling researchers pointed out, the use of 'real FL' is an absolute essential of second language communication. But the way in which it is introduced might involve first language use without loss of communicative intent. In applying this criterion to language teaching we have to be sensitive to the underlying principles of instruction.

Information gap

This important characteristic of natural conversation clearly distinguishes the experiential strategy from the practice and rehearsal type of exchange which occurs in the analytic treatment of language. For example, the question-and-answer exchanges which occur after reading a text are often not genuine, in the sense that the teacher already knows the answer beforehand and the students realize that the response is meant to practise the use of language rather than provide information. If we want to create in the language class the conditions for real communication, we have to introduce an element of unpredictability, i.e. an information gap between speaker and listener.

Prabhu (1987) points out that it may also be useful to introduce a reasoning gap, implying true inference, and an opinion gap, in which case the interlocutors do not know in advance what comment is likely to be made. The COLT scheme makes a sound distinction between non-communicative display requests (for example, 'What is the weather like today?' in order to provide structural practice) and information requests ('What's the weather going to be like tomorrow?' as a genuine question by someone who has not heard the forecast). COLT also distinguishes relatively predictable and relatively unpredictable information, the latter being considered more communicative than the former. It must, however, be pointed out that real communication also includes many predictable conventional routines, such as enquiries about health, greetings, and farewells which, in spite of their predictability, have genuine communicative value. Information gap as a characteristic of ordinary talk does not only apply to conversation. It is also a feature of learning any new area of knowledge, listening to lectures, or reading a text. It is, therefore, also a typical feature of the activities associated with substantive topics that occur in an experientially oriented language class.

Sustained speech

The COLT authors convincingly argue: 'If practice with normally sustained discourse is considered to be important for the development of fluent speaking and listening skills, then it is necessary for the teacher to create situations where such practice can take place' (Allen *et al.* 1987: 32). Accordingly, COLT distinguishes between ultra-minimal (one word) utterances, minimal (one clause or sentence) utterances, and sustained speech in the language class. The COLT designers hope to capture the difference between experiential and analytic ways of teaching through this criterion, because it has been characteristic of audiolingual classes to foster single-word or single-clause responses.

We must bear in mind that in ordinary conversation many verbal exchanges consist of what Brown and Yule (1983a) have called short turns, whereas long turns are more demanding to produce and somewhat less frequent, even in native language exchanges. Clearly, it is necessary for anyone learning a language to be able to follow sustained discourse and also to give more than one-word or single-clause responses. However, it is not an inherent part of the analytic strategy that we should avoid longer stretches of speech and writing. Therefore, this criterion does not in principle distinguish the analytic from the experiential strategy. It does, however, serve to differentiate between older forms of conventional practice and the more challenging demands of recent communicative language teaching.

Reaction to message, not code

What distinguishes an experiential response from one in the analytic mode is that it is like an ordinary conversational exchange; i.e. it constitutes a reaction to the message, its content and meaning rather than a reaction to the code, for example to document whether what was said was grammatically correct or not.

Incorporation of preceding utterances

Some ways of responding to the utterances of other people indicate an analytic, and others a more experiential type of strategy. In a truly conversational exchange, as it occurs between a child and parent for example, the parent might rephrase the child's statement to ensure that what was said has been correctly interpreted. Often a parent comments on what the child has said, expands on it, or provides further elaboration. It is this kind of co-operation in true conversational exchanges to which so much importance is attached in first language development (Wells 1981a, 1986). The same kind of interaction is cultivated in the communicative classroom, partly because it helps the topic of conversation to be more adequately dealt with and partly because this treatment contributes to the development of the learner's proficiency. Topic incorporation is less likely to be a feature of the analytic mode. In a classroom with an analytic orientation the teacher may comment on a student's utterance, but usually the focus is on felicity or accuracy of expression rather than on the substance of what has been said.

Discourse initiation

In many conventional language classes it is the teacher who regularly initiates talk and elicits responses from students, often in predictable and fairly repetitive ways. This is done not because it is natural but because it supplies opportunities for practice. If classroom discourse is to reflect the characteristics of ordinary conversation as it occurs among adults or children, the initiative for starting talk or determining topics should not be exercised by the teacher alone. There should be opportunities for students to take the initiative, and speech roles should be diversified, as is made possible through small group or pair work. For an experiential strategy, shifts in discourse initiation (or 'topic control' as COLT calls it) are essential attributes. There is no reason why analytic classrooms should not provide for similar shifts of discourse initiation. The fact is, however, that the study and practice of different speech roles is not typically a feature of the analytic strategy.

Control of linguistic form

It was characteristic of traditional classes that the linguistic forms to which learners were exposed were grammatically and lexically restricted. Indeed it was one of the main tenets of audiolingualism that linguistic forms should be introduced gradually, and the lack of control of earlier approaches was criticized. However, if the language class is to provide the experience of real communication then there must be exposure to the natural language without linguistic controls and restrictions. The COLT scheme distinguishes restricted and unrestricted use of the second language, on the assumption that an experiential approach is less restricted, while an analytic strategy implies stricter control of the language input. It is quite clear that an analytic strategy can apply linguistic restriction more easily than an experiential one. Teachers who are concerned about accuracy and avoidance of linguistic errors will tend to exercise linguistic control and relax it only gradually. The critics of communicative language teaching have accused it of being too open and relaxed in its handling of linguistic forms, resulting in an unsatisfactory pidgin-like interlanguage.

However, it would be wrong to assume that the experiential strategy is always completely unrestricted. Krashen's concept of comprehensible input, for example, implies an intuitively teacher-applied restriction guided by the learner's level of proficiency. Moreover, Krashen's principle of giving priority to reception over production exercises is also a restriction of skill development. Yet, if the experiential strategy is to do justice to the variety of situations, topics, and roles, it is bound to be less restrictive than has been customary in traditional language teaching. The two categories of restrictiveness identified by the COLT scheme can be considered a continuum. The experiential strategy tends towards openness of linguistic form, while the analytic strategy tends to maintain a greater control of language input and output.

Priority of meaning and fluency over error avoidance and accuracy

It is a characteristic of the experiential strategy that it encourages learners to make sense of written and spoken texts and to get meaning across in production. The experiential strategy tries to counteract the excessively slow and painstaking struggle against error; it adopts instead the developmentally more optimistic belief that errors will gradually disappear as the result of a rich and varied language experience. On the other hand, as we have seen, critics of this kind of communicative teaching (Higgs and Clifford 1982) have accused it of encouraging fluency too early and arresting learners at too low a level of proficiency. So far, there is little evidence to support either side of this argument. Provisionally, it seems right to assume that the attempt to encourage meaning and fluency is justified provided it is matched by an equivalent attempt to develop accuracy. The specific function of an experiential strategy is to develop fluency and meaning and to downplay linguistic error.

The communicative use of the four skills

Another criterion which should be added to those of the COLT scheme is the treatment of the four skills. The COLT analysis focuses on discourse in the classroom, the typical verbal exchanges in a lesson. Many language learning activities, however, are concerned with the four skills—systematic listening, speaking, reading, or writing—and not only with teacher-student exchanges. Each skill can be treated abstractly as something to be developed, so to speak, for its own sake. This is typical of an analytic approach. On the other hand, the skills can form a natural part of a purposeful set of activities: giving a talk, listening to a recording, participating in a group discussion, writing a report or a letter. The more these activities occur in a specified context, and the more they involve clearly identified interactants and have well defined aims, the more they meet experiential criteria. In this way, we can distinguish between the four skills as experiential or analytic activities.

Social interaction

If the language class is meant to be a place where individuals can experiment with communication in the second language, it is important to establish a social climate in which students are not inhibited, aggressive, or afraid. They should feel encouraged by the classroom context and see the teacher as a helper and facilitator. The importance of human relations in language pedagogy and the affective state of mind of the class was increasingly recognized during the 1970s. In the first place, this was a reaction against the somewhat mechanical types of treatment which prevailed during the previous decade. The popularity of some humanistic techniques and methods, such as Counseling-Learning, Suggestopedia, or the Dartmouth Method, is symptomatic of the need felt by many people to modify the social relations and the affective climate in the language class as one way of improving language teaching. Secondly, the increased emphasis on social and affective factors served to bring language pedagogy into line with general educational developments. These developments are important for an experiential strategy because they create the right conditions for communicativeness in a learning group.

Another social arrangement that can be helpful is the use of pair work and small group work. A good many communicative activities can best be done in a language class which operates with a socially flexible organization. We have already pointed out that real-life discourse involves contact with a variety of speakers in different kinds of social settings. Such variety cannot be entirely replicated in a language class; but group work and pair work can be used to approximate some characteristics of the socially diverse settings in which language is normally used.

A further social feature that encourages communication is co-operation among students. Helping one another is not only emotionally satisfying, it creates the right conditions for learning. There is no single interpersonal prescription for an experiential strategy. But an awareness of the social aspect of learning and making use of the language class as a way of encouraging social interaction is an essential aspect of the experiential strategy. Several of the features we have described, such as discourse initiation, topic control, conversational exchanges, the communicative use of the four skills, imply a diversification of interpersonal relations in the language class. Social interaction is an important strategy in its own right. As such it is relevant to a number of teaching strategies and can be used in combination with them. In the present context it is necessary to point out that an experiential strategy demands a clear awareness on the part of the teacher of the class as a social group and the importance of interpersonal relations that can be modified and made use of to encourage communication and experience as a way of language learning.

Summary

To sum up, the criteria for an experiential strategy are: (a) focus on substantive topics; (b) activities that emphasize fluency rather than language study and practice; (c) talk that has the characteristics of ordinary conversation, and normal communicative uses of reading and writing; (d) encouragement of a variety of social interactions in the classroom. In the application of the experiential strategy we may find any one of these features present. If all four are present, the strategy is being applied more integrally than if only one or two of the criteria are met.

Combination of the analytic and experiential strategies

In the foregoing sections we have treated the analytic and experiential strategies separately in order to throw into relief the distinct contribution of each. We have also borne in mind the possible shortcomings of both strategies. We see no reason to assume that one strategy alone offers the royal road to proficiency. Therefore, some kind of combination of these two approaches appears to be the best policy to adopt pending more convincing evidence of the greater effectiveness of either one or the other. A combination of both strategies is probably the policy that is tacitly most widely subscribed to, although in reality teachers have not clearly identified the specific contribution of each. In language pedagogy today we find no theoretician who firmly asserts that only one of these two strategies—the analytic or the experiential—is valid under all circumstances.

In practice, however, there are biases in the analytic or experiential direction. Traditional teaching approaches are heavily analytic. Classroom observation studies in search of experiential teaching, such as the Stirling study in Britain (Mitchell *et al.* 1981) and the core French study in Canada (Allen *et al.* 1987), have tended to conclude that analytic teaching is dominant and an emphasis on experiential teaching is the exception. An examination of language course materials largely confirms this view. Teachers do not deny the value of experiential activities; but very often they do not see them as part of an organized language course or, as we have already noted, they do not know exactly how to implement an experiential strategy. The experiential component is often viewed as an extra-curricular addition, to be accomplished, for example, through student exchanges, travel, or residence and work in the target language community. On the other side of the continuum, there are only a few theoreticians who have adopted a radically experiential position (for example, Krashen 1982, 1985). Most theorists have not gone along with this position. Instead, they have tended to adopt a more balanced combination of the two strategies. The main differences among the different viewpoints lie in the emphasis and timing of the strategies.

The changing point of view on this issue can be illustrated by Rivers' writings during the last twenty years. In the early 1970s, at a time when there was a noticeable shift in pedagogic viewpoints, Rivers clearly expressed the idea that language teaching requires both skill-getting, i.e. an analytic approach, to be followed by skill-using activities, that is an experiential approach (Rivers 1972). In the course of the 1970s, however, Rivers repeatedly pointed out that skill-using should not be delayed. Thus, in 1975 she offered a diagram which seemed to indicate that skill-getting and skill-using were introduced together (Figure 11.4). The author comments:

> This is not a sequential but a parallel schema, in the sense that skill getting and skill using are continually proceeding hand in hand. There is genuine interaction from the beginning, with students exploring the full scope of what is being learned.
> (Rivers 1975: 4)

The position advocated by Higgs and Clifford (1982) is a reaction against what they considered the premature use of an experiential strategy. In their view, too early a use of experiential teaching leads to a premature arrest in proficiency development. Hence, they advocate systematic teaching and, within the analytic strategy, a shifting emphasis on different aspects of the target language: vocabulary, pronunciation, grammar, discourse, and sociolinguistics. When all these come together at a fairly

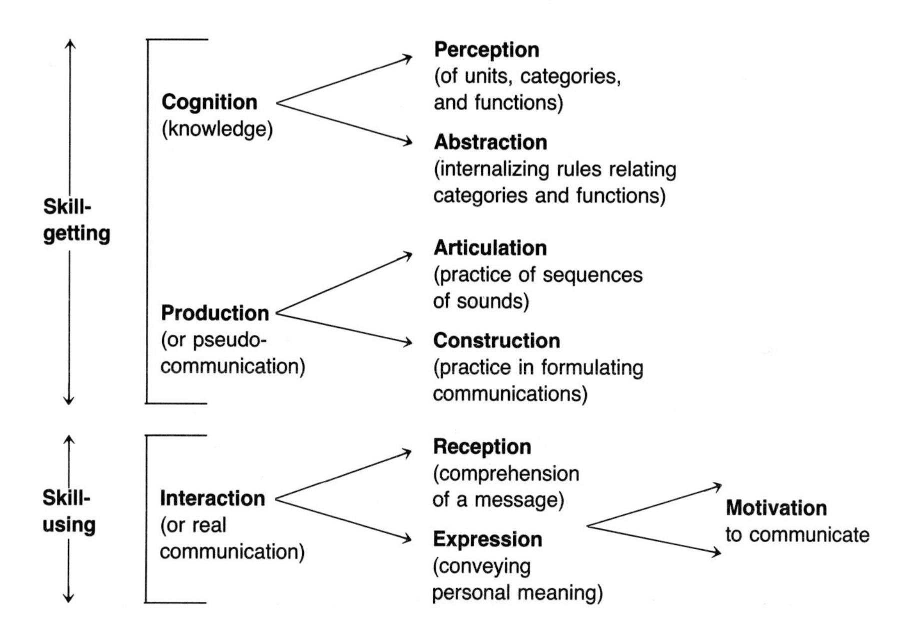

Figure 11.4 Processes involved in learning to communicate (Rivers 1975)

advanced stage, Higgs and Clifford seem to envisage a move towards a more experiential strategy. In other words, they do not share Rivers' view that the skill-using experiential strategy should be introduced early in the language course. They resist the 'push toward communication' and instead recommend delay.

Much of the argumentation for or against ways of combining or sequencing analytic and experiential procedures is speculative. The arguments are plausible, but there is little concrete evidence in support of these different viewpoints. One example of empirical research is an experimental study at the school level which focused on the specific language learning difficulties of French immersion students (Harley 1989). It has been observed that immersion pupils have difficulties with some grammatical features of French which do not automatically disappear through experiential teaching. Harley chose one such difficulty, the distinction between two tenses, the *passé composé* and the *imparfait*, for experimental teaching. The teaching method employed deliberately mixed analytic and experiential teaching, arguing for a hypothesis that

> the grammatical competence of immersion students, with respect to the use of the imparfait and the passé composé, can be enhanced: (1) by providing focused L2 input that promotes perception and comprehension of functional contrasts between these two verb tenses; and (2)

> by providing more opportunities for students to express these functions in the realization of interesting, motivating tasks.
> (Harley 1989: 335)

Six French immersion classes which received the experimental treatment were compared with six classes which did not receive the treatment and simply continued their ordinary teaching programme. The experimental treatment, a set of activities called *Parlons du passé*, consisted of eight units which were spread over an eight-week period, each taking up between one or two hours of teaching time per week. All had some bearing on the particular grammar difficulty. The basis of this set of tasks was, therefore, analytic in its conception.

The first task consisted of the reading of a French Canadian legend on the werewolf (*Le loup garou et le châle*). It was preceded by a discussion of French Canadian oral literary tradition, and followed by comprehension questions. This unit was designed to give the teachers a chance of informally observing the use of the two tenses by the students in a situation in which their attention was focused on the subject matter, not on a grammatical feature. In this unit the experiential emphasis was so dominant that 'there were no comments with respect to students' use of the past tense in class discussions' (Harley 1989: 349). Instead, the teachers reported interest in the legend and animated discussions about werewolf films and other substantive comments. The partly analytic intention of the designers of this unit may have been missed by the teachers no less than by the students.

The third unit, on the other hand, was more clearly analytic. It presented to the students contrasting pictures, to illustrate the aspectual difference between the two past tenses: for example, one picture showed someone falling downstairs (*il dégringolait l'escalier*) and the other someone having fallen downstairs (*il a dégringolé l'escalier*). Students were asked to illustrate contrasting sentences of a similar kind through drawings of their own (for example, *Le second cheval a dépassé le premier*, *Le second cheval dépassait le premier*). According to the teachers, this analytic activity proved to be very useful in clarifying the differences between the two tenses and was also found enjoyable by the students. The outcome of this study was that the combination of analytic with experiential activities was helpful in accelerating the development of grammatical competence even in 'an area of French grammar that poses subtle problems for advanced anglophone learners' (ibid.: 357).

In Harley's study the analytic strategy was dominant and the experiential one was in a secondary role. We can also imagine situations in which the experiential strategy is dominant and the analytic one subordinate. This would apply to another experiment which has already been previously mentioned in another context. In this study (Wesche 1984), French-speaking university students learning English and English-speaking students learning French, both groups at an intermediate level of proficiency, took part in a 'sheltered class' experiment. In such classes subject matter is taught in the second language so that students will learn the subject matter and simultaneously advance in the second language. The subject matter for both groups was psychology. Linguistically, the course was adjusted by the instructors in that they relied more on written outlines and weekly short answer quizzes instead of a research paper; but in content the course was equivalent to an 'introduction to psychology' offered to native speakers either in English or French. The two experimental courses were presented as psychology courses, not as language courses. Consequently the treatment, as far as the second language is concerned, can be regarded as experiential.

The psychology instructor was helped by a language teacher who provided approximately fifteen minutes of instruction in each ninety-minute class period. The language instruction was not intended to offer any explicit grammar teaching, but to clarify points of language or substance covered in the lecture and to provide help to the students in reading and note taking. The language instruction was geared to the students' difficulties, and constituted, broadly speaking, an analytic component within a predominantly experiential approach. The result of this experiment was that: (a) the students compared favourably in subject matter with students who had attended the equivalent psychology course in their native language, English or French, and (b) they gained significantly in second language proficiency, again approximately as much as students of similar proficiency level in well-taught, 45-hour courses in English and French as second languages. A third benefit of the course was that the students gained greatly in confidence in using the second language. They commented on the satisfaction they derived from 'doing something real' in their second language (Wesche 1984: 23).

In this instance, the experiential strategy was made more effective by analytic support which was offered on a limited scale. A similar relationship is achieved in certain ESL classes which are sometimes offered to foreign students who have difficulty in following regular university courses (Brinton *et al.* 1989). In these cases the ESL course is subject-oriented. It may provide help with essay writing or support in a particular subject, for example, history, science, or mathematics. While concentrating on subject matter—implying an experiential strategy—the course simultaneously pays attention to the language difficulties the course presents to foreign students, and for this purpose it uses an analytic strategy. The balance between analytic or experiential teaching is likely to vary according to the nature of the problems encountered by the students.

Concluding comments

Now that the nature of these two strategies is more clearly identified it should be possible to experiment with them in different proportions according to the students' age and cognitive maturity, language background, and interest in the subject matter or language. It is relatively easy to shift the emphasis in teaching from an experiential to a more analytic approach or vice versa. So long as research results on these options are in short supply it is best for teachers to be open to the specific merits and drawbacks of the two strategies, and to mix them in accordance with their personal judgement on the benefits to be derived.

Notes

1 See for example, McLaughlin (1978, 1987); Seliger (1979); Sharwood Smith (1981); Littlewood (1984); Widdowson (1987); Rutherford (1987); and Lyster (1990).

2 This exercise presupposes that students understand the principle of the partitive. If they do not, they will miss the point of the exercise.

3 Analytic techniques also imply a judgement on the part of the curriculum developer or teacher who has to decide whether the feature is important enough to be taught.

4 The anomaly is that in spite of the criticisms the analytic strategy is the most widely and often the only strategy used.

5 There are a few books on language teaching methodology which convey this entirely positive sense of the analytic study of the L2. Among the classics, Sweet's *Practical Study of Foreign Languages* (1899) is the best example. More recent writings include Rivers' *Practical Guide to the Teaching of French* (1975), and Gilbert's *Clear Speech* (1984).

6 On the Humpty Dumpty effect see FCLT: 183–4.

7 Valentine goes on to provide a further illustration: One Scottish teacher told me that to correct the frequent use of 'went' for 'gone' (as in 'He has went home') he once set a boy after school to write 'He has gone out' fifty times. After a time the teacher left the boy to himself. On his return he found the imposition on his desk—'He has gone out' duly written fifty times. However, the boy had added at the bottom of the page: 'I have done the work, and I have went home'. As Lightbown (1985) points out, practice does not necessarily make perfect.

12 The explicit–implicit dimension

Introduction

A key issue in second language pedagogy is whether the learner should be taught to approach the learning task consciously as an intellectual exercise, or whether he should be encouraged to avoid thinking about the language and absorb it intuitively. We propose to call the former teaching strategy 'explicit' and the latter 'implicit'. There is no established terminology for these two concepts. We have chosen the terms that have been in use since the research on this issue by the Swedish GUME Project (see below). What is meant by this dimension will become clearer if we look at the examples in Figure 12.1 below. In relation to our overall set of teaching strategies, we do not regard an explicit strategy as synonymous with the analytic approach, even though it often constitutes a characteristic part of that approach. On the other

Explicit ←	→ **Implicit**
rational/formal/intellectual	intuitive
conscious	automatic/latent
conscious learning	subconscious acquisition
consciousness-raising	automatization
monitoring	
reflective	unreflective
deliberate	incidental
studial capacities (Palmer 1922)	spontaneous capacities (Palmer 1922)
problem-solving	analogy
analysis	global understanding
cognitivism	behaviourism
abstract	practical
rule learning	
metacognitive and metalinguistic strategies	
inferencing	mimicry and memory
rationalist approach	empiricist approach
systematic study	exposure to language in use

Figure 12.1 The explicit–implicit dimension in language teaching and learning strategies

hand, an implicit strategy may coincide with the experiential approach, but it goes beyond this to encompass implicit code-focused presentation and practice techniques which fall within the analytic strategy. Intralingual and crosslingual strategies in our scheme can each be either explicit or implicit.

A distinction between explicit and implicit ways of learning and teaching did not begin to crystallize until the mid-1960s. Before that time, language pedagogy did not make a systematic distinction between more or less conscious approaches to learning. Although it has always been part of the folk wisdom that languages can be deliberately studied and practised or acquired intuitively through use in the natural environment, language teaching traditionally relied on explicit techniques of grammar and vocabulary teaching. The late nineteenth century reform movement did not introduce this particular distinction into its learning theory or its approach to pedagogy. The direct method in its original form relied just as much on an explicit teaching strategy as did the grammar–translation method.

Palmer (1922) was one of the first methodologists to be aware of the issue presented by the dimension we are discussing. He distinguished spontaneous (implicit) and studial (explicit) capacities which, in his view, jointly contributed to successful language learning. Among the studial capacities, however, he made a further distinction between those which were more intellectual and others which were less intellectually demanding and which emphasized habit formation. It was these latter—requiring repetition, memorizing, and automatization—which, according to Palmer, were most useful for language learning. Palmer was very insistent on this point, and expressed his view forcefully in a chapter on 'habit forming and habit-adapting', thus anticipating the kind of implicit yet analytic pedagogy that was so strongly advocated first by Bloomfield and later by audiolingualism.

Bloomfield (1933), agreeing with Palmer, saw in behaviouristic psychology a simple but sound theoretical basis for an approach to language learning which would encourage habit formation through imitation, repetition, and memorization. That is, he laid emphasis on relatively low-level cognitive activities in which thinking about language was less important than acquiring automatic responses. The ground was thus prepared for mimicry and memorization as key concepts in the American wartime courses and for the non-intellectual ways of language learning advocated by audiolingualism in the early 1960s. Audiolingualism brought the options of the explicit–implicit dimension to the fore by its critique of traditional language teaching and grammatical explanation, firmly opting for pattern practice, habit formation, and analogy as preferable approaches over the intellectual, problem-solving methods of the past.

One of the main principles of audiolingualism was that language learning should be viewed as the acquisition of new forms of behaviour which had to become 'automatic habits'. Language training was thus seen as a means of developing these habits in the learner. As a result, much emphasis was laid on 'habit formation' and 'automatic control' in which deliberation, insight, or problem-solving played little or no part. Language learning, it was said, is teaching *of* the language, not teaching *about* the language. Therefore, rote learning, repetition, imitation (mimicry), memorization, and pattern practice in the classroom or the language laboratory were encouraged so as to bypass or minimize explicit learning techniques. 'The acquisition of non-thoughtful responses is the very core of successful language learning' as Nelson Brooks, the leading theoretician of audiolingualism, expressed it (Brooks 1964: 62). All accounts of the audiolingual method include ample illustrations of this strong preference for mechanical and non-thinking techniques of language learning.

From this point of view, Skinner's learning paradigm in terms of stimulus, response, and reinforcement was useful because it was strictly behaviouristic and dispensed with any reference to a thinking mind which does the learning. Many pattern drills were designed—in line with Skinnerian programmed instruction—in such a way that sequences of small items could be practised successfully without involving techniques of slow problem-solving. In this way, it was argued, language learning could be made more active, less intellectual, more practical, and more readily accessible to ordinary learners. The contrast with grammar-translation exercises of the previous era was striking. It should be noted that the audiolingual theory did not rely entirely on the implicit principle. If grammar was first presented through the drilling of structures, the process was completed by the expression of simple 'generalizations'. In other words, the generalization summed up what had already been practised, thus ensuring that grammatical explicitness was allotted a secondary role.

During the period 1965 to 1970 the mechanical techniques of audiolingual pedagogy were very much on the defensive while the cognitive approach was gaining ground. The behaviouristic interpretation of learning, which dominated audiolingualism, had suffered under the attack of Chomsky (1959). In this context, an experiment by Carton in the mid-1960s signalled a shift of emphasis from an implicit to an explicit orientation. Reacting against the unthinking techniques of the audiolingual method, Carton experimented with deliberate training in intelligent guessing in second language comprehension, described as 'inferencing'. The cues the learner was trained to take note of in Carton's experimental studies were intralingual if they were supplied by the target language; interlingual if they exploited cognates and loans between languages, and extralingual if they invited the learner to relate the text to the 'real world'.

These procedures are widely used in language teaching but what makes them interesting in the historical context was that they represented 'a sharp departure from those views of language study which put exclusive emphasis on mimicry and memory' (Carton in Pimsleur and Quinn 1971: 56). Carton's conclusion illustrates well the case for an explicit strategy:

> A language pedagogy that utilizes inferencing removes language study from the domain of mere skills to a domain that is more closely akin to the regions of complex intellectual processes. Language study becomes a matter of problem solving and the entire breadth of the student's experience and knowledge may be brought to bear on the processing of language.
> (Carton, op. cit.: 57–8)

During the same period, several researchers were anxious to explore the conflict between a more explicit approach to language learning as expressed in Carroll's description of cognitive code and the more implicit approach to grammar represented by audiolingual pattern drill. In one such study, Chastain and Woerdehoff (1968) compared groups of students taught Spanish audiolingually with equivalent groups taught 'cognitively'. In this particular study, the results 'favoured the cognitive code-learning theory' (op. cit.: 279). In Sweden, a series of studies was undertaken around the same time by the GUME Project (Lindblad 1969). In this group of studies the explicit–implicit issue was the key question.

Official Swedish language teaching methodology strongly favoured an implicit approach, whereas some Swedish researchers had doubts about the validity of this position. The conflict of views had led to a public debate which was even carried on in the press of the day. In one of these experiments students were taught the use of 'do' in English as, in 'Do you read the newspaper?' or 'I helped you, but you didn't help me'. In this case, the implicit method was found to be the most successful and of the two explicit approaches, that which used Swedish for the explanation proved to be superior to the one that used English. The interpretation of the results was interesting in that the 'terminology and the novelty of the transformational approach may have been part of the reason for the comparatively poor results' in the two explicit groups (Lindblad 1969: 96).

The acrimoniousness of the debate went beyond the preference of one teaching strategy over another; it comprised two different philosophies, one based on behaviourism and the audiolingual pedagogy as it had developed in the early 1960s and the other representing cognitivism, rationalism, and a nativist view of language learning. A telling illustration of this heated controversy is Diller's book *Generative Grammar, Structural Linguistics, and Language Teaching* (1971) which appeared in 1978 in a revised version under the new title *The Language Teaching Controversy*. Diller distinguished the two philosophies as the 'empiricist approach' (behaviourism) and the 'rationalist approach' (cognitivism), characterizing both vividly while expressing a distinct preference for the rationalist position.

In 1964 a well-known paper by J. B. Carroll had initiated a debate on the conceptual distinction between 'audiolingual habit theory' and 'cognitive code-learning theory'.[1] In a further paper, Carroll (1971) insisted on the complementary nature of these two approaches. Language learning, he argued, does involve habit. He criticized the rejection of the concept of habit by the 'new orthodoxy', and suggested that its replacement by the term 'rule' was just a 'terminological overlay'. At the same time cognition could play a valuable role in language learning: 'the concepts of cognition and of habit formation can be accommodated to each other' (Carroll 1971: 110), not as an eclectic compromise but because 'a knowledge and comprehension of the facts and formal rules of the language . . . can indeed be of help in guiding the formation of appropriate language habits' (ibid.: 112). In other words Carroll, who had opened the debate in 1964, closed it in 1971 by arguing that an explicit and implicit strategy are compatible with one another; in other words, the differences between the two had been exaggerated.[2]

In the early 1970s, the interest of researchers shifted to communication as a key concept without completely resolving the earlier issue of a more or less explicit pedagogy. During the 1970s, research experience was gathered on language learning in the natural environment, in bilingual situations, and through immersion schooling. In all of these situations a language is not acquired through systematic study but absorbed largely unconsciously through exposure to the language in use. The meaning of 'implicit' learning thus gradually shifted from unthinking practice techniques to subconscious absorption of the second language under conditions of spontaneous communication.

The argument about the explicit–implicit option in this new guise was taken up in the mid-1970s by Krashen's Monitor theory and continued into the 1980s. According to Krashen, some language learners are Monitor over-users, while others are Monitor under-users. Ideally, a learner should be an optimal Monitor user: 'An overemphasis on conscious grammar has the undesirable result of encouraging over-use of the Monitor. But completely eliminating grammar robs our students of the chance to use conscious learning as a supplement for acquisition' (Krashen and Terrell 1983: 45). In other words, Krashen has not opted entirely for an implicit learning strategy; he recognizes that explicit learning has a certain role to perform, although it is limited. As we will see later, Krashen's interpretation of an explicit learning strategy is quite narrow. It is entirely confined to the notion of 'grammar rules'. In our view, a conscious learning strategy covers a much wider range of activities, and consequently an explicit teaching strategy is not restricted to what in Krashen's terms is described as grammar teaching alone.

In 1978, Bialystok developed a model of second language learning including three knowledge sources which she labelled: 'other knowledge', 'explicit knowledge', and 'implicit knowledge' (Bialystok 1978). This model, therefore, acknowledges that it is possible to know some things about a language explicitly, and others only implicitly. The model also claims that there is an interaction between explicit and implicit knowledge. Bialystok did not assume—as Krashen did—that there is no movement from explicit to implicit or vice versa. In fact, Bialystok has experimented with ways of finding out how the explicit and implicit knowledge sources interact with one another (Bialystok 1979).

In one experiment, students who were learning French had to make three kinds of judgement: after listening to a number of sentences in French, they were first asked simply to say whether a sentence they had heard was right or had a grammatical error in it. In the second condition they had to state in which part of the sentence the ungrammatical sentence was wrong, and in the third condition they were given a set of grammar rules and had to identify the particular rule that was broken in the incorrect sentence. This study led to the conclusion that both implicit and explicit knowledge have a contribution to make to language learning. The study pointed out the differential role of intuitive and formal information: 'Learners' intuitions must be developed and encouraged and efficient strategies for consulting explicit knowledge when necessary must be trained' (Bialystok 1979: 100–1). Thus, Bialystok did not dismiss either implicit or explicit knowledge as without value to the learner, and the pedagogical implication of her study was that both should be developed.

However, it was implicit learning—in its newer guise as intuitive acquisition—that once more became persuasive as a relatively sound and simple way of acquiring second language proficiency. To counteract this over-optimism about implicit learning, some writers in the 1980s have advocated a more balanced view. Typical of these attempts to redress the balance are the writings of Sharwood Smith and Faerch. Both these authors evolved models which consider the option between explicit and implicit learning not as dichotomous, but as a continuum in which the two approaches complement each other. They recognize that some linguistic phenomena are acquired in an unconscious way, and others are learnt more deliberately. Moreover, it is possible to move from explicit to implicit, the process of automatization, or from implicit to explicit, the process of consciousness-raising, and in both presentations we find diagrammatic models of explicitness and implicitness as continua. Thus, Sharwood Smith (1981) represents consciousness-raising by two orthogonal continua, one of which refers to the overtness of the explicit approach, and the other to degrees of elaboration:

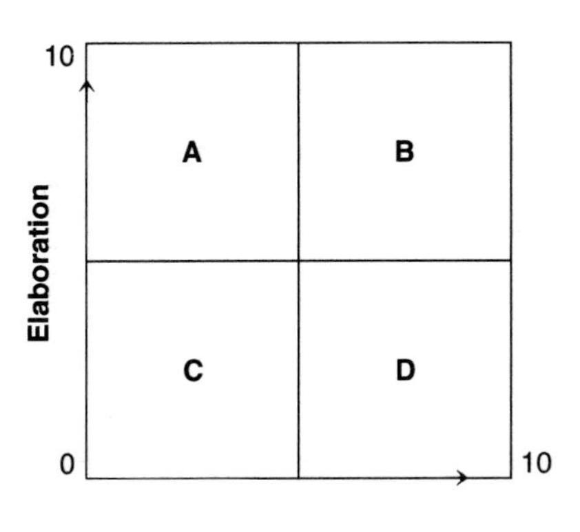

Figure 12.2 Consciousness-raising in language teaching (Sharwood Smith 1981)

Faerch *et al.* (1984) describe the interrelation between implicit, explicit, automatization, and consciousness-raising by another diagram suggesting a flow from implicit to explicit and vice versa in both directions, as follows:

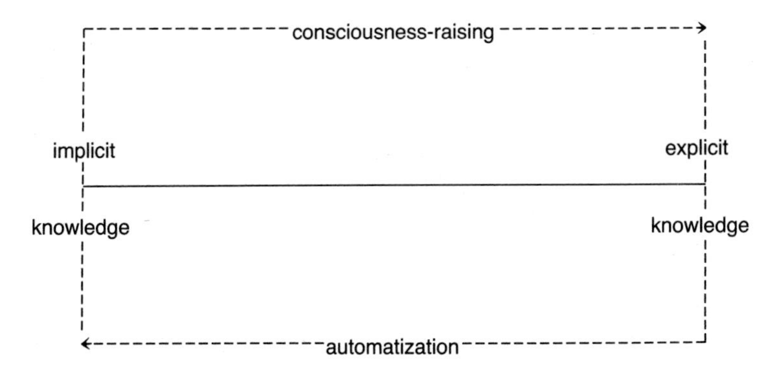

Figure 12.3 The interrelation between implicit and explicit language learning (Faerch et al. *1984:203)*

According to Faerch *et al.*, rules—whether they are teacher-made or devised from a textbook—offer the opportunity for intellectual or explicit learning, while textual input encourages intuitive and implicit learning.

In the following discussion of the explicit-implicit dimension, we associate ourselves with the point of view which is represented by Bialystok, Sharwood Smith, and Faerch. From our perspective, Krashen's view of explicitness, as expressed in his Monitor theory, is too restricted because it does not allow for a movement from explicit to implicit or vice versa. At the same time, we must acknowledge the contribution that Krashen's theory has made to the discussion of many issues which relate to the explicit–implicit dimension. In particular, it recognizes the importance of implicit learning which had previously been under-rated by the cognitivists, or had been too narrowly interpreted as a mechanical process of habit formation.

On the basis of what has been said up to this point, we conclude that both explicit and implicit knowledge sources exist, that they complement one another, and that both contribute to proficiency development. It is advantageous for learners to have access to both ways of learning and to be offered the possibility of shifting from a more cognitive to a more intuitive command, or in the opposite direction, that is, from implicit learning to consciousness-raising. Movement back and forth is advantageous for language learning. It may well be that some learners have a preference for more implicit ways of learning while others prefer more explicit approaches. For a teacher, it is important to be aware of different techniques which provide the opportunity for both implicit and explicit learning and respect the preferences of learners.

The explicit teaching strategy

Advocates of an explicit teaching strategy assume that second language learning is, for many people, a cognitive process leading to an explicit knowledge of the language. Such learners focus on the characteristic features of the language, and make an effort to acquire a conscious and conceptual knowledge of it. Learners who use an explicit learning strategy want to know how the language functions, how it hangs together, what words mean, how meaning is conveyed, and so on. Any efforts in this direction can be described as leading to an explicit knowledge store. Many students consciously plan and organize their learning activities, setting themselves goals and choosing ways and means to reach them, for example through 'academic' study or practice, or through other procedures such as immersing themselves in the language environment. Research on learning in or out of the classroom has revealed that many students make insightful observations on their own performance. They prove to have a good understanding of their own command (or lack of command) of the second language. They can usually also comment on what they expect of their teacher and what they themselves regard as more or less efficient techniques of instruction.

It is known that students do not tackle language learning in a uniform way. Some may express a clear preference for treating learning as a cognitive task, in which case it is natural to employ an explicit teaching strategy; others may reject this approach entirely or use an explicit strategy with many reservations. An explicit teaching strategy is designed to throw into relief the cognitive aspects of language learning. This may be done so as to correspond with the students' natural learning styles, or with the purpose of developing strategies in those who feel less confident about their use. An explicit teaching strategy may also serve to promote the declared cognitive objectives of a particular language course. An explicit teaching strategy has a particular bearing on the knowledge objective (see Chapter 3). It cultivates a systematic and orderly command of different aspects of the language. The technical terminology of linguistics or of traditional grammar will certainly not be avoided, but it is not essential. An explicit strategy encourages the students to look upon learning as an intellectually challenging and worthwhile task.

It is often argued that second language teaching in which explicitness is emphasized gives the learner an inefficient command of the target language. The learner is over-conscious of rules and lacks an intuitive native-like competence. Thus, as we have seen, Krashen's Monitor theory severely restricts the role of any conscious knowledge and deliberately planned approaches to the second language. However, Sharwood Smith and Faerch, among others, have argued convincingly that there is much more movement in both directions between explicit and implicit knowledge than is allowed for in the Krashen model. Language items and sequences can become automatic even though they have been consciously learnt at the beginning. A language user can also revert to a more conscious command if need be even if an item has become automatic. In other words, an explicit strategy does not hinder the acquisition of an implicit command nor does it necessarily impede proficiency; on the contrary, it enhances it and is likely to make language items more learnable, more durable, more flexible, and more easily retrievable.

Many writers on second language pedagogy, particularly those who are sceptical about an explicit teaching strategy, delight in evoking the image of clumsy and incomprehensible rules followed by difficult and obscure practice with little or no useful application in real language use. Nothing could be further from the efficient use of this strategy. The main point about using an explicit strategy is to make the language clear and transparent, to help learners understand the underlying principles, and to give them a sense of order, consistency, coherence, and systematicity about the way the language operates. The techniques within this strategy fall into two broad groups which jointly direct, guide, or support the deliberate efforts of learners in acquiring and using the second language. One group may be described as metacognitive counselling techniques; the other can best be summarized as guided cognitive learning techniques.

The first group of *metacognitive counselling techniques* brings together various acts of advice to learners which occur during the course of instruction. Informally, teachers have always more or less deliberately advised students about efficient methods of language learning. Sometimes this advice consists of hints on what to do and what not to do in order to learn efficiently. There may be admonitions, words of encouragement, or specific suggestions on how to memorize, how to learn, how to note vocabulary items, how to respond to error correction, how and when to apply what has been studied, and so on. Since the early 1970s, there has been increasing interest in the strategies of language learners (Rubin 1975; Stern 1975; Wenden and Rubin 1987; O'Malley and Chamot 1990; Oxford 1990). As a result, teachers are beginning to experiment with counselling in order to help students develop more efficient strategies. In Chapter 9 we discussed the possibility of a syllabus of 'learning how to learn' including techniques of learner training. The techniques involved—whether or not they constitute a formal part of the curriculum—can easily be incorporated into second language teaching.

The second group of *guided cognitive learning techniques* support the cognitive learning strategy we have previously described. Examples of such techniques are observation, conceptualization, explanation, mnemonic devices, rule discovery, relational thinking, trial and error, explicit practice, and monitoring. These activities may arise in the language syllabus with reference to phonology, grammar, lexis, semantics, discourse, or sociolinguistics. They may also occur in the treatment of the culture syllabus. In a communicative activities syllabus explicit strategy episodes are less prominent, but they may occur spontaneously with reference to individual linguistic or cultural items as they arise in the course of other language-related activities or in general language use. Cognitive techniques in this wider sense can be seen as aids in creating mental links in second language acquisition, stimulating observation or trial and error, and establishing networks of verbal relations in the minds of the learners, thus helping them to store information efficiently and retrieve data more easily. These techniques will now be briefly described.

Observation. From an early stage, learners can be made aware of critical linguistic features, and be taught to identify them in texts, and to distinguish them from other features by comparison or contrast. These activities can apply to phonology, grammar, lexis, functional characteristics, and cultural features. At an early stage of learning French, for example, it is useful to be able to distinguish masculine from feminine nouns. The difference is indicated by definite and indefinite articles and by the agreement of adjectives and some participles. To an expert user of French this distinction is so obvious that it is hardly worth mentioning. In the case of learners, however, it may be necessary to draw attention to these gender markers. At a more advanced stage it may be confusing for a learner of French when *le* or *la* functions as an article before a noun for example, *la porte* (the door), and in other contexts functions as a pronoun, for example, with reference to a new shirt, *je la porte* (I'm wearing it). In this case, the learner must distinguish differences in meaning and function of a language form in different contexts, although the forms are outwardly identical. Perceiving, observing, and studying are central to a cognitive grasp of the second language. They help learners to familiarize themselves with difficult, subtle, or puzzling but crucial aspects of the language. Prompting observation is not dependent on a technical vocabulary. The language phenomena can be pointed out by gestures, various typographical devices, or by the use of simple labels.

Conceptualization. What kind of abstract concepts we can introduce into language instruction depends on the learner's background, maturity, ability, and objectives. The criterion is the extent to which learners are likely to be helped or hindered by abstractions about the second language.

Explanation. An explanation may be presented by the teacher as a general principle which is then exemplified by one or two illustrations and applied through practice in exercises or drills. This so-called deductive technique is widely used in language instruction. The rule, together with one or two examples, serves not only as a guidepost but also as a reminder or handy mnemonic which can be referred to whenever this particular language problem arises. The explanation may be a teacher-made rule of thumb (Faerch 1986), or it may be expressed in terms of a particular linguistic model.[3] The explanation can come early, late, or in the middle of a practice sequence. According to Cooke (1974), there is a case to be made for introducing explanation early with regard to a given item 'in order to promote productive hypotheses, and possibly to help in monitoring hypothesis-testing . . . during language performance' (Cooke 1974: 59).

Mnemonic devices. Teacher-made rules of thumb, as Faerch (1986) has rightly pointed out, serve not only as explanations but also as mnemonic devices. For example, Faerch recalls from his own childhood the following mnemonic rhyme for prepositions which govern the accusative in German:

> durch – für – gegen – ohne – wieder – um –
> kennst du nicht den Akkusativ
> dann bist du wirklich dumm!
> (Faerch 1986: 131)

Rule discovery. Instead of presenting an explanation or rule before application, the explanation may be deliberately withheld in order to encourage students to discover the underlying principle for themselves. Excessive use of the rule-and-application sequence (deduction) which had characterized the grammar-translation method in the 1800s prompted influential reformers by the turn of the century to recommend a 'method of inductive grammar' (Sweet 1899) or 'inventional grammar', according to which 'the object of the pupils must be to discover the principle of usage' (Jespersen 1904: 172).

Relational thinking. This technique includes differentiating, comparing, and contrasting. A weakness of much explicit teaching is that it treats a linguistic phenomenon in isolation instead of comparing it with other aspects of the language system. What difference in meaning is signalled by using this particular form? What change of meaning results if another form is used? In an effective use of the explicit strategy attention will be paid not only to the item to be learnt but also to the way it compares and contrasts with other related items. At the same time, it is important to avoid excessively subtle distinctions which exceed the level of proficiency of the learner.

Trial-and-error. One simple way of stimulating explicit learning is to get learners to experiment with a new form, word, phrase, or intonation pattern, and to find out how it works and what it conveys to an interlocutor. This is not just a matter of random tryouts. It can involve systematic hypothesis testing, for instance, about language rules or the meaning of new words.

Explicit practice. Repeated observation, exercises, or drills as part of the explicit strategy presupposes that the activity is undertaken with a consciousness of the language phenomenon that is being practised. This cannot be taken for granted. Drills are sometimes practised without any awareness on the part of the learner as to what the specific purpose of the exercise may be. Consequently, the drill is treated as a school task to be completed in the easiest and most painless way. Think-aloud protocols have revealed that some learners complete a drill correctly but fail to understand the purpose of the drill and, therefore, miss its intended value. Explicit practice, if correctly done, is undertaken with an understanding of what is being practised and why. Even if an exercise is done repeatedly and is becoming increasingly automatic, the learner in the explicit mode should always be able to raise the rule or principle involved to the level of consciousness if need be.

Monitoring. While engaged in meaningful communication the learner is encouraged to be vigilant about the rules of the language, and to check what he reads or writes in relation to his explicit knowledge. Monitoring is needed by second language learners because their command of the language is not as intuitive as it is in the case of the mother tongue. The learner should develop some insight as to how vigilant he has to be about language use, and how much editing is needed. There is a constant need for learners to balance the demands of fluency against those of accuracy. Krashen is right in drawing attention to the possibility of under-monitoring, that is, of being overconfident, as well as the possibility of over-monitoring and thus becoming hesitant and excessively slow both in language reception and production. Optimal monitoring is somewhere between these two extremes. It is not a fixed entity. In order to progress and not to get bogged down in a 'fossilized' use of language errors, a learner may have to adjust the degree of monitoring.

Taking the metacognitive and the cognitive techniques together, language learning can be an intellectually challenging task at any stage. The extent to which an explicit teaching strategy will be emphasized depends partly on the objectives of the course and partly on the teacher's intentions and assessment of the learners' needs. Whatever the decision, it can be firmly asserted that an explicit teaching strategy must be balanced against an implicit strategy if the instructor wants to do justice to different learning approaches.

The implicit teaching strategy

The techniques subsumed under this heading encourage the learner to approach the new language globally and intuitively rather than through a process of conscious reflection and problem-solving. The rationale for an implicit strategy can be set out as follows:

(a) Languages are much too complex to be fully described. Even if we accept the validity of linguistic descriptions, they only take us so far. There is always a large residue of underlying rules which have not been clearly formulated, or which are not fully understood even by the experts.
(b) Even if the entire rule system could be described, it would be impossible to keep all the rules in mind and to rely on a consciously formulated system for effective learning. The learner would be

handicapped rather than helped by an attempt to grasp the target language system in its entirety. The teaching and learning of a second language must therefore rely largely on an intuitive absorption of many features of the language.

(c) According to some theories of language acquisition (for example, Krashen 1982), languages are acquired at a psychologically 'deeper' level if they are experienced unreflectively in meaningful, authentic contexts.

(d) Even if we do not accept Krashen's argument, there are always some learners who express a preference for intuitive rather than intellectual modes of learning. Some students are afraid of linguistic abstractions or claim to be unable to cope with metalinguistic concepts. An implicit teaching strategy can meet the demands of learners who fall into this category.

In the psychological literature, it is regarded as an undisputed fact that learning can occur with different degrees of consciousness. It is accepted without question that some learning—so-called blind, unconscious, incidental, or latent learning—takes place outside the awareness of the learner. Procedures have been developed to induce changes in the behaviour of individuals regardless of their conscious participation. In many learning tasks an explicit and self-conscious approach is not always successful. Thus, in learning a stroke in golf or tennis, dissection of the stroke is not necessarily the best way of acquiring the skill in question. In such cases, an intuitive perception of the whole movement may be more effective.

When the first language is learnt in early childhood, development takes place imperceptibly in the course of social interaction between parent and child. In later life, when a second language is learnt without tuition in the natural environment, conscious efforts directed to the formal features of the language are only part of the learning process. The learner may not have the time, inclination, or opportunity to study the formal characteristics of the second language. Much of the learning appears to occur below the level of consciousness, while the learner is busy using the language in the course of daily life. It is, therefore, perfectly reasonable to encourage unconscious language acquisition, and to vary the thinking load. Three different types of implicit teaching techniques have evolved: implicit audiolingual techniques, experiential teaching techniques, and techniques for creating a state of receptiveness in the mind of the learner.

Implicit techniques of audiolingualism

A number of implicit, yet analytic, techniques which focus on the language but attempt to reduce the mental effort in coping with it were developed in the 1950s and 1960s within the audiolingual framework. At the time, they were enthusiastically received as simple, practical, and effective innovations, and their influence on teaching materials and classroom teaching was widespread.[4] While these techniques have not proved as powerful as they were thought to be at the time, it would be a mistake to completely reject them. They have provided students with useful ways of practising language items without having to think hard. A number of techniques were designed to provide plenty of active practice and at the same time to bypass or minimize more intellectual activities, for example: repetition, rote learning, imitation of sounds and sentence patterns, memorization of dialogues or narratives, pattern practice, and choral practice.

An example from Lado (1964) will help us to understand the rationale. According to Lado, 'language operates largely on the basis of habit' (1964: 105), and therefore it is important to establish these habits. In his view 'pattern practice is rapid oral drill on problem patterns with attention on something other than the problem itself' (1964: 105). For example, if we want to teach the question pattern *do you* + verb as in 'Do you understand?' the focus on new lexical items, for example, *see*, *believe*, *approve*, *try*, diverts the student's attention from the question pattern, which is practised 'automatically'. That at least is the theory.

The various audiolingual procedures were based on the principle that it is the practice itself that creates the habit and that time spent on such practice constitutes a more valuable use of learning time than slower explicit techniques. Carefully graded audiolingual practice is still valuable today because it provides an opportunity for exercising language patterns in a way which is cognitively undemanding. Even if we never again give pattern practice the central role it occupied during the audiolingual era, we would be justified in re-examining the principles and recommendations which are discussed in the writings of Brooks (1964); Lado (1964); Rivers (1968, 1975, 1981); and others.

Experiential teaching techniques

While the implicit techniques of audiolingualism focus on the mechanics of the language but invite practice with a minimum of reasoning, experiential techniques shift the learner's attention away from the language altogether and direct it to topics, tasks, activities, and substantive content (see Chapter 11). If we deliberately introduce an experiential element into the classroom we create opportunities for implicit language learning similar to those offered by a natural target language environment. An experiential teaching strategy thus assumes a mainly implicit strategy. It is, of course, possible to emphasize language in a subject- or topic-oriented classroom and to apply an explicit language teaching strategy; but this must be done circumspectly, otherwise the subject matter would be neglected. Focus on content and the use of an implicit strategy raise a number of questions:

(a) At what level of proficiency can a focus on content be introduced so that the subject matter is accessible to learners and helps them to learn language as well as substance? We would like to assume that topics of real interest and value can be offered from the very beginning of language instruction.
(b) Should the level of language be adjusted to the proficiency level of the learners or should the subject matter be offered without adaptation more or less as it occurs in the natural environment? Krashen (1982) suggests that the language level needs to be adapted so that the learners can cope with it. In his view only 'comprehensible input' slightly above the level of proficiency so that there is an element of challenge—expressed in the formula 'i + l'—can lead to further development of proficiency; i.e. not indiscriminate exposure to the language as it occurs in the natural environment.
(c) To what extent is it legitimate in a content-oriented course to focus on language (vocabulary and grammatical features, for example), without detracting from the character of the course and denying the value of implicit learning? During instruction which takes real-life topics and uses them as the basis for an implicit learning strategy, the focus on language must be limited to what is necessary so that the subject-matter is made accessible. Within this context, subject-matter takes precedence on the grounds that a great deal of language is learned when the substantive interests of learners are aroused.
(d) Is it realistic to believe that in an ordinary language class we can create opportunities for implicit learning which are equivalent to the experiences of a second language environment or of an immersion-type programme? Unfortunately, even under the best of circumstances, a student in a classroom is always at a disadvantage. This is particularly so when the classroom setting is physically distant or psychologically remote from the target language environment, for example when English is learnt in Latin America or Japan, or Russian in the United States or Canada. On the other hand, one could argue that the less propitious the circumstances, the more important it is to offer students opportunities for implicit learning. Such opportunities should occur repeatedly during the language course and replace some of the formal practice.

The implicit strategy and the four skills. The implicit strategy can be applied to any of the four skills. Listening to a story or reading a familiar text gives confidence in the receptive skills. In applying an implicit approach, the class would not focus on grammatical features, vocabulary items, or stylistic matters. The students' main attention would be entirely directed to the content and its intrinsic interest. Students who are familiar with hockey or football, for example, might get a great deal from listening to a radio sports commentary, even though linguistically it might be well above their level of proficiency. In an implicit approach, we would be concerned less with the details of understanding and more with the fluency of listening comprehension directed to the overall content.

Where speaking and writing are concerned we can focus on content and deliberately withhold comments on accuracy. In a 'brain-storming' session, the learners try to say what they think even though their speech may be faulty and hesitating. If we wanted to emphasize implicit learning, we would withhold comment on many of the points which indicate linguistic difficulty in the interests of building up confidence and the experience of thinking and communicating in the second language. We could also contribute by responding to what students say and helping them to express themselves more correctly. On these occasions, it is not important for the students to repeat the corrected version. In an implicit language learning session, it is meaning, fluency, speed, and readiness of expression that should be emphasized. Particularly students who are slow, hesitant, and laboured in their attempts to speak might need this kind of treatment. At the same time it is important for students to understand what is meant by an implicit teaching strategy, and to enlist their co-operation so that they enter into the spirit of what we are attempting to do.[5]

For much the same reason it is useful at regular intervals to present radio and television programmes, films, and videos as well as providing opportunities for listening to native speakers of the second language—not so that the students can observe specific language phenomena, but so they can experience 'language in action' in a real-life context. The effect of global exposure on a regular basis is likely to be different for different learners. The experience can be guided by preparatory or follow-up discussions. For the most part, however, the activity can be left to make its impression without detailed study of the language. Detailed study has its place as well; but there are times when learners should be confronted by the language in its undiluted reality.

Creating states of receptiveness

We should consider under the heading of implicit teaching the various attempts that have been made to create a state of receptiveness in the mind of the learner. The purpose of this is to overcome the deeper psychological resistances to second language learning which are difficult to reach by purely rational approaches. For example, a number of attempts have been made under the heading of hypnopedia, to induce learning by activating a sound-receiving pillow with language items in the expectation that learners will be subconsciously receptive to them while they are asleep. In assessing techniques of this kind it is not necessary to assume that a high level of proficiency will be attained through hypnopedia alone. Even if the treatment were able to create a state of greater readiness for learning or if it could consolidate learning previously achieved on a more conscious level, it would have something to contribute to the total language learning enterprise and particularly to our efforts to understand various forms of implicit learning.

In this context we might also consider Suggestopedia which gave rise to a good deal of controversy in the 1970s.[6] Suggestopedia makes very determined attempts to create a state of receptiveness by paying particular attention to certain features which influence learners indirectly: for example, a comfortable physical environment, a sympathetic attitude on the part of the teacher, and the association of soft classical music with readings in the foreign language. In a similar way, The Lozanov Method draws on yoga as a means of helping students to attain a relaxed state of mind. No evidence is available to show whether these techniques have the intended effect on learners, or whether they are beneficial to language learning at all. They illustrate, however, some recent attempts to circumvent intellectual inhibitions by appealing to the affective state of mind of the student. Richards and Rodgers (1986: 149) show how much Suggestopedia relies on implicit learning: 'Learners must not try to figure out, manipulate, or study the material presented but maintain a pseudo-passive state, in which the material rolls over and through them.' In short, we see here a distinct preference for an implicit over an explicit teaching strategy.

The implicit strategy, then, has manifested itself in three ways: (a) through implicit practice, i.e. techniques which minimize thinking about the language and avoid metalinguistic concepts; (b) through experiential approaches which focus the learner's attention on interesting activities and content involving the use of the second language, but without focusing on the language system and its rules; (c) through creating a receptive state of mind in the learner, principally by paying attention to the affective tone of the language class. Although implicit techniques have been discussed in the context of various methods, their applicability is not confined to the methods we have referred to here. Implicit teaching and learning is a necessary complement to an explicit teaching strategy and has a function to perform in any type of language programme. It follows that in developing a policy on second language education, an important consideration is the nature of the balance we wish to achieve between implicit and explicit teaching strategies.

Combination of the explicit and implicit strategies

In this chapter we have presented the case first for an explicit and then for an implicit teaching strategy. Many discussions are flawed by the fact that they tend to favour either an explicit or an implicit approach, and this makes it difficult to get a balanced view of both strategies. Thus, the audiolingual literature tended to lean towards implicit practices in order to counteract the heavy emphasis on explicit teaching of earlier methods. The cognitive theorists reacted against the implicit teaching policy of audiolingualism and reverted to a much more explicit approach. Subsequently, Krashen argued strongly for implicit experiential techniques. However, a number of recent writers, including Faerch and Sharwood Smith, have reacted once more against the over-emphasis on implicit learning that they found in such policy statements as Krashen and Terrell's *The Natural Approach* (1983) and have made their case for a more explicit orientation. In order to develop a policy for ourselves, we want to bear both strategies in mind and treat the explicit and implicit options as opposite ends of a continuum. In practice, we expect the two strategies to be combined, but the mix will be varied according to the language topic, the course objectives, the characteristics of the students, and the needs of the teaching situation.

As we have already seen, some topics are more easily managed implicitly, while others are better handled explicitly. We saw this issue arising in pronunciation teaching where a great deal of technical knowledge is available. It is questionable, however, to what extent students are helped in acquiring a good pronunciation by being exposed to this knowledge. In Chapter 4 we outlined various options in the treatment of pronunciation problems, based on a continuum devised by Strevens (1977). A review of these pages will indicate how, on this particular issue, implicit and explicit techniques need to be interwoven. For example, one approach we suggested in pronunciation teaching was listening, observation, and imitation. While these techniques do not require abstractions and metalinguistic concepts and are therefore more implicit than explicit, the learner's attention may still need to be drawn to salient features to observe and imitate, and these techniques represent an increase in explicitness. In other aspects of language such as grammar, lexis, or functional analysis the linguistic sophistication that can go into the treatment of any language topic is considerable. The question we have to ask in each instance is whether students are likely to be helped or hindered by treating language consciously and deliberately or whether it is better to leave conceptualizations alone and to let the particular language aspect be absorbed at a less conscious level.

Many of these considerations will fall into place if we bear in mind the context of a course and its objectives. For example, students studying a language as part of a university programme may be predisposed towards a more cognitive approach, and this may lead us towards the explicit end of the strategy continuum. On the other hand, if we are teaching a second language to Canadian immigrants, our main task may be to give them a high level of practical proficiency as quickly as possible. We might find that some learners prefer an explicit approach, while others consider it an imposition to have to deal with grammatical and other linguistic abstractions. In this situation we would probably reduce explicit techniques to a necessary minimum and emphasize implicit procedures as much as possible.

An important consideration in the choice of an appropriate emphasis is undoubtedly the learning style of the students. Language learners are likely to differ with regard to their preference for explicit or implicit language learning. To some extent, choosing a point on the continuum is a question of age, maturity, and previous educational experience. Students who are younger, illiterate, or lacking in educational background may have difficulties in coping with metalinguistic concepts; in this case explicit techniques would have to be handled cautiously. On the other hand, adult students whose educational background has given them a general knowledge of language processes may have a strong preference for explicit techniques, and this in turn can influence the teaching emphasis. It should go without saying that the preference of students for an explicit strategy ('I wish you would teach us the grammar in a straightforward way') or for implicit teaching ('I hate grammar') is not the only factor to take into consideration. Students whose demand for explicit teaching or whose refusal to accept it is excessive (Krashen's Monitor overusers and underusers) should be persuaded to try a different type of strategy, if the teacher feels that this is what they need.

Finally, a given teaching situation may suggest ways of sequencing explicit and implicit teaching. The two strategies can be treated as different phases of the learning process. In the late 1960s, some theorists attempted to overcome the conflict between audiolingualism and cognitivism by treating implicit and explicit procedures as early and late phases of language teaching. Thus, Rivers (1968) treated 'manipulation' (a relatively mechanical type of practice) as a first phase preceding a second phase of more intelligent control in which deliberate 'selection' and a deeper understanding of linguistic processes would be involved. In a similar way, Strevens (1972, 1977) in his discussion of pronunciation teaching gives preference to an implicit teaching of sounds as a first phase ('the principle of innocence'), while more explicit teaching ('the principle of sophistication') will be applied if the simpler methods do not work, or to meet the demands of older and more sophisticated learners who want to progress more quickly. On the other hand, Campbell

(1970), on the basis of an experimental study, argues in favour of explicit teaching to begin with: 'certainly in the teaching of grammar to adults (and probably to anyone over twelve) explication of the rules to be acquired is advantageous' (1970: 43). Once the principle of an explicit approach has been established, Campbell introduces implicit practice techniques, beginning with 'mechanical, manipulative drills', and culminating with 'the most realistic communicative experiences possible' (ibid: 47).

Concluding comments

In this chapter we have considered the arguments for and against explicit and implicit strategies in second language pedagogy. We have seen that, since the 1960s, a plausible case has been made for treating one strategy as an early phase and the other as a later phase. On purely theoretical grounds, one can make an equally good case for placing either one or the other strategy first. It makes perfectly good sense to start off with a relatively atheoretical approach, as Rivers and Strevens propose, and to reserve consciousness-raising techniques for more advanced and more sophisticated learners. But it is equally plausible to argue for a more cognitive orientation to begin with which will become more automatic and habitual at a later stage. The fact that we can make a plausible case for either direction indicates that it would be unwise to be too dogmatic on this issue.

Notes

1 J. B. Carroll first presented these ideas at an international conference in Berlin in 1964. The paper was published in the proceedings of this conference (Müller 1965). It appeared again in a revised version in 1965 in the *Modern Language Journal* (Carroll 1965) and a year later in a collection of papers on current trends in language teaching edited by Valdman (1966). Rivers (1964), who examined audio-lingualism in the light of current psychological thought, described the preference of audiolingualism for unthinking approaches to grammar teaching and demonstrated some of the inconsistencies of the audiolingual position in relation to contemporary views on learning. In general psychology, as well as in educational psychology and educational theory, there was strong preference for cognitive approaches, exemplified in the writings of Ausubel (e.g. 1968), Bruner (e.g. 1966), and an influential book on cognitive psychology by Miller, Galanter, and Pribram, *Plans and the Structure of Behavior* (1960).

2 For an assessment of the ideological situation in the early 1970s see a

1972 AILA plenary address in Copenhagen (Stern 1974: 95), which makes reference to 'the rational-intuitive parameter' and hypothesizes 'that the rational and intuitive aspects are not irreconcilable because language learning needs both'. Subsequently, the issue that was left open in the early 1970s also formed part of the areas included in the *Good Language Learner* studies which were undertaken by the Modern Language Centre between 1973–1976 (Naiman *et al.* 1978).

3 Faerch (1986: 130) gives examples of teacher-made rules of thumb which teachers use in the teaching of English in Denmark. These examples include the following: '1. Use the *s*-genitive about persons, *of* about things. 2. *Any* is used in interrogative (Dan. "spørgende"), negative ("naegtende") and conditional (*if*) clauses—the SNIF rule. 3. Use *as* about cause, *when* about time'.

4 They were of course not entirely new. Some, for example memorization, had had a long history in education, others, like pattern practice, had been strongly advocated half a century earlier, by Palmer (1922). However, in emphasis and in the combinations and context in which they appeared they were new.

5 Krashen and Terrell (1983: 74–5), who strongly emphasize implicit learning, invite the students' co-operation with their methodology with the following suggestions: When you do try to speak in the new language, the teacher is interested in what you have to say—not whether you have said it perfectly. Neither you nor the teacher will be overly concerned with grammar in your speech while you are a beginner. Remember that as long as you understand what the teacher is saying you are acquiring French. This means that you should focus on what is being said, the message, rather than how it is being said.

6 For further details on Suggestopedia see Oller and Richard-Amato (1983) and a concise and sober analysis and appreciation in Richards and Rodgers (1986).

Conclusion[1]

Introduction

Recent discussions of second language curriculum have been characterized by two main trends. On the one hand, we have seen an increasing tendency to define the field in terms of two or more contrasting approaches, or 'paradigms' in the Kuhnian sense. The other, complementary, trend is to seek for commonalities between the various theoretical positions, in the hope of providing a richer, multidimensional framework for classroom decision-making. In his writings on curriculum, Stern has made a major contribution to both aspects of this debate. First, as a theorist keenly interested in the underlying disciplines, he was responsible for a number of important conceptual clarifications, represented in this book by his clear definition of the different syllabuses and teaching strategy options. Second, as a researcher committed to the improvement of practical language teaching, he saw clearly the need to break away from narrow prescriptivism and to emphasize the role of each syllabus as a collection of resources from which individuals are free to choose in order to implement their own programmes.

A key question raised in the context of this book is how the multidimensional curriculum that Stern proposes might be integrated at the policy and practical action levels. In this Conclusion, our main purpose is to examine this issue, drawing on the author's previous publications and on the experience of a Canadian project in curriculum renewal based on his multidimensional approach (LeBlanc 1990). Firstly, however, we need to draw attention to the fact that there were further chapters planned for this volume in the areas of social strategies, timing strategies, resources, and student evaluation, as well as a chapter on vocabulary to be incorporated in the language syllabus. With these chapters, Stern had intended to round out his language teaching analysis as outlined in Chapter 1. Before embarking on our discussion of the integration issue, therefore, we will endeavour briefly to provide an indication of the author's thinking in these areas. Our sources are his existing publications, together with some unpublished papers serving as background to this volume and lecture notes for a course on language teaching methodology that he taught at the Ontario Institute for Studies in Education until 1987.

Rounding out the framework

Social strategies

Under the heading of social strategies, Stern proposed to examine language teaching policy and practice in the areas of: (a) class size, (b) group composition, and (c) interpersonal relationships.

(a) Class size
Class size, he observed, is more often determined by administrative factors such as the availability of teachers, classroom space, programme demand, and economic considerations than it is by pedagogical factors alone. Even where pedagogical considerations are in the forefront, there is no simple equation for determining the optimal size for a language class. The teacher's perception of his/her role together with the students' age, maturity, aptitude, and prior language learning experience are seen as important considerations. The optimal class size, according to Stern, is one which allows for a variety of grouping patterns. Older, more able and experienced learners are seen as needing less personal help and being capable, therefore, of working more independently in larger groups, while younger, slower, or less experienced learners will need more help in smaller classes.

(b) Group composition
How to group students into classes that make educational sense is a much debated issue in language teaching. One widely used principle of classroom organization is the students' prior level of L2 proficiency, such that classes are divided into levels (for example, beginners, intermediate, advanced). Stern notes that determining proficiency criteria for such levels is problematic, and that even within levels there is liable to be considerable heterogeneity with respect to different aspects of proficiency, not to mention differences in aptitude, motivation, and other individual factors. The issue of how much heterogeneity is appropriate or tolerable in a language class is linked by Stern to broader philosophical issues. In Britain, for example, he notes that the tradition of 'streaming' or 'setting' secondary school classes according to ability has led to controversy between those who view it as a form of educational discrimination and social injustice, and those who view it as a realistic recognition of human differences and educational efficiency. In the United States, he observes that the streaming option has generally been shunned, with more attention being paid to the individualization of instruction as a way of catering to individual differences.

(c) Interpersonal relationships
Under this heading, Stern planned to discuss the advantages and disadvantages of different grouping arrangements within the class, the

extent to which teachers can influence the social climate of the class (see the section 'Social interaction', Chapter 11), and how they might encourage the development of initiative, responsibility, and independence among their students (see also Chapter 10). In a comment on the literature, he observes that language students are typically depicted as anxious, lacking in confidence, and resistant to language learning, and teachers are urged to surmount these affective barriers by being friendly, encouraging a relaxed attitude, and creating a non-threatening environment. In practice, he suggests, many teachers find their students too relaxed, over-confident, and lacking in persistence and adequate standards of achievement. To promote the requisite social conditions for productive learning and personal growth, teachers have to steer a middle course between the extremes of overprotection on the one hand and lack of necessary support and encouragement on the other.

Timing strategies

In an article published in the *TESL Canada Journal* in 1985, Stern discusses the time factor in L2 teaching from the perspective of overall curriculum design. He notes that the question of time allocation for a language course is largely a matter of tradition and that the issues involved in different time allocations have received very little study. Generally speaking, however, increases in time allocation have been associated with higher proficiency (for example, Carroll 1975). A key question is whether concentrating time over a shorter overall time span is beneficial. A compact foreign language course at the secondary school level is seen as attractive at first sight because it offers relief from 'the relentlessness and inflexibility of the monotonous long-term language course' (Stern 1985: 18), and because it permits courses in more than one language or provides more time for other school subjects. But little is known about how it would work out in practice.[2] Stern warns against over-enthusiastic wholesale adoption of such courses on the grounds that 'in many countries the issue is not that too much time is squandered in poor foreign language instruction but rather that too little time is made available for effective teaching' (1985: 24). In addition to 'macro' planning decisions with respect to time allocation for a language programme, Stern recognized that there were important 'micro' timing decisions to be made by the classroom teacher, with numerous issues surrounding the distribution of time among different types of classroom activities. Here, he would doubtless also have pointed to student factors such as age, aptitude, and prior language experience as important intervening variables.

Resources

Stern emphasizes that language teaching materials are a component of the curriculum and are not synonymous with the curriculum itself. For widely taught languages, present-day materials include much more than the traditional textbook (see Figure C.1). The teacher's main problem is one of selection from an *embarras de richesses*. However, there may be the opposite problem for less commonly taught languages where even the most basic grammars and texts may be lacking.

1 coursebooks, textbooks
2 audio-visual courses
3 audiolingual courses
4 integrated courses or programmes
5 courses for special purposes
6 courses for independent self-study, programmed courses, material for computer-assisted instruction
7 dictionaries, vocabularies, glossaries
8 pedagogical grammar, teaching grammars, review grammars
9 reference grammars
10 books of drills, exercises and practice, workbooks
11 composition books
12 conversation books
13 readers
14 literary texts
15 poetry collections
16 song books
17 works on culture and civilization
18 materials designed for teaching a subject through the medium of the L2
19 flash cards
20 film loops
21 film strips and slides
22 pictures, wall charts, overhead transparencies
23 disc recordings
24 reel-to-reel and cassette tape recordings
25 video tapes and films
26 wall maps
27 games
28 authentic documents, realia
29 multi-media kits, modules
30 language tests
31 teachers' guides, curriculum guides
32 additional books, pamphlets, leaflets on methods of L2 teaching

Figure C.1 Second language teaching materials as a component of curriculum

Stern categorizes materials according to their nature, function, and mode of presentation. Thus, they may be designed for teachers (for example, guidelines) or students, for classroom instruction or private consumption, as core or supplementary materials, and they may be comprehensive or specific in purpose. They may be closely defined and organized or loosely organized, flexible, and modular, teacher-made or formally published, while different components may consist of L2 texts/input, information about L2, or language practice material. The mode of presentation may be print or non-print, audio, visual, or audio-visual. Choices from this wide variety should be made on a principled basis bearing in mind programme objectives and student needs. In order to decide how closely defined and organized the materials for a particular course should be, consideration must be given to the relative homogeneity of the student body, the distribution of responsibilities for the course, the training and experience of the teachers, and the amount of time they have available for materials development.

While teachers have reacted negatively to the rigid imposition of a detailed programme, the absence of any direction or ordering has also been found wanting. According to Stern, within some form of sequencing and organization, there should be opportunities for choice in accordance with students' learning needs and interests. He believed that there will always be a place for informal teacher-made materials prepared with a specific group of students in mind, alongside published materials which have the advantage of professional preparation. Published materials, he argued, should be submitted to rigorous development procedures as well as careful evaluation; they should state unambiguously for whom they are designed, on what research and documentation they are based, and under what field conditions they have been tried. Figure C.2 presents the steps he considered necessary in the 'curriculum processes' (see Chapter 2) of materials development and evaluation.

Student evaluation

Viewed as an integral part of language teaching policy and practice, student evaluation encompasses, for Stern, a wide range of activities ranging from the informal momentary withholding of help to a formally scheduled examination (see FCLT: 439–40). He saw tests and other forms of assessment as having a variety of possible functions: to help teachers and students estimate progress and identify weaknesses (i.e. a formative and diagnostic function), to direct attention to course objectives (a washback function), or to provide information for decision-making (a summative function). In Figure C.3 he presents in schematic form the different stages of the testing process, and exemplifies some types of evaluation activity on a formative–summative continuum.

Stern identified influences from a variety of language-related disciplines that have had an impact on evaluation practices in language teaching, and saw as an issue the 'puzzling mixture of established conventions and novel procedures' which are hard to reconcile in theory and in practice. He observes, for example, that the statistical procedures of educational psychology and psychometrics have long been applied in

Sequence of development stages

I Selection stage
The need for new materials of a specific kind is identified (general area, subject matter, target group, intended treatment).

II Research and documentation stage
Sources for the new materials are found, and if necessary, direct studies are undertaken so that the validity and authenticity of the content is assured.

III Design stage
(a) specific objectives of unit and content are defined.
(b) Manner of presentation is established: format, media.
(c) Texts, practice materials, explanations, etc. are drafted or selected.

IV Pilot testing stage
The draft materials are tried on a small scale by a few teachers in their regular classes.

V Revision stage
In response to the pilot testing and evaluation at the pilot stage, the materials are revised.

VI Field trials
The materials are distributed in draft form to a sample of classes representing the intended potential users, and tried in their classes.

VII Final version
On the basis of the field trials, the final draft of materials is made ready for publication or distribution.

Sequence of evaluation stages

Stage I
The evaluator assists with needs assessment and confirms needs by special inquiries, surveys, questionnaires, reviews of existing materials. Characteristics of target audience are established.

Stage II
Expert opinions are sought to guarantee that the content has a high degree of validity: e.g., on linguistic data, linguists qualified in this area; on topical data, specialists knowledgeable in the field.

Stage III
(a) Objectives and content, manner of presentation, texts, practice materials, explanations, etc. are reviewed by evaluators in consultation with practitioners.
(b) Observation schedules and testing programmes for pilot testing and subsequent field testing are established. Tests and questionnaires are developed. Pilot testing schedules are set up.

Stage IV
The evaluators observe and investigate teachers' and students' attitudes and reactions by means of interviews, attitude tests, achievement tests, and questionnaires. The findings are communicated to developers with recommendations for revisions.

Stage V
The evaluators assess field trials by means of tests and questionnaires. The findings are communicated to developers with recommendations for the final version.

Stage VI
The evaluators adapt some of the instruments used for formative evaluation as tests for use with the materials and as forms for summative user evaluations of the published materials.

Figure C.2 The sequence of stages in materials development and corresponding stages in formative evaluation

Types of evaluation

Stages of evaluation	**Formative**		**Summative**
	Informal	**Formal**	
1. Setting tasks/test items/ test/battery of tests/examination	Day-to-day quizzes tasks slip tests checks	Occasional class tests progress tests 'mock' examinations	Internal examinations External examinations Tests at mastery levels Schemes of continuous assessment
2. Assessment in relation to criterion	**Student performance** Observation of process, inspection of product Judgements: right-wrong, approval-disapproval, rating/marking/scoring, pass-fail, etc.		
3. Decision-making	reteach? explain? practice? new approach? remediation? advances? (etc.)		promotion to next course? placement in appropriate stream or set? discontinue? professional promotion? change of status? entitlement? (etc.)

Figure C.3 Types and stages of evaluation

language tests aiming for precision and objectivity (see, for example, Henmon 1929), and that the associated concept of reliability has challenged traditional 'subjective' methods of examining students. Conventional language examinations (including free composition, renarration, translation from and into L2, précis, and dictation) have none the less persisted alongside newer testing techniques, although in some educational systems there is new concern for inter-rater reliability and a fusing of traditional and objective testing techniques is taking place. Owing to the influence from psychometrics, Stern points out that test developers today have access to a considerable body of knowledge on test construction, including how to determine item difficulty, the importance of standardizing format and instructions, the concepts of validity and reliability, the difference between norm-referenced and criterion-referenced tests, and so on (see Bachman 1990 for definitions of these terms in relation to language testing).

A second major influence Stern identified is that of structural linguistics. In his book *Language Testing*, Lado (1961/1964) was to introduce the idea that language tests should be solidly founded on linguistic descriptions. Also reflecting the influence of structural linguistics was the adoption of the diagnostically useful notion of discrete-point testing, and the emphasis on test items based on a contrastive analysis of the L1 and the L2. Such ideas were embodied in a number of major tests first produced in the 1960s in the United States (for example, the MLA Cooperative Foreign Language Tests). Stern points out that since it became anchored in linguistics, language testing has inevitably been affected by changes in linguistic theory. Thus, further influences on testing have come from generative grammar and sociolinguistics, leading to a rejection of contrastive analysis as a guiding principle of test construction and to an emphasis on global, integrative ways of testing communicative competence, including cloze tests and oral interviews as opposed to decontextualized test items that pinpoint specific phonological or grammatical distinctions. Stern refers here to the still unresolved problems in designing communicative tests (for recent discussion see, for example, Canale (1988) and Hart, Lapkin, and Swain (1987)).

Finally, Stern notes an influence from educational theory and research which is seen to have left its mark on language teaching in the notions of formative and summative evaluation, the distinction between student evaluation and curriculum evaluation (see Chapter 2), the role of feedback in student evaluation, and the recognition that testing needs to be supplemented by other forms of evaluation such as observation and peer- and self-evaluation, conducted with the help of checklists and questionnaires. While summative examinations are generally recognized as having a washback effect on classroom practice, Stern draws attention to the fact that the daily formative evaluation of student progress has so far been very little investigated in language teaching research. The question of how much and what kind of evaluation is most productive for second language learning has scarcely been asked.

This brief sampling of Stern's views on the topics of social strategies, timing strategies, resources, and student evaluation is obviously far from the comprehensive analysis he had envisaged for the relevant chapters. What it does make clear, however, is that he saw numerous important issues and options in all these aspects of language teaching that call for careful analysis at the policy level and for empirical research at the level of classroom practice.

Integration of the multidimensional curriculum

As we have seen, Stern's multidimensional curriculum contains a set of four syllabuses, with a range of objectives and teaching strategy options. The language teaching syllabus deals analytically with descriptive aspects of the target language, including phonology, grammar, and discourse; the communicative activities syllabus provides opportunities for natural unanalysed language use; the cultural syllabus provides sociocultural knowledge and contact with the target language community; and the general language education syllabus serves to broaden the scope of the L2 curriculum to include as an integral component general issues of language, culture, and language learning. In Figure C.4 we represent a form of conceptual integration that Stern (1983b) envisaged for a foreign language curriculum at the school level, in which content, objectives, and teaching strategies are brought together in a single scheme. Here, each syllabus is cross-referenced with suggested major and minor objectives as well as being associated with characteristic teaching strategies. As Stern (1983b: 136) puts it: 'Such a model can express not only the multidimensionality of the foreign language curriculum content but also the multiplicity of major and minor *objectives* and of associated teaching *strategies*.'

In the same article, Stern discussed several strategies for integration that would avoid the danger of overloading the curriculum and making it unworkable in the limited time available.

(1) Recognize the complementary nature of the syllabuses

First, he considered it vital for teachers to be aware that the four syllabuses complement one another and that they are not separated by hard and fast boundaries. Rather, he saw each syllabus as representing a change of perspective. The language and cultural syllabuses require the learner to focus respectively on the target language and culture as objects of study; the communicative activities syllabus requires the learner to take on the role of a participant; and with the general

Content	Objectives				Main strategies
	Proficiency	**Knowledge**	**Affect**	**Transfer**	
Language syllabus	Suggested **major** emphasis	Suggested minor emphasis	Suggested minor emphasis	Suggested minor emphasis	Analytic: study and practice
Culture syllabus	Suggested minor emphasis	Suggested **major** emphasis	Suggested minor emphasis	Suggested minor emphasis	Analytic: study (knowledge about second culture)
Communicative activities syllabus	Suggested **major** emphasis	Suggested minor emphasis	Suggested minor emphasis	Suggested minor emphasis	Experiential: communicative activities
General language education syllabus	Suggested minor emphasis	Suggested minor emphasis	Suggested minor emphasis	Suggested **major** emphasis	Comparative (crosslingual/ crosscultural)

Figure C.4 An integrated L2 curriculum model (based on Stern 1983b) language education syllabus the learner changes roles again, standing back and looking at language and culture from a more detached perspective. Stern visualized such shifts of perspective as occurring either momentarily within a single lesson, or in the form of particular focuses which could extend over a long period of time.

(2) Build bridges from syllabus to syllabus
While for practical reasons Stern foresaw development of each syllabus as the responsibility of a different individual or team, he none the less stressed the importance of avoiding compartmentalization. During the development process, he anticipated a need for each developer to keep the other syllabuses in mind, to seek out common ground and make cross-references wherever possible. As an example, he cites forms of address which would be included in the language syllabus as grammatical items, but which are at the same time of sociocultural relevance and thus also part of the cultural syllabus.

(3) Develop and use teaching materials which cut across the syllabus divisions
Another approach to integration suggested by Stern is to use materials focused on one syllabus but clearly related at the same time to another syllabus, or to develop materials that focus specifically on previously neglected areas, thus creating a better overall balance of activities. Thus, Stern was himself involved for several years in the development of modules that were designed to inject a more substantive cultural element into Canadian curriculums in French as a second language where the emphasis had been solidly on language (Stern *et al.* 1980). The purpose was 'to shift the emphasis gradually away from a narrowly linguistic progression, to stress cultural themes and to demonstrate at the same time that the linguistic progression does not suffer. On the contrary it is enriched by the other emphases' (Stern 1983b: 135).

(4) Start from one syllabus and work towards the others
In this approach to integration, Stern saw the curriculum developer starting from one syllabus, for example the language syllabus, and referring to it in order to define proficiency or knowledge objectives. For each linguistic topic so determined, an inventory of sociocultural themes and communicative activities could then be chosen to contribute towards the given objectives. Alternatively, he suggested, one might equally well start from another syllabus and determine relevant objectives: for example, decide on the kind of knowledge about the target community that learners should have at a given stage of the curriculum (the cultural syllabus); the kind of communicative experiences that learners should participate in (the communicative activies syllabus); or the general knowledge about language and culture that the learners should have (the

general language education syllabus). In short, any one of the syllabuses can serve as the starting point and the implications can be worked out for the other syllabuses.

(5) Establish a longitudinal, proportional pattern of syllabus content
In a subsequent article (Stern and Harley 1988), an additional integration strategy was suggested that would establish relative weights for each syllabus at different stages of the curriculum, on the assumption that the content of any individual teaching unit could in principle be derived from one syllabus, or in equal proportions from two, three, or even four syllabuses. A possible four-stage longitudinal pattern is illustrated in relation to the core French second language programme in Canada extending from the primary grades to the end of high school. At the first stage, the primary-junior grades, the communicative activities syllabus might dominate the curriculum with the other syllabuses assuming a minor role; then in the junior-intermediate stage, equal weight might be given to the communicative activities and language syllabuses, with culture and general language education still playing a subsidiary role. At stage 3, intermediate to senior grades, culture could take on added weight together with communicative activities and language; and finally at the senior level, all four syllabuses might receive equal prominence.

From the five integration strategies that have been proposed we can see that Stern clearly considered integration of the multidimensional curriculum to be a matter of deliberate policy, for the most part carefully preplanned prior to implementation of the curriculum in the L2 class. Only the first strategy, involving the professional development of teachers, suggests that integration can also occur spontaneously during classroom interaction at the implementation stage. The other four strategies imply that an integration policy is established either during or after the process of syllabus development, which is assumed to take place outside the classroom itself. How an integration policy is in fact translated into classroom practice in any particular context remains, of course, an issue to be investigated at the practical action level of Stern's analytic framework.

Applying the multidimensional curriculum approach

In this section we describe a Canadian project in L2 curriculum renewal explicitly based on the multidimensional approach elaborated by Stern. The project, entitled the National Core French Study, was initiated with a view to broadening and strengthening the 'core French' regular French L2 programme in English-speaking schools across Canada, in order to promote higher levels of L2 proficiency and increase the programme's educational impact.[3] The 3½ year project involved the design of a master plan for a four-syllabus core French curriculum, extending from grade 4 to grade 12 and assuming an average of 40 minutes of instruction in French per day. In addition to the major task of syllabus design, a policy for integration of the multidimensional curriculum was worked out and a concrete example of integration in the form of a teaching unit for the grade 10 level was developed and piloted in classes across the country. As proposed by Stern (1983b), who himself directed the project from 1985 to 1987, each syllabus was the responsibility of a different team of researchers, whose leaders met on several occasions to exchange and discuss draft documents. Feedback at the development stage was also provided by committees in each province composed of teachers, core French administrators, and ministry of education personnel. A complete account of the project is provided in LeBlanc (1990). Here we limit ourselves to an overview of some major characteristics of each syllabus and a brief account of the integration policy and the piloting of the integrated teaching unit.

The language syllabus

The point of departure for this syllabus (Painchaud *et al.* 1990) is the stated aim of core French programmes to develop communicative competence in the L2 and not simply knowledge of the grammatical system. Four general teaching objectives are stated: (a) to develop students' ability to interpret different types of discourse, including authentic written and oral texts; (b) to develop their ability to express progressively more complex messages that do justice to their intentions and conform to the rules of French; (c) to make explicit the relationship between form and function in a wide range of oral and written texts; and (d) to develop an awareness of rules of use in French. An inventory of linguistic content includes, in addition to traditional grammatical categories, functional units such as speech acts and discourse features contributing to coherence in oral and written French. None of this linguistic content is to be taught for its own sake, however, but is to be introduced in motivating contexts provided by the other syllabuses. Analytic study and practice are regarded as a means to immediate communicative ends, taking place in response to the learners' needs for more effective communication in the given contexts. There is no rigid ordering of linguistic content in this language syllabus; instead the content is divided into three levels (grades 4–6, 7–9, 10–12) with teaching objectives specified for each level. Learning objectives in the form of mastery levels, on the other hand, are not specified, but are left open for decision at the provincial level.

The communicative/experiential syllabus

Corresponding to Stern's communicative activities syllabus (see Chapter 7), this syllabus (Tremblay, Duplantie, and Huot 1990) is designed to contribute to French proficiency by offering experience in using the second language for authentic communicative purposes. The intent is to provide motivating, non-arbitrary themes and activities that will be personally and educationally relevant to students, increasing their communication skills and at the same time enriching their experience in a variety of areas. A number of domains of experience are identified which can be treated in different ways for different age groups and at various stages of linguistic development. These are organized in five broad categories: physical, social, civic, leisure, intellectual. As part of the physical category, for example, the following domains are proposed: nutrition, physical exercise, clothing, self-protection, hygiene, the senses; and under the social heading, domains include: school, family, friends, native peoples, immigrants, holidays and celebrations, trades and professions. These domains are designed to be treated experientially (see Chapter 11) for the intrinsic interest of their substance, with the learners taking the role of participants in the relevant communicative activities, projects, and tasks which are intended to build on their prior life experiences. The question of task and text complexity is addressed, with implications for sequencing of syllabus content. Attention is given, for example, to principles such as familiarity of topic, intrinsic interest, motivation to communicate, cultural affinity, and features of text such as predictability, length, vocabulary range, visual or verbal support, abstractness, and redundancy.

The culture syllabus

In the culture syllabus (LeBlanc, Courtel, and Trescases 1990) the focus is on contemporary small-c culture—on francophone people of today, where and how they live, and what it means to be a francophone in the Canadian context. The objectives of the syllabus are: (a) to sensitize students to francophone culture; (b) to prepare them to function comfortably and effectively within the context of a bilingual Canada; (c) to broaden students' cultural horizons; and (d) to enhance their communicative competence in French. Cultural content is seen as more central to the core French curriculum than has generally been the case, reflecting the view that cultural competence is an essential dimension of successful communication. Topics proposed for this syllabus move outward gradually from local and regional to national and international, and progress from an emphasis on simple facts at early grade levels to a concern with broader issues at higher grades. Topics in Canadian francophone culture include focuses on concrete manifestations of the presence of francophones, the historical context of Canadian francophones, their speech—including regional and social variations, their daily life, and various aspects of the phenomenon of bilingualism. A more general scheme for exploring francophone culture beyond Canada is also provided. The position is taken in this syllabus that culture should be taught in French. A wide variety of learning activities is envisaged both inside and outside the classroom, drawing on authentic written and oral documents and contacts with francophones through classroom visits, the media, pen-pals, and exchanges.

The general language education syllabus

This syllabus (Hébert 1990) aims to encourage students' reflection on the nature of language and culture, to promote openness towards other language groups, and to develop an active, self-reliant approach to language learning that will both improve skills in French and transfer to other learning contexts. As in Chapter 9, three main topic areas are identified: language awareness, cultural awareness, and learning how to learn a language. General observations about the nature of language and culture are seen as providing sources for specific topics in language and cultural awareness, for example the productivity of language, its creativity, recognition that it is stable yet continually evolving, its social variability, the relative communicative success with which it is used by its speakers, and its fundamental form–meaning duality. Similarly, in the realm of culture, recognition that cultures are dynamic, stable yet changeable, diverse, invested with their own codes and symbols, transmitted in many different ways, and participated in with varying degrees of success provides a series of headings for topics in cultural awareness. The syllabus is also concerned with developing competence in, and awareness of, various kinds of learner strategies: cognitive learning strategies including operations such as inferencing, reasoning, and practising; metacognitive learning strategies of planning and monitoring; communication strategies to repair and circumvent problems in online communication; and social strategies to enhance opportunities for L2 use. Teaching strategies proposed for this syllabus are comparative analysis and reflection arising from an initial language- or culture-learning experience, and designed to lead to reinvestment in further learning experiences. Learning activities are seen to include case studies, role-playing, simulation, work in multicultural groups, problem solving, and so on.

A policy for integration

The issue of how to integrate the multidimensional curriculum so that it becomes practically manageable in the limited time available for core French, and theoretically viable as a coherent whole, is discussed in the synthesis of the National Core French Study prepared by Raymond LeBlanc (1990), who directed the project from 1987. Like Stern, LeBlanc finds it necessary to develop a preplanned policy for integration rather than leaving it to happen at the implementation stage. While he notes the desirability of Stern's second strategy of building bridges from syllabus to syllabus at the development stage, he observes that, in practice, the relative isolation of the different groups of syllabus developers was not conducive to any major emphasis on integration during the syllabus development process, although areas of natural overlap between syllabuses were identified. Instead, the main strategy for integration adopted in the project was, in effect, an elaboration of Stern's fourth strategy: 'Start from one syllabus and work towards the others'. This approach to integration was based on the principle that as a prime means of communication, language is global and functional in nature, and that given the main core French objective of communicative competence, this implied a major emphasis on the instrumental use of language in authentic communicative situations.

In keeping with this view, LeBlanc argues that an experiential teaching approach should be privileged in a core French programme and should serve as the basis for integration of the multidimensional curriculum. Any teaching unit would thus be based on an experiential domain derived in most cases from the communicative/experiential syllabus, but also on occasion from the culture and general language education syllabuses. The chosen domain then serves to motivate the integration of content from other syllabuses. As already noted above (The language syllabus), content from the language syllabus is not introduced as an end in itself but as a means to achieving the communicative objectives of a specific teaching unit. This does not, however, imply a necessarily minor role for language content in proportional terms.

An integrated teaching unit

In order to demonstrate in concrete terms how integration of syllabus content can be realized in classroom practice, an experimental teaching unit for the grade 10 level was designed in the context of the national study and piloted in thirty-nine core French classes across Canada. The theme of the teaching unit, entitled 'Se lancer en affaires avec un jeu' (Tremblay, Painchaud, LeBlanc, and Godbout 1989) is derived from the communicative/experiential syllabus. Students take part in a business venture designed to develop their experience in this domain and foster their creativity. A series of activities intended to take approximately ten hours of class time involves the invention and marketing of a game about the francophone world. Cultural content is thus closely integrated with the experiential theme, as is content from the language syllabus which includes, for example, an analytic focus on the language of instructions that students need to use in writing rules for their games. Content from the general language education syllabus concentrates on developing comprehension strategies and reflecting on the general phenomenon of regional accents. This reflection takes place after students have listened to recordings of francophones from different countries in gathering information for their games.

The unit consists of four components, all in French: a student booklet and audio-cassette containing information and ideas for the design and marketing of the games; a student workbook; and a teacher's guide with step-by-step instructions for use of the materials. Teachers taking part in the piloting of the integrated teaching unit were introduced to the material via an in-service workshop for which a professional development kit was provided (Roy *et al.* 1989), and feedback on the unit was obtained through questionnaires from teachers, students, and observers (Harley and d'Anglejan 1990). The findings of the pilot study suggested a number of implications for further curriculum planning of an integrated, multidimensional nature.

In the first place, there was a largely positive reaction to the integrated multidimensional approach illustrated in the teaching unit. Three quarters of the teachers fully approved of the central role accorded to the communicative/experiential component of the unit and two thirds expressed clear agreement with the way in which opportunities for language work were motivated by the experiential domains treated. The cultural content was found by 70 per cent of teachers to be appropriate and to be better integrated than in their regular programme, while 65 per cent found the strategy training and awareness activities more or less suited to their students' learning needs, and 25 per cent considered them well suited. Overall, the approach to integration was regarded as successful by 62 per cent and more or less successful by 35 per cent, with the great majority (79 per cent) of teachers seeing the approach as appropriate throughout a core French programme.

This general endorsement of an integrated multidimensional approach to the core French curriculum was accompanied by a number of suggestions for revision of the pilot teaching unit. One finding, for example, was that the unit was too long to be completed in the allotted ten hours, and useful suggestions were made for the pruning of activities regarded as either redundant, overly complex, or time-consuming. At the same time, a substantial proportion (61 per cent) of teachers indicated that they had found it necessary to add language work to help students cope with some of the activities, and this no doubt added to the time required.

Keeping in mind the pilot nature of the teaching unit introduced midstream into existing programmes, it was, of course, to be expected that the materials might represent an unusual challenge for at least some classes for whom a communicative/experiential orientation was a novelty. The issue of appropriate time distribution among different kinds of activities and components of the curriculum remains, none the less, an important one for future multidimensional curriculum development, along with the recognition that teachers need sufficient flexibility at the implementation stage to balance activities in a way that best meets the immediate needs of their students. In the present case, the adaptation appears to have taken the form of adjusting the proportion of analytic language content while maintaining the essential experiential orientation of the teaching unit. Referring to Stern's first strategy for integration we can see here the crucial importance of teachers understanding the intended complementary relationship among the syllabuses.

Concluding comments

The last few years have been marked by a rapid growth in classroom-oriented research, which focuses on various aspects of teacher-student interaction, and attempts to determine the relationship between such behaviours and learning outcomes (cf. Allwright 1988; Chaudron 1988; Van Lier 1988). Although this interest in the classroom is to be welcomed, there is a danger that we could become over-concerned with the minutiae of classroom discourse, and begin to lose touch with the curriculum as a whole. In Stern's view, if we are to make sense of our classroom observations, we must be prepared to place them in a broader context of language teaching analysis. What is needed is a comprehensive scheme which can be used for the analysis of teaching in general, rather than one which is designed to focus on a particular type of classroom. Such a scheme should be broad enough to relate to a wide range of situations, and precise enough to capture the uniqueness of any given programme. A scheme of this sort would have a number of applications. It could be used for teacher education and programme evaluation, and it could be used by individual teachers as a basis for their own decision-making.

Stern's curriculum model as set out in this book provides a general schematic framework at the policy level, but it does not in itself constitute a plan for teaching at the practical action level. It is best regarded as a set of guidelines for developing a bank or library of resources which can be drawn upon and implemented in different ways by those who are engaged in developing actual language programmes. The heart of the proposal lies in the provision of four major content areas or syllabuses. In the past, L2 curriculums have tended to be too narrowly focused on language proficiency in isolation. As Stern (1983b) points out, a multiple approach is more theoretically defensible, as well as more educationally desirable, because it reflects the social nature and cultural embeddedness of language. As we have seen, Stern's proposal implies: (a) a more systematic approach to the other syllabuses relative to the language syllabus, (b) a weighting of the emphasis in curriculum design which will be more evenly spread over the different components, and (c) an integration of the four syllabuses. The overall intention is to provide a more substantial and viable approach than has been possible within a unidimensional curriculum design.

The multidimensional L2 curriculum as it evolved in the National Core French Study provides a specific curriculum plan at the policy level of Stern's framework, while the integrated pilot teaching unit brings his proposal for an enriched four-syllabus approach to L2 teaching into the realm of practical action. We look forward in the coming years to further long-term application of his ideas in a variety of second language programmes in Canada and elsewhere. In this volume, we see clearly the author's abiding concern for non-prescriptivism in language teaching, and his recognition that different circumstances will call for different kinds of policy decisions. Above all, his aim has been to provide practitioners with a clear and comprehensive framework for making principled choices in L2 curriculum matters. In so doing, he has not hesitated to point to the numerous issues that remain unresolved and where he believed it is crucial to keep an open mind.

Notes

1 Since we were unable to find a conclusion among Dr Stern's papers, this chapter was compiled by the editors.
2 An intensive ESL programme for French-speaking students at the elementary school level in Quebec is yielding interesting results in this regard (e.g. Spada and Lightbown 1989).
3 This project was conducted under the auspices of the Canadian Association of Second Language Teachers with funding from the Secretary of State for Canada.

Bibliography and citation index

Acton, W. 1984. 'Changing fossilized pronunciation'. *TESOL Quarterly* 20:207–25. [124(n13)]

Agard, F. B. and **Di Pietro, R. J.** 1965. *The Sounds of English and Italian*. Chicago: University of Chicago Press. [123(n5)]

Ahmad, K., Corbett, G., Rogers, M. and **Sussex, R.** 1985. *Computers, Language Learning and Language Teaching*. Cambridge: Cambridge University Press. [10]

Alatis, J. E., Altman, H. B. and **Alatis, P. M.** (eds.) 1981. *The Second Language Classroom: Directions for the 1980s*. Essays in honour of Mary Finocchiaro. New York and Oxford: Oxford University Press. [Krashen 1981b, Stern 1981a, Valette 1981, Widdowson and Brumfit 1981]

Alexander, L. G. 1979. 'A functional-notional approach to course design'. *Audio Visual Language Journal* 17:109–13. [166]

Allan, K. 1986. *Linguistic Meaning* (2 vols.) London: Routledge and Kegan Paul. [176(n1)]

Allen, E. D. and **Valette, R. M.** 1977. *Classroom Techniques: Foreign Languages and English as a Second Language*. Second edition. New York: Harcourt Brace Jovanovich. [109, 113, 138, 144, 152(n1), 154(n12), 206, 225, 235(n1), 239(n23), 240(n26, n27, n28, n30), 241(n34), 242(n37, n39, n40, n41, n43), 289, 307, 310]

Allen, J. P. B. 1973. 'Applied grammatical models in a remedial English syllabus' in S. P. Corder and E. Roulet (eds.) *Theoretical Linguistic Models in Applied Linguistics*. Brussels: AIMAV and Paris: Didier. [152(n1)]

Allen, J. P. B. 1983. 'A three-level curriculum model for second language education'. *The Canadian Modern Language Review* 40/1:23–43. [166, 303]

Allen, J. P. B. and **Corder, S. P.** (eds.) 1974. *Techniques in Applied Linguistics*. The Edinburgh Course in Applied Linguistics, Vol 3. London: Oxford University Press. [Howatt 1974]

Allen, J. P. B. and **Howard, J.** 1981. 'Subject-related ESL: An experiment in communicative language teaching'. *The Canadian Modern Language Review* 37/3:535–50. [169]

Allen, J. P. B. and **Carroll, S.** 1987. 'Evaluation of classroom processes in a Canadian core French Programme' in *Evaluation and Research in Education* 1/2:49–61. [306]

Allen, J. P. B., Carroll, S., Burtis, J. and **Gaudino, V.** 1987. 'The core French observation study' in B. Harley, P. Allen, J. Cummins, and M. Swain, *The Development of Bilingual Proficiency: Final Report. Volume II; Classroom Treatment*. Toronto: Ontario Institute for Studies in Education. [317, 322]

Allen, J. P. B., Fröhlich, M. and **Spada, N.** 1984. 'The communicative orientation of second language teaching: An observation scheme' in J. Handscombe, R. A. Orem, and B. P. Taylor (eds.) *On TESOL '83: The Question of Control*. Washington, DC: TESOL. [53, 57, 314, 315]

Allen, J. P. B., Swain, M., Harley, B. and **Cummins, J.** 1990. 'Aspects of classroom treatment: towards a more comprehensive view of second language education' in Harley *et al.* (eds.) 1990. [152(n1), 154(n13)]

Allen, J.P.B. and **Widdowson, H.G.** 1974. 'Teaching the communicative use of English'. *IRAL* 12/1. [169]

Allwright, R.L. 1975a. 'Problems in the study of the language teacher's treatment of learner error' in M.K. Burt and H.C. Dulay (eds.) 1975. [50, 57(n5)]

Allwright, R.L. 1975b. 'Language learning through communication practice'. *ELT Documents* 3:2–14.

Allwright, R.L. 1979. 'Language learning through communicative practice' in C.J. Brumfit and K. Johnson (eds.) *The Communicative Approach to Language Teaching*. Oxford: Oxford University Press. [204(n12)]

Allwright, R.L. 1980. 'Turns, topics, and tasks: patterns of participation in language learning and teaching' in D. Larsen-Freeman (ed.) 1980. [50]

Allwright, R.L. 1988. *Observation in the Language Classroom*. London: Longman. [49, 366]

Anderson, A. and **Lynch, T.** 1988. *Listening*. Oxford: Oxford University Press.

Armstrong, L.E. 1947. *The Phonetics of French*. London: Bell. [122(n3)]

Asher, J. 1977. *Learning Another Language through Actions: The Complete Teacher's Guide Book*. Los Gatos, Calif.: Sky Oaks Production. [204(n11)]

Asher, J., Kusudo, J. and **de la Torre, R.** 1983. 'Learning a second language through commands: the second field test' in J.W. Oller and P.A. Richard-Amato (eds.) 1983. [204(n11)]

Ashworth, M. 1985. *Beyond Methodology: Second Language Teaching and the Community*. Cambridge: Cambridge University Press. [35]

Astley, H. 1983. *Get the Message!* Cambridge: Cambridge University Press. [270(n9)]

Astley, H. and **Hawkins, E.** 1985. *Using Language*. Cambridge: Cambridge University Press. [253, 270(n9)]

Austin, J.L. 1962. *How to Do Things with Words*. Oxford: Clarendon Press and Cambridge, Mass.: Harvard University Press. [159]

Ausubel, D.P. 1968. *Educational Psychology: A Cognitive View*. New York: Holt, Rinehart and Winston. [347(n1)]

Avery, P. and **Ehrlich, S.** 1992a. 'Preliminary considerations in the teaching of pronunciation' in P. Avery and S. Ehrlich. 1992b. [111]

Avery, P. and **Ehrlich, S.** 1992b. *Teaching American English Pronunciation*. Oxford: Oxford University Press.

Bachman, L.F. 1990. *Fundamental Considerations in Language Testing*. Oxford: Oxford University Press. [356]

Bachman, L.F. and **Palmer, A.S.** 1982. 'The construct validation of some components of communicative proficiency'. *TESOL Quarterly* 16/4:449–65. [73]

Bailey, K.M. 1976. 'The Use of Two Observation Instruments in Supervised ESL Teaching'. Unpublished M.A. thesis, University of California, Los Angeles. [49]

Bailey, N. 1989. 'Theoretical implications in the acquisition of the English simple past and past progressive: putting together the pieces of the puzzle' in S. Gass, C. Madden, D. Preston, and L. Selinker (eds.) *Variation in Second Language Acquisition: Psycholinguistic Issues*. Clevedon: Multilingual Matters. [153(n6)]

Balyayev, B.V. 1963. *The Psychology of Teaching Foreign Languages*. Oxford: Pergamon.

Beretta, A. 1986. 'Toward a methodology of ESL program evaluation'. *TESOL Quarterly* 20/1:144–55. [47]

Berman, R.A. 1979. 'Rule of grammar or rule of thumb?' *IRAL* 17/4:279–302. [132, 147, 150, 152(n1, n2, n4), 154(n12)]

Berns, M. 1990. 'Why language teaching needs the sociologist'. *The Canadian Modern Language Review* 46/2:339–53. [235(n1)]

Bialystok, E. 1978. 'A theoretical model of second language learning'. *Language Learning* 28:69–83. [332]

Bialystok, E. 1979. 'Explicit and implicit judgements of L2 grammaticality'. *Language Learning* 29:81–103. [332]

Bialystok, E. 1990. *Communication Strategies: A Psychological Analysis of Second Language Use*. Oxford: Blackwell. [273(n32)]

Bibeau, G. 1984. 'No easy road to bilingualism' in H.H. Stern (ed.) 1984. [305]

Bickley, V. (ed.) 1989. *Language Teaching and Learning Styles Within and Across Cultures*. Hong Kong: Institute of Language in Education. [235(n1)]

Birdsong, D. 1988. *Metalinguistic Performance and Interlinguistic Competence*. New York: Springer-Verlag. [268(n4)]

Birkmaier, E.M. (ed.) 1969. *Foreign Languages Education: An Overview*. ACTFL Review of Foreign Language Education 1. Lincolnwood, Ill.: National Textbook Co. [Seelye 1969]

Bishop, G.R. (ed.) 1960. *Culture in Language Learning*. Middlebury, Vt.: Northeast Conference on the Teaching of Foreign Languages. [236(n8)]

Bloom, B.S. (ed.) 1956. *Taxonomy of Educational Objectives: The Classification of the Linguistic Society of America*. Baltimore: Linguistic Society of America. [65, 80]

Bloomfield, L. 1933. *Language*. New York: Holt, Rinehart and Winston. [328]

Bloomfield, L. 1942. *Outline Guide for the Practical Study of Foreign Languages*. Special publications of the Linguistic Society of America. Baltimore: Linguistic Society of America. [259, 271(n20)]

Bodmer, F. and **Hogben, L.** 1944. *The Loom of Language*. London: Allen and Unwin. [82, 258]

Bongers, H. 1947. *The History and Principles of Vocabulary Control*. Woerden: Wocopi.

Born, W.C. (ed.) 1975. *Goals Clarification, Curriculum, Teaching, Evaluation*. New York: Northeast Conference on the Teaching of Foreign Languages.

Born, W.C. (ed.) 1976. *Language and Culture: Heritage and Horizons*. Conference Reports. New York: Northeast Conference on the Teaching of Foreign Languages. [236(n8)]

Born, W.C. (ed.) 1977. *Language: Acquisition, Application, Appreciation*. New York: Northeast Conference on the Teaching of Foreign Languages.

Born, W.C. (ed.) 1978. *New Contents, New Teachers, New Publics*. New York: Northeast Conference on the Teaching of Foreign Languages.

Bosco, F.J. and **Di Pietro, R.J.** 1970. 'Instructional strategies: their psychological and linguistic bases'. *IRAL* 8:1–19. [31]

Bowen, J.D. 1975. *Patterns of English Pronunciation*. Rowley, Mass.: Newbury House. [123(n6)]

Boyer, P., Charbonneau, S. and **Nault, C.** 1982. *Les Passe-Partout de la Conversation*. Ottawa: Ministre des Approvisionnements et Services Canada. [174]

Brée, G. (ed.) 1955. *Culture, Literature, and Articulation*. New York: Northeast Conference on the Teaching of Foreign Languages. [236(n8)]

Breen, M.P. 1983. 'How would we recognise a communicative classroom?' in B. Coffey (ed.) *Teacher Training and the Curriculum: The 1982 Dunford House Seminar*. London: The British Council. [43]

Breen, M.P. 1984. 'Process syllabuses for the language classroom' in C.J. Brumfit (ed.) 1984. [20, 272(n28)]

Breen, M.P. 1987. 'Contemporary paradigms in syllabus design (parts 1 and 2)'. *Language Teaching* 20:81–92 and 157–74. [43]

Breen, M. P. and **Candlin, C. N.** 1980. 'The essentials of a communicative curriculum in language teaching'. *Applied Linguistics* 1:89–112. [25]
Breen, M. P., Candlin, C. N., Dam, L. and **Gabrielsen, G.** 1989. 'The evolution of a teacher training program' in R. K. Johnson (ed.) 1989. [272(n28)]
Brindley, G. 1989. 'The role of needs analysis in adult ESL programme design' in R. K. Johnson (ed.) 1989. [43, 98(n3)]
Brinton, D. M., Snow, M. A. and **Wesche, M. B.** 1989. *Content-Based Second Language Instruction*. New York: Newbury House. [170, 192, 193, 325]
Brooks N. 1964. *Language and Language Learning*. New York: Harcourt Brace. [206, 208, 235(n1, n6), 238(n19), 239(n24), 281, 329, 341]
Brooks, N. 1968. 'Teaching culture in the foreign language classroom'. *Foreign Language Annals* 1:204–17. [236(n6)]
Brooks, N. 1969. 'The meaning of bilingualism today'. *Foreign Language Annals* 2:304–9. [236(n6)]
Brooks, N. 1971. 'A guest editorial: culture—a new frontier'. *Foreign Language Annals* 5:54–61. [233, 236(n6)]
Brown, G. 1977/1990. *Listening to Spoken English*. London: Longman. [123(n7, n8), 125(n20)]
Brown, G. and **Yule, G.** 1983a. *Discourse Analysis*. Cambridge: Cambridge University Press. [159, 161, 176(n1), 200, 317]
Brown, G. and **Yule, G.** 1983b. *Teaching the Spoken Language: An Approach Based on the Analysis of Conversational English*. Cambridge: Cambridge University Press. [123(n8)]
Brown, H. D. 1980/1987. *Principles of Language Learning and Teaching*. Englewood Cliffs, NJ: Prentice-Hall. [216, 271(n16)]
Brown, J. D. 1989. Language program evaluation: a synthesis of existing possibilities' in R. K. Johnson (ed.) 1989. [47, 48]
Browne, S. C. and **Huckin, T. N.** 1987. 'Pronunciation tutorials for nonnative technical professionals: a program description' in J. Morley (ed.) *Current Perspectives on Pronunciation*. Washington, DC: TESOL. [125(n22)]
Brumfit, C. J. 1980a. *Problems and Principles in English Teaching*. Oxford: Pergamon.
Brumfit, C. J. 1980b. 'From defining to designing: communicative specifications versus communicative methodology in foreign language teaching' in K. E. Müller (ed.) 1980. [137, 165]
Brumfit, C. J. 1981. 'Notional syllabuses revisited: a response'. *Applied Linguistics* 2:90–2. [165]
Brumfit, C. J. (ed.) 1984. *General English Syllabus Design*. ELT Documents 118. Oxford: Pergamon. [Breen 1984, Candlin 1984]
Brumfit, C. J. 1988. 'Applied linguistics and communicative language teaching' in R. B. Kaplan (ed.) *Annual Review of Applied Linguistics* 8.
Brumfit, C. J. and **Carter, R. A.** 1986. *Literature and Language Teaching*. Oxford: Oxford University Press.
Bruner, J. S. 1966. *Toward a Theory of Instruction*. Cambridge, Mass.: Harvard University Press. [347(n1)]
Bruner, J. S. 1973. *Beyond the Information Given: Studies in the Psychology of Knowing* (edited by J. M. Anglin). London: Allen and Unwin and New York: Norton. [258]
Buckby, M., Bull, P., Fletcher, R., Green, R., Page, B. and **Roger, D.** 1981. *Graded Objectives and Tests for Modern Language: An Evaluation*. London: Schools Council.
Bühler, K. 1934. *Sprachtheorie*. Jena: Fischer. [158]
Bullock Report. 1975. *A Language for Life*. Report of a Committee of Inquiry

appointed by the Secretary of State for Education and Science under the chairmanship of Lord Bullock. London: H.M.S.O. [247]

Bundesarbeitsgemeinschaft Englisch an Gesamtschulen, Protokolle der Arbeitstagungen. 1975. *Diskursstruktur und Übungstypologie.* Fuldatal (HILF). [173]

Bundesarbeitsgemeinschaft Englisch an Gesamtschulen 1977. *Leistungsmessung und Beurteilung im Kommunikativen Englischunterricht.* Fuldatal (HILF). [289]

Burstall, C., Jamieson, M., Cohen, S. and **Hargreaves, M.** 1974. *Primary French in the Balance.* Windsor: NFER Publishing Company. [32, 47, 287, 288]

Burt, M.K. and **Dulay, H.C.** (eds.) 1975. *New Directions in Second Language Learning, Teaching and Bilingual Education.* Washington, DC: TESOL. [Allwright 1975a]

Buttjes, D. and **Byram, M.** 1991. *Mediating Languages and Cultures: Towards an Intercultural Theory of Foreign Language Education.* Clevedon, Avon: Multilingual Matters. [235(n1)]

Byrnes, H. 1991. 'Reflections on the development of cross-cultural communicative competence in the foreign language classroom' in B.F. Freed (ed.) *Foreign Language Acquisition Research and the Classroom.* Lexington, Mass.: Heath. [235(n1)]

California State Department 1980. *Foreign Language Framework for California Public Schools, Kindergarten Through Grade Twelve.* Sacramento.

Callamand, M. 1981. *Méthodologie de l'enseignement de la prononciation.* Paris: Nathan. [115, 123(n7, n8)]

Callamand, M. and **Pedoya, E.** 1984. 'Phonétique et enseignement'. *Le français dans le monde* 182:56–8. [110, 124(n12)]

Campbell, R. 1970. 'An evaluation and comparison of present methods of teaching English grammar to speakers of other languages'. *TESOL Quarterly* 70:37–48. [346–7]

Campbell, R. and **Wales, R.** 1970. 'The study of language acquisition' in J. Lyons (ed.) *New Horizons in Linguistics.* Harmondsworth: Penguin. [162]

Canale, M. 1983. 'From communicative competence to communicative language pedagogy' in J.C. Richards and R.W. Schmidt (eds.) *Language and Communication.* London: Longman. [75, 115, 156, 164]

Canale, M. 1988. 'The measurement of communicative competence'. *Annual Review of Applied Linguistics* 8:67–84. [356]

Canale, M. and **Swain, M.** 1980. 'Theoretical bases of communicative approaches to second language teaching and testing'. *Applied Linguistics* 1:1–47. [75, 115, 156, 164]

Candlin, C.N. 1983. 'Applying a systems approach to curriculum innovation in the public sector'. 18th RELC Seminar on Syllabus Design. Singapore, April 1983. [20]

Candlin, C.N. 1984. 'Syllabus design as a critical process' in C.J. Brumfit (ed.) 1984. [20, 272(n28)]

Candlin, C.N. 1987. 'Towards task-based language learning' in C.N. Candlin and D. Murphy (eds.) 1987.

Candlin, C.N. and **Murphy, D.** (eds.) 1987. *Language Learning Tasks.* Englewood Cliffs, NJ: Prentice-Hall. [203(n9), Candlin 1987]

Caré, J.M. and **Debyser, F.** 1978. 'Lire la rue dans la rue'. *Le Français dans le monde* 141:52–9. [204(n13)]

Carrell, P.L. 1985. 'Facilitating ESL reading by teaching text structure'. *TESOL Quarterly* 19:727–52. [174]

Carroll, J.B. 1964. *Language and Thought.* Englewood Cliffs, NJ: Prentice-Hall.

Carroll, J.B. 1965. 'The contributions of psychological theory and educational

research to the teaching of foreign languages'. *Modern Language Journal* 49:273–81. [347(n1)]
Carroll, J. B. 1967. 'Foreign language proficiency levels attained by language majors near graduation from college'. *Foreign Language Annals* 1:131–51. [299(n2)]
Carroll, J. B. 1971. 'Current issues in psycholinguistics and second language teaching'. *TESOL Quarterly* 5:101–14. [331]
Carroll, J. B. 1975. *The Teaching of French as a Foreign Language in Eight Countries*. New York: Wiley. [32, 287, 351]
Carter, R. 1987. *Vocabulary: Applied Linguistic Perspectives*. London: Unwin Hyman. [104(n1)]
Carter, R. and **McCarthy, M.** (eds.) 1988. *Vocabulary and Language Teaching*. London: Longman. [104(n1), 308]
Carton, A. S. 1971. 'Inferencing: a process in using and learning language' in P. Pimsleur and T. Quinn (eds.) 1971. [330]
Catford, J. C. 1987. 'Phonetics and the teaching of pronunciation: a systemic description of English phonology' in J. Morley (ed.) 1987. [117, 125(n17)]
Celce-Murcia, M. 1985. 'Making informed decisions about the role of grammar in language teaching'. *TESOL Newsletter* 19/1:4–5. [127, 129, 130, 133, 142, 143, 151, 152(n1)]
Celce-Murcia, M. 1987. 'Teaching pronunciation as communication' in J. Morley (ed.) 1987. [109, 115, 123(n8), 124(n15)]
Celce-Murcia, M. and **Hilles, S.** 1988. *Techniques and Resources in Teaching Grammar*. New York: Oxford University Press. [152(n1)]
Celce-Murcia, M. and **Larsen-Freeman, D.** 1984. *The Grammar Book: An ESL/EFL Teacher's Course*. Rowley, Mass.: Newbury House. [132]
Chamot, A. and **Kupper, L.** 1989. 'Learning strategies in foreign language instruction'. *Foreign Language Annals* 22/1:13–24. [272(n26)]
Chastain, K. 1976/1988. *Developing Second Language Skills: Theory to Practice*. Chicago: Rand McNally. [141, 208, 223, 235(n1), 238(n19), 239(n20, n24), 240(n28, n29, n30), 241(n33), 242(n39, n41, n43)]
Chastain, K. 1987. 'Examining the role of grammar explanation, drills and exercises in the development of communicative skills'. *Hispania* 70:160–6. [154(n11)]
Chastain, K. D. and **Woerdehoff, F. J.** 1968. 'A methodological study comparing the audio-lingual habit theory and the cognitive code-learning theory'. *Modern Language Journal* 52:268–79. [330]
Chaudron, C. 1988. *Second Language Classrooms: Research on Teaching and Learning*. Cambridge: Cambridge University Press. [49, 154(n13), 203(n5), 366]
Chomsky, N. 1959. Review of *Verbal Behavior* by B. F. Skinner. *Language* 35:26–58. [329]
CILT Reports and Papers 14. 1976. *Bilingualism and British Education: The Dimensions of Diversity*. London: Centre for Information on Language Teaching and Research. [Dodson 1976]
Clark, E. 1978. 'Awareness of language: some evidence from what children say and do' in A. Sinclair, R. Jarvella, and W. Levelt (eds.) *The Child's Conception of Language*. New York: Springer-Verlag. [268(n4)]
Clark, H. H. and **Clark, E. V.** 1977. *Psychology and Language: An Introduction to Psycholinguistics*. New York: Harcourt Brace Jovanovich.
Clark, J. L. 1987. *Curriculum Renewal in School Foreign Language Learning*. Oxford: Oxford University Press.
Clarke, D. F. 1989. 'Communicative theory and its influence on materials production'. *Language Teaching* 22/2:73–86. [203(n9)]
Cohen, A. 1990. *Language Learning: Insights for Learners, Teachers and Researchers*. New York: Newbury House. [272(n26)]

Coleman, A. 1929. *The Teaching of Modern Foreign Languages in the United States*. New York: Macmillan. [62]

Collins, H.F. 1934. 'England and Wales: modern languages' in Lord E. Percy (ed.) *The Yearbook of Education*. London: Evans. [280]

Cook, G. 1989. *Discourse*. Oxford: Oxford University Press.

Cook, V.J. 1979. *Young Children and Language*. London: Edward Arnold. [271(n16)]

Cooke, D.A. 1974. 'The Role of Explanation in Foreign Language Instruction'. University of Essex, unpublished Ph.D. thesis. [146, 337]

Corder, S.P. 1973. *Introducing Applied Linguistics*. Harmondsworth, Middlesex: Penguin Books. [136, 138, 139]

Corder, S.P. 1978. 'Language-learner language' in J.C. Richards (ed.) *Understanding Second and Foreign Language Learning: Issues and Approaches*. Rowley, Mass.: Newbury House. [299(n1)]

Corder, S.P. 1981. *Error Analysis and Interlanguage*. Oxford: Oxford University Press.

Coulthard, M. 1977/1985. *An Introduction to Discourse Analysis*. London: Longman. [167, 176]

Council of Europe. 1979. *A European Unit Credit System for Modern Language Learning by Adults*. Report of the Ludwigshafen Symposium. Strasbourg: Council of Europe.

Council of Europe. 1981. *Modern Languages (1971–1981)*. Report presented by CDCC Project Group 4 with a résumé by J.L.M.Trim, Project Adviser. Strasbourg: Council for Cultural Co-operation of the Council of Europe. [26, 268(n3), Trim 1981]

Crawford-Lange, L.M. and **Lange, R.L.** 1984. 'Doing the unthinkable in the second-language classroom: a process for the integration of language and culture' in T.V.Higgs (ed.) 1984. [232, 236(n8), 238(n17), 241(n36)]

Crombie, W. 1985. *Discourse and Language Learning: A Relational Approach to Syllabus Design*. Oxford: Oxford University Press.

Cross, D. 1977a. 'Organizational changes in foreign language teaching'. *Modern Languages* 58:64–9. [269(n8)]

Cross, D. 1977b. 'The intensive course at Archbishop Michael Ramsey School'. *Modern Languages* 58:175–81. [269(n8)]

Cross, D. 1978. 'A pilot investigation into the effects of a delayed start in foreign language learning followed by an oral-based intensive course'. *Modern Languages* 59:82–96. [269(n8)]

Cross, D. 1979. 'An investigation into the effects of a delayed start in main foreign language learning'. *Modern Languages* 60:92–101. [269(n8)]

Cross, D. 1980. 'An investigation into the effects of a delayed start in main foreign language learning'. *Modern Languages* 61:89–98. [269(n8)]

Cross, D. 1981. 'An investigation into the effects of a delayed start in main foreign language learning'. *Modern Languages* 62:85–92. [269(n8)]

Curran, C.A. 1976. *Counseling-Learning in Second Languages*. Apple River, Ill.: Apple River Press. [271(n23)]

Curtain, H.A. and **Pesola, C.A.** 1988. *Languages and Children: Making the Match*. Reading, Mass.: Addison-Wesley. [269(n6, n7)]

Damen, L. 1987. *Culture Learning: The Fifth Dimension in the Language Classroom*. Reading, Mass.: Addison-Wesley. [83, 206, 236(n7)]

Delattre, P. 1965. *Comparing the Phonetic Features of English, French, German and Spanish*. London: Harrap and Heidelberg: Julius Groos Verlag. [123(n5)]

Dickens, P. and **Woods, E.** 1988. 'Some criteria for the development of communicative grammar tasks'. *TESOL Quarterly* 22:623–46.
Dickinson, L. 1987. *Self-Instruction in Language Learning*. Cambridge: Cambridge University Press. [244]
DiLaura, S. J. 1983. 'Teaching without grammar: Title XII experience at the University of Delaware'. *Foreign Language Annals* 16/5:339–42. [149]
Diller, K. C. 1971. *Generative Grammar, Structural Linguistics, and Language Teaching*. Rowley, Mass.: Newbury House. [331]
Diller, K. C. 1978. *The Language Teaching Controversy*. Rowley, Mass.: Newbury House. [331]
Diller, K. C. 1990. 'The non-linearity of language learning and "post modern" language teaching methods'. Paper presented at the Tenth Second Language Research Forum, University of Oregon.
Di Pietro, R. J. 1983. 'From literature to discourse: interaction with texts in the ESL/FSL classroom'. *The Canadian Modern Language Review* 40/1:44–50.
Di Pietro, R. J. 1987. *Strategic Interaction: Learning Languages through Scenarios*. Cambridge: Cambridge University Press. [176(n6), 198]
Dodge, J. W. (ed.) 1972. *Other Words, Other Worlds: Language-in-Culture*. Middlebury, Vt.: Northeast Conference on the Teaching of Foreign Languages. [236(n8)]
Dodson, C. J. 1962. *The Bilingual Method: Another Approach to the Learning of Modern Languages*. Aberystwyth: Faculty of Education, University College of Wales. [282]
Dodson, C. J. 1967. *Language Teaching and the Bilingual Method*. London: Pitman. [282]
Dodson, C. J. 1976. 'Foreign language teaching and bilingualism'. In CILT Reports and Papers 14. [178]
Dodson, C. J. 1978. *Bilingual Education in Wales*. London: Schools Council.
Donmall, G. (ed.) 1985. *Language Awareness*. National Congress on Languages in Education. NCLE Papers and Reports 6. London: Centre for Information on Language Teaching and Research. [248, 250, 251, 270(n11, n13), Quinn and Trounce 1985]
Dubin, F. and **Olshtain, E.** 1986. *Course Design*. Cambridge: Cambridge University Press.
Duff, A. 1989. *Translation*. Oxford: Oxford University Press. [282]
Dulay, H. C., Burt, M. K. and **Krashen, S.** 1982. *Language Two*. New York: Oxford University Press. [141, 153(n9), 154(n13)]
Dunkin, M. J. and **Biddle, B. J.** 1974. *The Study of Teaching*. New York: Holt, Rinehart and Winston. [35]
Dunlea, A. 1985. *How Do We Learn Languages?* (Awareness of Language Series). Cambridge: Cambridge University Press. [257, 270(n9)]
Duplantie, M., LeBlanc, R. and **Tremblay, R.** 1986. *Initiation au voyage*. Winnipeg: Canadian Association of Second Language Teachers. [195]

Eddy, P. A. 1980. 'Present status of foreign language teaching: A Northeast Conference survey' in T. H. Geno (ed.) 1980.
Edmondson, W. and **House, J.** 1981. *Let's Talk and Talk About It*. Munich and Baltimore: Urban and Schwarzenberg. [172, 173, 174]
Edwards, H., Wesche, M., Krashen, S., Clément, R. and **Kruidenier, B.** 1984. 'Second-language acquisition through subject-matter learning: a study of sheltered psychology classes at the University of Ottawa'. *The Canadian Modern Language Review* 41:268–82. [193]
Elkins, R. J., Kalivoda, T. B. and **Morain, G.** 1972. 'Teaching culture through the audio-motor unit'. *Foreign Language Annals* 6:61–7. [241(n33)]

Ellis, R. 1984. 'Can syntax be taught? A study of the effects of formal instruction on the acquisition of WH questions by children'. *Applied Linguistics* 5/2:138–55. [141, 145]

Ellis, R. 1985. *Understanding Second Language Acquisition*. Oxford: Oxford University Press. [123(n9), 151, 176(n4), 271(n16), 273(n32)]

Ellis, R. 1987. 'Does remedial instruction work? An L2 acquisition perspective' in J. Coleman and R. Towell (eds.) *The Advanced Language Learner*. London: Centre for Information on Language Teaching and Research.

Ellis, R. 1990. *Instructed Second Language Acquisition*. Oxford: Blackwell. [271(n16)]

Enright, D. S. and **McCloskey, M. L.** 1988. *Integrating English*. Reading, Mass.: Addison-Wesley.

Ervin, S. M. and **Osgood, C. E.** 1954. 'Second language learning and bilingualism' in C. E. Osgood and T. A. Sebeok (eds.) 'Psycholinguistics: A survey of theory and research problems'. *Journal of Abnormal and Social Psychology* 49: Supplement. [280, 281]

Faerch, C. 1986. 'Rules of thumb and other teacher-formulated rules in the foreign language classroom' in G. Kasper (ed.) *Language Teaching and Communication in the Foreign Language Classroom*. Aarhus: Aarhus University Press. [337, 338, 348]

Faerch, C., Haastrup, K. and **Phillipson, R.** 1984. *Learner Language and Language Learning*. Clevedon, Avon: Multilingual Matters. [333]

Faerch, C. and **Kasper, G.** (eds.) 1983. *Strategies in Interlanguage Communication*. London: Longman.

Fanselow, J. 1977. 'Beyond Rashomon—conceptualizing and describing the teaching act'. *TESOL Quarterly* 11:17–39. [50]

Fantini, A. E. *et al.* (eds.) 1984. *Beyond the Language Classroom: A Guide for Teachers*. Brattleboro, Vt.: The Experiment in International Living.

FCLT. See Stern 1983a.

Fiedler, F. E., Mitchell, T. and **Triandis, H. C.** 1971. 'The culture assimilator: an approach to cross-cultural training'. *Journal of Applied Psychology* 55:95–102. [226]

Finocchiaro, M. and **Brumfit, C.** 1983. *The Functional-Notional Approach*. New York: Oxford University Press. [152(n1, n3), 167, 174]

Firth, S. 1992a. 'Pronunciation syllabus design: a question of focus' in P. Avery and S. Ehrlich. 1992b. [117, 124(n15), 125(n17)]

Firth, S. 1992b. 'Developing self-correcting and self-monitoring strategies' in P. Avery and S. Ehrlich. 1992b. [125(n22)]

Fisiak, J. (ed.) 1981. *Contrastive Linguistics and the Language Teacher*. Oxford: Pergamon. [297, Sajavaara 1981]

Flanders, N. A. 1970. *Analyzing Teaching Behavior*. Reading, Mass.: Addison-Wesley.

Flege, J. 1988. 'A critical period for learning to pronounce foreign languages?' *Applied Linguistics* 8/2:162–75. [123(n9)]

Foley, J. 1991. 'A psycholinguistic framework for task-based approaches to language teaching'. *Applied Linguistics* 12/1:62–75. [203(n9)]

Freedman, A., Pringle, I. and **Yalden, J.** (eds.) 1983. *Learning to Write: First Language/Second Language*. London: Longman.

Freudenstein, R. (ed.) *Multilingual Education Through Compact Courses*. Munich: Hueber and Oxford: Pergamon.

Fries, C. C. 1945. *Teaching and Learning English as a Foreign Language*. Ann Arbor: University of Michigan Press. [135]

Fröhlich, M. 1976. 'Case studies of second language learning'. Unpublished M.A. thesis, University of Toronto. [259]

Fröhlich, M., Spada, N. and **Allen, J. P. B.** 1985. 'Differences in the communicative orientation of L2 classrooms'. *TESOL Quarterly* 19/1:27–52. [305]

Gairns, R. and **Redman, S.** 1986. *Working with Words: A Guide to Teaching and Learning Vocabulary*. Cambridge: Cambridge University Press. [105(n1), 308]

Gauthier, R. 1964/1967. *Fifth Form French Reader*. London: Pergamon.

Genesee, F. 1987. *Learning Through Two Languages: Studies of Immersion and Bilingual Education*. Cambridge, Mass.: Newbury House. [47, 304]

Genesee, F. 1988. 'Neuropsychology and second language acquisition' in L. M. Beebe (ed.) *Issues in Second Language Acquisition: Multiple Perspectives*. New York: Newbury House. [123(n9)]

Geno, T. H. (ed.) 1980. *Our Profession: Present Status and Future Directions*. New York: Northeast Conference on the Teaching of Foreign Languages. [Eddy 1980, Lafayette 1980]

Geno, T. H. (ed.) 1981. *Foreign Language and International Studies*. New York: Northeast Conference on the Teaching of Foreign Languages.

George, H. V. 1972. *Common Errors in Language Learning: Insights from English*. Rowley, Mass.: Newbury House. [137]

Gilbert, J. B. 1984. *Clear Speech: Pronunciation and Listening Comprehension in American English*. Cambridge: Cambridge University Press. [114, 123(n10), 124(n13, n14), 125(n23, n24), 307, 326(n5)]

Gougenheim, G., Michéa, R., Rivenc, P. and **Sauvageot, A.** 1964. *L'élaboration du français fondamental (1er degré): Etude sur l'établissement d'un vocabulaire et d'une grammaire de base*. Paris: Didier.

Gouin, F. 1880. *L'art d'enseigner et d'étudier les langues*. Paris. Translated by H. Swan and V. Bétis as *The Art of Teaching and Studying Languages*. London: George Philip, 1892. [256]

Grice, H. P. 1975. 'Logic and conversation' in P. Cole and J. L. Morgan (eds.) *Syntax and Semantics 3: Speech Acts*. New York: Academic Press.

Grittner, F. M. 1977. *Teaching Foreign Languages*. New York: Harper and Row. [11, 70]

Gudschinsky, S. C. 1967. *How to Learn an Unwritten Language*. New York: Holt, Rinehart and Winston. [271(n21)]

Guntermann, G. and **Philips, J. K.** 1981. 'Communicative course design: developing functional ability in all four skills'. *The Canadian Modern Language Review* 37:329–43. [188, 196, 202]

Hakes, D. 1980. *The Development of Metalinguistic Abilities in Children*. New York: Springer-Verlag. [268(n4)]

Halliday, M. A. K. 1973. *Explorations in the Functions of Language*. London: Edward Arnold.

Halliday, M. A. K., McIntosh, A. and **Strevens, P.** 1964. *The Linguistic Sciences and Language Teaching*. London: Longman. [80, 135, 136]

Hammerly, H. 1982. *Synthesis in Second Language Teaching*. Blaine, Washington: Second Language Publications. [110, 124(n11), 125(n21), 206, 210, 212, 213, 214, 216, 223, 229, 234, 235(n1), 237(n13), 238(n18, n19), 239(n20, n21), 240(n28, n29, n30, n32), 241(n36), 242(n43)]

Hammond, R. 1988. 'Accuracy versus communicative competency: the acquisition of grammar in the second language classroom'. *Hispania* 71:408–17.

Hanna, G., Smith, A. H., McLean, L. D. and **Stern, H. H.** 1980. *Contact and Communication: An Evaluation of Bilingual Student Exchange Programs*. Toronto: OISE Press. [242(n42)]

Harding, A., Page, B. and **Rowell, S.** 1980. *Graded Objectives in Modern Languages*. London: Centre for Information on Language Teaching and Research. [272(n25)]

Harley, B. 1984. 'How good is their French?' in H. H. Stern (ed.) 1984. [305]

Harley, B. 1986. *Age in Second Language Acquisition*. Clevedon, Avon: Multilingual Matters. [271(n16)]

Harley, B. 1988. 'Effects of instruction on SLA: issues and evidence' in R. B. Kaplan (ed.) *Annual Review of Applied Linguistics* 9.

Harley, B. 1989. 'Functional grammar in French immersion: a classroom experiment'. *Applied Linguistics* 10/3:331–59. [150, 323, 324]

Harley, B., Allen, P., Cummins, J. and **Swain, M.** (eds.) 1990. *The Development of Second Language Proficiency*. Cambridge: Cambridge University Press. [Allen *et al.* 1990]

Harley, B., Cummins, J., Swain, M. and **Allen, J. P. B.** 1990. 'The nature of language proficiency' in Harley *et al.* (eds.) 1990.

Harley, B. and **d'Anglejan, A.** 1990. 'Report on the piloting of "Se lancer en affaires avec un jeu": An integrated teaching unit designed for grade 10 core French classes'. Winnipeg: Canadian Association of Second Language Teachers. [365]

Harley, B. and **Swain, M.** 1984. 'The interlanguage of immersion students and its implications for second language teaching' in A. Davies, C. Criper, and A. P. R. Howatt (eds.) *Interlanguage*. Edinburgh: Edinburgh University Press. [129, 142]

Harrison, B. (ed.) 1990. *Culture and the Language Classroom*. ELT Documents 132. London: The British Council. [235(n1)]

Harrow, A. J. 1972. 'A taxonomy of the psychomotor domain; a guide for developing behavioral objectives'. New York: McKay. [65]

Hart, D., Lapkin, S. and **Swain, M.** 1987. 'Communicative language tests: perks and perils'. *Evaluation and Research in Education* 1/2:83–94. [356]

Hatch, E. 1978. 'Discourse analysis and second language acquisition' in E. Hatch (ed.) *Second Language Acquisition*. Rowley, Mass.: Newbury House. [167, 174]

Hawkins, E. 1981. *Modern Languages in the Curriculum*. Cambridge: Cambridge University Press. [247, 254, 268(n1), 269(n6)]

Hawkins, E. 1983. *Spoken and Written Language*. Cambridge: Cambridge University Press. [253, 270(n9)]

Hawkins, E. 1984/1987. *Awareness of Language: An Introduction*. Cambridge: Cambridge University Press. [248, 253, 254, 268(n1), 269(n6), 270(n9)]

Hébert, Y. 1990. *Le Syllabus Formation Langagière Générale*. Etude nationale sur les programmes de français de base. Winnipeg: Canadian Association of Second Language Teachers. [363]

Heid, M. (ed.) 1984. *Literarische Texte im Kommunikativen Fremdsprachenunterricht*. New York: Goethe-Institute. (203(n7)]

Henmon, V. A. C. 1929. *Achievement Tests in the Modern Foreign Languages*. Prepared for the Modern Foreign Language Study and the Canadian Committee on Modern Languages. New York: Macmillan. [356]

Henmon, V. A. C. *et al.* 1929. *Prognosis Tests in the Modern Foreign Languages*. Reports prepared for the Modern Foreign Language Study and the Canadian Committee on Modern Languages. New York: Macmillan.

Higgs, T. V. (ed.) 1982. *Curriculum, Competence and the Foreign Language Teacher*. Skokie, Ill.: National Textbook Company. [Higgs and Clifford 1982]

Higgs, T. V. (ed.) 1984. *Teaching for Proficiency: The Organizing Principle*. ACTFL Foreign Language Education Series, 15. Lincolnwood, Ill.: National Textbook Company. [Crawford-Lange and Lange 1984, Liskin-Gasparro 1984, Omaggio 1984]

Higgs, T. V. and **Clifford, R. E.** 1982. 'The push toward communication' in T. V. Higgs (ed.) 1982. [305, 319, 322]

Hiple, D. V. 1987. 'A progress report on the ACTFL Proficiency Guidelines, 1982–1986' in H. Byrnes and M. Canale (eds.) *Defining and Developing Proficiency.* Lincolnwood, Ill.: National Textbook Company. [272(n25)]

Holec, H. 1980a. 'Learner training: meeting needs in self-directed learning' in H. B. Altman and C. V. James (eds.) *Foreign Language Teaching: Meeting Individual Needs.* Oxford: Pergamon. [271(n22)]

Holec, H. 1980b. 'Learner-centred communicative language teaching: needs analysis revisited'. *Studies in Second Language Acquisition* 3:26–33. [271(n22)]

Holec, H. 1981. *Autonomy and Foreign Language Learning.* Oxford: Pergamon Press. [271(n22)]

Holec, H. 1985. 'On autonomy: some elementary concepts' in P. Riley (ed.) *Discourse and Learning.* London: Longman. [271(n22)]

Holec, H. 1987. 'The learner as manager: managing learning or managing to learn?' in A. Wenden and J. Rubin (eds.) 1987. [260, 262, 271(n22)]

Horwitz, E. K. 1987. 'Surveying student beliefs about language learning' in A. Wenden and J. Rubin (eds.) 1987. [268(n5)]

Hosenfeld, C. 1975. 'The new student role: individual differences and implications for instruction' in G. A. Jarvis (ed.) *Perspective: A New Freedom.* ACTFL Review of Foreign Language Education, 7. Skokie, Ill.: National Textbook Company. [292]

Howatt, A. P. R. 1974. 'The background to course design' in J. P. B. Allen and S. P. Corder (eds.) 1974. [139]

Howatt, A. P. R. 1984. *A History of English Language Teaching.* Oxford: Oxford University Press. [122(n1, n3), 271(n17), 272(n31), 280, 289]

Hudson, R. A. 1980. *Sociolinguistics.* Cambridge: Cambridge University Press. [176(n1)]

Hutchinson, T. and **Waters, A.** 1987. *English for Specific Purposes: A Learning-Centred Approach.* Cambridge: Cambridge University Press. [40(n2), 44]

Hymes, D. 1967. 'Models of the interaction of language and social setting' in J. Macnamara (ed.) *Problems of Bilingualism.* Special issue of *Journal of Social Issues* 23. [157, 162]

Hymes, D. 1972. 'On communicative competence' in J. B. Pride and J. Holmes (eds.) *Sociolinguistics: Selected Readings.* Harmondsworth: Penguin. [73]

Ilson, R. 1985. *Dictionaries, Lexicography and Language Learning.* ELT Documents 120. Oxford: Pergamon. [104(n1)]

Jakobovits, L. A. 1968. 'Implications of recent psycholinguistic developments for the teaching of a second language'. *Language Learning* 18:89–109. [303]

Jakobovits, L. A. 1970. *Foreign Language Learning: A Psycholinguistic Analysis of the Issues.* Rowley, Mass.: Newbury House. [163]

Jakobovits, L. A. 1972. 'Introduction: authenticity in FL teaching' in S. J. Savignon, *Communicative Competence: An Experiment in Foreign Language Teaching.* Philadelphia, Pa.: The Center for Curriculum Development. [303]

Jakobovits, L. A. and **Gordon, B.** 1974. *The Context of Foreign Language Teaching.* Rowley, Mass.: Newbury House. [233]

Jakobson, R. 1960. 'Closing statement: linguistics and poetics' in T. A. Sebeok (ed.) *Style in Language.* Cambridge, Mass.: MIT Press. [158]

Jarvis, G. A. 1968. 'A behavioral observation system for classroom foreign language skill acquisition activities'. *Modern Language Journal* 52:335–41. [50, 53]

Jarvis, G. A. (ed.) 1974a. *Responding to New Realities.* ACTFL Review of Foreign

Language Education, 5. Lincolnwood, Ill.: National Textbook Company. [Nostrand 1974]

Jarvis, G. A. (ed.) 1974b. *The Challenge of Communication.* ACTFL Review of Foreign Language Education, 6. Skokie, Ill.: National Textbook Company.

Jarvis, G. and **Adams, S.** 1979. *Evaluating a Second Language Program.* Washington, DC: Center for Applied Linguistics. [48]

Jespersen, O. 1904. *How to Teach a Foreign Language.* London: Allen and Unwin. [338]

Johnson, K. 1982. *Communicative Syllabus Design and Methodology.* Oxford: Pergamon. [188, 196, 197]

Johnson, R. K. 1989. 'A decision-making framework for the coherent language curriculum' in R. K. Johnson (ed.) 1989. [41, 46]

Johnson, R. K. (ed.) 1989. *The Second Language Curriculum.* Cambridge: Cambridge University Press. [Breen *et al.* 1989, Brindley 1989, Brown 1989, Johnson 1989]

Jones, B. 1984. *How Language Works.* Cambridge: Cambridge University Press. [253, 254, 255, 270(n9)]

Jones, D. 1909. *The Pronunciation of English.* Cambridge: Cambridge University Press. [122(n3)]

Jones, D. 1917. *An English Pronunciation Dictionary.* London: Dent. [122(n3)]

Jones, R. L. and **Spolsky, B.** (eds.) 1975. *Testing Language Proficiency.* Arlington, Va.: Center for Applied Linguistics. [64, Wilds 1975]

Kachru, B. B. (ed.) 1982. *The Other Tongue: English Across Cultures.* Urbana, Ill.: University of Illinois Press. [98]

Kachru, B. B. 1985. 'Standards, codification and sociolinguistic realism: the English language in the outer circle' in R. Quirk and H. G. Widdowson (eds.) *English in the World: Teaching and Learning the Language and Literatures.* Cambridge: Cambridge University Press. [98]

Kalivoda, T. B., Morain, G. and **Elkins, R. J.** 1971. 'The audio-motor unit: a listening comprehension strategy that works'. *Foreign Language Annals* 4:392–400. [241 (n33)]

Kaplan, R. B. 1966. 'Cultural thought patterns in international education'. *Language Learning* 16:1–20. [176(n3)]

Kaplan, R. B. 1988. 'Contrastive rhetoric and second language learning: notes toward a theory of contrastive rhetoric' in A. C. Purves (ed.) *Writing Across Languages and Cultures: Issues in Contrastive Rhetoric.* Newbury Park, Calif.: Sage. [176(n3)]

Kasper, G. (ed.) 1986. *Language Teaching and Communication in the Foreign Language Classroom.* Aarhus: Aarhus University Press. [Faerch 1986]

Kelly, L. G. 1969. *25 Centuries of Language Teaching.* Rowley, Mass.: Newbury House. [61, 107]

Kenney, M. and **Fiddes, T.** 1985. *Le Français en action.* Toronto: Heath.

Klein, W. 1986. *Second Language Acquisition.* New York: Cambridge University Press. [271(n16)]

Klippel, F. 1984. *Keep Talking: Communicative Fluency Activities for Language Teaching.* Cambridge: Cambridge University Press. [198, 289]

Kramsch, C. 1979. 'Word watching: learning vocabulary becomes a hobby'. *Foreign Language Annals* 12/2:153–8. [105(n1)]

Kramsch, C. 1984. *Interaction et discours dans la classe de langue.* Paris: Hatier/Credif. [188]

Krashen, S. D. 1981a. *Second Language Acquisition and Second Language Learning.* Oxford: Pergamon. [25]

Krashen, S. D. 1981b. 'Effective second language acquisition: insights from research' in J. E. Alatis, H. B. Altman, and P. M. Alatis (eds.) 1981.
Krashen, S. D. 1982. *Principles and Practice in Second Language Acquisition*. Oxford: Pergamon. [25, 179, 322, 340, 342]
Krashen, S. D. 1984. 'Immersion: why it works and what it has taught us' in H. H. Stern (ed.) 1984. [189, 192, 303, 304]
Krashen, S. D. 1985. *The Input Hypothesis: Issues and Implications*. London: Longman. [179, 322]
Krashen, S. D. and **Seliger, H.** 1975. 'The essential contribution of formal instruction in adult second language learning'. *TESOL Quarterly* 9:173–83. [31]
Krashen, S. D. and **Terrell, T.** 1983. *The Natural Approach—Language Acquisition in the Classroom*. Oxford: Pergamon. [113, 114, 148, 189, 203(n6), 204(n11), 303, 331, 345, 348]
Krathwohl, D. R., Bloom, B. S. and **Masia, B. B.** 1964. *Taxonomy of Educational Objectives: The Classification of Educational Goals*. Handbook 2: *Affective Domain*. New York: McKay. [65, 85]
Krumm, H. J. 1980. 'Communicative processes in the foreign language classroom: preconditions and strategies' in K. E. Müller (ed.) 1980.

Lado, R. 1957. *Linguistic Across Cultures: Applied Linguistics for Language Teachers*. Ann Arbor: University of Michigan Press. [135]
Lado, R. 1961/1964. *Language Testing: The Construction and Use of Foreign Language Tests*. London: Longman and New York: McGraw-Hill. [356]
Lado, R. 1964. *Language Teaching: A Scientific Approach*. New York: McGraw-Hill. [341]
Lafayette, R. C. 1978a. *Language in Education: Theory and Practice*. Washington, DC: Center for Applied Linguistics. [236(n7)]
Lafayette, R. C. 1978b. *Teaching Culture: Strategies and Techniques*. Language in Education series: Theory and Practice. Washington, DC: Center for Applied Linguistics. [206, 212, 226, 236(n7)]
Lafayette, R. C. 1980. 'Toward an articulated curriculum' in T. H. Geno (ed.) 1980.
Lafayette, R. C. 1981. 'Approches formelles et approches non-linguistiquement structurées pour l'enseignement du français langue seconde'. 5th World Congress of FIPF, Rio de Janeiro.
Lafayette, R. C. and **Strasheim, L. A.** 1980. 'Foreign language curricula and materials for the twenty-first century' in D. L. Lange (ed.) 1980. [237(n14), 238(n18), 239(n20, n22, n23, n24)]
Lambert, W. E. and **Gardner, R. C.** 1972. *Attitudes and Motivations in Second Language Learning*. Rowley, Mass.: Newbury House. [85]
Lambert, W. E. and **Tucker, G. R.** 1972. *Bilingual Education of Children: The St. Lambert Experiment*. Rowley, Mass.: Newbury House. [47]
Lange, D. L. (ed.) 1980. *Proceedings of the National Conference on Professional Priorities*. American Council on the Teaching of Foreign Languages. Hastings-on-Hudson, NY: ACTFL Materials Center. [Lafayette and Strasheim 1980, Rivers 1980, Valdman 1980b, Warriner-Burke 1980, Zais 1980]
Larsen-Freeman, D. (ed.) 1980. *Discourse Analysis in Second Language Research*. Rowley, Mass.: Newbury House. [174, Allwright 1980]
Larsen-Freeman, D. and **Long, M. H.** 1991. *An Introduction to Second Language Acquisition Research*. London: Longman.
Larson, D. N. and **Smalley, W. A.** 1972. *Becoming Bilingual—A Guide to Language Learning*. New Canaan, Conn.: Practical Anthropology. [265, 271(n21)]
Leather, J. 1983. 'Second-language pronunciation learning and teaching'. *Language Teaching* 16/3:198–219. [113, 114, 124(n11, n17), 125(n19, n21)]

LeBlanc, R. 1990. *Le Rapport Synthèse*. Etude nationale sur les programmes de français de base. Winnipeg: Canadian Association of Second Language Teachers. [270(n10), 349, 361, 364]

LeBlanc, C. and **Courtel, C.** 1990. 'Executive summary: the culture syllabus'. *The Canadian Modern Language Review* 47/1:82–92. [242(n44)]

LeBlanc, R., Courtel, C. and **Trescases, P.** 1990. *Le Syllabus Culture*. Etude nationale sur les programmes de français de base. Winnipeg: Canadian Association of Second Language Teachers. [270(n10), 362]

Leech, G. N. 1983. *Principles of Pragmatics*. London: Longman. [176(n1)]

Léon, M. 1964. *Exercices systématiques de prononciation française*. Vol. 1: Articulation. Vol. 2: Rythme et intonation. Collection le français dans le monde. Paris: Librairies Hachette et Larousse.

Léon, P. R. 1966. *Prononciation du français standard*. Paris: Didier. [123(n6)]

Léon, P. and **Léon, M.** 1964. *Introduction à la phonétique corrective*. Collection le français dans le monde. Paris: Librairies Hachette et Larousse. [123(n6)]

Levano, A. W. and **Pfister, G. G.** 1980. 'An analysis of surface culture and its manner of presentation in first-year college French textbooks'. *Foreign Language Annals* 13:47–52.

Levinson, S. C. 1983. *Pragmatics*. Cambridge: Cambridge University Press. [157, 159, 176(n1, n2)]

Lewy, A. (ed.) 1977. *Handbook of Curriculum Evaluation*. Paris: Unesco and New York: Longman. [47]

Lightbown, P. M. 1985. 'Great expectations: second language acquisition research and classroom teaching'. *Applied Linguistics* 6:173–89. [326(n7)]

Lipton, G. C. 1988. *Practical Handbook to Elementary Foreign Language Programs*. Lincolnwood, Ill.: National Textbook Company. [269(n6, n7)]

Lindblad, T. 1969. *Implicit and Explicit: An Experiment in Applied Psycholinguistics, Assessing Different Methods of Teaching Grammatical Structures in English as a Foreign Language*. GUME-projektet 1. Sweden: Göteborgs Universitet. [330]

Liskin-Gasparro, J. E. 1984. 'The ACTFL proficiency guidelines: a historical perspective' in T. V. Higgs (ed.) 1984.

Littlewood, W. 1981. *Communicative Language Teaching: An Introduction*. Cambridge: Cambridge University Press. [170, 171, 204(n12)]

Littlewood, W. 1983. 'Contrastive pragmatics and the foreign language learner's personality' in K. Sajavaara (ed.) *Cross-Language Analysis and Second Language Acquisition*, Jyväskylä Cross-Language Studies 9.

Littlewood, W. 1984. *Foreign and Second Language Learning: Language Acquisition Research and Its Implications for the Classroom*. Cambridge: Cambridge University Press. [326(n1)]

Livingstone, C. 1983. *Role Play in Language Learning*. London: Longman. [198]

Long, M. H. 1984. 'Process and product in ESL program evaluation'. *TESOL Quarterly* 18/3:409–25. [48]

Long, M. H. 1985. 'A role for instruction in second language acquisition: task-based language teaching' in K. Hyltenstam and M. Pienemann (eds.) *Modelling and Assessing Second Language Acquisition*. Clevedon, Avon: Multilingual Matters. [203(n9)]

Long, M. H. 1987. 'Second language acquisition and the language curriculum: an interview with D. Nunan'. *Prospect* 2/3.

Long, M. H. 1988. 'Instructed interlanguage development' in L. M. Beebe (ed.) *Issues in Second Language Acquisition: Multiple Perspectives*. New York: Newbury House. [152]

Long, M. H. 1990. 'Maturational constraints on language development'. *Studies in Second Language Acquisition* 12/3:251–85. [123(n9)]

Lynch, B.K. 1990. 'A context-adaptive model for program evaluation'. *TESOL Quarterly* 24/1:23–42. [47]

Lyons, J. 1977. *Semantics*. London and New York: Cambridge University Press. [158, 176(n1)]

Lyster, R. 1990. 'The role of analytic language teaching in French immersion programs'. *The Canadian Modern Language Review* 47/1:157–76. [326(n1)]

MacCarthy, P. 1975. *The Pronunciation of French*. London: Oxford University Press. [123(n7, n8)]

MacCarthy, P. 1978. *The Teaching of Pronunciation*. Cambridge: Cambridge University Press. [123(n7)]

Mackay, R. and **Mountford, A.** (eds.) 1978. *English for Specific Purposes*. London: Longman. [40(n2)]

Mackay, R. and **Palmer, J.D.** (eds.) 1981. *Languages for Specific Purposes: Program Design and Evaluation*. Rowley, Mass.: Newbury House. [48]

Mackey, W.F. 1965. *Language Teaching Analysis*. London: Longman. [135]

Macnamara, J. 1973. 'Nurseries, streets, and classrooms: some comparisons and deductions'. *Modern Language Journal* 57:250–4. [128, 179, 303]

Mager, R. 1962. *Preparing Objectives for Programmed Instruction*. Palo Alto, Calif.: Fearon. [67]

Maley, A. and **Duff, A.** 1978. *Drama Techniques in Language Learning*. Cambridge: Cambridge University Press. [198]

Marcel, C. 1853. *Language as a Means of Mental Culture and International Communication*. London: Chapman and Hall.

Marckwardt, A.H. 1981. 'What literature to teach: principles of selection and class treatment'. *Forum* 19/1. [229]

Marland, M. 1987. *Multilingual Britain*. London: Centre for Information on Language Teaching and Research. [254]

Martin, M.A. 1978. 'The application of spiraling to the teaching of grammar'. *TESOL Quarterly* 12/2:151–60. [139]

Maslow, A. 1970. *Motivation and Personality*. New York: Harper and Row. [237(n12)]

McCandless, P. and **Winitz, H.** 1986. 'Test of pronunciation following one year of comprehension instruction in college German'. *The Modern Language Journal* 70/4:355–62. [124(n15), 125(n19)]

McCarthy, M. 1990. *Vocabulary*. Oxford: Oxford University Press. [104(n1), 308]

McKay, S. 1987. *Teaching Grammar: Form, Function and Technique*. New York: Prentice-Hall. [152(n1)]

McLaughlin, B. 1978. 'The monitor model: some methodological considerations'. *Language Learning* 28:309–32. [326(n1)]

McLaughlin, B. 1987. *Theories of Second Language Learning*. London: Edward Arnold. [176(n4), 271(n16), 326(n1)]

McNair, J. 1980. *Progress in Modern Languages Teaching: Aspects of Education 22*. Institute of Education, University of Hull. [51]

McNerney, M. and **Mendelsohn, D.** 1992. 'Suprasegmentals in the pronunciation class: setting priorities' in P. Avery and S. Ehrlich. 1992b. [125(n17)]

McRae, J. 1985. *Using Drama in the Classroom*. Oxford: Pergamon. [198]

Mead, R.G. (ed.) 1982. *The Foreign Language Teacher: The Lifelong Learner*. New York: Northeast Conference on the Teaching of Foreign Languages.

Mead, R.G. (ed.) 1983. *Foreign Languages: Key Links in the Chain of Learning*. Middlebury, Vt.: Northeast Conference on the Teaching of Foreign Languages. [236(n8), Omaggio 1983, Stern 1983b]

Meade, B. and **Morain, G.** 1973. 'The culture cluster'. *Foreign Language Annals* 6/4:331–8. [225]
Miller, G. A., Galanter, E. and **Pribram, K. H.** 1960. *Plans and the Structure of Behavior*. New York: Holt, Rinehart and Winston. [347(n1)]
Ministère de l'Education du Québec. 1980a. *Programme d'études primaire: Anglais langue seconde*. Québec: Ministère de l'Education.
Ministère de l'Education du Québec. 1980b. *Programme d'études primaire: Français langue seconde*. Québec: Ministère de l'Education.
Mitchell, R. 1988. *Communicative Interaction in Practice*. London: Centre for Information on Language Teaching and Research. [305]
Mitchell, R., Parkinson, B. and **Johnstone, R.** 1981. *The Foreign Language Classroom: An Observation Study*. Stirling: University of Stirling Press. [53, 56, 148, 236(n9), 287, 305, 322]
Modern Studies. 1918. 'The report of the committee (appointed by the Prime Minister) on the position of Modern Languages in the educational system of Great Britain (The Leathes Committee report)'. London: H.M.S.O. [205]
Mohan, B. A. 1986. *Language and Content*. Reading, Mass.: Addison-Wesley. [170, 193]
Morain, G. G. 1968. 'French folklore: a fresh approach to the teaching of culture'. *The French Review* 41:675–81. [241(n37)]
Morain, G. G. 1969. *French Culture: The Folklore Facet*. [241(n37)]
Morain, G. G. 1971. 'Cultural pluralism' in D. L. Lange (ed.) *Pluralism in Foreign Language Education*. Skokie, Ill.: National Textbook Company. [236(n7, n8)]
Morgan, B. Q. 1928. *German Frequency Wordbook*. New York: Macmillan.
Morgan, J. and **Rinvolucri, M.** 1986. *Vocabulary*. Oxford: Oxford University Press. [105(n1)]
Morley, J. 1979. *Improving Spoken English: An Intensive Personalized Program in Perception, Pronunciation, Practice in Context*. Ann Arbor: University of Michigan Press. [123(n6)]
Morley, J. (ed.) 1987. *Current Perspectives on Pronunciation*. Washington, DC: TESOL. [Browne and Huckin 1987, Catford 1987, Celce-Murcia 1987, Wong 1987]
Moskowitz, G. 1967. 'The Flint system' in A. Simon and E. G. Boyer (eds.) *Mirrors for Behaviour: An Anthology of Observation Instruments*. Philadelphia: Research for Better Schools.
Moskowitz, G. 1978. *Caring and Sharing in the Foreign Language Class: A Sourcebook of Humanistic Techniques*. Rowley, Mass.: Newbury House. [49, 57]
Moulton, W. G. 1962. *The Sounds of English and German: A Systematic Analysis of the Contrasts between the Sound Systems*. Chicago: University of Chicago Press. [115, 123(n5)]
Moulton, W. G. 1966. *A Linguistic Guide to Language Learning*. New York: Modern Language Association of America. [271(n21)]
Mounin, G. 1984. 'Sens et place de la civilisation dans l'enseignement des langues'. *Le Français dans le monde* 188:34–6. [235(n3), 237(n11)]
Müller, G. (compiler) 1965. *International Conference: Modern Foreign Language Teaching Report*. Berlin: Pädagogisches Zentrum und Cornelsen. [347(n1)]
Müller, K. E. (ed.) 1980. 'The Foreign Language Syllabus and Communicative Approaches to Teaching: Proceedings of a European-American Seminar'. Special issue of *Studies in Second Language Acquisition* 3/1. [Brumfit 1980b, Krumm 1980, Stern 1980b]
Munby, J. 1978. *Communicative Syllabus Design: A Sociolinguistic Model for Defining the Content of Purpose-Specific Language Programs*. Cambridge: Cambridge University Press. [43, 78, 155]

Naiman, N. 1992. 'A communicative approach to pronunciation teaching' in P. Avery and S. Ehrlich. 1992b. [115, 124(n15), 125(n17, n22)]

Naiman, N., Fröhlich, M., Stern, H. H. and **Todesco, A.** 1978. *The Good Language Learner*. Research in Education Series no. 7. Toronto: OISE Press. [259, 268(n5), 348(n2)]

Nation, I. S. P. 1990. *Teaching and Learning Vocabulary*. New York: Newbury House. [104(n1)]

Neufeld, G. G. 1988. 'Phonological asymmetry in second language learning and performance'. *Language Learning* 38/4:531–59. [123(n9)]

Newmark, L. 1966. 'How not to interfere with language learning'. *International Journal of American Linguistics* 32:77–83.

Newmark, L. 1971. 'A minimal language-teaching program' in P. Pimsleur and T. Quinn (eds.) 1971. [179]

Newmark, L. and **Reibel, D.** 1968. 'Necessity and sufficiency in language learning'. *IRAL* 6/2:145–64. [303]

Nida, E. A. 1957. *Learning a Foreign Language: A Handbook Prepared Especially for Missionaries*. Friendship Press for the National Council of Churches. [271(n21), 273(n34)]

Nisbet, J. D. and **Shucksmith, J.** 1986. *Learning Strategies*. London: Routledge and Kegan Paul. [271(n19)]

Nostrand, H. L. 1966. 'Describing and teaching the sociocultural context of a foreign language and literature' in A. Valdman (ed.) *Trends in Language Teaching*. New York: McGraw-Hill. [236(n7)]

Nostrand, H. L. 1968. 'Levels of sociocultural understanding for language classes' in H. N. Seelye (ed.) 1968a. [233]

Nostrand, H. L. 1973. 'French culture's concern for relationship: relationism?' *Foreign Language Annals* 6:469–80. [236(n7)]

Nostrand, H. L. 1974. 'Empathy for a second culture: motivations and techniques' in G. A. Jarvis (ed.) 1974a. [223, 228, 229, 236(n7, n8), 240(n28), 241(n35, n36, n37), 242(n38, n39, n40, n41)]

Nostrand, H. L. 1978. 'The "emergent model" applied to contemporary France'. *Contemporary French Civilization* 2:277–94. [209, 236(n7), 237(n11), 238(n18, n19), 239(n20, n21, n22, n23, n24)]

Nunan, D. 1988a. *The Learner-Centred Curriculum*. Cambridge: Cambridge University Press. [25, 43, 272(n28)]

Nunan, D. 1988b. *Syllabus Design*. Oxford: Oxford University Press. [203(n9)]

Nunan, D. 1989. *Designing Tasks for the Communicative Classroom*. Cambridge: Cambridge University Press. [203(n9), 204(n12, n14)]

Odlin, T. 1989. *Language Transfer*. Cambridge: Cambridge University Press. [176(n4)]

Oller, J. W. 1979. *Language Tests at School: A Pragmatic Approach*. London: Longman.

Oller, J. W. and **Richard-Amato, P. A.** (eds.) 1983. *Methods That Work: A Smorgasbord of Ideas for Language Teachers*. Rowley, Mass.: Newbury House. [25, 271(n23), 348(n6), Asher *et al.* 1983]

Omaggio, A. C. *et al.* 1983. 'Foreign languages in the secondary school: reconciling the dream with the reality' in R. G. Mead (ed.) 1983. [269(n7)]

Omaggio, A. C. 1984. 'The proficiency-oriented classroom' in T. V. Higgs (ed.) 1984. [174]

Omaggio, A. C. 1986. *Teaching Language in Context: Proficiency-Oriented Instruction*. Boston, Mass.: Heinle and Heinle. [289, 310, 311]

O'Malley, J. M., Chamot, A. V., Stewner-Manzanares, B., Pusso, R. P. and **Küpper, L.** 1985. 'Learning strategy applications with students of English as a second language'. *TESOL Quarterly* 19:557–84. [272(n29)]

O'Malley, J. M. and **Chamot, A. V.** 1990. *Learning Strategies in Second Language Acquisition*. Cambridge: Cambridge University Press. [336]

Ontario Ministry of Education. 1980. *French, core programs 1980: Curriculum Guidelines for the Primary, Junior, Intermediate, and Senior Divisions*. Toronto: Ontario Ministry of Education.

Oskarsson, M. 1975. 'On the role of the mother tongue in learning foreign language vocabulary: an empirical investigation'. *IRAL* 27:19–32. [288]

Oxford, R. 1989. 'Use of language learning strategies: a synthesis of studies with implications for strategy training'. *System* 17/2:235–47. [272(n27)]

Oxford, R. 1990. *Language Learning Strategies: What Every Teacher Should Know*. New York: Newbury House. [271(n19), 272(n26), 336]

Oxford, R. and **Crookall, D.** 1989. 'Research on language learning strategies: methods, findings, and instructional issues'. *The Modern Language Journal* 73/4:405–19.

Paikeday, T. M. 1985. 'May I kill the native speaker?' *TESOL Quarterly* 19:390–5. [238(n16)]

Painchaud, G. with **de Boyko, J., LeBlanc, R., Ruf, T., St-Pierre, M.** and **Thibault, P.** 1990. *Le Syllabus Langue*. Etude nationale sur les programmes de français de base. Winnipeg: Canadian Association of Second Language Teachers. [361]

Palmer, F. R. 1976. *Semantics: A New Outline*. London: Cambridge University Press. [175(n1)]

Palmer, H. E. 1922. *The Principles of Language Study*. London: Harrap. [328, 348(n4)]

Palmer, H. E. and **Redman, H. V.** 1969. *This Language Learning Business*. First edition London: Harrap, 1932. Reissued in Language and Language Learning Series. London: Oxford University Press. [71]

Parent, P. P. and **Belasco, S.** 1970. 'Parallel-column bilingual reading materials as a pedagogical device: an experimental evaluation'. *The Modern Language Journal* 54/7:493–504. [288]

Park, P. and **Fullan, M.** 1986. *Ontario Curriculum 1986: Issues of Professional Development*. Toronto: Ontario Teachers' Federation. [46]

Passy, Paul E. 1906. *Petite phonétique comparée des principales langues européennes*. Leipzig: B. G. Teubner Verlagsgesellschaft. [122(n3)]

Paulston, C. B. 1970. 'Structural pattern drills: a classification'. *Foreign Language Annals* 4/2:187–93.

Paulston, C. B. 1981. 'Notional syllabuses revisited: some comments'. *Applied Linguistics* 2/1:93–5. [165]

Paulston, C. B. and **Bruder, M. N.** 1975. *From Substitution to Substance: A Handbook of Structural Pattern Drills*. Rowley, Mass.: Newbury House. [128, 141, 144, 149, 152(n1), 154(n12), 290]

Pennington, M. C. and **Richards, J. C.** 1986. 'Pronunciation revisited'. *TESOL Quarterly* 20/2:207–25. [123(n7, n8)]

Peters, R. S. 1965. 'Education as initiation' in R. D. Archambault (ed.) *Philosophical Analysis and Education*. London: Routledge and Kegan Paul.

Pfister, G. B. and **Borzilleri, P. A.** 1977. 'Surface cultural concepts: A design for the evaluation of cultural material in textbooks'. *Die Unterrichtspraxis* 10:102–8. [237(n14)]

Pimsleur, P. and **Quinn, T.** (eds.) 1971. *The Psychology of Second Language Learn-*

ing. Cambridge: Cambridge University Press. [330, Carton 1971, Newmark 1971]

Pomphrey, C. 1985. 'Language varieties and change'. Cambridge: Cambridge University Press. [253, 254, 270(n9)]

Porcher, L., Huart, M. and **Mariet, F.** 1980. *Adaptation de 'Un niveau-seuil' pour des contextes scolaires*. Strasbourg: Council of Europe.

Prabhu, N. S. 1987. *Second Language Pedagogy*. Oxford: Oxford University Press. [137, 179, 202(n3), 203(n4), 316]

Prator, C. H. and **Robinett, B. W.** 1972. *Manual of American English Pronunciation* (Third edition). New York: Holt, Rinehart and Winston. [123(n7)]

Quinn, T. J. and **Trounce, M.** 1985. 'Some aspects of Australian experience with language awareness courses' in G. Donmall (ed.) *Language Awareness*. NCLE Papers and Reports no. 6. London: Centre for Information on Language Teaching and Research. [247, 249]

Quirk, R., Greenbaum, S., Leech, G. and **Svartvik, J.** 1985. *A Comprehensive Grammar of the English Language*. London: Longman. [132]

Rahmenrichtlinien Neue Sprachen Sekundarstufe. 1980. Der Hessische Kulturminister. Frankfurt: Diesterweg. [189]

Rampton, M. B. H. 1990. 'Displacing the "native speaker": expertise, affiliation, and inheritance'. *ELT Journal* 44/2:97–101. [98]

Redman, S. and **Ellis, R.** 1990. *A Way with Words: Vocabulary Development Activities for Learners of English, Book 2*. Cambridge: Cambridge University Press. [105(n1)]

Richards, J. C. 1981. 'Introducing the progressive'. *TESOL Quarterly* 15/4:391–402. [153(n6)]

Richards, J. C. and **Rodgers, T. S.** 1986. *Approaches and Methods in Language Teaching: A Description and Analysis*. Cambridge: Cambridge University Press. [40(n1), 204(n11), 344, 348(n6)]

Richterich, R. 1980. 'Definition of language needs and types of adults' in J. L. M. Trim, R. Richterich, J. A. van Ek, and D. A. Wilkins (eds.) *Systems Development in Adult Language Learning: A European Unit Credit System for Modern Language Learning by Adults*. Oxford: Pergamon. [43]

Richterich, R. and **Chancerel, J. L.** 1977. *Identifying the Needs of Adults Learning a Foreign Language*. Strasbourg: Council of Europe and Oxford: Pergamon. [43]

Rinvolucri, M. 1984. *Grammar Games: Cognitive, Affective and Drama Activities for EFL Students*. Cambridge: Cambridge University Press. [203(n10), 289]

Rivers, W. M. 1964. *The Psychologist and the Foreign Language Teacher*. Chicago: University of Chicago Press. [347(n1)]

Rivers, W. M. 1968/1981. *Teaching Foreign-Language Skills*. Chicago: University of Chicago Press. [11, 109, 152(n1), 153(n10), 154(n12), 206, 227, 235(n1), 240(n26, n27, n28, n30), 241(n34, n35), 242(n37, n38), 310, 341, 346]

Rivers, W. M. 1971. 'The language learner: reaching his heart and mind'. *The Canadian Modern Language Review* 28/1:7–16.

Rivers, W. M. 1972. 'Talking off the tops of their heads'. *TESOL Quarterly* 6/1:71–81. [149, 246, 304, 322]

Rivers, W. M. 1975. *A Practical Guide to the Teaching of French*. New York: Oxford University Press. [109, 123(n6), 144, 289, 310, 322, 323, 326(n5), 341]

Rivers, W. M. 1976. *Speaking in Many Tongues: Essays in Foreign Language Teaching*. Rowley, Mass.: Newbury House.

Rivers, W. M. 1980. 'Practical implications of new trends and directions' in D. L. Lange (ed.) 1980.

Rivers, W. M. 1983. 'The foreign language teacher and cognitive psychology' in W. M. Rivers (ed.) *Communicating Naturally in a Second Language*. Cambridge: Cambridge University Press.

Roberts, J. T. 1986. 'The use of dialogues for teaching transactional competence in foreign languages' in C. J. Brumfit (ed.) *The Practice of Communicative Teaching*. ELT Documents 124. Oxford: Pergamon. [176(n6)]

Robinson, G. L. N. 1985. *Crosscultural Understanding*. New York: Pergamon. [83, 214]

Robinson, G. L. N. 1987. 'Culturally diverse speech styles' in W. M. Rivers (ed.) *Interactive Language Teaching*. Cambridge: Cambridge University Press. [206, 229, 236(n7)]

Robinson, P. 1980. *ESP (English for Specific Purposes)*. Oxford: Pergamon. [40(n2)]

Roy, R., Ardanaz, N., Hainsworth, H. and **Ullmann, R.** 1989. *Integration in Action: A Professional Development Kit for Teachers of French as a Second Language*. Winnipeg: Canadian Association of Second Language Teachers. [365]

Rubin, J. 1975. 'What the "good language learner" can teach us'. *TESOL Quarterly* 9:41–51. [259, 262, 336]

Rubin, J. 1987. 'Learner strategies: theoretical assumptions, research history and typology' in Wenden and Rubin (eds.) 1987. [261, 263, 264, 272(n27, n29, n30)]

Rubin, J. and **Thompson, I.** 1982. *How to Be a More Successful Language Learner*. Boston, Mass.: Heinle and Heinle. [262, 263, 271(n23)]

Rulon, K. and **McCreary, J.** 1986. 'Negotiation of content: teacher-fronted and small group interaction' in R. R. Day (ed.) *Talking to Learn: Conversation in Second Language Acquisition*. Rowley, Mass.: Newbury House. [167]

Rutherford, W. E. 1987. *Second Language Grammar: Learning and Teaching*. London: Longman. [139, 152, 153(n8), 153(n10), 326(n1)]

Rutherford, W. E. and **Sharwood Smith, M.** 1985. 'Consciousness-raising and universal grammar'. *Applied Linguistics* 6/3:274–82.

Rutherford, W. E. and **Sharwood Smith, M.** (eds.) 1988. *Grammar and Second Language Teaching: A Book of Readings*. New York: Newbury House. [152(n1)]

Sajavaara, K. 1981. 'Contrastive linguistics past and present and a communicative approach' in J. Fisiak (ed.) *Contrastive Linguistics and the Language Teacher*. Oxford: Pergamon. [123(n5)]

Samarin, W. F. 1967. *Field Linguistics: A Guide to Linguistic Field Work*. New York: Holt, Rinehart and Winston. [271(n21)]

Sanderson, D. 1982. *Modern Language Teachers in Action*. A report on classroom practice. Language Teaching Centre, University of York. [51, 52, 112, 148, 206, 287]

Savignon, S. J. 1972. *Communicative Competence: An Experiment in Foreign Language Teaching*. Philadelphia: Center for Curriculum Development. [164, 173, 179, 198, 304, Jakobovits 1972]

Savignon, S. J. 1983. *Communicative Competence: Theory and Classroom Practice*. Reading, Mass.: Addison-Wesley. [152(n1)]

Saville-Troike, M. 1982. *The Ethnography of Communication*. London: Blackwell. [176(n1)]

Scarcella, R. 1989. 'Conversational analysis in L2 acquisition and teaching' in R. B. Kaplan (ed.) *Annual Review of Applied Linguistics* 9:72–91.

Schumann, J. H. 1978. 'The acculturation model for second language acquisition' in

Gingras (ed.) *Second Language Acquisition and Foreign Language Teaching*. Arlington, Va.: Center for Applied Linguistics. [216, 283]

Scriven, M. 1967. 'The methodology of evaluation' in R. W. Tyler, R. M. Gagné, and M. Scriven (eds.) *Perspectives of Curriculum Evaluation*. AERA Monograph Series on Curriculum Evaluation 1. Chicago: Rand McNally. [47]

Searle, J. R. 1969. *Speech Acts: An Essay in the Philosophy of Language*. Cambridge: Cambridge University Press. [159]

Seelye, H. N. (ed.) 1968a. *A Handbook on Latin America for Teachers: Methodology and Annotated Bibliography*. Springfield, Ill.: Office of Public Instruction. [Nostrand 1968]

Seelye, H. N. 1968b. 'Culture in the foreign language classroom'. *Illinois Journal of Education* 59:22–6. [236(n7)]

Seelye, H. N. 1969. 'Analysis and teaching of the cross-cultural context' in E. M. Birkmaier (ed.) 1969. [236(n8)]

Seelye, H. N. (ed.) 1970a. *Perspectives for Teachers of Latin American Culture*. Springfield, Ill.: State Superintendent of Public Instruction. [Taylor 1970]

Seelye, H. N. 1970b. 'Performance objectives for teaching cultural concepts'. *Foreign Language Annals* 3:566–78. [212, 236(n7)]

Seelye, H. N. 1972. *Teaching Cultural Concepts in Spanish Classes*. Springfield, Ill.: Illinois Office of Education. [233]

Seelye, H. N. 1984. *Teaching Culture*. Lincolnwood, Ill.: National Textbook Company. [206, 208, 209, 210, 212, 225, 229, 236(n7, n8), 238(n15, n17, n18, n19), 240(n25, n30, n31, n32), 241(n34, n36), 242(n40)]

Seliger, H. 1979. 'The nature and function of language rules in language teaching'. *TESOL Quarterly* 13: 359–69. [326(n1)]

Selinker, L. 1972. 'Interlanguage'. *IRAL* 10/3:219–31. [283]

Sharwood Smith, M. 1981. 'Consciousness-raising and the second language learner'. *Applied Linguistics* 11:159–68. [139, 326(n1), 333]

Sims, W. D. and **Hammond, S. B.** 1981. *Award-Winning Foreign Language Programs: Prescriptions for Success*. Skokie, Ill.: National Textbook Company. [246, 269(n7)]

Singleton, D. 1989. *Language Acquisition: The Age Factor*. Clevedon, Avon: Multilingual Matters. [271(n16)]

Skehan, P. 1986. 'Cluster analysis and the identification of learner types' in V. Cook (ed.) *Experimental Approaches to Second Language Acquisition*. Oxford: Pergamon. [272(n24)]

Skehan, P. 1989. *Individual Differences in Second Language Learning*. London: Edward Arnold. [272(n24)]

Slagter, P. J. 1979. *Un nivel umbral*. Strasbourg: Council of Europe.

Smith, C. and **Tager-Flusberg, H.** 1982. 'Metalinguistic awareness and language development'. *Journal of Experimental Child Psychology* 34:449–68. [268(n4)]

Smith, L. E. (ed.) 1981. *English for Cross-Cultural Communication*. London: Macmillan. [98(n2)]

Smith, L. E. (ed.) 1983. *Readings in English as an International Language*. Oxford: Pergamon. [98(n2)]

Smith, L. E. 1987. *Discourse Across Cultures*. New York: Prentice-Hall. [176(n3)]

Somerville, A. A. 1936. *A Primer of French Grammar*. London: Rivingtons. [140]

Spada, N. and **Lightbown, P. M.** 1989. 'Intensive ESL programmes in Quebec primary schools'. *TESL Canada Journal* 7/1:11–32. [367(n2)]

Spilka, I. V. 1976. 'Assessment of second-language performance in immersion programs'. *The Canadian Modern Language Review* 32:543–61. [305]

Spolsky, B. 1968. *Some Psycholinguistic and Sociolinguistic Aspects of Bilingual Education*. New Mexico: University of New Mexico. [163]

Spolsky, B. 1978. *Educational Linguistics: An Introduction*. Rowley, Mass.: Newbury House. [163]

Standwell, G. J. B. 1973. 'The phoneme, a red herring for language teaching?' *Audio Visual Language Journal* 11:119–22. [124(n17)]

Steele, R. 1989. 'Teaching language and culture: old problems and new approaches' in J. E. Alatis (ed.) *Georgetown University Round Table on Languages and Linguistics*. Washington: Georgetown University Press. [235(n1)]

Stern, H. H. 1970. *Perspectives on Second Language Teaching*. Toronto: OISE Press. [x]

Stern, H. H. 1973. 'Language teaching materials: the next phase' in G. Rondeau (ed.) *Some Aspects of Canadian Applied Linguistics*. Montreal: Centre Educatif et Culturel.

Stern, H. H. 1974. 'Directions in language teaching theory and research' in J. Qvistgard, H. Schwarz, and H. Spang-Hanssen (eds.) *Applied Linguistics: Problems and Solutions*. Heidelberg: Julius Groos Verlag. [348(n2)]

Stern, H. H. 1975. 'What can we learn from the good language learner?' *The Canadian Modern Language Review* 31/4:304–18. [259, 262, 271(n21), 336]

Stern, H. H. 1976. 'Mammoths or modules?' *Times Educational Supplement*. 8 October 1976. [47]

Stern, H. H. 1978. 'Bilingual schooling and foreign language education: some implications of Canadian experiments in French immersion' in J. E. Alatis (ed.) *International Dimensions of Bilingual Education*. Georgetown Round Table on Languages and Linguistics. Washington, DC: Georgetown University Press. [302]

Stern, H. H. 1980a. 'Directions in foreign language curriculum development' in American Council on the Teaching of Foreign Languages 12–17. [27]

Stern, H. H. 1980b. 'Some approaches to communicative language teaching in Canada' in K. E. Müller (ed.) 1980.

Stern, H. H. 1980c. 'Language learning on the spot: some thoughts on the language aspect of student exchange programs'. *The Canadian Modern Language Review* 36/4:659–69. [203(n6)]

Stern, H. H. 1981a. 'Communicative language teaching and learning: toward a synthesis' in J. E. Alatis, H. B. Altman, and P. M. Alatis (eds.) 1981.

Stern, H. H. 1981b. 'The formal-functional distinction in language pedagogy: A conceptual clarification' in J. G. Savard and L. Laforge (eds.) *Proceedings of the 5th Congress of the International Association of Applied Linguistics*. Quebec: Laval.

Stern, H. H. 1982. 'French core programs across Canada: How can we improve them?' *The Canadian Modern Language Review* 39/1:34–7. [270(n10)]

Stern, H. H. 1983a. *Fundamental Concepts of Language Teaching*. London: Oxford University Press. [3, 31, 72, 262]

Stern, H. H. 1983b. 'Toward a multidimensional foreign language curriculum' in R. G. Mead (ed.) *Foreign Languages: Key Links in the Chain of Learning*. Middlebury, Vt.: Northeast Conference. [357, 358, 359, 361, 367]

Stern, H. H. (ed.) 1984. 'The Immersion Phenomenon'. Special issue of *Language and Society* 12. [Bibeau 1984, Harley 1984, Krashen 1984, Wesche 1984]

Stern, H. H. 1985. 'The time factor and compact course development'. *TESL Canada Journal* 3:13–27. [270(n10), 351]

Stern, H. H. *et al.* 1976. *Three Approaches to Teaching French: Evaluation and Overview of Studies Related to the Federally-Funded Extensions of the Second*

Language Learning (French) Programs in the Carleton and Ottawa School Boards. Toronto: Ontario Ministry of Education.

Stern, H.H. and **Harley, B.** 1988. 'Second language curriculum renewal: The National Core French Study, a 3-year Canadian project in progress'. *Australian Review of Applied Linguistics* 11/1:147–57. [360]

Stern, H.H., Ullmann, R., Balchunas, M., Hanna, G., Schneidermann, E. and **Argue, V.** 1980. *Module Making: A Study in the Development and Evaluation of Learning Materials for French as a Second Language*. Toronto: Ontario Ministry of Education. [203(n8), 359]

Stevick, E.W. 1976. *Memory, Meaning and Method*. Rowley, Mass.: Newbury House. [154(n11)]

Stevick, E.W. 1980. *Teaching Languages: A Way and Ways*. Rowley, Mass.: Newbury House. [271(n23)]

Stockwell, R.P. and **Bowen, J.D.** 1965. *The Sounds of English and Spanish*. Chicago: University of Chicago Press. [123(n5)]

Strevens, P.D. 1972. 'Language teaching' in T.A. Sebeok (ed.) *Current Trends in Linguistics* 9/1. The Hague: Mouton. [346]

Strevens, P.D. 1977. *New Orientations in the Teaching of English*. Oxford: Oxford University Press. [109, 111, 119, 120, 345, 346]

Strevens, P.D. 1982. 'World English and the world's English—or, whose language is it anyway?' *Journal of the Royal Society of Arts*, June, 412–28. [98]

Strong, M. 1983. 'Social styles and the second language acquisition of Spanish-speaking kindergarteners'. *TESOL Quarterly* 17:241–58. [273(n34)]

Stubbs, M. 1983. *Discourse Analysis: The Sociolinguistic Analysis of Natural Language*. Chicago: University of Chicago Press. [160, 176(n1)]

Suter, R. 1976. 'Predictors of pronunciation accuracy in second language learning'. *Language Learning* 26/2:233–53. [125(n24)]

Swaffar, J.K. and **Stephens, D.S.** 1981. 'What comprehension-based classes look and feel like in theory and practice' in H. Winitz (ed.) *The Comprehension Approach to Foreign Language Instruction*. Rowley, Mass.: Newbury House.

Swain, M. 1984. *Studies on Immersion Education: A Collection for United States Educators*. Sacramento, Calif.: State Department of Education. [175]

Swain, M. and **Lapkin, S.** 1982. *Evaluating Bilingual Education: A Canadian Case Study*. Clevedon, Avon: Multilingual Matters. [47, 304]

Sweet, M. 1899. *The Practical Study of Languages: A Guide for Teachers and Learners*. London: Dent. Reprinted in the Language and Language Learning Series. Oxford: Oxford University Press, 1964. [82, 110, 114, 122(n2), 258, 326(n5), 338]

Taylor, H.D. and **Sorenson, J.L.** 1961. 'Culture capsules'. *Modern Language Journal* 45:350–4. [224, 237(n14)]

Taylor, J.S. 1970. 'Direct classroom teaching of cultural concepts' in H.N. Seelye (ed.) 1970a. [224]

Temperley, M.S. 1983. 'The articulatory target for final –s clusters'. *TESOL Quarterly* 17/3:421–36. [123(n8)]

Terry, R.M. 1981. 'Concepts of pastness: the passé composé and the imperfect'. *Foreign Language Annals* 14/2:105–10. [153(n6)]

The Canadian Modern Language Review 47/1. 1990. Issue on the National Core French Study.

Thorndike, E.L. 1921. *The Teacher's Word Book*. New York: Teachers College Press.

Tickoo, M.L. (ed.) 1987. *Language Syllabuses: State of the Art*. Singapore: SEAMEO Regional Language Centre. [Widdowson 1987]

Tremblay, R., Painchaud, G., LeBlanc, R. and **Godbout, R.** 1989. *Se lancer en affaires avec un jeu: an integrated teaching unit for the NCFS.* Winnipeg: Canadian Association of Second Language Teachers. [364]

Tremblay, R., Duplantie, M. and **Huot, D.** 1990. *The Communicative/Experiential Syllabus.* National Core French Study. Winnipeg: Canadian Association of Second Language Teachers. [362]

Trim, J. L. M. 1980. *Developing a Unit Credit Scheme of Adult Language Learning.* Oxford: Pergamon. [43, 155]

Trim, J. L. M. 1981, 'Résume' in Council of Europe, 1981.

Trimble, L. 1985. *English for Science and Technology: A Discourse Approach.* Cambridge: Cambridge University Press. [40(n2)]

Trudgill, P. (ed.) 1984. *Applied Sociolinguistics.* London: Academic Press.

Tumposky, N. R. 1984. 'Behavioural objectives, the cult of efficiency and foreign language learning: are they compatible?' *TESOL Quarterly* 18/2:295–310. [98]

Tursi, J. A. (ed.) 1970. *Foreign Languages and the "New" Student.* New York: Northeast Conference on the Teaching of Foreign Languages.

Ullmann, R. (n.d.) *The Module Making Project and Communicative Language Teaching in the Core French Program.* Toronto: Ontario Institute for Studies in Education.

Ullmann, R. 1981. 'Thematic and activity approach to communicative language teaching in second language classrooms'. Paper presented at the Canadian Association of Applied Linguistics meeting, Ottawa, May 1981.

Ullmann, R. 1982. 'A broadened curriculum framework for second languages'. *ELT Journal* 36:255–62. [27]

Ullmann, R. 1987. 'The Ontario experience: a modular approach to second language teaching and learning' in S. Savignon and M. Berns (eds.) *Initiatives in Communicative Language Teaching, Vol. 2.* Reading, Mass.: Addison-Wesley. [203(n8)]

Ullmann, R. 1990. 'Materials development as a professional development process'. *The Canadian Modern Language Review* 46/4:714–22. [203(n8)]

Ullmann, R., Balchunas, M. and **Pritchard, C.** 1980. *Visitons et Explorons.* Toronto: OISE Press.

Ullmann, R. and **Geva, E.** 1984. 'Approaches to observation in second language classes' in J. P. B. Allen and M. Swain (eds.) *Language Issues and Education Policies.* ELT Documents 119. Oxford: Pergamon. [54, 57]

Ullmann, R., Geva, E., Mackay, L. and **Stern, H. H.** 1983. *The York Region Core French Evaluation Project.* Toronto: Ontario Instiute for Studies in Education. [54, 148]

Ur, P. 1984. *Teaching Listening Comprehension.* Cambridge: Cambridge University Press.

Ur, P. 1988. *Grammar Practice Activities: A Practical Guide for Teachers.* Cambridge: Cambridge University Press. [152(n1), 154(n10)]

USA. 1979. *Strength through Wisdom: A Critique of U.S. Capability.* The President's Commission on Foreign Language and International Studies. November 1979. Washington, DC: US Government Printing Office. [206]

Valdes, J. M. (ed.) 1986. *Culture Bound: Bridging the Cultural Gap in Language Teaching.* Cambridge: Cambridge University Press.

Valdman, A. (ed.) 1966. *Trends in Language Teaching.* New York: McGraw-Hill. [347(n1), Nostrand 1966]

Valdman, A. 1975. 'Error analysis and pedagogical ordering' in S. P. Corder and

E. Roulet (eds.) *Some Implications of Linguistic Theory for Applied Linguistics.* Brussels: AIMAV and Paris: Didier.

Valdman, A. 1980a. 'Communicative ability and syllabus design for global foreign language courses'. *Studies in Second Language Acquisition* 3/1:81–96. [137, 144, 145]

Valdman, A. 1980b. 'The incorporation of the notion of communicative competence in the design of the introductory foreign language course syllabus' in D. L. Lange (ed.) 1980.

Valentine, C. W. 1950. *Psychology and Its Bearing on Education.* London: Methuen. [312]

Valette, R. M. 1969. *Directions in Foreign Language Testing.* New York: ERIC Clearinghouse on the Teaching of Foreign Languages and of English in Higher Education, and Modern Language Association. [68, 80, 86]

Valette, R. M. 1971. 'Evaluation of learning in a second language' in B. Bloom, J. Y. Hastings, and G. Madaus (eds.) *Handbook of Formative and Summative Evaluation of Student Learning.* New York: McGraw-Hill. [44, 68, 80, 91]

Valette, R. M. 1977. *Modern Language Testing.* Second edition. New York: Harcourt Brace Jovanovich. [29, 212, 213, 218, 237(n12)]

Valette, R. M. 1981. 'The evaluation of second language learning' in J. E. Alatis, H. B. Altman, and P. M. Alatis (eds.) 1981. [29, 44, 68, 80]

Valette, R. M. and **Disick, R. S.** 1972. *Modern Language Performance Objectives and Individualization: A Handbook.* New York: Harcourt Brace Jovanovich. [67, 68, 69, 80, 86, 91]

Vander Beke, C. Z. 1929. *French Word Book.* New York: Macmillan.

van Ek, J. A. 1975. *The Threshold Level in a European Unit/Credit System for Modern Language Learning by Adults.* Strasbourg: Council of Europe. [166]

van Ek, J. A. 1976. *The Threshold Level for Modern Language Learning in Schools.* London: Longman.

van Ek, J. A. and **Alexander, L. G.** 1977. *Systems Development in Adult Language Learning: Waystage.* Strasbourg: Council of Europe.

van Ek, J. A. and **Trim, J. L. M.** (eds.) 1984. *Across the Threshold: Readings from the Modern Languages Project of the Council of Europe.* Oxford: Pergamon. [155]

van Lier, L. 1988. *The Classroom and the Language Learner.* London: Longman. [49, 366]

Varonis, E. M. and **Gass, S.** 1985. 'Nonnative/nonnative conversations: a model for negotiation of meaning'. *Applied Linguistics* 6:71–90. [167]

Vollmer, H. J. 1983. 'The structure of second language competence' in A. Hughes and D. Porter (eds.) *Current Developments in Language Testing.* London: Academic Press. [73]

Wallace, M. 1982. *Teaching Vocabulary.* London: Heinemann.

Wardhaugh, R. 1986. *An Introduction to Sociolinguistics.* Oxford: Blackwell. [176(n1)]

Warriner-Burke, H. P. 1980. 'Reactions: curriculum and materials' in D. L. Lange (ed.) 1980.

Wells, G. (ed.) 1981a. *Learning Through Interaction: The Study of Language Development.* Cambridge: Cambridge University Press. [271(n18), 318, Wells 1981b]

Wells, G. 1981b. 'Becoming a communicator' in G. Wells *Learning Through Interaction: The Study of Language Development.* Cambridge: Cambridge University Press.

Wells, G. 1986. *The Meaning Makers: Children Learning Language and Using Language to Learn*. London: Heinemann. [271(n18), 318]

Wenden, A. 1986. 'What do second-language learners know about their language learning? A second look at retrospective accounts'. *Applied Linguistics* 7:186–201. [268(n5), 272(n29)]

Wenden, A. 1987a. 'Conceptual background and utility' in A. Wenden and J. Rubin (eds.) 1987. [261]

Wenden, A. 1987b. 'How to be a successful language learner: insights and prescriptions from L2 learners' in A. Wenden and J. Rubin (eds.) 1987. [268(n5)]

Wenden, A. and **Rubin, J.** (eds.) 1987. *Learner Strategies in Language Learning*. Englewood Cliffs, NJ: Prentice-Hall. [261, 336, Holec 1987, Horwitz 1987, Rubin 1987, Wenden 1987a]

Wesche, M. B. 1981. 'Language aptitude measures: streaming, matching students with methods, and diagnosis of learning problems' in K. C. Diller (ed.) *Individual Differences and Universals in Language Learning Aptitude*. Rowley, Mass.: Newbury House. [272(n24)]

Wesche, M. B. 1984. 'A promising experiment at Ottawa University' in H. H. Stern (ed.) 1984. [192, 193, 200, 325]

Wesche, M. 1985. 'What can the universities offer to the bilingual student?' *The Canadian Modern Language Review* 41/5:956–61. [193]

Wesche, M., Canale, M., Cray, E., Jones, S., Mendelsohn, D., Tumpane, M. and **Tyacke, M.** 1987. *The Ontario Test of English as a Second Language (OTESL): A Report on the Research*. Toronto: Ontario Ministry of Education. [175]

West, M. 1926. *Learning to Read a Foreign Language: An Experimental Study*. New York: Longmans Green. [62]

White, R. V. 1988. *The ELT Curriculum: Design, Innovation and Management*. Oxford: Blackwell. [41]

Widdowson, H. G. 1978. *Teaching Language as Communication*. Oxford: Oxford University Press. [40(n2), 155, 169, 299(n3)]

Widdowson, H. G. 1979. *Explorations in Applied Linguistics*. Oxford: Oxford University Press. [281]

Widdowson, H. G. 1983. *Learning Purpose and Language Use*. Oxford: Oxford University Press. [40(n2), 176(n5)]

Widdowson, H. G. 1987. 'Aspects of syllabus design' in M. L. Tickoo (ed.) *Language Syllabuses: State of the Art*. Anthology Series 18. Singapore: SEAMEO Regional Language Centre. [98, 326(n1)]

Widdowson, H. G. and **Brumfit, C. J.** 1981. 'Issues in second language syllabus design' in J. E. Alatis, H. B. Altman, and P. M. Alatis (eds.) 1981.

Wilds, C. P. 1975. 'The oral interview test' in R. L. Jones and B. Spolsky (eds.) *Testing Language Proficiency*. Arlington, Va.: Center for Applied Linguistics. [64]

Wilkins, D. A. 1976. *Notional Syllabuses*. London: Oxford University Press. [48, 128, 137, 155, 165]

Wilkins, D. A. 1981. 'Communicative language teaching: some misconceptions and some proposals' in *Bulletin de l'acha*, Automne 1981:90–105. Actes du 12e Colloque annuel. [165]

Willems, G. M. 1987. Communication strategies and their significance in foreign language teaching'. *System* 15/3:351–64. [273(n32)]

Willis, D. 1990. *The Lexical Syllabus: A New Approach to Language Teaching*. London and Glasgow: Collins. [104(n1)]

Willis, D. and **Willis, J.** 1988. *Collins COBUILD English Course, Book 1*. London and Glasgow: Collins. [104(n1)]

Wing, B. H. 1986. *Listening, Reading and Writing: Analysis and Application*. Middlebury, Vt.: Northeast Conference on the Teaching of Foreign Languages.
Wittrock, M. C. (ed.) 1986. *Handbook of Research On Teaching*. Third edition. New York: Macmillan. [271(n19)]
Wong, R. 1987. 'Learner variables and prepronunciation considerations in teaching pronunciation' in J. Morley (ed.) 1987. [111, 117, 124(n15)]
Wong-Fillmore, L. 1976. 'The second time around'. Unpublished doctoral dissertation, Stanford University. [273(n34)]

Yalden, J. 1983. *The Communicative Syllabus: Evolution, Design and Implementation*. Oxford: Pergamon. [43, 166]
Yorkey, R. C. 1970. *Study Skills for Students of English as a Second Language*. New York: McGraw-Hill. [271(n21)]

Zais, R. S. 1980. 'Curriculum and materials development: A jeremiad on the past—A standard for the eighties' in D. L. Lange (ed.) 1980.

Index

The Index covers the Introduction, Chapters 1 to 12, and the Conclusion.

Entries are arranged in letter-by-letter alphabetical order, in which spaces between words are ignored; 'affective strategies' is therefore listed before 'affect objective'.

References to chapter notes are indicated by page and note number, e.g. 'error analysis 176n4'.